WEST AFRICAN RESISTANCE

BY MICHAEL CROWDER

Pagans and Politicians
The Story of Nigeria
Senegal: A Study of French Assimilation Policy
Nigeria: A Modern History for Schools (joint author)
West Africa under Colonial Rule
History of West Africa (joint editor), 2 vols.
Revolt in Bussa: A Study of British Native Administration in
    Nigerian Borgu 1902–1936
West Africa: An Introduction to Its History
Colonial West Africa: Collected Essays

West African Resistance

The military response to colonial occupation

Edited by
Michael Crowder

Hutchinson University Library for Africa

HUTCHINSON UNIVERSITY LIBRARY FOR AFRICA
Hutchinson & Co. (Publishers) Ltd
3 Fitzroy Square, London W1P 6JD

London Melbourne Sydney Auckland
Wellington and agencies
throughout the world

First published 1971
New edition with corrections 1978

© Hutchinson & Co. (Publishers) Ltd 1971 and 1978

Set in Monotype Garamond

Printed in Great Britain by litho at The Anchor Press Ltd
and bound by Wm Brendon & Son Ltd
both of Tiptree, Essex

ISBN 0 09 134031 4

Contents

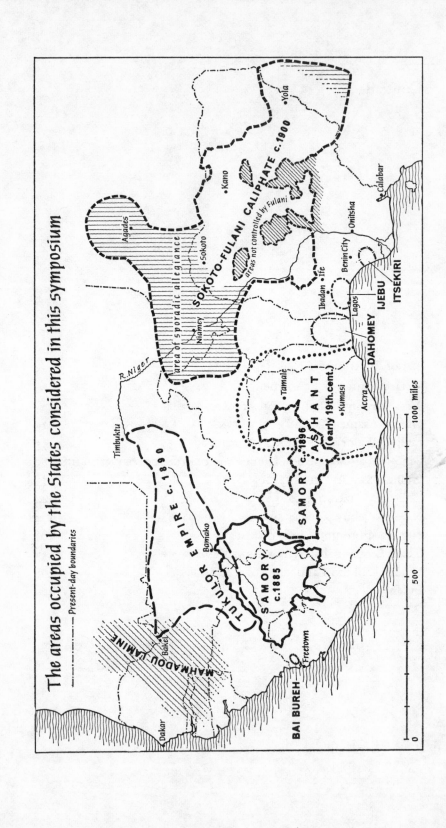

The areas occupied by the States considered in this symposium

——— Present-day boundaries

SOKOTO-FULANI CALIPHATE c.1900

area of sporadic allegiance

areas not controlled by Fulani

TUKULOR EMPIRE c.1890

MAHMADOU LAMINE

SAMORY c.1885

SAMORY c.1890

SAMORY c.1896

ASHANTI (early 19th.cent.)

BAI BUREH

DAHOMEY

IJEBU

ITSEKIRI

Yola

Kano

Agades

Sokoto

Calabar

Onitsha

Benin City

Ife

Ibadan

Lagos

Niamey

R.Niger

Tamale

Kumasi

Accra

Timbuktu

Baniako

Bakel

Freetown

Dakar

0   500   1000 miles

Illustrations and maps

A survivor of the Fulani-British wars.

Brevet-Major Cunningham, Lieutenant J. A. Burdon, Major A. J. Arnold.
From the Burdon Collection, by courtesy of A. H. M. Kirk Greene.

Maps in text

The maps were specially drawn for this book by Leon Vernon.

List of contributors

MICHAEL CROWDER is Research Professor in the Centre for Cultural Studies, University of Lagos. He has a wide experience in West Africa and has published a number of books on West African history and politics, the most recent of which is *Colonial West Africa: Collected Essays* (Cass, 1978).

J. K. FYNN is Research Fellow in the Institute of African Studies, University of Ghana. He has his doctorate from the University of London and his *Ashanti and her Neighbours, c. 1700–1807* was published by Longman in 1972.

A. S. KANYA-FORSTNER's doctoral thesis on the French military penetration of the Western Sudan was published by Cambridge University Press as *The Conquest of the Western Sudan: A Study in French Military Imperialism*.

OLATUNJI OLORUNTIMEHIN is Professor of History at the University of Ife and Dean of Administration. He gained his doctorate at Ibadan University. He is author of *The Segn Tukulor Empire*, published by Longman.

YVES PERSON is a former colonial administrator and now Professor of History at the University of Paris. He has written a large number of articles on Guinea and on Samori, whose definitive biography he has published.

ROBERT SMITH, formerly an Associate Professor of History in the University of Lagos, is co-author of *Yoruba Warfare in the Nineteenth Century* and author of *Kingdoms of the Yoruba, Warfare and Diplomacy in Pre-Colonial West Africa,* and *The Lagos Consulate, 1851–1861* (forthcoming), as well as articles on West African history. He was the first (acting) Head of the Department of History in the University of Ife. He is currently Senior Lecturer in History at the University of Ibadan.

OBARO IKIME is Professor and Head of the Department of History at Ibadan University where he gained his doctorate. He is author of a biography of Nana Olumu. *Merchant Prince of the Niger Delta, Niger Delta Rivalry* and *The Fall of Nigeria: The British Conquest.*

LARAY DENZER has been lecturing at the University of Illinois, Chicago Circle, and has recently gained her PhD from the University of Birmingham. She has made a special study of Bai Bureh.

D. J. M. MUFFETT, O.B.E. is a former Senior Resident in Northern Nigeria and author of *Concerning Brave Captains,* a book about the British conquest of Northern Nigeria. He is now Assistant Professor of Hausa at Duquesne University.

MICHAEL CROWDER

Preface to the First Edition

The idea for this symposium on the nature of the African military response to colonial occupation was first suggested to me in 1967 by Graham Nicol when he was my editor at Hutchinson. Having just read the account of resistance in West Africa to the imposition to colonial occupation in the manuscript of my *West Africa under Colonial Rule* he had been surprised how much stronger this resistance had been than was generally supposed. He suggested a collection of essays on the military aspects of African resistance to the colonial forces would be opportune and the result is this symposium.

I am grateful to Mr. Nicol for suggesting the idea of this symposium and to Mr. Ronald Lewin, my present editor at Hutchinson, for the very great assistance he has given me in preparing the manuscript for press. In editing this symposium it has been very comforting to have the advice of a distinguished military historian like Mr. Lewin, especially as my own martial experience has been largely limited to trying to keep broken-down army motor transport going over laterite roads in Northern Nigeria in 1953–4.

I should like to thank contributors to the symposium for the promptness with which they delivered their manuscripts and for offering criticisms of my introduction. I should also like to thank colleagues who read various chapters for me, namely Professor I. A. Akinjogbin, Professor J. F. Ade Ajayi, Dr. R. A. Adeleye, Professor Robin Horton and Dr. B. Olatunji Oloruntimehin, himself a contributor.

I am indebted to Dr. Joan White for her excellent translation from the French of the chapter on Samori.

Finally, it was found impossible to adopt a standard spelling for the names of people and places in the book since contributors vary in the orthography they adopt and in the absence of a standard orthography for African names, we have decided to allow each contributor the orthography of his choice. We apologise to non-specialist readers for the inconvenience this may cause, but on the other hand until the urgently needed standard orthography is established it is difficult to insist on the adoption of any particular one, especially as some Africanists are vehement in the defence of the particular orthography they follow.

Preface to the New Edition

West African Resistance: The military response to colonial occupation, which was first published in 1971, has had a greater success than either the editor or the contributors could have envisaged for what was conceived as a somewhat specialised symposium. Continuing demand for the book has persuaded the publishers to re-issue the volume in their new Hutchinson University Library for Africa in which it is one of the first titles to be published. Only slight non-substantive revisions have been made by contributors to this edition of *West African Resistance* so that in essence it is the same in the 1971 edition.

MICHAEL CROWDER
Lagos 1978

MICHAEL CROWDER

West African Resistance

1

In 1861 the administration of the newly acquired British colony of
Lagos commissioned Captain A. T. Jones to make a report on the
army of their north-western neighbours, the Egba. Jones summed
up their military strategy with the same contempt so many European
historians have subsequently shown for pre-colonial African armies,
describing it as 'the irregular marching and skirmishing of the
barbarous horde'.[1] Because so many European historians of Africa
have dismissed African armies as little better than slave-hungry
rabbles, easy prey for the disciplined, well-equipped European armies
of occupation, very little attention has been paid to the African
military response to the European invasion.

Indeed the history of the Scramble for Africa has largely been
written with reference to its implications for European history.
For the majority of the European historians of the quarter-century of
African history from 1880–1905, during which the European
conquest was largely completed, the most important events have
been European ones. In a well-known history of Africa the chapter
on the European Scramble for Africa devotes only one short para-
graph to West African military resistance, and makes no reference to
the military quality of this resistance.[2] Yet one of the reasons why the
European occupation of West Africa took over twenty-five years was
the strength of African resistance. Parts of Ivory Coast, Mali, Niger,
south-eastern Nigeria, the plateau of northern Nigeria, and Mauri-
tania were not 'pacified' until the second decade of the twentieth

century. Not only was resistance bitter, it was often skilful. It was provided not by a few states with well-developed armies like Dahomey or Asante but by a very wide range of peoples. Indeed, it is rarely appreciated that a good majority of the states of West Africa, large and small, as well as most of the people living in segmentary societies, opposed European occupation with force.[3]

The conquest has been seen as an unequal contest, and as such little interest has been shown either in the scale, organisation or effectiveness of resistance. Yet though it *was* an unequal contest—the Europeans had Maxim guns, for which African military leaders, however brilliant, had no ultimate answer—the Africans in many cases gave their European opponents a much stiffer battle than the latter had anticipated and the cost of conquest in terms of men and money was much higher than has generally been appreciated. Experience of the determination of African resistance, even if easily overcome with superior weapons, slowed down the rate of occupation, since each advance had to be worked out with regard to the scale of opposition likely to be encountered. This is borne out by the journals of the European military commanders, who though they necessarily saw the battles they fought in terms of their own preconceptions of military strategy, were rather more generous in their assessment of the military capabilities of their opponents than most historians of colonial rule have been.[4]

While many European historians have seen, and still do see, the period 1880–1905 largely in terms of the diplomatic negotiations between European powers and accept that once agreement had been arrived at as to which power should have what part of Africa, effective occupation was only a question of time, the contemporary African historian naturally sees the period through a different optic. He is interested to know why African military resistance was not more effective, why some states resisted, and others did not, why some states were able to adapt their armies to deal with the military strategies of their European opponents, why others fought entirely in traditional terms. Where the heroes of the European histories of this period are Archinard, Gallieni, Dodds, Lugard, Garnet Wolseley and Texeira Pinto, those of the African are Samori, Bai Bureh, Lat Dior, Nana of Ebrohimi, Behanzin and Attahiru Ahmadu. Battles are seen not in terms of the success of the conquerors but of the prowess of the defeated leaders in the face of overwhelming odds. And these battles, fought only seven or eight decades ago, are still vivid in oral tradition.

Such an attitude is understandable in purely nationalistic terms, but it is also historically justified. What can be more absurd than to record the history of these twenty-five years almost exclusively in European terms, without looking at the African response to the immense upheaval in African society that was brought about by the European partition? For the African the heroes of the resistance are the heroes of the new nations of Africa. Samori in Guinea and Bai Bureh in Sierra Leone are obvious examples.[5] Thus, shortly after Nigeria's independence the white flag of Caliph Attahiru I, captured by the British after his defeat and death at Burmi, was returned to his descendant, Sultan Sir Abubakar of Sokoto.[6] Moreover the military prowess demonstrated by the African during the occupation had to be borne in mind during colonial rule. Even where the French in the Western Sudan had smashed the armies that opposed them, during the 1914–18 War, when the French were at a disadvantage, large areas of the Western Sudan rose in revolt and slipped from French control for nearly two years.[7] The British and Germans in Central and East Africa learnt that occupation did not mean an end to resistance when many whites were slaughtered during the Shona and Ndebele risings in 1896–7 in Southern Rhodesia[8] and the Maji Maji rising in Tanganyika in 1905–6.[9] Lugard, despite the apparent ease with which he had conquered the Sokoto Caliphate, was well aware that a small miscalculation in his subsequent administration and diplomacy with the Emirs might lead to a revolt which he could not put down.

While a number of historians, both European and African, have in recent years undertaken studies of resistance to colonial occupation and rebellions against colonial rule once it had been established, they have been primarily concerned with the questions as to *why* Africans offered armed resistance. Little attention has, however, been paid to the actual *mechanics* of resistance.

This symposium is an attempt to redress this imbalance in existing historical studies and to look at nine major instances of resistance by African armies to colonial occupation from the point of view of the strategies adopted by these armies. The different studies show that though such strategies were unsuccessful, they were not those of 'barbarous hordes' but of generals, often with long years of experience, some so sophisticated that they taxed European forces, despite their possession of superior weapons, to the utmost; others so hide-bound by traditional military thinking that, like the French at the opening of the Second World War, they were unable to appreciate that old methods were not suitable for dealing with armies equipped with revolutionary new arms, in this case the Maxim and Gatling guns. It seeks to look at some of the major battles of the Scramble as two-sided affairs, which all battles, of course, are. In so doing one recalls the change in character of the 'Western' film in recent years. Most old 'Westerns' showed a wild horde of all but naked Indians attacking the 'Cowboys' with seemingly no discipline or plan of attack. The 'Cowboys' were always triumphant since films had to have happy endings for an audience which was heir to the cowboy culture. In recent years more sophisticated films have shown the 'Cowboys' and 'Indians' pitting their wits against each other, with the latter sometimes triumphing, as indeed they did, and as indeed African armies sometimes did. Few films have been made of African battles, though there are great opportunities for them. When they are made it is to be hoped that, as with *Zulu*, that remarkable film of the near defeat of the British at Rourke's Drift, both sides will be given credit for their generalship and strategic abilities, though it must also be hoped that their account of actual events will not be so romanticised and distorted as in this film.

The papers of this symposium describe the organisation of the African armies in question, the weapons available to them, the nature of their generalship, the strategy employed against the Europeans, and in particular the way diplomacy was used by leaders as a means of staving off military confrontation when they were convinced that the outcome would be unfavourable to them. Such was particularly the concern of Ahmadou of the Tukolor empire, as Kanya-Forstner shows in his essay. Finally the combined chapters show why the European conquest was, as so many writers have rightly observed, ultimately a matter of time. But demonstration of this fact relies not on an assumed superiority of European generalship but a careful analysis of the options open to the African leaders involved in the confrontation and why African strategies failed in the face of the technologically superior, but usually numerically far inferior, enemy.

2

The nine case studies in this volume are concerned with the confrontation of African and European armies, and as such do not cover the resistance of segmentary societies or peoples divided into numerous petty chiefdoms which had no co-ordinated military organisation beyond the level of the village. Nevertheless, such societies—in particular the peoples of the Benue valley in Nigeria and the peoples of the southern Ivory Coast—provided some of the stiffest resistance the colonial forces of occupation experienced. Since each village offered its resistance, there was no identifiable army to defeat among the Igbo as there was, say, among the Tukulor, the Emirates of Nigeria, or Samori's Mandingo empire. Each village or federation of hamlets had its own war-leader. These societies conducted what was in effect guerilla warfare against the invading armies, quite the best tactic that could have been adopted in the circumstances. Unfortunately no detailed study has yet been made of the military nature of the resistance of these societies against the European invaders.

Each case study is concerned with the opposition to the European forces by an organised army of a centralised state. The size and complexity of these states varied considerably. The smallest of the armies was that of Bai Bureh of Kasseh, a tiny Temne state in northern Sierra Leone, barely more than 400 square miles in area. As a war-leader of long-standing reputation, as well as chief of Kasseh, he was, however, able to unite the forces of most other Temne chiefdoms against the British and provide them with some of the toughest opposition they met in their occupation of West Africa. Nana Olomu, Governor of the Benin river, ruled over a state more conspicuous for its prosperity than its size. The military forces he used to maintain his monopoly of trade on the Benin river were used to defend it against the British who had to bring into play most of the forces at their disposal in West Africa. Ijebu was a Yoruba kingdom which seems never to have been brought under the rule of Oyo, which controlled most of Yorubaland as well as Dahomey during the eighteenth century. In the nineteenth century, with the opening of the Lagos lagoon to regular trade with Europe, it prospered on the middleman trade in goods and firearms with the interior, and became during the civil wars of the nineteenth century one of the most powerful of the Yoruba states. It was the only one to offer any effective military resistance to the British and, despite internal dissension, fielded an army of between 7,000 and 10,000, larger than that of Federal Nigeria at the beginning of the Civil War. It was defeated, however, in a short engagement, but acquitted itself with greater success than the British forces had ever anticipated.

Asante and Dahomey had both been founded in the seventeenth century and owed their expansion as states in great measure to their sophisticated military organisation. Though Dahomey was tributary to Oyo during the eighteenth century, and only secured its independence between 1818 and 1822, its army, with its famed Amazons, was one of the most impressive in West Africa. Asante, a much larger state, based on its resources in gold, kolanuts and slaves, had by the beginning of the nineteenth century made most of what is modern Ghana tributary to it. In 1823 it became the first major West African power to fight a war against the Europeans, in this case the British. In all it fought eight major engagements with the British, and in two of these it achieved significant victories, thus being the only West African army decisively to defeat the Europeans in more than one major engagement.

Four of the states considered here were products of the Islamic revival that swept the Western Sudan: the Sokoto Caliphate, founded in 1804; the Tukolor empire, founded in 1852; the Mandingo empire of Samori, which almost immediately after its foundation in 1870 came up against French expansionist ambitions in the Western Sudan; and the short-lived Sarakole empire of Mahmadou Lamine, which threatened both French Senegal and the Tukolor empire, so that the Tukolor, whilst intent on resisting French encroachments on their own territory, saw Mahmadou Lamine as a more immediate threat and allied with the French against him.

These studies represent a sample, we believe significant, of the way in which West African armies acquitted themselves against the Europeans. They have been chosen principally because they show not only the varied success of African armies in their resistance to the Europeans, but also why, in the long-run, even the best of them were doomed to failure. They have been selected, also, because they are armies on which research has been carried out. The military history of West Africa is in its infancy. Other obvious candidates for inclusion, had there been the necessary research, would have been Lat Dior and Ali Bouri of Senegal, and the Mossi of Upper Volta.

In this introductory essay the following points of common interest to the nine case studies will be discussed:

The size, composition and equipment of the invading armies.

The size, composition and equipment of the African armies which opposed them.

The reasons for the failure of African armies.

3

Perhaps the most striking feature of the invading armies was their small size in comparison with the African armies which opposed them. For instance, Colonel Kemball took Sokoto with a force of only 1,200, half of which consisted of carriers, yet Sokoto had an army estimated at nearly 30,000. The British expedition against Ijebu-Ode in 1892 comprised just over 1,000, more than half of whom were again carriers, while the Ijebu fielded a force seven to ten times larger. Again General Dodds led an expeditionary force of only 2,000 against the Dahomeyan army of nearly 12,000. There were, however, exceptions to this disproportion. While the British considered at the outset that only a small force was necessary to deal with Bai Bureh's army of 3,000 they ended up with almost the same number of troops and carriers in the field before they could bring him to bay. Again, while French armies in the early campaigns against Samori had been greatly outnumbered, by 1891–2 the French and Samorian armies opposing each other were of roughly the same size.

The composition of the European forces varied, but for the most part they were only European in leadership. French and British officers and N.C.O.s led African troops, trained in their drill and weapons, against their fellow Africans. The use of European other ranks was limited: Wolseley sent three British battalions to Kumasi in the Asante War of 1874. More regularly employed by the British were West Indian troops, who were better adapted to the climate and were permanently stationed in Freetown, Gold Coast and Lagos. They fought in the wars with Bai Bureh, the Asante and the Ijebu among others. The French armies were based on the *Tirailleurs Sénégalais*—founded by General Faidherbe in St. Louis in 1857. They were recruited from among local Africans, who were officered by Frenchmen. In the early years French troops were used in the rank and file: at the battle of Guemou against El Hajj Omar, in 1859, 320 European soldiers as against 760 African soldiers fought in the French army. Nearly half the Senegal garrison in 1874 was composed of French *disciplinaires* sent to Senegal as a punishment. By contrast with British practice some Africans did gain commissions in the French forces and it was an African lieutenant, Yaro Coumba, who successfully defended the French post at Senedoubou against Mahmadou Lamine. Medina was defended against El Hajj Omar by Paul Holle, who was a *métis* from St. Louis, as was General Dodds who conquered Dahomey. The reluctance of the invading armies to use European troops was the result of the high death rate from the climate and tropical illnesses, in particular malaria and yellow fever, though by the time of the conquest the regular use of quinine as a prophylactic reduced deaths from the former. Cardwell, at the War Office, instructed Wolseley in 1873: 'If the employment of Europeans shall become a necessity, every preparation should be made in advance; and no European force should be landed on the Coast until the time for decisive action has arrived.' Wolseley was urged to use troops only during the 'period when the risk of loss from the climate is at a minimum . . . [and to] spare to the utmost of your power the exposure of European soldiers or marines to the climate of the Gold Coast'.[10]

The fact that the invading armies were able to defeat African armies which sometimes outnumbered them 10–1 was due in part to the possession of superior weapons, and in part to the superior manipulation of those weapons which the African armies also possessed. The chief advantage of the European forces was that they had access to the most recent advances in military technology. While African forces were able to purchase small-arms, and some artillery, their own supplies were not only sparser than those of their European adversaries, but also less up to date. However, European forces did not have a decisive technological advantage over the Africans before the 1860s, since any superiority in small-arms, such as their possession of breech-loaders as against the muzzle-loaders employed by African armies, could be compensated for by the greater numbers their opponents could mass against them, and any superiority their cannon might possess was countered by the difficulty of transporting them into action. But the development of machine guns was to place the odds substantially in the European's favour. In the 1860s the Gatling gun, consisting of a number of small barrels, rotated by a crank, was invented, giving much more rapid fire than the single-round, breech-loaded gun. This was followed by the Mitrailleuse, which consisted of thirty-seven barrels of rifle calibre fixed together, also operated by a crank. These and further similar developments in artillery, such as the Gardner and the Nordenfeld, when use was made of their light weight and greatly improved manœuvrability, increased the forward fire-power of the possessors enormously, and greatly compensated for imbalance in numbers. The major development in Western military technology as far as Europe and Africa were concerned was the single-barrel Maxim gun, the force of the recoil of which operated loading, firing, extraction and ejection at the rate of eleven shots a second. Much lighter than the Gatling gun and the Mitrailleuse, it could be used easily by the forward troops, and its devastating fire-power could hold down an army of much vaster numbers. The Gatling and its relatives were used by European forces in West Africa from the early 1870s onwards, and the Maxim from the early 1890s. No West African army appears ever to have obtained either of these machine-guns for use against their European opponents, though Johnson, the historian of the Yoruba, quotes a claim that the Ijesha had a Gatling gun in their war with Ibadan at Kiriji. The Amakiri faction in the state of New Calabar acquired a Gatling for use in the Civil War of 1879–82. This weapon stands in the Abbi compound in Buguma today. Also during the Satiru 'rebellion' against the British in Northern Nigeria in 1906 the 'rebels' captured a Maxim gun, but its water jacket was slashed and it could not be used.

Over and above their superiority in weapons the Europeans were also heirs to systems of drill and tactics devised to make maximum use of their weapons. African armies which did acquire relatively up-to-date European weapons rarely appreciated instruction in their mechanical and tactical advantages. Thus the Ijebu, as Smith points out, never took advantage of the fact that with a breech-loading rifle you can fire prostrate, thus presenting a smaller target to the enemy: they continued to fire them standing, as they had had to with muzzle-loaded guns. On the other hand Samori deliberately sent his soldiers to enlist clandestinely in the French Army to learn how to use the new arms to best effect. In addition he recruited African soldiers who had served the British and French armies. Over and above these, there was no means of learning the tactical advantages of the new weapons except through direct experience of battle with the Europeans.

Apart from Samori, few of the generals of the West African armies that opposed the British appear to have realised that the new weapons they were acquiring needed special drills and gave specific tactical advantages. Herein lay the second major key to the success of the European armies: using African soldiers, they were much better drilled and disciplined than most of their opponents. The 'square' which the invading armies invariably used in any open engagement was, if it held fast, invincible. Disciplined troops, with rapid-fire rifles and fortified with Gatling and Maxim guns, could mow down opponents with vastly superior numbers, whether foot-soldiers or cavalry.

While the invading forces had clear advantages in weapons and discipline which compensated for differences in numbers, they suffered the severe disadvantage that they were fighting on foreign ground, with which their European officers were usually completely unfamiliar. They all too often had very extended lines of communication, having to rely on carrier pigeons, or runners, to keep in touch with headquarters. Their artillery was cumbersome, and they were much more heavily equipped on the march with both clothing and gear than their African opponents. Too often military dress in the tropics was conceived on a pattern more suitable for Europe, so that quick movement was impeded by the exhaustion heavy clothing would bring on. It is not surprising that the Colonel commanding the expedition against Bai Bureh died of 'Heat Apoplexy'.[11] Nevertheless Wolseley in his expedition to Kumasi did design a light-weight uniform more suitable for the tropics than the domestic uniform.

The greatest disadvantages of all faced by the invading armies was the fact that the only method of advance in the bush was in single file along narrow paths. The extended column, in particular with unarmed carriers trailing at the rear, was particularly vulnerable to attacks from behind or to ambushes from the side, as Bai Bureh and Samori showed. Bai Bureh in particular used bush-fires to cut off the advance or retreat of the British forces. The lack of knowledge of the countryside, however, was partially compensated for by the use of local scouts, the presence of African allies, and the use of African troops themselves.

4

The armies which resisted the European invasion of West Africa varied considerably as to size, organisation and equipment. But they all faced the same dilemma. Their organisation, tactics and equipment had evolved to deal with local military situations, which continued to threaten them, at the same time as the presence of European forces demanded that they re-think their strategy to deal with the different tactics and superior weapons of their new opponents. Thus even if army commanders, one of whose common characteristics is their conservatism, had been inclined to devise new tactics to deal with the invading Europeans, there were powerful arguments in favour of sticking to the existing organisation, since for the most part they had still to deal with their African enemies, both external and internal. This was acutely the dilemma of the Sokoto Caliphate, as Muffett shows. And the European enemies were not, at least in the short-run, always considered the more dangerous foe. Thus Ahmadu of Segou allied with the French against Mahmadou Lamine; Tieba of Sikasso with the French against Samory; and Ibadan with the British against the Ijebu, who also had to cast nervous glances over their shoulders at a dissident Ijebu army led by their Seriki, Kuku.

To deal successfully with the European invading forces would have necessitated a complete reorganisation of the army in terms of strategy and equipment. Of those studied in this book only Bai Bureh, Samori and to a certain extent Nana and the Asante managed to effect this. Bai Bureh adopted the strategy of guerilla warfare, avoiding direct confrontation with the enemy, which was so characteristic of the battles fought between African and European forces. Samori not only adopted guerilla warfare as a strategy but also managed to achieve some parity in arms with his adversaries. This he did not only through a remarkable network of commercial contacts but also by manufacturing effective copies of the European originals. This enabled him to stave off the Europeans for longer than any other African military commander in tropical Africa, but ultimately he was doomed, as he himself knew, because he did not have the weapons the Europeans possessed. He never obtained anything more than rapid-fire rifles and his fire-power could never equal that of the French. Nana's untrained riflemen, just by taking advantage of the natural defences of Ebrohimi, forced the British to withdraw on three occasions. The Asante used their superior knowledge of the forest to attack the British on the flanks where they were most vulnerable.

The major problem for all African armies was the difficulty of obtaining supplies of European arms. Before 1890, when the European powers formally forbade the export of arms to West Africa, obsolete European arms had been a staple of the export-import trade. Even after 1890 arms could still be obtained from European traders. Samori obtained his arms from British traders in Freetown to fight the French, the Ijebu from French traders to fight the British. Bai Bureh obtained supplies from merchants of the very country he was fighting. Indeed Joseph Chamberlain, the British Colonial Secretary, was considering a charge of treason against one such merchant.[12] But even where they did obtain arms from European merchants these were very rarely the modern ones which the European armies, supplied by metropolitan military ordnance, had access to. None of the armies considered here ever got hold of a Maxim gun. The African armies became the dumping ground for discarded European models, which could give them immense advantage over African rivals who did not possess them, but left them, with the rapid development of gun technology at the end of the nineteenth century, often several jumps behind the European invading forces. This policy of dumping obsolete weapons on African armies continued in some cases into colonial days. When the British and French invaded Togo in 1914 they found the local forces equipped with rifles from the Franco-Prussian War of 1870–1.[13] Even where African armies did obtain modern arms, repair was difficult. Samori solved this by sending his armourers covertly to St. Louis to gain experience from the French armoury.

African armies, apart from guns, relied on a variety of weapons—

swords, spears, lances, bows and arrows—the complexity of which is indicated by Muffett's study of the weaponry of the Hausa-Fulani armies.[14] But these were ineffective, except as irritants, against the enemy. As late as 1916, in the Borgu rebellion against the French in Dahomey, the rebels met gun-fire with bows and arrows, albeit poisoned. The number of French forces killed in the two-month-long engagement, in which eleven battles were fought, was only ten, with thirty-three wounded. Of these only two were European: one under-officer killed, one under-officer wounded. The African rebels suffered losses which they admitted after the war to be very heavy. Two months after the war only 611 dane-guns (flintlocks) had been confiscated from the rebels.[15]

Too often the African armies fell back in defeat on their walled cities or stockaded towns. Designed to withstand long sieges against an enemy with no marked superiority of weapons, they were delightful targets for cannon and projected flares which could set alight the thatched roofs of the houses, a trick also used by the Fulani.[16]

Where most African states did not have standing armies as such, they had the mechanisms for the rapid recruitment and formation of an army of soldiers who had had military training. In most African societies youths were expected to learn the arts of warfare, so that in times of emergency they could be called up. Some states had a small standing army which formed the nucleus of the much larger army formed from the 'reserves' in times of war. The standing army might consist of just the recognised military commanders and the palace guard or be a regular force such as the Amazons in Dahomey, the war-boys of northern Sierra Leone or Samori's *sofa*.

Usually soldiers were expected to equip themselves: part of Samori's success lay in keeping his men supplied with rifles. The King of Dahomey equipped his standing army with flintlocks or carbines, though flintlocks were replaced for at least half the standing army with rapid-firing rifles immediately prior to the wars with the French. Soldiers usually brought their own supplies with them, and often, in traditional siege-type warfare, they were followed by their wives, who during the long static battles cultivated crops behind the lines.[17] In fast-moving battles soldiers lived of necessity off the land. The organisation of the armies again varied greatly from state to state, and these case studies give some idea of the varieties of their organisation. It is certainly impossible at this stage to generalise about them, except that in every African society, whatever its organisation, there was the obligation for young men to undertake military service in times of need, and train for it in advance.

5

While the European forces had great advantages in weapons and discipline over their African opponents, they had all the disadvantages of the invading army coupled with paucity of numbers. Why in these circumstances did the African armies not mount more effective opposition to the Europeans?

Though the great majority of West African peoples cherished their independence, they were invariably faced with a series of potential threats to that independence. Not only was their attention divided between African and European threats to their independence, but at times the European seemed less of an immediate threat to that independence, and was, as we have seen, called in as an ally, or was joined in his conquest of a mutual enemy. In many of the case studies in this book the Europeans were assisted by African enemies of their immediate protagonist. In some cases there were enemies within the state. Thus the British allied with the Fante against the Asante; the French with the Yoruba of Ketu against Dahomey; the British with the Ibadan against Ijebu; the French with the Bambara and other dissident groups against the Tukolor;[18] the French with the Tukolor against Mahmadou Lamine; the British with Dogho and other trade rivals of Nana Olomu in their expedition against Ebrohimi. Indeed the Europeans, though strangers, proved much more skilful in their diplomacy with regard to forging military alliances with African states than these states did among themselves. The major weakness of African resistance was that it was undertaken state by state, where alliances of threatened states might not only have inflicted defeats on the Europeans but put the cost of conquest higher than the metropolitan powers were prepared to pay. As it was, the high costs of the Sudan campaign evoked violent criticism in the French Chamber of Deputies between 1891 and 1893.[19] The fiasco of the British expedition against Ashanti in 1863 was in large part responsible for the decision of the 1865 British Parliamentary Select Committee's decision to limit British commitments on the West Coast. However, there was only one major attempt to combine forces against the Europeans and this was more significant as an exception in the pattern of resistance than as the threat it posed to the Europeans. Between 1889 and 1893, a number of states and groups allied to resist the French in the Western Sudan.[20] Unfortunately, while they all shared a common goal in seeking to preserve their independence from the French, within the alliance were groups who were equally anxious to preserve their independence from other members of the alliance. Thus Tieba of Sikasso joined an alliance in which his long-standing enemy Samori was a leading member; the Bambara allied with the son of their erstwhile conqueror, El Hajj Omar, against the French. But by the time the coalition had brought together all its members—Tieba did not join until 1890, the Bambara till 1891—the French had gained sufficient ground in the Western Sudan to make their conquest only a matter of time. Had, however, such an alliance been forged at the outset, the task of the French military would have been very much more difficult than it was. Attacked on all sides, without firm bases, they would have had to commit far more troops. Furthermore the African armies, freed from looking over their shoulders at potential and actual African enemies, could have devoted all their energies to the defeat of the Europeans. Just as the Europeans followed a policy of divide and conquer, so some African leaders followed a policy of divide and survive. Unfortunately the Europeans, though bitterly divided at home, managed to settle their differences amicably in Africa despite high tension in Borgu and the Gold Coast hinterland. The British in Sierra Leone turned down Samori's request for protection, a request which was designed to stave off the French. The Mogho Naba of the Mossi tried to play off the French and the British and so preserve his independence. But in the circumstances the British, French and Germans in West Africa, though greedy for as much land as they could obtain, were not prepared to do so at the cost of a local African war that might provoke clashes in Europe.

Even though Africans were unable successfully to pool their resources, and even though they were unable to play off one European power against another, the African armies, despite their inferior weapons, their shortage of supply of arms and ammunition, and their less-advanced discipline and drill, could have put up a better fight if they had been more tactically adaptable. If all African generals had appreciated, like Samori and Bai Bureh, that head-on clashes with the enemy's army, or the taking up of defensive positions in walled cities, gave the Europeans the fullest tactical advantage for their weapons, and had accordingly resorted to guerilla warfare, the story of the European conquest would have been very different. The forest regions were, of course, much better suited to guerilla warfare than the savannah areas, though we must remember that the savannah was then much more densely wooded than it is today, denuded as it is of trees by the cultivation of groundnuts. The European armies were particularly vulnerable at night, but for the most part they were only attacked by African armies by day, since many of the troops were too superstitious of the night to fight in the dark. The most difficult conquests for the Europeans were those where the African armies abandoned conventional warfare and resorted to guerilla tactics. Nana of Ebrohimi used to fullest advantage his superior knowledge of the creeks along which the British had to sail to reach Ebrohimi and made what the British thought would be a casual African conquest one of their most difficult. Bai Bureh appreciated that the African troops used by the British depended intimately on their white leaders, and instructed his men to pick off the Europeans. Similarly he saw that the most vulnerable part of the British columns was the line of carriers, and concentrated attacks on them. Samori took advantage of the extended lines of communication of his opponents, which forced them to live off the land, by pursuing a scorched-earth policy. The longest war fought by the Europeans in West Africa after that against Samori was against the peoples of the southern Ivory Coast, in particular the Baoule, who resisted occupation village by village, using to maximum advantage the dense forests of the area.

Even when African armies did adapt their tactics to meet the European threat there was a sense of inevitability about the European conquest. Even Samori, the most successful of the resisters, knew he was doomed but refused to surrender. So, too, did Ahmadu, but here he chose to stave off the inevitable by diplomacy. Threatened from within by rivals to the throne and by recently conquered subject groups, he knew he could not win against the French. Islam, whose hatred of subjection to the infidel could have provided, as it did for a short while between 1889 and 1893 in the Western Sudan, a unifying theme for resistance against the French and British, also held the seeds of a fatalist acceptance of the inevitable. It is clear that in the Sokoto Caliphate the leadership had given much thought to *hijra,* or the obligatory flight from the infidel, when there was no hope of resisting his rule. Caliph Attahiru Ahmadu thus after the conquest of Sokoto led a *hijra* to the east, where the British finally overtook him at Burmi and killed him after two bitterly fought engagements. However, many of his followers continued to the Sudan where their descendants still live today under the chieftaincy of his grandson, Mohammadu dan Mai Wurno. For many African leaders the confrontation between themselves and the technologically superior and vastly different European must have held something of the trauma of the encounter between Cortes and Montezuma and Pizarro and the Inca, so vividly portrayed in *The Royal Hunt of the Sun.* Furthermore, the myth of the white man's invincibility was enhanced by each conquest. Added to that was the ruthlessness of his methods of conquest. Much has been made of the bloodthirsty methods of the Africans in their wars with each other: too little of those of the Europeans in their wars with Africans when they often resorted to standards of warfare they would not have tolerated in Europe. In the British campaigns against Bai Bureh a policy of systematic burning of villages was followed. Crozier reported that the Hausa-Fulani wounded after the battle for Sokoto were shot 'to put them out of their misery'.[21] The French in their conquest of the Western Sudan held out to their African troops the prospect of African slaves as the reward for their services. The Voulet and Chanoine columns' ruthlessness in sacking towns, killing innocent women and children and enslaving adult males caused a major scandal in France. Above all, the Maxim gun, and the Gatling before it, evoked wonder and fear among the Africans. After the conquest of Ijebu, Carter trekked round Yorubaland displaying his Maxim gun. In the war with Ashanti the British forces in 1874 made a point of showing off their Gatling gun to the concealed but watching enemy.[22]

Guerilla warfare could only have staved off the inevitable. West Africa was an agricultural society with limited resources to finance a long-term war, whereas the Europeans came from an industrial society which had, by comparison, infinite resources, in particular the resources of fire-power.[23] Furthermore, at this stage the Europeans were not at war at home, and could devote all their energies to the African conquest. Twenty years later, when the European powers fought each other, and had limited resources to spare for Africa, their African subjects were able seriously to embarrass them in the Western Sudan and Dahomey, which rose up against the French taking advantage of their weakness. Lugard feared that in sending African troops to East Africa the British might become vulnerable in Nigeria. The Egba and Iseyin risings were treated very seriously. The tiny rebellion against the British-imposed Native Authority in Bussa caused concern because of the shortage of troops available.[24] It was Africa's misfortune that the Scramble for Africa occurred at a time of peace in Europe, when Europeans, instead of using their newly acquired weapons on each other, used them on Africa.

NOTES

1 'Report of Captain A. T. Jones', appendix to J. F. Ade Ajayi and R. S. Smith, *Yoruba Warfare in the Nineteenth Century,* London, 1964, p. 139.

2 Roland Oliver and J. D. Fage, *A Short History of Africa,* London, 1962, pp. 194–5.

3 For a general account of the European conquest of West Africa see Michael Crowder *West Africa Under Colonial Rule,* London, 1968, Part II.

4 See for instance, J. S. Gallieni, *Deux campagnes au Soudan français 1886–1888,* Paris, 1891; C. Braithwaite Wallis, *The Advance of Our West African Empire,* London, 1903; one of the notable exceptions to this is Lugard, whose reports, as Muffett shows in his chapter on the conquest of the Sokoto Caliphate, deliberately played down the importance of Hausa-Fulani resistance.

5 President Sekou Touré claims descent from Samory; in Sierra Leone when Colonel (later Brigadier) Juxon-Smith took over power he cited as the national heroes of Sierra Leone Bai Bureh, I. T. A. Wallace Johnson and Sir Milton Margai, *Daily Mail* (Freetown), 1 April 1967.

6 D. J. M. Muffet, *The Story of Sultan Attahiru I,* revised edition, Lagos, 1971, pp. 117–118.

7 National Archives of Senegal, 4D 45 Recrutement indigène: Execution —comptes rendus des colonies—1915–16. See also Michael Crowder *West Africa and the 1914–18 War Bulletin de l'IFAN,* T.xxx, sér B., No. 1, 1968, pp. 227–45.

8 T. O. Ranger, *Revolt in Southern Rhodesia 1896–7,* London, 1967.

9 John Iliffe, *Tanganyika under German Rule 1905–1912,* Cambridge, 1969.

10 Quoted in Alan Lloyd, *The Drums of Kumasi,* London, 1964, p. 68.

11 P.R.O./C.O. 267/437, Govt. to Sec. of State, Conf., 31 March 1898.

12 P.R.O./C.O. 267/438, Draft reply dated 24 June 1898 to Gov.'s Secret (Conf.) of 28 May 1898.

13 Sir Charles Lucas, *The Gold Coast and the War,* London, 1920, p. 18.

14 See also Robert S. Smith, 'Yoruba Armament', *Journal of African History,* VIII, 1, 1967.

15 National Archives of Senegal, I.D. 178.

16 H. Clapperton, *Journal of a Second Expedition into the Interior of Africa from the Bight of Benin to Soccatto,* London, 1829, p. 62.

17 See S. A. Akintoye 'The Ekitiparapo and the Kiriji War', Ph.D. thesis, Ibadan, 1966.

18 For a detailed study of dissident groups within the Tukolor Empire see B. Olatunji Oloruntimehin 'Resistance Movements in the Tukolor Empire', *Cahier's d'Etudes Africaines,* 29, vol. viii, No. 1, 1968, pp. 123–43.

19 See A. S. Kanya-Forstner, *The Conquest of the Western Sudan: A Study in French Military Imperialism,* Cambridge, 1969, pp. 202–9.

20 See B. Olatunji Oloruntimehin, 'The Anti-French Coalition of States and Groups in the Western Sudan 1889–1893' *Odu: A Journal of West African Studies,* New Series No. 3, April 1970.

21 Brigadier F. P. Crozier, *Five Years Hard,* London, 1932.

22 Lloyd, *Drums of Kumasi,* p. 97.

23 See J. B. Wester, *et al. The Growth of African Civilization: The Revolutionary Years: West Africa since 1800.* London, 1967, pp. 243–4.

24 Nigerian Archives, Kaduna, SNP/331p Telegram Lt. Gov. Northern Provinces to Resident Kontagora of 17 June 1915 and Lt. Gov. Northern Provinces to Governor-General, Lagos, 17 June 1915.

J. K. FYNN

Ghana–Asante (Ashanti)

Of all the states of West Africa involved in resistance against European occupation, Asante had by far the longest experience. Her armies first clashed with British forces in 1823. The following year they defeated a British army and killed the British Governor of the Gold Coast settlements. And although the Asante army was driven back to its capital in Kumasi they returned to fight the British and their allies at a place near Dodowa in 1826. But the Asante army proved no match for the British, who wielded Congreve rockets. Nevertheless, though the Asante were defeated, the British abandoned their administrative obligations in the Gold Coast to a company of British merchants.

George Maclean, who became the President of this Council of Merchants, revived British power and jurisdiction on the Gold Coast and in 1843 the British Government returned to the coast. But Maclean's successors lacked his ability and prudence and in 1863 the Asante again attacked and defeated the British. This defeat forced the British to review their commitments along the whole of the West Coast of Africa.

Though in 1874 they were disastrously defeated by the British, the Asante clung tenaciously to their independence. It was not until 1896 that the British entered Kumasi to establish their protectorate over Asante. The Asantehene, Prempeh I, and his chiefs offered no resistance to the large, well-equipped, invading force, for they had estimated in the light of past experience that the Asante were no match for the British. However, though the British deported Prempeh I and tried to establish their authority in Asante, the Asante did not consider that they had been conquered. In 1900 they rose up against the British and gave them their last as well as the hardest battle the latter had ever fought in their long-standing attempts to control and finally subjugate Asante.

During the second half of the seventeenth century various Akan-speaking peoples were organised into the Asante kingdom. The principal architects of this political union were the famous Osei Tutu and his wise companion Okomfo (Priest) Anokye. These two men were, and are still, much respected, revered and regarded with awe in Asante for their sagacity and statesmanship.[1]

After the chiefs of the original Asante divisional states—Kumasi, Mampong, Kokofu, Bekwai, Dwaben, Asumegya and Nsuta—had accepted the policy of union, Osei Tutu and his advisers determined that the Asante Union should last. To that end a number of state-building instruments—some inherited and others devised—were put to use. For example, Osei Tutu removed his court from Kwaman, the capital of his predecessors, and established himself at Kumasi, which to this day remains the capital of Asante. Moreover, the songs and recitals connected with traditional history were couched in terms calculated to disseminate the notion of common origin. The most potent of these unifying instruments, however, were the Asante national army, the Odwira festival, the Asante constitution, the Great Oath and the Golden Stool.

Asante was fundamentally a military union which aimed at economic expansion. This policy of military expansion was so successful that by the end of the eighteenth century Asante was in control of a territory much larger than modern Ghana.[2] Apart from the original divisions, the Asante state included Gonja, Dagomba, Denkyera, Adansi, Akyem, Assin, Sefwi, Aowin, Wassa, Twifo, Akuapem, Akwamu, Ga-Adangbe and a number of the Boron states. The only independent state on the Gold Coast was the Fante kingdom on the coast.

At the beginning of the eighteenth century Fante was a small kingdom. But like Asante, Fante also responded to the new economic demands arising out of the development of trade with Europeans and embarked upon a policy of expansion. Between 1700 and 1750, partly to stem the tide of Asante expansion but mainly to ensure their middleman position in the trade between the interior and the

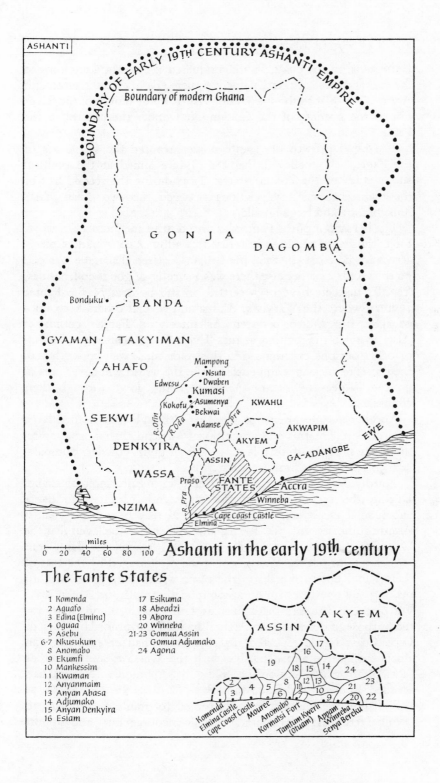

BOUNDARY OF EARLY 19TH CENTURY ASHANTI EMPIRE

Boundary of modern Ghana

G O N J A

D A G O M B A

Bonduku • • B A N D A

GYAMAN • TAKYIMAN

• AHAFO

Mampong
• Nsuta
Edwesu • • Dwaben
Kumasi
Kokofu • Asumenya
• Bekwai
• Adanse

R. Ofin

R. Oda

R. Pra

KWAHU

AKYEM

AKWAPIM

EWE

SEKWI

DENKYIRA

ASSIN

GA-ADANGBE

WASSA

Praso

FANTE
STATES

Accra
Winneba

R. Pra

NZIMA

Cape Coast Castle
Elmina

miles

| 0 | 20 | 40 | 60 | 80 | 100 |

Ashanti in the early 19th century

The Fante States

1 Komenda
2 Aquato
3 Edina (Elmina)
4 Oguaa
5 Asebu
6-7 Nkusukum
8 Anomabo
9 Ekumfi
10 Mankessim
11 Kwaman
12 Anyanmaim
13 Anyan Abasa
14 Adjumako
15 Anyan Denkyira
16 Esiam

17 Esikuma
18 Abeadzi
19 Abora
20 Winneba
21-23 Gomua Assin
    Gomua Adjumako
24 Agona

AKYEM

ASSIN

Komenda
Elmina Castle
Cape Coast Castle
Mouree
Anomabo
Kormatsi Fort
Tamtum Kweril
(Otuam)
Appam
Winneba
Senya Bereku

Europeans on the coast, Fante conquered the coastal kingdoms to the east and west of them, namely Aguafo, Fetu, Asebu, Acron and Agona. This placed the stretch of coast from the mouth of the River Pra to the borders of the Ga kingdom under the control of the Fante.[3]

The rapid growth of Asante power aroused the suspicions of the Fante, who believed that the Asante aimed at the political subjugation of the coastal states. Thus during the second half of the eighteenth century relations between the two Akan states remained by and large hostile.

The behaviour of the Fante was provocative in a number of ways. First, the Fante persistently refused to allow Asante traders direct access to the coast. In 1764 the British declared that trade was bad on the Gold Coast because there was a surplus of goods and, besides, 'regular markets have been settled on the borders of the Fantee country where the Warsaws, Akims and several others keep up a constant intercourse between Ashantee and Fantee country'.[4] Also, in 1778, the report was that 'Every judicious master of a ship or other persons experienced in this trade must well know that all the presents, messages and entreaties in the world will never prevail on the Fantees to let the Ashantee come down through their country. . . .'[5]

Another Asante grievance was that although they needed large quantities of firearms and amunition to defend their huge empire, the Fante prohibited 'by a law' the sale of guns, powder, iron bars, lead and pewter to Asante traders.[6]

Thirdly, the Fante greatly interfered in Asante internal affairs. During the second half of the eighteenth century the Fante encouraged Denkyera, Wassa, Twifo and Akyem to rebel against Asante authority. In 1753, for instance, when they believed that the Wassa might regularise relations with the Asante, the Fante sent messengers to tell the Wassa 'not to be discouraged by the loss of their King, but to remain in the place where they were, without making any overtures for an accommodation with the Ashantees'.[7] Furthermore, Fante formed alliances with these rebellious states for the purpose of defeating the Asante. In 1766 Governor Hippisley of Cape Coast Castle reported that the Fante had entered into 'an alliance offensive and defensive with the Warsaws and Tufferoes (Twifo) to which Amoniaha, King of Appolonia (Nzima) had acceded' in order to defeat Asante.[8]

Fourthly, the Fante were accustomed to granting sanctuary to criminal refugees from Asante. It was the encouragement and support which the Fante gave to the rebellious Assin Chiefs Tsibu and Aputai which precipitated the Asante–Fante war of 1807 which resulted in the defeat of the Fante.[9]

Asante–Fante hostility had European repercussions. From a purely commercial point of view, all the three principal European trading nations on the Gold Coast, namely, Britain, Holland and Denmark, were anxious to establish peaceful relations with Asante. In particular, it became a matter of considerable importance for the Governor and Council at Elmina, Cape Coast and Christiansborg castles to court the friendship and goodwill of the Asantehene. For instance, Sir Dalby Thomas, the Agent-General of the Royal African Company from 1703 to 1711, informed his company that 'trade to Ashantee is so important and the King's friendship so valuable that you can't be too generous to the King'. And a Danish Governor declared in the 1790s that 'it is a custom to send messengers and presents etc. etc. to Ashantee'.[10]

Nevertheless, the European nationals viewed differently the prospect of Asante as the political master of the coastal states. By and large, the Danes and the Dutch were indifferent as to whether or not the Asante defeated the Fante and ruled the coastal seaboard. In 1744, when Asante had acquired dominion over the Ga-Adangbe area, Danish Governor Billsen noted that 'as we at present have Ashantee as overlord so we have to maintain a firm friendship with that nation'.[11] And it was in recognition of the Asantehene's overlordship over the Ga-Adangbe area that the Danes invited Osei Kwame (1777–1801) to send 10,000 troops to the coast to re-establish law and order in the Lower Volta area in 1792.[12] Also, as early as 1715, when the Dutch heard that an Asante army under Amankwa Tia had arrived in the Wassa country, they had been greatly pleased because it was believed that 'the Ashantees were coming to settle nearer the coast'.[13]

The British merchants, on the other hand, were opposed to the establishment of Asante authority on the coast. There were a number of reasons for this. Firstly, the British believed that their Dutch rivals would be the greatest beneficiaries if the Asante were in control of the seaboard because the Dutch had all along made the Asantehene regard the British 'as his enemies or at least the allies of his enemies, the Fantees'.[14]

Secondly, the British regarded the Asante king as an absolute monarch like the King of Dahomey and they feared that if the Asante gained dominion over the coast all the European settlements between Cape Appolonia and the estuary of the Volta would 'become as much dependent on the king of Ashantee as the Forts at Whydah are on Dahomey'.[15]

Thirdly, apart from the fact that the British had had a long trading connection with the Fante, all the major British settlements were located in Fante country and it was largely through Fante assistance that British traders were able to hold their own in the face of bitter commercial rivalry with other Europeans. Thus, in 1772, when it was widely believed that the Asante intended invading Fante territory, the Governor and Council at Cape Coast Castle resolved that 'as most of our forts are situated in the Fantee country, and that nation having always lived in friendship with us, we will grant them every assistance consistent with reason should their adversaries, the Ashantee attack them; this Council being clearly of opinion that the Fantees . . . are, as neighbours far preferable to the Ashantees, who are a rude and unpolished set of men governed by a despotic tyrannical Prince, with whom we might find it very hard, (if practicable) to live on any terms. . . .'[16]

During the second half of the eighteenth century, then, partly as a result of European commercial rivalry and partly because of British involvement in Fante trade and politics, the British traders on the coast were gradually committed to a policy of having to defend the Fante should they be attacked by the Asante.

This pro-Fante policy and the failure to establish a lasting peace with Asante did not find favour in London. The official British policy, and indeed that of all the European nations trading on the Gold Coast, was non-involvement in African affairs.[17] Thus the Board of Trade and Plantations which had general oversight of the British settlements expressed disagreement with the prevailing opinion on the Gold Coast that an Asante conquest would endanger the European establishments there. The Board of Trade made its views known to the London Committee of Merchants and in 1766 the Committee wrote thus to Cape Coast: 'we differ somewhat . . . in regard to the danger of the British forts and settlements if the Ashantees should force their way to the coast, apprehending in that case it will be as much the interest of these people to live in harmony with us as it is at present that of the Fantees and a great increase of trade may be expected by the Ashantees having a direct communication with the ships; this event will also be a just punishment on the Fantees for their perfidious conduct'.[18]

It was in 1807 that the fear of an Asante conquest of the coastal states which had dominated European thinking throughout the eighteenth century crystallised. In a fiercely contested battle which lasted a few months Fante resistance was broken. The Governor of Cape Coast Castle reported that 'the king of Ashantee with a most powerful army invaded the coast. He has made rapid progress and actually cut his way through the heart of the Fantee country. The Fantees give way on every side and the Ashantees have taken Cormantyne (Kormantsi) Fort'.[19] Danish Governor Schioning also noted that 'the Assianthees, with sword and fire murder and destroy everything they meet with. The very large town of Anomabo was burnt down close under the strongest fort cannons in Africa . . . many thousands of people not shot in battle, were murdered in cold blood'.[20]

The Asante followed this victory by two more invasions of the coast in 1811 and 1816 and by 1820 Asante was 'indisputably the greatest and the rising power of Western Africa'.[21] J. Dupuis, who was appointed British Consul to Kumasi shortly after the Asante victories, wrote that 'the kingdom of Ashantee [-north-] west to [-south-] east i.e. from Gaman to the Volta River, embraces about four degrees longitude; and from south to north, i.e. from Cape Coast Castle to the tributary kingdom of Ghofan (Buipe) about four degrees latitude'.[22] T. E. Bowdich, who led a British mission to Asante in 1817, also noted that the Comoe river in modern Ivory Coast was regarded as the limit of Asante jurisdiction to the north-west and that to the north-east Ghamba (Gambaga?) was considered 'the boundary of the Ashantee authority', though Asante influence, through the medium of Dagomba, was held to penetrate as far as the Niger.[23]

The Asante forces which achieved such spectacular successes in the eighteenth and nineteenth centuries were not regular troops. Like the armies on the Gold Coast (Ghana) during this period all able-bodied Asante men were mobilised as and when required. Every Asante divisional state supplied its quota of men according to the overall requirements of the projected campaign.[24]

As was to be expected, Asante, as a forest state, had no cavalry. The main strength of the army lay in the infantry—musketeers, bowmen and spearsmen. The musketeers commanded the greatest prestige, and it was most probable that great importance was placed upon maintaining a superiority in the possession of muskets. It appears, however that the bow and arrow played an important role in the military efficiency of the Asante army. As late as 1807, when the bow and arrow had been abandoned by most of the coastal peoples, the British at Cape Coast discovered that the Asante fought with 'musquets, bows and arrows'.[25] The retention of these weapons was probably due to the fact that the muzzle-loading guns of that period could not be depended upon to sustain a heavy volume of concentrated fire. The superior power of the muskets, however, could be supplemented by the rapidity of fire attainable with the bows and arrows.

The Asante purchased their guns, powder, lead and pewter from the Europeans on the coast. This was the reason why they were prepared to go to war to open the trading routes linking Asante with the coast when these were closed by the intervening states. For example, in 1766 the Fante, the Twifo, the Akyem and the Wassa formed an alliance to end the political and economic domination of Asante by cutting off Asante traders from their supply of firearms. The Asante decided to force a way through to the coast and Governor John Hippisley remarked that 'the Ashantees could not see with Tranquility all access to the waterside cutt off and no way left to open it but war'.[26]

There were two means of acquiring these firearms. First of all, the bulk of guns and gunpowder were purchased by traders who came down purposely for those commodities. For example, in 1748 the Danes at Christiansborg Castle, Accra, reported that about 2,000 Asante traders, who were accompanied by Akwamu sharp-shooters, arrived at Great Ningo with slaves and ivory and that they bought nothing but guns and gunpowder.[27] Secondly, the Asantehene often demanded that the ground rents for the European settlements at Accra and Elmina should be paid in arms. In 1772, for instance, Osei Kwadwo asked the governors of the three European forts at Accra to credit him with four years' salary payable in guns, powder, lead and pewter.[28]

The successful employment of the Asante army as the instrument of rapid territorial expansion presupposes a highly developed system of military organisation. Rattray has described in some considerable detail the military organisation of the Asante divisional states of Asumegya, Bekwai, Kokofu, Dwaben, Kumawu, Mampong and Nsuta. The Asante national army was comprised of a body of scouts (Akwansrafo), an advance-guard (Twafo), a main body (Adonten), the King's personal body-guard (Gyase) a rear-guard (Kyidom) and two wings—left (Benkum) and right (Nifa). Moreover, the mere domestics of the King's household were not spared the rigours of campaigning. Stool-carriers, drummers, horn-blowers, umbrella-carriers, elephant-tail switchers, fan-bearers, hammock-carriers, sword-bearers, gun-bearers, minstrels and executioners were all liable for active service at a moment's notice.[28]

As the military tradition grew, the Asante warrior became highly disciplined. Evasion of military service was punished by death and the warrior usually took a very disdainful view of personal risk. The Asante, and the Akan in general, have a saying that *'fere ne owuo efenim owuo'*—that is, 'if it is a matter of choosing between disgrace and death then I should choose death'. Guided by this principle, an Asante war-lord would normally commit suicide rather than fall into enemy hands. Each army group took its supplies of ordnance and food to war. The Asante army also had well-trained medical orderlies, the Esumankwafo, a combat class who gave aid to the wounded and helped to remove the dead from the field.

Before setting out on a campaign the national priests or necro-mancers sacrificed to the gods and the ancestors to help them achieve victory. During the last three decades of the eighteenth and through-out the nineteenth centuries the Asante warriors also sought the prayers of the Moslem community in Asante to help them achieve victory in their wars. Dupuis noted that Osei Bonsu (1801–24) 'does not neglect to supplicate the Moslems for their prayers. . . .' The usefulness of the Moslems, however, was not confined to matters of prayer. Some of the Moslems accompanied the Asante army 'to make the great laws', i.e. the peace settlements, and it seems that such treaties were sometimes drawn up in Arabic.

The Asante warriors also believed that the amulets and talismans containing parchments inscribed with fragments of the Koran were efficacious in battle and all the great captains wore garments studded with these.[29] In 1807 Governor George Torrane noticed that the Asante army which defeated the Fante included 'many Moors, and every Ashantee man has a Gregory or Fitisch, which is a little square cloth inclosing some little sentences of the Al Koran; some have many'.[30] Indeed, the Asante soldiers had such belief in the potency of these talismans that, according to Bowdich, 'several Ashantee captains offered seriously to let us fire at them'.[31]

It was clear, however, that in the nineteenth century the British could not establish peaceful relations with the Asante. The Abolition of the Slave Trade Act of 1807 'gave notice of the British nation's resolve to stop the flow of West Africans from the Guinea Coast across the Atlantic'.[32] This act of the British Parliament made it illegal for British subjects to engage in the pernicious traffic in human beings. Apart from the Act itself, the British Government also signed treaties by means of which foreign nationals were similarly restricted. Furthermore, an African squadron of the British Navy was instituted to police the West African coast so as to seize contraband cargo that the British or foreign vessels might attempt to ship across the Atlantic to the Americas and the Caribbean islands. Finally, the British Government took over the administration of Sierra Leone in 1808 to provide a depot for slaves so seized.

Thus, since the British Government, urged on by the humanitarians and other interested bodies, was determined to stop the slave trade, it was almost impossible for the British to establish peaceful relations with Asante, which had, by 1820, become the main source of slaves on the Gold Coast. The British therefore reverted to their traditional policy of support for the coastal peoples against Asante.

A second reason why the British found themselves involved in the conflicts of Asante and the coastal states was also humanitarian. The British were not only interested in seeing the slave trade abolished and trade in natural products developed; they also wanted to ensure the promotion of Western education and civilisation. But most British officials and traders were convinced that such objectives could never be achieved until Asante's hold on the coastal states was broken.

A third reason was economic. British merchants were convinced that if Asante power could be destroyed, a vast field for commerce would be opened to them. In fact, it was partly this economic motive which had decided Governor Torrane and his Council to reverse the traditional British policy of hostility towards Asante. In 1807 Torrane wrote this to the African Committee: 'I have received a message from the King [of Asante], reporting that as soon as the war shall be over, he will return and form his camp near Annomaboo, to the end that we may arrange all points for the future of the country, and the regulations of trade; and here let me observe that an intercourse securely opened with Ashantee, offers prospects of the highest advantage; and the more so, as the Slave Trade is now at an end. The Ashantees have ivory and gold in great abundance, and the Fantees have ever thrown impediments in the way, so as to prevent their intercourse with us; but it appears to hold an object of more national importance, and one, if I can be the happy instrument of bringing about, I shall consider my services in Africa not altogether misapplied. I mean a thorough knowledge of the source of the Niger, and a direct and safer way of going to Tombuctu. . . .'[33]

As far as the Asante were concerned, their primary objective was to preserve their huge empire. This involved the continuation of the slave trade which had become a basis of the Asante economy; the establishment of a firm hold on the coastal states; the payment by the Europeans of ground rents for the forts and castles they occupied in Fante country; the return of criminals and runaway slaves from Asante; the payment of tributes by the vassal states; free access to Asante traders resorting to the coast for their trade; and, finally, respect for the Asante and their institutions.

At first the British tried to resolve their differences with the Asante peacefully. In 1817 a British mission led by F. James, Governor of James Fort, Accra, visited Kumasi. A treaty signed by T. E. Bowdich, who had superseded James, on behalf of the British Company and Asante, declared that 'there are no palavers now existing and that neither party has any claim upon the other'. But if Osei Bonsu by this agreement allowed the Governor and Council of Cape Coast Castle to mediate in disputes between himself and the coastal states he nonetheless regarded the coastal peoples as his subjects. In fact the Bowdich mission nearly failed to achieve its objectives because, although the British had been paying the ground rent for their fort at Accra, they had refused to pay the rents for their settlements in the Fante country. Governor Hope Smith (in office 1817–22) did not recognise Asante sovereignty over the coastal towns in which stood the British forts. He even took strong exception to the demands levied on Cape Coast and Anomabo by way of tribute and fines for various alleged offences.

The situation was saved, temporarily, by the arrival of Joseph Dupuis, who had been appointed first British Consul to Kumasi. Dupuis disliked the attitude of the British traders on the coast and he referred to them contemptuously as 'servants of a mercantile body'.[34] He was therefore inclined to sympathise with the Asante and he concluded a treaty with them which explicitly conceded Asante sovereignty over the coastal towns. The Council at Cape Coast Castle, of course, repudiated the Dupuis treaty and prepared to resist what it considered exhorbitant demands, hoping to satisfy the Asantehene with small token payments in the interest of trade. Thus when the British Government took over from the Company in 1822 the rupture between the British authorities on the coast and Asante was complete.

On 27 March 1822 Sir Charles Macarthy, who had already gained a high reputation in England for his handling of affairs in Sierra Leone, arrived on the Gold Coast to take charge of the British settlements. It has been argued that Macarthy did not come to the Gold Coast determined to provoke a rupture with the Asante. Be that as it may, it was certainly the case that Sir Charles had nothing but contempt for Asante and its institutions. He already saw the coastal states as a British protectorate which must be encouraged and assisted to help themselves against the 'barbarous' Asante.

Sir Charles Macarthy's contempt for Asante is shown in a number of ways. First when he arrived on the coast an Asante embassy was actually at Cape Coast to seek an assurance from the British authorities there that British intentions were peaceful. Macarthy not only ignored this embassy but also described its message as 'insulting'. Secondly, Sir Charles completely disregarded the authority of the Asantehene by failing to send a message to Kumasi as the courtesies of the country demanded.

Later in the year another incident occurred which further illustrates Macarthy's contempt for Asante institutions. A Fante serving as a sergeant in the British garrison at Anomabo took the Asantehene's name in vain. Now, under Asante customary laws the penalty for abusing the King was death and the sergeant was seized and carried to Abura Dunkwa where he was slapped in chains. For a while Osei Bonsu prudently held his hand, hoping that the British would make some favourable overtures for an accommodation. But none came, and in February of the following year the sergeant was put to death. The Asante further demanded that the Anomabo people should openly declare where their loyalty lay.

Sir Charles and his military authorities took it that this was clearly intended to affirm Asante sovereignty over Anomabo and the Fante, a claim which they could not tolerate. For Macarthy the Fante sergeant was a British subject and on hearing that an Asante prince and a few captains, together with 200 or 300 retainers were still at Abura Dunkwa, Macarthy summoned his officers and announced that the time had come to give the Asante 'an example [such] as would prevent a similar occurrence', and by 'chastisement to render the commission of crime hideous in their eyes'.[35] He resolved that since Asante spies were all over the place, the expedition to Abura Dunkwa should march out in the night and attack the Asante forces in the half-light of dawn the next morning. At 7 p.m. both the regular colonial troops and the volunteers started the twenty-mile journey to Abura Dunkwa.

It was calculated that this journey should have been covered by 4 a.m., but either intentionally or not the African guides misled the troops. Then, exhausted by several hours of struggling through the thick forest and scrambling over slippery rocks, the column was suddenly attacked by the Asante from the banks of a rugged defile.

Within a short time several dozen men had been killed, including Lieutenant Swanzy of the Royal African Corps.

The strength of the Asante ambush was unknown because its position was well chosen. Nevertheless, the 2nd Wes⁺ India Regiment, officered by a Captain Laing, continued to push on at the same time returning fire. But operating in an unknown country they soon lost their way and when the last remnants of the column eventually struggled to the safety of the British settlement at Anomabo more than fifty men were listed as wounded, killed or missing.

Far from 'seeing reason', Osei Bonsu announced that he would march on Cape Coast and Anomabo and destroy everybody there, black or white. Macarthy responded by organising the coastal peoples into a 'Grand Alliance'. On 10 May 1823 he announced the conclusion of a solemn oath of alliance involving 'the whole of the Fantee chiefs, only one excepted'. The primary objective of this alliance was to secure the independence of all the states from the Tano river in the west to the Volta in the east.

The British received information that the Asante were moving down into Wassa country and Macarthy planned a three-pronged advance to deal with them. A Captain Blenkerne, with a force consisting mainly of militiamen and African levies, was to make a looping march from the east to take the enemy either in the rear or on the flank. Laing, with a division of Fante troops, was to march along the Cape Coast–Kumasi road and create a diversion in Assin country. Finally, Macarthy, assisted by Major Chisholm with 2,500 men, including the Royal African Colonial Corps, a body of the 2nd West Indians and the Cape Coast Militia, marched towards Wassa to meet the enemy. Sir Charles was followed by his brigade-major, Ricketts, with the supplies.

At about 2 p.m. on 22 January 1824 the British and their allies met the Asante army, numbering more than 10,000, near the village of Bonsaso. Macarthy gave orders for the band of the Royal African Corps to strike up 'God Save the King'. To this the Asante replied with their own lively music.

It was not long before the Asante forces opened fire and it soon became clear that they not only outnumbered the British and their allies but also they were better tacticians. The Asante forces encircled their foes and engaged them in fierce battle. At one point De Graft, an African lieutenant in the British alliance, hauled a small brass cannon into position, loaded it with powder and loose musket balls and let fly at the advancing Asante. The Asante replied by rushing forward and killing those operating the cannon. At the height of the action Brandon, the British civilian storesman, returned from Cape Coast where he had been sent for the reserve ammunition. But when the ammunition boxes he brought were opened they were found to be full of biscuits.

In the meantime Sir Charles, who had been wounded three times, tried to order a retreat, but he was quickly overpowered by the Asante and his head was cut off.[36]

Macarthy's extravagance, followed by his defeat and death, damned his policy in the eyes of the British. His successors, Major-General Turner and Sir Neil Campbell, saw nothing to be gained by continuing his policy and no good reason for staying on the Gold Coast at all.

In the meantime British honour had been retrieved by the defeat of the Asante by the British and the allies in a series of battles. By an odd coincidence, Osei Bonsu died the same day that Macarthy was killed. But his successor, Osei Yaw Akoto, threw himself into the the war against the allies and swept all before him until he reached the outskirts of Cape Coast. But on July 1824 Major Chisholm, assisted by a few marines and seamen from British ships, succeeded in driving the Asante back to Kumasi.

The Asante were still confident of victory and they invaded the coast again. But this time they made a tactical error. They attacked the British and their allies on the open plains at Akatamanso near Dodowa in 1826. Though they were primarily experts in fighting in the bush, the Asante fought valiantly in the grassy plains of Accra, and at one point it looked as if their valour might still bring them victory. But the British commander, Colonel Purdon, called up his reserves and ordered them to open fire with Congreve rockets. 'The noise they made', wrote Claridge, 'the long tail of fire they left behind them, the local explosions, and the fearful wounds, led the enemy to believe that the English had some great "fetish" and were fighting them with thunder and lightning.'[37] Osei Yaw and his army withdrew to Kumasi and it soon became clear that the battle of Akatamanso had removed any immediate threat from Asante.

Nevertheless, after 1826 the British Government decided to wash its hands of Gold Coast affairs. There was no hope of a peaceful settlement of affairs largely because the coastal peoples were not magnanimous in victory. Having defeated the Asante, the coastal peoples expected the Asantehene and his chiefs to come and beg for peace. On the other hand, the British authorities feared that the Asante, smarting under a defeat at the hands of the coastal peoples, would never rest until they had 'glutted in the blood of their conquerors and destroyed every vestige of civilisation from their own frontier to Cape Coast and the River Volta'.[38]

In the circumstances the British handed over the settlements to a committee of three London merchants and granted them an annual subsidy of £4,000 for the upkeep of the forts. The merchants, however, were specifically asked to exercise their authority and jurisdiction only over the people living within the forts and not in any way to interfere in African trade and politics. On the Gold Coast the settlements were to be administered by a council elected by the merchants resident at Cape Coast and Accra who had been there for more than a year. The council was to be under a president elected by its members.

Captain George Maclean was appointed President of the Council in October 1829. He arrived in Cape Coast in February 1830 and stayed on until his death in May 1847.[39] Maclean was a realist who realised that neither trade nor missionary activities would flourish unless law and order was re-established. He therefore ignored his instructions and involved his administration in African affairs.

Soon after his arrival he negotiated for a peace treaty with Asante. This treaty was successfully concluded in April 1831. By the terms of the treaty the Asantehene recognised the independence of the coastal states and agreed to refer all disputes between Asante and the former vassal states to Cape Coast Castle for peaceful settlement. The southern states, in turn, undertook to keep the trading paths open and free to all persons engaged in lawful trade; not to force them to trade in any particular market, and not to insult the King of Asante. Finally, all parties to the treaty agreed to stop human sacrifices and to stop 'panyarring', that is, forcibly seizing debtors or their relations and enslaving them or selling them.

George Maclean was a wise administrator who by tact and exertion brought peace and prosperity to the peoples of the Gold Coast during his term of office. As a result of his work, peace was not only established between Asante and the southern states in the 1830s and 1840s but also British power and jurisdiction replaced that of Asante on the coast. In a word, Maclean converted the southern states into a British Protectorate.

Nevertheless, though Maclean's exertions had greatly extended British jurisdiction on the Gold Coast, his actions had no legal basis. Also, his enemies accused him of condoning and conniving at the slave trade. It was mainly for these reasons that upon the recommendations of a Parliamentary Select Committee of 1842 the British Government resumed direct responsibility for the administration of the forts. But because Maclean's judicial work was considered beneficial to the Africans he was given the minor post of a Judicial Assessor.

It was clear, however, that the succeeding British administrators had neither the tact nor the competence of Maclean to maintain law and order in the country. Thus after 1843 the old abuses, insults and attacks on Asante traders began again. The inability of his successors to maintain peace with Asante was recognised by Maclean himself. In 1846 he wrote: '. . . the present state of affairs is precisely one of these crisis which I have so often predicted would occur, and with which the Government, as now constituted, is utterly powerless and unable to deal. This day three years, I would, with the power and influence which I then wielded have set matters right again in ten days time. As things stand now, the result may be a new Ashantee war.'[40]

Maclean's fear of an Asante invasion of the 'Protectorate' materialised in 1863–4. Since the period of Maclean there had been an unspoken bargain to return criminal refugees. The failure of the British authorities to return an Asante Chief, Kwasi Gyani, and a runaway slave boy to the Asantehene led to an Asante invasion of the southern states in 1863. The British Governor, Richard Pine, who was in an acute moral dilemma, wrote thus to London: 'If against the old man there is the slightest shadow of a *prima facie* case of criminality, my course would be clear; but as it is, I dare not deliver him up, much less the runaway boy. Their blood will be upon my head; and yet I feel I am estranging, if not exasperating, the most powerful King on this coast, and upon whom, according to his ideas, I am committing a gross injustice.'[41]

King Kwaku Dua I, who seriously felt that the British could never be depended upon to keep their word, ordered his armies to invade the southern states. On two occasions the Asante forces defeated the allied forces under a Major Cochrane. They burnt more than thirty towns and villages and then recrossed the River Pra.

Governor Pine decided to mount an expedition to the Pra with six companies of West Indian troops. The plan of the campaign was badly organised, and the troops apparently had little appetite for the venture. The troops arrived at the Pra in the dry season and spent most of their time building stockades and a bridge. But soon the rains set in and dysentery and fever struck officers and men by the dozen. After lingering on for five months the last remnants of the expedition, more than half of them sick, returned to the coast.

Not a shot had been fired, yet the bulk of the ammunition had disappeared together with the guns and stores. This drew the cynical comment from the Asantehene that 'the forest is stronger than the whiteman's cannon'.[42]

The failure of Pine's expedition did nothing to inspire the people of the Protectorate with confidence in British power. In Britain popular indignation nearly unseated Lord Palmerston's government and a Parliamentary Select Committee was hastily appointed to enquire into the British West African settlements. This Commission, appointed in 1865, recommended *inter alia* 'that all further extension of territory or assumption of Government or new treaties offering any protection to native tribes, would be inexpedient and that the object of our policy should be to encourage in the natives the exercise of those qualities which may render it possible for us more and more to transfer to them the administration of all the Governments with a view to our ultimate withdrawal from all except, probably Sierra Leone'.[43]

In the 1860s, then, Britain's incompetent rule on the Gold Coast, coupled with Asante incursions into the Protectorate, forced the British Government to accept the policy of retrenchment advocated by 'Little Englanders' and merchants who wanted a free hand in West Africa without governmental interference.

But if British policy-makers and British public opinion were veering towards minimum commitments in West Africa, British administrators on the Gold Coast stood for greater involvement in African affairs. They held the view that trade and civilisation could not flourish in an atmosphere of instability and they therefore disregarded the recommendations of the 1865 Select Committee and continued their expansionist policies.

As early as 1850 the British authorities had bought the Danish settlements for £10,000 and in 1867 they agreed with the Dutch to exchange forts on the Gold Coast. According to this 'Sweet River Convention' all the Dutch forts and settlements and 'rights of sovereignty and jurisdiction', east of the Sweet River (i.e. River Kakum) near Elmina were to be taken over by the British whilst the Dutch were to take over those of the British to the west. Secondly, the Fante Confederation which sought to replace the weak British administration on the coast was destroyed by the British administrators. Both Ussher and Salmon saw the Fante national movement as a real challenge to British power and jurisdiction in the country and directed their hostile attention to the leaders of the Confederation who were described as half-educated rascals. In fact, in 1871,

Salmon, the acting administrator, caused the arrest and detention of the Executive Officers of the Confederation on the ridiculous charge of treason. The Colonial Office, of course, condemned Salmon's action and ordered the immediate release of the officials, but the Confederation never recovered from that perfidious conduct.[44]

This extension of British power and jurisdiction was resented by the chiefs of the Protectorate and the Asantehene. Early in 1865 King Aggery of Cape Coast criticised Maclean, who had, he said, 'in a very peculiar imperceptible and unheard of manner wrested from the hands of our Kings, Chiefs and headmen their power to govern their own subjects'.[45] The Asantehene Kofi Karikari, on the other hand, wanted to recover the lost provinces and also to ensure that Elmina did not fall into British hands. It was therefore with some surprise that he learnt that Dutch Governor Nagtglas was persuading the Elmina to join the Fante in alliance.

Kofi Karikari and his chiefs interpreted this action of Nagtglas as a 'sell-out' and dispatched troops under the intrepid Asante war-lord, Akyeampong, to protect Elmina. Akyeampong and his troops committed atrocities in the Dutch coastal districts, especially at Elmina, and since the Dutch were unable to impose law and order in their territories, they started negotiations to transfer their forts to the British.

King Kofi Karikari protested vigorously when he heard of the proposed treaty whereby the British would purchase all the Dutch possessions, including Elmina. In November 1870 the Asantehene wrote objecting to the transfer of Elmina to the British claiming it as his right, and saying that Elmina had, since time immemorial, paid annual tribute to his ancestors. The British Governor wrote to his Dutch counterpart that his government 'could not and would not purchase forts from the Netherlands Government which lay under the suspicion of being feudatory to a powerful native prince, the traditional enemy of its protected tribes'.[46] The Dutch denied the Asantehene's claim, saying that 'the King of Ashantee has no recognised claim upon the territory or people of Elmina. . . .'[47] They maintained that although they had paid an annual sum to the Asante, it was not a tribute but a present to keep up friendly relations. The Dutch further produced a fictitious document, the so-called 'A Certificate of Apology', bearing the mark of the Asantehene withdrawing his claim to Elmina and stating that his earlier letter had been 'a mistake'. King Kofi Karikari was furious when he later heard of this document which was clearly forged by the Dutch messenger, Plange.[45] Nevertheless the British authorities declared themselves satisfied and the cession of the Dutch settlements was duly ratified. The Dutch possessions were then formally handed over in April 1872, and the British authorities flattered themselves that all would be well.

But it soon became clear that the Asante were resolved not to accept the loss of Elmina. With the final departure of the Dutch, it became clear that the strengthened British position was a direct threat to Asante interests, and a determination to drive the Europeans out was added to their long-standing ambition to win back the southern states. The scale of the operation was commensurate with this wider aim.

The Asante general, Adu Bofo, who captured the Basel missionaries, Ramseyer and Kuhne, and the French trader, J. Bonnat, in the Krepi country in 1869,[49] was instructed to march to Denkyira with 4,000 or 5,000 men; the chief of Marawere, with a small force of 2,000 or 3,000 moved off to keep the Akyem in check, while Amankwa Tia, Bantamahene and Kontihene of Kumasi, led some 20,000 warriors and reserves drawn from all the Asante divisions to the coast along the Cape Coast–Kumasi road. These Asante warriors wore necklaces of razor-sharp knives and carried the long, red-stocked muskets known as Dane guns. The great captains, under their multi-coloured umbrellas, wore plumes of eagles' feathers draped with horse-tails. After five days of continuous ferrying across the Pra, the Asante army burned and plundered a few nearby villages and then proceeded to capture the first allied camp at Assin Nyankumasi. The Asante invasion swept forward successfully to the outskirts of Cape Coast and was joined by several of the former Dutch tribes, notably at Sekondi, Shama, Axim and Dixcove.

However anxious the British might have been to withdraw from the coast in 1865, they were not now prepared to be driven out by the Asante. R. W. Harley, the Administrator-in-Chief, who underestimated Asante intentions by asserting that he did not believe the move to be a prelude to an Asante war, was relieved of his post.

General Sir Garnet Wolseley was appointed civil administrator and military commander with full powers to free the Protectorate from the Asante 'menace'. His subordinates were a remarkable group of young enthusiasts, sometimes known as the 'Wolseley Ring'.

Sir Garnet's orders were to try to raise a force from the tribes of the Protectorate, stiffen it with his special service officers and lead it against the Asante. Having destroyed the invading Asante army, he was to obtain a peace treaty with the Asantehene, together with a large indemnity of gold and the release of the European prisoners.

But it was clear that though the British Government had at last decided that Asante power must be broken once and for all, it was not intended to achieve that objective with British troops. They should be called in only as a last resort. On his arrival at Cape Coast, therefore, Wolseley called a meeting of the chiefs of the Protectorate at which he told them that the Queen of England was much concerned by their sufferings and had sent him to help them. At the same time, Her Majesty would help only those who help themselves, and they should know that it was not an English war but a Fante war. This was old stuff to the assembled chiefs. They knew that British assistance had achieved very little in the past. Furthermore, it was quite obvious that the Asante invasions disrupted British trade as much as it disturbed the peace of the Protectorate. However, they politely replied that they would do their best to help. In actual fact only a few thousand African levies were prepared to join Wolseley's forces and he had to write to London for British troops.

On his arrival on the Gold Coast in October 1873, Sir Garnet Wolseley found about 20,000 Asante forces occupying threatening positions within an easy march of Elmina and Cape Coast. He therefore decided to attack them and it was later claimed that within a fortnight he had succeeded in precipitating the flight of the Asante army to Kumasi. The truth of the matter was that Amankwa Tia, the Asante general, had already decided to go home. His forces were battle worn and they were ravaged by smallpox and dysentery. Even so, their return was not a precipitate flight but a calculated withdrawal characteristic of a disciplined force. As Brackenbury, the military secretary of Wolseley, admitted later, 'the army of a civilised nation need not have been ashamed of a retreat conducted with such skill and such success'.[50]

On 9 December 1873 the long-awaited British troops arrived to join Wolseley's African levies. These troops comprised the 2nd Battalion of the Rifle Brigade, the 23rd Royal Welch Fusiliers and the 42nd Highlanders, with detachments of Engineers, Artillery and auxiliary services. The 1st West India Regiment also arrived from Jamaica.

The plan of the campaign was that Captain Glover R.N., with a small body of Hausa troops, was to raise an allied force in Accra and the south-east and advance towards Dwaben. Captain Butler was to raise a force of the Akyem and advance more or less parallel with Glover towards Kumasi. Captain Dalrymple was to advance with a force to Wassa and Denkyira and attack the Asante from the south-west. The main column, under Sir Garnet Wolseley himself, was to advance straight up the main Cape Coast–Kumasi road across the Pra.

At the same time, Sir Garnet sent to Kofi Karikari the ultimatum he had been instructed to send by three messengers. But these were intercepted by Amankwa Tia who sent a reply as follows:

Sir,

I have received those two letters which you sent to me in order to send them to the King of Ashantee. For what purpose I came here is that: Assin, Dankra [Denkyira], Akyem, Wassaw. Those four nations belong to the King of Ashantee and they refused to serve the King . . . and when you deliver Assin, Dankra, Akyem and Wassaw unto me, I shall bring unto the King there is no any quarrel with you.[51]

On 7 January 1874 an advance party of the allied troops occupied Asaman north of the Pra, to serve as a bridgehead for the bridge constructed by the Engineers. Sir Garnet then wrote to Kumasi, warning the Asantehene that he was about to begin his advance. He also offered the following armistice terms: all prisoners in Asante to be delivered, an indemnity of 50,000 ounces of gold to be paid; Sir Garnet with an escort of 500 men to visit Kumasi and sign a formal treaty after hostages had been given for his safety.

The Asante, of course, did not intend to comply with these requests, but the situation was certainly serious, for on the day on which the General's letter was written a big sacred tree, planted in Kumasi by the famous Okomfo Anokye, fell down. This led the Asanteman Council to release all the Europeans. Kofi Karikari wrote to Wolseley on 23 January promising to make Amankwa Tia personally responsible for the indemnity, because he had exceeded his instructions in attacking Elmina. Sir Garnet replied by insisting on the release of all Fante prisoners, the payment of half the indemnity as a first instalment and the delivery of Efua Kobiri, the Queen-Mother, the heir to the Golden Stool, and the heirs to the stool of Dwaben, Mampong, Kokofu and Bekwai. This was asking for the impossible and the Asante prepared for war.

Amankwa Tia was superseded as commander of the Asante national army by Kwabena Dwumo, the Omanhene of Mampong, in accordance with Asante military tradition. Moreover, Asamoa Nkwanta, the veteran Asante warrior, was instructed to take charge of the Adanse forces, who were to delay the British as much as possible. The Asante plan was that the Adanse and other advanced troops should offer stiff resistance to entice the British well into the country in the hope of an easy victory; that the defensive position at Amoafo should occupy the whole attention of the invader for some days at least; and that while the British were being detained here, the Dwaben should make a great detour to the east, break down the bridge at Praso, and hold the crossing of the Pra, cutting the British off from the sea.

The fiercest battle of the war was fought at Amoafo near Bekwai. The landscape was thickly forested. The Asante army flanked the advance of the British as they came down the first hill, and enclosed them in a semi-circle. The commander of the leading British column, Brigadier Sir Archibald Alison, a veteran of the Crimea, has described the battle of Amoafo thus: 'The peculiarities of Ashanti warfare were now strongly developed. We were in the midst of a semi-circle of hostile fire, and we hardly ever caught sight of a man. As company after company of the 42nd descended . . . into the ravine, they were almost immediately lost sight of in the bush, and their position could only be judged from the sharp crack of their rifles. Another difficulty developed when a company was sent to support another in action, it saw nothing but bush in its front, and speedily came under heavy fire of slugs from the enemy.'[52] Asante skirmishers caused considerable confusion by slipping between columns, lying down, and firing at both. This had the effect of making it impossible for the British to know whether fire was coming from their own side or their enemy.

Though the Asante stood their ground admirably and kept up the heaviest of fires, the battle of Amoafo was won by the British due to superiority in weapons. The rifles were, of course, superior to the muzzle-loading guns used by the Asante and the continual advance of the Black Watch gave the Asante too little time to reload. Even so, seven companies of the Black Watch and a company of the Royal Welch Fusiliers could make little impression on the Asante position until the two seven-pounder guns were brought into action. Against these, of course, the Asante could not make a reply. The Asante losses were unknown; 150 of their dead were buried by the British, and many more were carried by the Asante themselves. The British lost one officer, a Major Baird, and three men killed, twenty-one officers and 173 men wounded. The heaviest losses were among the Black Watch. But the bravery, disposition and skill of the Asante army were proved as conclusively at Amoafo as was the inadequacy of their weapons.

The British and their allies spent the next day, 1 February, in bringing up supplies, and in attacking and destroying Bekwai. On the 3rd the invading army arrived on the Oda river. At this point Sir Garnet Wolseley became anxious of his time-table. The advance was slow because of the difficulty of bringing up supplies through a predominantly hostile country and guarding the line of communications against attack. He decided, therefore, to form an advance base and to make a quick dash for Kumasi. His object was that such a bold venture might end the fighting and bring the Asante to ask for peace.

At six o'clock the advance began, and after two hours hard fighting the advance guard of the Rifle Brigade led by Colonel Wood reached the village of Odaso. Wolseley's column took three hours to cover the 500 yards to Odaso, repeating the process of short rushes by artillery and infantry which had won Amoafo. By 11 a.m. the British troops were defending Odaso fiercely from Asante counter-attacks.

The veteran Asante war-lord, Asamoa Nkwanta, had laid the plans for the defence of Odaso and the Asantehene himself was present. Asamoah's plan was that a large force was to be held in reserve to the flank of the road, with orders to close in and cut the British communications if they succeeded in forcing their way to the village. This was done, but the advance of the Highlanders, so gallantly carried out, was contrary to Asante war strategy. The Asante regarded an army to be in great danger if threatened on the flank, and ruined if threatened in the rear. The Black Watch broke through all opposition and reached Kumasi at half past five, having been marching and fighting for nearly twelve hours after a night spent in grass huts under a torrential rainstorm. Sir Garnet Wolseley arrived soon after six, and, forming up in the main street of Kumasi, the troops gave three cheers for the Queen.

The British and their allies had reached Kumasi but Asante power had not been broken. Kofi Karikari was out of reach, no hostages had been given, no indemnity paid and no treaty signed. Sir Garnet therefore sent another letter to the Asantehene demanding that either the King, the Queen-Mother or the heir to the Golden Stool should appear to negotiate, and that if these people did not come, others of high rank should be sent.

But this was of no effect because during the night all the citizens left Kumasi with their belongings so that the place was completely deserted in the morning; while the Fante prisoners who were released looted and set fire to the town.

The British General was greatly worried. He had over sixty wounded to carry back and he had to get back before his supplies failed, and all the afternoon it rained in torrents. He decided to wait no longer than one day, and as the Asantehene's messengers did not appear, he had the town fired and the Asantehene's palace blown up. On the morning of 6 February 1874 Sir Garnet began his march back to the coast.

On 13 February envoys from the Asantehene overtook Wolseley at Fomena, the Adansi capital, and promised that the King would accept his conditions. They produced 1,040 ounces of gold, and they took back with them a draft treaty for signature.

The Treaty of Fomena, which was signed by Kofi Karikari and nine Kumasi chiefs and by representatives of Dwaben, Bekwai, Kokofu, Kuntanase, Nsuta, Mampong and five other states, was executed at Cape Coast on 14 March. The main points of the treaty was that the Asante agreed to pay an indemnity of 50,000 ounces of gold; the King renounced all allegiance from Denkyera, Assin, Akyem and Adansi; the King also renounced Asante claims on Elmina and all payments from the British in respect of any of the forts. The Asante also agreed to withdraw their troops from the south-west and to keep open the trade routes. Finally, the Asantehene promised to do his best to stop human sacrifices. This treaty was meant to replace the Maclean Treaty of 1831 as the basis of relations between the British and Asante.

The fall of Kumasi shook the Asante kingdom to its foundations. By the treaty of Fomena, it was clear that Asante had lost the southern provinces for good. The Boron states to the north and north-west as well as Dagomba and Gonja also took advantage of the confusion in Asante to assert their independence. Furthermore, metropolitan Asante was on the point of disintegration. Adansi had decided to join the British colony of the Gold Coast, whereas Dwaben, Kokofu, Bekwai and Nsuta became disaffected.

Kofi Karikari himself was soon destooled for rifling the royal mausoleum. It was clearly a dismembered and demoralised remnant of an empire that Kwaku Dua III (Agyeman Prempeh) inherited in 1888.

Agyeman Prempeh's accession to the Golden Stool[53] was opposed by Kokofu, Mampon and Nsuta, and these states rose in rebellion soon after his enstoolment. Prempeh's task therefore was to rebuild the empire and he did this through diplomacy and war. He attacked and defeated the Kokofu with the help of the Bekwai. He then turned northwards and crushed the revolts of Nsuta and Mampon. Finally, though the Dwaben were still living in the colony, Yao Sapon, a member of the royal family, was recognised as the Dwabenhene. Thus within a few months after his accession Prempeh was able to prevent the Asante Union from dissolving into its component parts.

But he realised that Asante's greatest enemy was the British on the coast. It was common knowledge that the disaffection of the Dwaben, Kokofu and Adansi had the full backing of the British. And now that a determined central authority was emerging in Prempeh, the British became openly hostile. They decided to extend their protection to all who cared to desert the Asantehene and come into British territory or accept British protection. They had extended their protection over Sefwi in 1887 and a British mission visited Bondugu in 1888 in an unsuccessful bid to bring that country under British rule.

It was against this background that Prempeh wrote to the British Governor in 1889 objecting to the extension of British protection to Kwawu and other Asante dominions. He followed this up in July 1890 with a large mission to the Governor to ask for British help in re-establishing his authority over the rebellious states, and demanded the repatriation of all Asante refugees in the British colony.

But the British fear of the revival of Asante power was reinforced by the knowledge that the Germans and the French were closing in on the Gold Coast hinterland from Togo and the Ivory Coast respectively. Since the 1874 Anglo–Asante War, the international situation had changed fundamentally because the Partition of Africa was now in full swing. Therefore, they not only ignored the King's demands but went on to declare a protectorate over Atebubu. Furthermore they added insult to injury by sending an officer to Kumasi to invite the Asantehene to place his country under British protection.

King Prempeh rejected this invitation politely but firmly: 'The suggestion that Asante in its present state should come and enjoy the protection of Her Majesty the Queen and Empress of India I may say is a matter of very serious consideration, and which I am happy to say we have arrived at this conclusion, that my kingdom of Asante will never commit itself to any such policy. Asante must remain independent as of old, at the same time to remain friendly with all white men. I do not write this in a boastful spirit, but in the clear sense of its meaning . . . the cause of Asante is progressing and there is no reason for any Asante man to feel alarm at the prospects or to believe for a single instant that our cause has been driven back by the events of the past hostilities.'[54] After sending this reply Prempeh turned his attention to the north-west with the view of subduing the Boron states. In 1892 and 1893 he attacked and defeated the Nkoranza, the Mo and the Abease and only the timely arrival of a British contingent under Sir Francis Scott saved Atebubu. It was in 1893, too, that Asibe the Kokofuhene decided to return to Asante, but he was arrested and detained in Accra by the British.

In the meantime the British were so worried about Asante that when they received the King's reply they suggested that Prempeh should receive a British Resident at Kumasi in return for stipends to himself and his leading chiefs. When the Asante chiefs refused to be bribed new pressures were turned on. The British insisted that the Asante should now pay all the indemnity which Sir Garnet Wolseley had demanded in 1874. Torn between their desire to remain independent and their desire not to offend the British, the Asante chiefs decided to dispatch an embassy to England 'to go and see the Queen'. This Asante mission was led by Prince Owusu Ansa. The mission was unsuccessful because neither the Foreign Office nor the Colonial Office was prepared to receive them. Snubbed and bewildered, the Asante envoys were further dismayed when they learnt that the British were sending an expedition to Asante again. They hurried back to the Gold Coast only to discover that the British expedition had already reached the Pra.

The British expedition led by Sir Francis Scott consisted of a special Service Corps of picked men from several British regiments: the West Yorkshire Regiment, some West Indian troops, West African irregulars, Hausa artillery and an army of 10,000 carriers. But there was no fighting between Scott's army and the Asante. The Asante chiefs were not prepared to fight a war which they could not possibly win. Instead, they agreed, rather reluctantly, that they should submit to British protection. The Bekwai chief had already submitted and his town had been occupied peacefully by Robert Baden-Powell's column.

Asante envoys met Scott's army at the outskirts of Kumasi and informed them that the Asantehene was prepared to submit and that a treaty should be signed to that effect without the army entering Kumasi. Scott, however, was determined to enter the Asante capital and on 17 January 1896, after a raging tornado had cost the column a sleepless and miserable night, a British army entered Kumasi for the second time in history.

The Asantehene received the column seated on a raised dais in the square in front of the palace. He wore a black crown heavily worked with gold, a silk robe and embroidered sandals. Gold and silver ornaments dangled from his wrists. Beside him sat the Queen-Mother, a composed attractive woman, surrounded by a retinue of brightly clad female attendants. The lower portions of the dais were occupied by the other chiefs. After the customary greetings Scott thanked the Asantehene and his people for not offering any resistance to the British army and said that the Governor, who was the Queen's representative on the coast, would arrive the next day to negotiate.

Governor Sir William Maxwell arrived on Saturday and arranged to meet the King and his chiefs on Monday. At the meeting Maxwell stated that Prempeh had been unco-operative over the British ultimatums sent him, that he had allowed envoys to go to England in direct opposition to the wish of the government and that he had not fulfilled the terms of the treaty signed with Sir Garnet Wolseley. The Governor further alleged that human sacrifices had taken place since the signing of the treaty and the indemnity had not been settled. However, there was no need to depose Prempeh provided he now made his submission and paid 50,000 ounces of gold.

Whatever the King's feelings might have been, he now offered no comment. After waiting for a few minutes, clearly fighting his emotions, he and the Queen-Mother slipped off their sandals, walked across to where the British officers were sitting, prostrated themselves and embraced the feet of Maxwell and Scott. Then he declared that Asante was under the protection of the British Crown.

But the British were not now interested in formal submission by the Asantehene. They had decided that the annexation of Asante was necessary to the prosperity and growth of British interests in West Africa and they were bent on abduction of the Asantehene and other important chiefs in Asante. Thus, to the utter bewilderment of the assembled Asante, the King, the Queen-Mother, the King's father, his two uncles, his brother, the two war-chiefs and the kings of Mampong, Edweso and Offinso, as well as the Ansa brothers, were made prisoners and taken to Elmina Castle. The Asante captives were then taken to Sierra Leone and finally to the Seychelles Islands.

As soon as Prempeh was out of the way, Asante was declared a British Protectorate and a resident was stationed in Kumasi as the representative, under the Governor, of Her Britannic Majesty. The British also built a fort at Kumasi and forced the chiefs to provide transport and road gangs for the government. This effectively forestalled the French and the Germans who were closing in on Asante from modern Ivory Coast and Togo respectively.

Although deprived of their leader, the Asante had not been conquered; they had been tricked into submission and the indications were that they were determined to fight again for their independence. Bitterness united the Asante and large stores of weapons and ammunition were quietly and patiently amassed against the day they might strike for their liberation. Nevertheless, many of the older people felt that force would not be needed. It was believed that the Asantehene would soon return.

However, the newly appointed Governor, Sir Frederick Hodgson, added insult to injury by demanding the surrender of the Golden Stool, the very symbol of Asante unity and prosperity. In December 1899 Hodgson ordered his private secretary, Captain Armitage, to mount a small expedition of Hausas and carriers to search for the Stool. His mission, however, was unsuccessful and Armitage returned to the coast.

The failure of Armitage decided Governor Hodgson himself to go to Kumasi to supervise the search for the Golden Stool. He was accompanied by his beautiful wife, Lady Mary Alice Hodgson. At Kumasi, Hodgson addressed a large gathering of Asante chiefs and people. He informed the Asante that Prempeh would not be allowed to return to Asante; instead the King's powers of paramountcy would be vested in the British resident. He reminded the chiefs that the old war indemnity had not been paid. After saying all this Hodgson demanded that the Asante should surrender the Golden Stool because as the Queen's representative he alone was entitled to sit on it. In fact no Asantehene had ever sat on the Golden Stool and the suggestion that a British governor might do so was provocative in the extreme. Nevertheless, the Asante listened in silence, thanked His Excellency for meeting them, regretted that they were unable to pay the sums of money he had mentioned and returned home to make the final preparations for war.

Yaa Asantewaa, the Queen-Mother of Edweso, placed herself at the head of the war-party. The Asante attacked the Governor and his party and forced them to seek refuge in the fort which was besieged.[55]

In the meantime, on 25 April 1900, 250 soldiers, who had been hurried to the Gold Coast from Lagos in answer to Hodgson's urgent call for help, left Praso under a Captain Aplin with a seven-pounder gun and two Maxims. The column was within three miles of Kumasi when it was attacked by the Asante. A Maxim and the seven-pounder were used, but the reply was so devastating that the men serving the guns were quickly shot down. After some heavy fighting, the Maxims became overheated and jammed, while the seven-pounder ammunition had gone. Out of 250 men, five were dead and 139 wounded. All six officers were injured. The seven-pounder was abandoned on the way and Aplin's ammunition and supplies were exhausted.

At first the Asante tried to attack the fort itself, but the machine-guns on the bastions proved too effective for them and they settled down to a long and patient siege. Stockades were built on each of the tracks leading out of the town, and a war-path was cut through the forest in a complete circle around Kumasi, so that reinforcements could quickly be brought to bear on any position. Each Asante company had its allotted station in the cordon, while reserves were held at general headquarters, together with an intelligence department of spies, linguists and fetish men. A corps of crack shots, composed of professional hunters, was armed with rifles including a few .303 carbines and .22 rook rifles captured in Kumasi. The bulk of the Asante warriors, however, still had their ancient muskets.

The extraordinarily heavy fire brought to bear on the British columns was usually achieved by a fighting formation of three lines, each consisting of a company commanded by its own captain. The first line would fire and double to the rear for freshly loaded guns while the second line ran forward, discharged a volley, and was replaced by a third line, after which the first company was ready to begin the cycle again. For hand-to-hand fighting the Asante carried long knives in skin scabbards at their girdles, but usually they preferred the gun using their forest craft to remain hidden from the enemy. During the night the Asante camps kept up a morale-boosting ritual of question and answer by drums, roughly resembling the traditional claims and counter-claims of prowess exchanged elsewhere by European regiments.

Meanwhile the Governor and his party in the fort were running short of food and many were also suffering from smallpox. And as no relief column appeared Hodgson gave orders to march out fighting. The flight started at dawn on 23 June 1900. The British and their allies avoided the main Kumasi–Cape Coast road where the main Asante army lay in wait for them. Armitage led the way with a friendly Asante captain as his guide. The Gold Coast soldiers, under a Captain Legget, formed the advance guard. Then came Morris with a contingent from Gambaga which, with twenty men of the Coast Constabulary, formed the body-guard of Sir Frederick and Lady Hodgson, while the Lagos troops, under Aplin, brought up the rear.

But the runaways soon came face to face with an Asante stockade at Patase, a suburb of Kumasi. It was six feet high and five feet thick, built of immense tree-trunks with earth rammed between them. Armitage tried to charge with the leading soldiers but was beaten back, his guide hit in the arm and Legget mortally wounded. By sheer luck, the British and their allies succeeded in pushing on. There was a heavy downpour or rain and the Asante, hampered in their musket-loading, fought with reckless desperation for somewhere to pass the night and tend their wounds. Instead of pursuing the fugitives, they withdrew to their camps for the evening.

As soon as the Asante realised that the cordon at Patase had been broken, Antoa Mensa, a Kumasi chief, was detailed to give chase with 1,500 men. Mensa's men fell on the rear-guard of the escaping column and almost overwhelmed it. The carriers threw away their baggage, and Mensa, instead of keeping his men in hand and pressing home the attack, allowed them to stop and loot the British baggage.

Nevertheless, attacks continued on the column throughout the day from both front and rear. But the column pressed on till they reached Manso-Nkwanta, whose chief, Kwakye Nketsia, had remained pro-British throughout the rising. It was at Nkwanta that Hodgson and his fleeing party stopped and enjoyed a much-needed rest.

In the meantime Colonel Carter, commander of the forces from Southern Nigeria, had almost reached Dompoase with 350 troops and a seven-pounder when he fell into a devastating ambush. Carter was hit in the eye, while officers and men went down on all sides. The half-blinded commander had to order a retreat, and, with more than half its men killed or wounded, the force fell back to Fumsu.

By this time a company of the West African Frontier Force under a Captain Wilson had marched from another point with instructions to join Carter's line at Kwisa and assist his advance. Wilson's forces were also attacked by the Asante and Wilson himself was killed. The army had to retreat to Fumsu. A stronger force of the West African Regiment from Sierra Leone, under a Colonel Burroughs, next pushed forward to Bekwai. Here they were attacked by Kokofu warriors who enveloped Burroughs' column. Burroughs tried hard to deploy his companies outwards to meet the attack, but the Asante army, fighting with great coolness and skill, were more than a match. Burroughs was therefore forced to fall back to Asumegya.

In July, Willcocks, leading the main relief column, reached Fumsu. Divided and greatly out-armed, the Asante divisional armies defended their country with fierce vigour. Several towns had to be taken by the British and their allies by hand-to-hand fighting. In one instance an army of 4,000 levies under white officers was halted and driven back from Boankra by 250 Asante troops.

By September, however, a British force of nearly 2,000 troops was camped at Kumasi and the Asante chiefs began to send in flags of truce. The British promised amnesty early in October and announced that the Asante who put down their arms would not be treated as rebels. Only those found guilty of murder would be punished.

But Yaa Asantewaa, the Queen-Mother of Edweso, and a number of the Asante chiefs refused to negotiate. This led to the last and final battle at Aboaso, a few miles north-west of Kumasi. Willcocks met the Asante army on sloping land leading to the village. His force, supported by field-guns and machine-guns, consisted of 1,200 troops, including Central African Rifles, West African Rifles, West African Frontier Force and Sikhs. Once again the Asante army fought with great courage and skill. But however much they tried, they could not stand up to the superior arms of the enemy and they were defeated. Yaa Asantewaa was captured and sent, among some fifteen other leaders of the rising, to join Prempeh in the Seychelles Islands.

The conclusion of the last Asante war, in 1900, resulted in the formal annexation of Asante as a British possession. King Prempeh and his fellow exiles were not brought back until 1924. He was made Kumasihene in 1926 until his death in 1931. But the Asante recognised him as their king and his successor, Nana Sir Osei Agyeman Prempeh II, was recognised as the Asantehene in 1935 when the Asante Confederacy was restored in that year.

It is clear, then, that the Asante were defeated by the British and their allies not because they lacked courage and discipline but mainly because the enemy used modern weapons unknown to the Asante. Secondly, though the Asante were great fighters in the forest and used ambuscades to great effect, they did not resort to guerilla warfare. This was a great strategic error which greatly detracted from their efficiency. Finally, after 1874, the Asante were not able to to present a united front to the British. There were also pro-British Asante who contributed a lot to the final defeat of the Asante. This is particularly true of the Asante divisions of Agona and Mango Nkwanta.

ABBREVIATIONS USED IN NOTES

W.I.C.   Archives of the 2nd Dutch West India Company in the State Archives, The Hague.

V.G.K.   Danish West India and Guinea Company in the Royal Archives, Copenhagen.

N.B.K.G.   Archives of the Dutch Possessions in Guinea in the State Archives, The Hague.

T70   Treasury Papers in P.R.O. London.

C.O.   Colonial Office Papers in P.R.O. London.

P.R.O.   Public Record Office, London.

NOTES

1 On traditional histories connected with Osei Tutu and Okomfo Anokye see, for example, C. C. Reindorf, *A History of the Gold Coast and Asante,* Basle, 1897. Sir Francis Fuller, *A Vanished Dynasty: Ashanti,* London, 1921. R. S. Rattray, *Ashanti Law and Constitution,* London, 1929.

2 See map page 21

3 See map of Fante states.

4 T70/31. William Mutter, Cape Coast Castle, 27 May 1764.

5 T70/1536. Governor and Council, Cape Coast Castle, 1778.

6 See, for example, T70/31 Gilbert Petrie, Cape Coast Castle, 13 September 1766.

7 T70/30. Diary or Narrative of Transactions with the Fantees from the death of Intuffero, King of Warsaw. Entry dated 23 September 1753. Intsiful (Intuffero), rebelled against Asante Domination in 1726 and continued in that position till his death in 1752.

8 T70/31. John Hippisley, Cape Coast Castle, 13 September 1766.

9 See below.

10 T70/5. Abstract of letters received by the Royal African Company of England from the coast of Africa. Letter dated 8 May 1709.

11 V.G.K. Billesen, Christiansborg Castle, Accra, 21 July 1744.

12 On Asante–Danish relations during the 1790s see, for example, J. K. Fynn. 'Ashanti and Her Neighbours, c.1700–1807'. An unpublished Ph.D. thesis submitted to the University of London, 1964, ch. 5.

13 N.B.K.G. 82, William Butler, Axim, to Director-General H. Haring, Elmina, 6th February 1715.

14 T70/31. Gilbert Petrie, Cape Coast Castle, 6 November, 1767.

15 *Ibid.* same 9 October and 6 November 1767.

16 T70/152. Minutes of the Council at Cape Coast Castle, 11 August 1772. See also map of Fante states.

17 See Fynn 1964, *op. cit.,* pp. 221–4.

18 T70/26. Committee of Merchants, London, to John Hippisley, Cape Coast Castle, 3 September 1766.

19 T70/35. George Torrane, Cape Coast Castle, 12 June 1807.

20 V.G.K. Guinea Journal No. 1217. C. Schioning, Christiansborg Castle, Accra, 5 June 1811.

21 T. E. Bowdich, *A Mission from Cape Coast Castle to Ashantee,* London, 1819, p. 341.

22 J. Dupuis, *Journal of a Residence in Ashantee,* London, 1824, pt. 2, p. xxvi.

23 Bowdich, 1819, pp. 179 and 181–2.

24 William Bosman wrote thus of Gold Coast armies at the beginning of the eighteenth century. 'If I have before talk'd of Negroes who followed the wars you must not from thence infer that they make that their whole employment. No, it is but one part . . . all the Negroes in the country are soldiers as long as the war continues . . . the war ended each man applies himself to the exercise of his particular calling.' W. Bosman, *A New and Accurate Description of the Coast of Guinea divided into the Gold, the Slave and the Ivory Coasts,* London, 1705, p. 70.

25 T70/35. George Torrane, Cape Coast Castle, 20 July 1807.

26 T70/31. John Hippisley, Cape Coast Castle, 25 April 1766.

27 V.G.K. Joost Platfues, F. Roemer, Carl Engmann, Christiansborg Castle, Accra, 16 February 1784.

28 (a) T70/979. Accra Day Books. Entry for 1 July 1772.

28 (b) See, for example, Rattray, 1929, *op. cit.,* chs. XI–XXIII.

29 On the role of Islam in Asante see, especially, I. Wilks, *The Northern Factor in Ashanti History* (Institute of African Studies, Legon. 1961), pp. 14–29.

30 T70/35. George Torrane, Cape Coast Castle, 20 July 1807.

31 Bowdich, 1819, pp. 271–2.

32 Edmund Collins, 'The Panic Element in Nineteenth Century British Relations with Ashanti', in *Transactions of the Historical Society of Ghana,* vol. V, pt. 2, p. 92.

33 T70/35. George Torrane, Cape Coast Castle. 20 July 1807, Henry Meredith, who was second-in-command of Anomabo fort during the Asante invasion, also remarked that 'the Ashantees seem not to be unacquainted with the customs of a civilised people'. H. Meredith, *An account of the Gold Coast of Africa,* London, 1812, p. 148.

C

34 W. W. Claridge, *History of the Gold Coast and Ashanti,* London, 1915, p. 241.
35 C.O. 267/58. Charles Macarthy to Lord Bathurst, Cape Coast Castle, 7 April 1823; 16 May 1823.
36 The best authority on this war is H. J. Ricketts, *Narrative of the Ashantee War,* London, 1831.
37 Claridge, 1915, pp. 387–8.
38 C.O. 268/26. Bathurst to Campbell, 23 March 1827.
39 The best authority on Maclean's administration is G. E. Metcalfe, *Maclean of the Gold Coast,* London, 1962.
40 C.O. 96/12. George Maclean to B. Cruickshank, 19 December 1846.
41 C.O. 96/58. Richard Pine to the Duke of Newcastle 10 December 1862 and 12 May 1863.
42 On further details of the Anglo–Asante War of 1863-4. See G. E. Metcalfe, *Great Britain and Ghana, Documents of Ghana History 1807–1957,* London, 1964, pp. 291–301.
43 See *ibid.,* pp. 305–18.
44 On the Fante Confederation see, for example, D. Kimble, *A Political History of Ghana 1850–1928,* London, 1963, ch. VI.
45 C.O. 96/67. John Aggery to R. Pine, Cape Coast, 16 March 1865.
46 Colonial Office to Foreign Office, London, 3rd February, 1871.
47 Metcalfe, *Documents,* 1964, p. 333.
48 See, for example, D.S. Coombs, 'The Place of the Certificate of Apologie in Ghanaian History' in *Transactions of the Historical Society of Ghana,* iii, p. 182.
49 On this episode see Ramseyer & Kuhn, *Four Years in Ashante,* London, 1874.
50 H. Brackenbury, *Narrative of the Ashantee war,* London, 1874.
51 Alan Lloyd, *The Drums of Kumasi,* London, 1964, p. 76.
52 Quoted in *ibid,* p. 109.
53 On the reign and exile of Prempeh I. See W. Tordoff, *Ashanti under the Prempehs,* London, 1962.
54 See Metcalfe, *Documents,* 1964, pp. 448–51
55 This account of the Yaa Asantewaa war is based on Metcalfe, *Documents,* pp. 507–25, and A. Lloyd, *op. cit.,* pp. 161–97.

A. S. KANYA-FORSTNER

Mali–Tukulor

Militant Islam presented the greatest challenge and mobilised the sternest resistance to the European occupation of Africa in the nineteenth century. Muslim polities, with their written languages, their heritage of state-making and the cohesive force of a universal religion preaching the brotherhood of all believers, could generally organise resistance on a wider scale than political units whose extent was limited by the ties of common ancestry. Muslims also had a strong incentive to oppose the advance of Christian power. The practice of their religion involved the strict observance of ritual and social obligations, and this made it theoretically imperative for them to live in an Islamic community, governed by a righteous ruler according to the precepts of the law *(Sharia)*. Since the realms of politics and religion were supposedly inseparable, it was their duty to establish the political as well as the religious ascendancy of Islam and, when necessary, to defend their community by force of arms. Participation in the *jihad* or holy war was one of their fundamental obligations. Islamic ideals did not always correspond to reality; but during the eighteenth and nineteenth centuries the Muslim world experienced a profound religious revival which gave birth to a succession of militant, reformist empires, pledged to the forceful extension of the *dar al-Islam*. The rulers of these *jihad* states could not easily co-operate with Europeans; they could certainly not accept European suzerainty without jeopardising the religious sanctions for their political authority. They had to resist the pressures of European imperialism not merely to safeguard their political independence but also to preserve the religious integrity on which they sought to base their societies. Their resistance, therefore, was likely to be ferocious.

The French learned this lesson early in Algeria. Here the Islamic revival had expressed itself initially through the spread of religious confraternities. These *tariqas,* drawing many of their adherents from the indigenous tribes of the interior, had long played an important political role as leaders of Algerian resistance against Turkish rule. When the French overthrew the tottering Ottoman administration in 1830, they led the tribes against the new invader, proclaiming the *jihad* in 1832 and electing Abd al-Qadir, a prominent member of the Qadiriyya order, as their commander. During the next fifteen years Abd al-Qadir devoted all his considerable administrative, military and political talents to the creation of a unified Algerian state, governed by the *Sharia* and strong enough to withstand the military might of France. In the end the French needed 100,000 men, the flower of their army, to bring him to heel.

French officers observing developments in the Western Sudan during the 1850s could see many parallels with Algeria. The Muslim borderlands between the Sahara and the Guinea forest had been among the first to feel the impact of the revivalist movement. As early as 1725, migrant Fula herdsmen from the Upper Niger, led by missionaries of the Qadiriyya order, had proclaimed the *jihad* in Futa Jallon, and after half a century of war they established a theocratic state there. Inspired by their success, the fervently Muslim *torodbe* caste of the closely related Tukulor peoples along the Lower Senegal rebelled against the ruling *denyanke* nobility and seized control of the Futa region of Senegal. In decades to come, similar revolutions were to topple the *ardos* of Masina on the Upper Niger and the rulers of the Hausa states between the Niger and Lake Chad. By the mid-nineteenth century most of the West African interior had passed once more under Muslim sway.

For the French in their bases on the Lower Senegal, the most dangerous of the Sudanese *jihads* was that of Umar b. Said Tall. Umar was a Tukulor, born at the end of ᵗhe eighteenth century in Futa-Toro, one of the states in the new Futa confederacy. The member of a minor *torodbe* family, he received a strongly religious upbringing and was initiated at an early age into the Tijaniyya, a recently founded Algerian brotherhood which was to become the chief rival to the Qadiriyya in the Western Sudan. In 1826 Umar undertook the pilgrimage to Mecca, where he became a pupil of

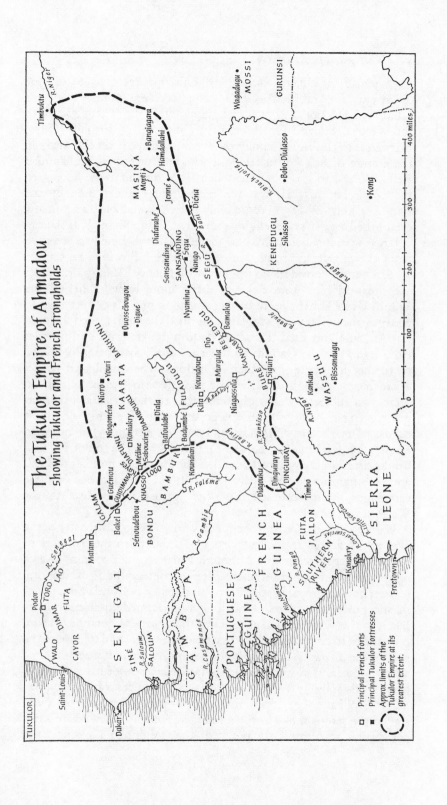

The Tukulor Empire of Ahmadou
showing Tukulor and French strongholds

R. Niger
Timbuktu

MOSSI
•Wagadugu
GURUNSI

•Bangiagara
MASINA
Homdallahi
•Morti
•Jenné
Diafarabé
Bandi Diéna
SANSANDING
Sansanding
Segu
SEGU R.
Nango

R. Black Volta

•Kong

KENEDUGU
•Sikasso

R. Bagoé

Ouossébougou•
•Digué
Nyamina
BAKHUNU
Dio
•Youri
Nioro
Niogoméra
KAARTA
Murgula
Bamako
KANGABA BELEDUGU
Diala
KHASSO
Kita
Koundou
BURÉ
•Siguiri
Nyagassola
R. Baoulé

Youri
DIAFUNU
Koniakry
Sabouciré DIAWARA
Guémou
KAYES

Kankan
WASSULU
R. Niger
•Bissandugu
Badumbé
FULADU
Bafoulabé
KHASSO LOGO
BAMBUK
Koundian
R. Bakhoy
R. Faléme
Diagouku
DINGUIRAY
Dinguiray
R. Tankisso
R. Bafing
•Timbo
GALAM
Bakel
Sénoudébou
BONDU
R. Gambia
FUTA JALLON
SOUTHERN
RIVERS
SIERRA
LEONE

Matam•
Podor
TORO
WALO
DIMAR FUTA
LAO
CAYOR
SENEGAL
SINÉ
R. Saloum
SALOUM
R. Casamance
GAMBIA
PORTUGUESE
GUINEA
FRENCH
GUINEA
R. Pongo
Rio Nunez
Réseau Scarcies
Rivière Scarcies
Kowaky
Freetown

Saint-Louis
R. Senegal
•Dakar

TUKULOR

□ Principal French forts
■ Principal Tukulor fortresses
⬛ Approx. limits of the
Tukulor Empire at its
greatest extent.

0   100   200   300   400 miles

Muhammad al-Ghali, *khalifa* or chief representative of the Tijaniyya in Arabia. Al-Ghali completed the young pilgrim's religious education and eventually appointed him Tijani *khalifa* to the Western Sudan.[1] On his return, Umar passed through Cairo, married into the ruling family of Bornu, and spent several years in the empire of Sokoto, marrying a daughter of Sultan Muhammad Bello. Forced to leave Sokoto when Bello died in 1837, he visited the empire of Masina, was imprisoned for a short time by the Bambara king of Segu, toured his native Futa-Toro, and finally established a *zawiyya* or religious hostel at Diagouku in Futa Jallon.

Umar's personal charisma and the prestige which he had acquired from the pilgrimage soon won him a large following, substantial wealth and considerable political influence. Many disciples accompanied him from Sokoto; many more joined him in Futa Jallon. While Umar sought new converts among his countrymen in Senegal, the community at Diagouku tilled the land, traded for gold dust in Buré and used the proceeds to purchase arms and powder from traders in the Gambia and Sierra Leone. Sympathisers helped to further his cause with their donations. The established *torodbe* aristocracy, although disturbed by the effects of his preaching on their own subjects, vied with each other in the lavishness of their gifts; even the King of Segu was persuaded to give him gold on his release. Umar's growing power, however, alarmed his hosts in Futa Jallon, and in 1849 he was forced to leave Diagouku for new headquarters in Dinguiray. From there he attacked a number of small animist kingdoms in the vicinity, and in 1852, during one of these campaigns, he proclaimed the *jihad* against all animists in the Western Sudan.

Within a decade, Umar's conquests were to make him master of the Western Sudan from the outskirts of Timbuktu to the frontiers of French Senegal (see map). Although Umar thought of himself as a religious reformer and professed himself contemptuous of temporal power, he was prepared to achieve his aims by political and military means. For he considered it his divinely appointed mission to purify Islam in the Western Sudan, to curb the abuses of corrupt Muslim potentates, to combat heresy, to extirpate animism, and to impose the rule of the *Sharia*. Accordingly, he set out to make himself ruler of an orthodox and powerful Islamic state. Members of his family and trusted disciples governed the various provinces of his empire; *talibés* (students of religion), for the most part Tukulors from Futa, staffed the senior ranks of the administration. A policy of enforced conversion was ruthlessly pursued; the prescribed Koranic taxes were levied on subject territories; *qadis* were appointed to administer Koranic law; religious observances were strictly enforced; mosques were built, and provisions were made for the spread of Koranic education. To strengthen the economy of the state, trade and local manufactures, particularly of textiles, were encouraged. Special efforts were also made to encourage the emigration of Muslim artisans from the European settlements along the coast.

Umar's armies were similarly infused with religious zeal. 'They march against our fire as if to martyrdom', wrote the French Governor of Senegal after the attack on Médine in 1857, 'it is clear that they wish to die.'[2] The *talibés,* many of them mounted on horses purchased from the Moorish tribes north of the Senegal, formed the élite corps of the army. Fula irregulars acted as auxiliary cavalry. Converted animists, serving either as professional *sofas* or as conscript *toubourrous,* formed the backbone of the infantry. *Talibés* responding to the call of the *jihad,* converts, and adventurers in search of booty kept the military establishment at full strength despite the heavy casualties suffered during the early campaigns. Umar's forces originally numbered about 12,000. Two thousand were lost during the conquest of Kaarta, yet 15,000 took part in the siege of Médine in 1857. The unsuccessful siege, famine and disease then reduced their number to 7,000; 2,000 more were lost in subsequent campaigns against the French and a further 1,000 at the start of the conquest of Segu. Yet by 1861 Umar was able to muster more than 30,000 men for the conquest of Masina. The troops were reasonably well trained and capable of executing basic tactical manœuvres. Most of the regulars were armed with muskets or rifles, some of them of recent vintage. In addition to supplies from the coast, some gunpowder was manufactured locally, and taxes were often collected in saltpetre. Gunsmiths accompanied the army; before the decisive battle in Masina, they were said to have manufactured 10,000 bullets a day. After 1858 Umar also possessed four cannons, two field-guns captured from the French at Bakel and two small mounted cannons taken from a French boat marooned on the Senegal. Samba N'Diaye, a former house-servant and trader from Senegal, acted as Master of Artillery and also supervised the construction of stone fortifications around the major garrison towns.

In military terms Umar certainly had the capacity to resist French expansion. He also had the political and religious incentive. His initial conquests carried him north-west towards the Senegal just at the time when the French themselves were beginning to advance up-stream and assert their influence over the Tukulor homelands in

Futa. A struggle for the control of these areas was bound to ensue. Early in 1855 Umar's supporters raided the French trading post at Bakel and kidnapped the commandant of the post at Sénoudébou. More menacingly, Umar himself declared war, promising to fight the French until they submitted and paid him tribute.[3] Two years later the Tukulor armies besieged the advance fort at Médine. For three months its tiny garrison, helped by a thousand allies from the surrounding villages, withstood repeated assaults and was only rescued in the nick of time when the rise in the water-level of the Senegal finally enabled reinforcements to move upstream from St. Louis. Although Umar's losses forced him to break off hostilities and retire to Koundian where he built a new fort, the Tukulors soon resumed the battle. From their fort at Guémou they intercepted caravans and harassed Bakel. Umar himself agitated in all the districts of Senegal from Bondu to Futa-Toro, and in 1859 he attacked the fort at Matam. The French, it seemed, were soon to have another Algeria on their hands.

But the issues at stake were not as simple as they appeared. The response of *jihad* states to European expansion was not limited to uncompromising, religiously inspired military resistance. Other options were open to them. They could attempt to oppose the European advance with the weapons of diplomacy instead of war; indeed, they could at times seek to establish bases for limited co-operation with the invaders. In Algeria, for example, the Tijaniyya was by no means hostile to the French. On the contrary, it accepted the invasion as divine punishment for Turkish misrule, steadfastly refused to participate in a *jihad* led by the rival Qadiriyya order, and collaborated wholeheartedly with the Christian enemy. Even Abd al-Qadir was quite prepared to negotiate with the French and keep the peace provided they kept to the coast and recognised his authority over the Algerian interior. Abd al-Qadir, moreover, was the leader of a proto-national resistance directed specifically against a European enemy. The Tukulor *jihad* was waged primarily against other Africans, and Umar could thus be expected to show still greater flexibility in his relations with the French.

The complexity of the Franco–Tukulor relationship was in fact made clear from the start. Although Umar had sound religious and political motives for opposing the French, he had equally important economic and military reasons for co-operating with them. Duties levied on French trade were a potentially valuable source of revenue for the new empire; arms and ammunition purchased from French traders were still more important for the maintenance of its military strength. These considerations at first outweighed any religious obligation to fight the Christians. During his tours of Senegal in the 1840s, Umar made contact with the local French commanders, assured them that his forthcoming campaigns would be directed only against animists, and offered his protection for French trade in return for the payment of duties and the sale of modern weapons. When the French reoccupied Podor, a stone's-throw from his native village, in 1854, he simply renewed his request for permission to buy arms. Only when the French refused and began to arm his enemies did his attitude change. Even after his declaration of war, he offered to make peace and support French trade if they paid him the customary duties and refrained from establishing a political as opposed to a commercial presence on the Senegal.

Nor were these gestures of conciliation entirely surprising. By 1855 the Tukulor armies were fully committed to the costly and difficult conquest of Kaarta, and Umar had neither the desire nor the necessary manpower to open a second front against the French. European rather than Tukulor policy made the clash inevitable. The French, already masters of a large Muslim population, were seriously alarmed by the rise of a militant religious empire on their doorstep. By now, moreover, they were planning to extend their own influence deep into the Sudanese interior, and they regarded Umar as the principal obstacle to be overcome. When Louis Faidherbe, a man with long Algerian experience, became Governor of Senegal in 1854, the anti-Tukulor trend in French policy intensified. Anxious to strengthen his colony's defences against possible Tukulor aggression and eager to open the routes into the interior, Faidherbe began to intervene more actively in the affairs of the Upper Senegal. Local rulers whose positions were threatened by the growth of Umari factions in their states were natural allies, and Faidherbe readily responded to their appeals for help. The construction of Médine in 1855 was intended to provide a refuge and rallying-point for the anti-Tukulor forces, and in particular to assist the ruler of Khasso, Sambala, in a civil war against the partisans of Umar who were led by his brother. French interference in a local struggle for power directly challenged Tukulor influence and could not be ignored. Although Umar remained opposed to a military confrontation, he had to contend with his aggressively anti-French *talibés* who were determined to free their homeland from European rule. The completion of the conquest in Kaarta gave Umar greater freedom of military manœuvre, and when the defeated Sambala took refuge at Médine, he finally sanctioned the attack.

The casualties and the loss of prestige suffered at Médine probably convinced Umar that further attempts to dispute French control over the Lower Senegal would be futile. Certainly, his subsequent campaign in Futa was not aimed at conquest; its objective was to coerce the population into emigrating. Futa had long provided most of Umar's *talibés;* his three premier regiments, the Guénar, Irlabé and Toro, were named after the three districts from which their *talibé* recruits originated. After Médine, Umar needed desperately to increase his following and reinforce his army before embarking upon a new series of campaigns; for by 1859 he had decided to divert his advance away from the French towards the kingdoms of the Upper Niger. As early as 1856 the rival empire of Masina had rejected his appeals for help in subduing Kaarta and had sent an army against him. Later, many rebels from Kaarta took refuge in the Bambara kingdom of Segu. Umar's relations with its ruler, Touroucoro Mari, were reasonably cordial; but when the latter was deposed by his brother Ali, Umar decided to act. The attack on Matam was his parting shot against the French, fired when he was on his way back to Kaarta to prepare for the campaign against Segu. The capture of the fort at Guémou in October 1859 removed the last serious threat to French supremacy on the Lower Senegal.

Having tacitly conceded victory to the French in the west in order to wage more promising campaigns in the east, Umar found it expedient to renew his overtures for peace, and this time Faidherbe accepted them. In August 1860 a truce was negotiated. A boundary was fixed along the Senegal and Bafing rivers; both sides undertook to support each other's trade and to refrain from coercing each other's subjects to emigrate, and provisions were made for the dispatch of a French ambassador to Umar's future capital. The terms of the treaty were not scrupulously observed, and Tukulor agitation continued to alarm the Senegalese authorities, but open hostilities were avoided. When Faidherbe, after an absence of two years, returned to Senegal in 1863, he was confident enough of Umar's intentions to envisage a French advance to the Niger in co-operation with the Tukulor empire. To secure this co-operation, he sent Lieutenant Mage to Segu in August 1863.

By the time Mage reached the Tukulor capital, however, the empire's fortunes had begun to turn. In 1861 Umar had easily defeated the Segu Bambaras, and the following year he had over-thrown Sultan Ahmadu of Masina. By 1863 his envoys were demanding tribute from Timbuktu. But the attempt to impose a Tukulor dynasty on the Muslim Fulas of Masina sparked off a serious rebellion which quickly spread throughout the new empire. Led by Ahmad al-Bakkai, head of the Bakkaiyya branch of the Qadiriyya and Umar's most influential religious opponent, the citizens of Timbuktu and their Tuareg allies drove the Tukulors from the town, capturing two of their cannon and killing Umar's most senior military commander. Next they joined the rebels in Masina and besieged Umar himself in the capital, Hamdallahi. Tukulor reverses in Masina then gave the signal for the subject Bambara of Segu to rise against their new masters. Communications between Segu and Masina were cut, and supplies bound for Hamdallahi were captured. In February 1864, a few days before Mage's arrival, Umar was killed in an attempt to break the siege.

Umar's death created further problems for the empire. Hitherto, its unity and strength had rested largely upon his own unquestioned politico-religious leadership and upon the determination which he inspired in his followers. Without him, its cohesion was bound to suffer. Umar had foreseen the danger and had tried to ensure an orderly succession; in 1860 he named Ahmadu, his eldest son, as heir apparent and later appointed him viceroy in Segu, ordering his other sons and senior commanders to swear allegiance to him. But problems arose nevertheless. Although Ahmadu was supposed to have inherited his father's *baraka,* he was clearly unable to exercise the same degree of influence over the *talibés* or to maintain the fanaticism of the army. Latent dissensions between the *talibé* and *sofa* regiments soon rose to the surface, and when Ahmadu refused to share out his father's treasure, the troops lost their appetite for war. The new Sultan continued to preach the virtues of the *jihad*, and in 1868 he proclaimed himself *amir al-muminin* (commander of the faithful) in an attempt to strengthen the religious basis of his position.[4] But the *talibés* were not impressed, and many of them deserted his ranks to return home to Futa. The losses inflicted by the rebels could not be made good, and by 1866 the army was said to number no more than 4,000 *talibés* and 11,000 *sofas*. Nor could Ahmadu, the son of a commoner, command the allegiance of Umar's better-born children who considered him their social inferior. These half-brothers became dangerous foci of disent, and in 1872 a group of them actually tried to throw off his authority altogether.

Factional strife in the army and disputes over the succession made it all the more difficult to deal with the rebellions which posed the greatest threat of all to the stability of the empire. Umar's policies towards his subjects were by no means totally oppressive; Mandinkas and Bambaras held several important territorial commands and exercised considerable power as *sofa* generals. But loss of independence and Umar's fanatical insistence on conversion undoubtedly created deep resentments which burst into flame as soon as Tukulor strength began to decline. The Bambara rebellion in Segu persisted long after Masina had been subdued, and at one point the capital itself came under imminent threat of attack. Trade was disrupted, and Nyamina, one of the principal trading centres on the Upper Niger, was for a time virtually deserted. After 1865 the turbulent region of Beledugu remained in a permanent state of insurrection, and Tukulor control over it was never effectively re-established. Rebellions in Kaarta were also frequent, and order was not finally restored there until the late 1870s.

Ahmadu, a skilful ruler if not a magnetic personality, did manage to save the empire from complete disintegration. Acting decisively against his rebellious brothers, he broke their conspiracy and imprisoned those most deeply implicated. He then increased his control over the provincial governors by forcing them to share power with councillors whom he appointed and who were directly responsible to him. To assure their loyalty still further, he ordered all governors to visit him once a year at Segu, and, as far as possible, he kept their armies supplied from the central treasury.[5] The rebellions in Segu and Kaarta were also suppressed. Fortunately, they were largely prompted by local grievances; they did not assume the proportions of a unified national movement against Tukulor rule and could thus be dealt with one by one. By the late 1870s Tukulor control over the two central provinces had been restored, and Tukulor influence was again being felt along the Senegal.

But Ahmadu's authority remained precarious. Jealous of the old *talibé* leadership and fearful of plots against the throne, the Sultan began to rely increasingly upon an entourage of personal favourites, many of them slaves or recent converts, and upon the *sofa* regiments of the army. The *talibés* grew correspondingly more disaffected with his rule. Yet Ahmadu could not afford to alienate them completely, for they continued to provide the bulk of the empire's administrative personnel. Accordingly, he allowed them to retain many of their privileges, including exemption from taxation, and made their life easy enough to attract the necessary reinforcements from Futa. Similarly, he had to show some favour towards the sons of Umar, for they still represented a serious potential threat to his authority. Most of his brothers were therefore given provincial governorships. Even the young Daye, who had supported the conspirators in 1872, was forgiven and allowed to remain in command of Diala.

The territorial limits of Ahmadu's power were also much reduced. He was not able to establish his authority over Masina which came to be ruled as an independent state by Umar's nephew Tijani. Dinguiray in the far south became an autonomous region under the Sultan's brother Aguibu. Ahmadu's own position in Segu was relatively secure, and most of his brothers in Kaarta remained loyal to him, but communications between the two regions were constantly interrupted by unrest in Beledugu. By the 1870s one could hardly talk of a unified Tukulor empire any more. Although Ahmadu's nominal suzerainty was generally accepted, the extent of his actual control over the various provinces was extremely limited, and few governors honoured their obligation to visit the capital regularly.

Ahmadu's personal difficulties, moreover, reflected the progressive decline and growing instability of the empire itself. The old unity of religious purpose was lost, and the Sultan virtually abandoned his father's evangelical mission. The *talibés,* once the shock troops of the *jihad,* became an oppressive and self-seeking aristocracy. The strength and morale of the army declined as it became more difficult to obtain reinforcements and as the *talibés* grew more unwilling to fight. And without a strong army there could be no guarantee of security against a largely hostile and imperfectly controlled Bambara population who bore the main burden of the administration and whom the exactions of the *talibés* constantly goaded into rebellion. Rent by dissensions from within and sapped by rebellions from below, Umar's once dynamic and self-confident community was gradually transformed into a rickety, alien and essentially secular empire of conquest.

Ahmadu's relations with the French must be viewed against the background of his empire's political and military decline. Certainly, the Sultan appreciated the dangers of allowing the French to establish themselves in his territories, and he adamantly rejected Mage's appeals for permission to build trading posts. But he also recognised the value of commercial contacts with Europeans and the importance of remaining on friendly terms with those who controlled the source of his reinforcements in Futa. He therefore opened the empire to French traders in return for the recognition of his authority, the payment of a 10 per cent import duty, and the guarantee of free communications between Segu and the Lower Senegal. Above all, Ahmadu wanted modern weapons to strengthen his army in its campaigns against the Bambaras; it was Mage's promise of cannon which finally persuaded him to negotiate. Although the Senegalese Government refused to ratify the agreement and the Sultan did not receive his artillery, he remained well disposed towards the French. He did not attempt to profit from the reduction of the Senegalese garrison after the Franco–Prussian War, and he continued to trade with Médine. In 1874, once he had quelled the rebellion of his brothers and placed his authority on a somewhat more stable footing, he made new overtures to the Governor of Senegal, asking for a revival of the Mage treaty and the sale of twelve mountain-guns.

Governor Valière was inclined to negotiate if not to provide the guns, but his more energetic successor, Brière de l'Isle, adopted a markedly less friendly policy. Since the gradual reassertion of Tukulor influence along the Senegal again seemed to threaten French security, Brière followed Faidherbe's example and intervened directly. French allies were given renewed military support against their pro-Tukulor rivals, and in September 1878 the French stormed Sabouciré, a Tukulor fortress in Logo which was then at war with Khasso. Having dealt with the immediate threat to security on the Senegal, Brière pressed hard for the extension of French power to the Niger. The French Government was thinking along the same lines; by 1880 plans had been drafted in Paris for the construction of a railway between the Senegal and the Niger and for the establishment of the political control which railway-building implied.[6] In February 1880, as part of this policy, Brière sent Captain Joseph Gallieni to conclude yet another treaty with Ahmadu in order to forestall Tukulor opposition to the French advance until the occupation of the Niger reduced the empire to impotence.

French policies seriously aggravated the empire's internal problems. Even under Valière, the Senegalese authorities had secretly assisted the rebels in Kaarta. Their destruction of Sabouciré destroyed Tukulor prestige throughout the Senegal–Niger valley. Mandinka villages which had previously vaccillated in their allegiance now flocked to the French with demands for protection and offers of support against the Tukulors. In the south-west the Tukulor fortress of Koundian was completely isolated and the sphere of influence of the fortress of Murgula much reduced. Further east, the Beledugu rebels gained new heart and intensified their attacks; in 1879 the important market town of Guigué was overrun and destroyed. Anxious to weaken the empire still further, the French maintained their pressure. On his way to Segu, Gallieni signed treaties with the chiefs of Kita permitting the construction of a French fort on their territory, and he promised French assistance to all who sought to free themselves from Tukulor rule. As proof of his intentions, he even avoided the safer route via Murgula and travelled instead through Beledugu.*

The Gallieni mission placed Ahmadu in a dilemma. The envoy's professions of friendship did not deceive him in the least, and he knew that the French were bent upon the occupation of at least part of his empire. But he also knew that he was too weak to oppose their plans by force, and he still clung to the possibility of an alliance with the one power whose support could tilt the military balance between him and his African enemies decisively in his favour. As in the past, his objectives were to limit the extension of French influence and to secure military aid against the Bambaras. Once more, his weapons were those of diplomacy, and these he employed with his customary skill. Although he received Gallieni as cordially as could have been expected, he refused to allow the mission into Segu and confined it instead to the village of Nango. Despite Gallieni's appeals, he obstinately postponed the start of negotiations, and in the meantime he deliberately exaggerated the extent of British influence in the empire. By the time the talks finally opened at the end of October, much of Gallieni's early self-confidence had been sapped, and subtle threats to conclude an alliance with the British in Sierra Leone soon broke down what remained of his resolution. The treaty of Nango was a clear diplomatic victory for the Tukulors. They did not insist on the destruction of Bafoulabé, the most recently constructed French fort; they allowed the French to build and maintain commercial routes through the empire; and they dropped their initial opposition to the construction of steamboats on the Niger. But in return for commercial privileges and exclusive navigation rights, the French had to recognise Ahmadu's authority over both his existing possessions and his future conquests, to guarantee his communications with Futa, and to undertake neither to invade nor to construct fortifications on his territory. Most important of all, Gallieni agreed to a single payment of four field-guns with full accessories and 1,000 rifles, and to a yearly rent of 200 rifles, 200 barrels of powder, 200 artillery shells and 50,000 flints. After some hesitation, Ahmadu signed the agreement and sent the mission back with gifts for the Governor.

Diplomatic barriers, however, could provide scant protection against the French advance. Gallieni himself had never meant to

* Gallieni was to pay dearly for this decision. On 11 May a group of Bambaras ambushed his convoy at Dio, killing fourteen men and capturing most of its baggage. Gallieni entered the territories of Segu more as a fugitive than as an ambassador.

honour his treaty, and his Government had no intention of arming the Tukulors.* At the end of 1880, moreover, the whole context of Franco–Tukulor relations was transformed by the creation of the Upper Senegal Military Command. The decision to place the execution of French policies in military hands meant that Ahmadu would in future have to contend with strong forces of African *tirailleurs* led by ambitious and aggressive officers of the French 'Marines'. The consequences were soon apparent. From the start, the objective of the French commander, Lieutenant-Colonel Borgnis-Desbordes, was the military occupation of the Senegal–Niger valley. After two inconclusive campaigns, he achieved his goal. Striking deep into Ahmadu's territory, his troops expelled the Tukulor garrison from Murgula, and in February 1883 they occupied Bamako on the Niger. A year later the first of the Niger gunboats was transported overland, reassembled, and made ready to sail.

Despite the gravity of the aggression, Ahmadu reacted with extraordinary moderation. At first, he simply expressed dismay that his new-found allies should send an army to invade his lands and demanded the evacuation of the forts at Bafoulabé and Kita as a sign of their good faith.[7] As Desbordes predicted, the Tukulors dared not risk an open clash with his expeditionary column and abandoned Murgula without a fight. Nor did they oppose the occupation of Bamako. Even the gunboat was allowed to operate unmolested. Although Ahmadu knew perfectly well that his capital was now directly threatened, he made no attempt to interfere with the gunboat's journey past Segu or to intercept it on its return. His only reprisal was to cut off trade. At no time during this crucial period did he oppose the French advance by force.

The internal weaknesses of the Tukulor empire rather than the overwhelming superiority of the French provide the explanation for the Sultan's failure to act in the years after 1883. In fact, the French were not nearly as formidable as they appeared. The rapidity of the military advance had created tremendous problems of communications and supply and had left them precariously established along an overextended and inadequately provisioned line of forts. In 1884,

* Gallieni's attitude is made clear in his final report, 12 October 1881, SOMAN Missions 16, Gallieni 1880. Despite his advice, the Government refused to ratify the treaty, primarily because of the clauses relating to the supply of arms. The official reason was the absence of the protectorate clause in the Arabic version of the treaty, but this discrepancy was not mentioned at the time. The Tukulor ambassador who accompanied Gallieni back to St. Louis was persuaded to sign a new treaty which did not provide for the supply of arms, but this agreement also remained unratified.

moreover, the military rashly invaded the territories of the powerful *imam* Samori and were quickly driven back to their bases at Kita and Niagassola.* Ahmadu was aware of these difficulties and for a moment seemed ready to profit from them. In 1884 he moved upstream from Segu towards Bamako, and at the end of the year he suddenly marched through Beledugu to Nioro, the capital of Kaarta on the exposed flank of the French line. But the Sultan's actions were not aimed against the French. He left Segu to take up a better position against the Beledugu Bambaras, not to threaten Bamako. The objective of his advance into Kaarta was to depose his brother Muntaga, grown too independent for his liking, not to gain a strategic advantage over the French. The protracted siege of Nioro further weakened the Sultan's armies, and he made no attempt to cut the highly vulnerable European line of communications.

Both the French position and their relations with the Tukulors continued to deteriorate during the campaign of 1885–6. The commander of the expeditionary force, Lieutenant-Colonel Frey, had no sooner dealt with the immediate challenge of Samori on the Upper Niger than he had to cope with the rebellion of the Sarrakule *marabout*, Mahmadu Lamine,† on the Upper Senegal. Having relieved Bakel and driven Mahmadu Lamine south towards the Gambia, Frey then led a punitive expedition through Guidimaka, still claimed by Ahmadu as part of his empire, in reprisal for the district's alleged help to the rebels. The Tukulors reacted firmly, tightening their trade ban and intercepting caravans bound for Médine; and Frey became convinced that all-out war was imminent. The French would have been hard pressed indeed to repel a determined assault; disease had decimated their ranks, and 400 men were already dead or out of action. But Ahmadu did not attack, and the crisis soon passed. There was no question of his helping Mahmadu Lamine, for the latter was a claimant to Umar's spiritual legacy and his sworn enemy. Having taken Nioro, moreover, Ahmadu was anxious to return to Segu; but his way back was barred by the rebels in Beledugu, and before he could force a passage he needed to replenish his arms supply. It was therefore necessary for him to persuade the French to lift the arms ban which they had imposed during the Guidimaka crisis. In exchange, he was prepared to reopen the trade routes to Médine, and he eased his commercial restrictions even when the French rejected his offer.

This gesture made a considerable impression on Frey's successor,

* For Samori's resistance to French expansion, see the chapter by Yves Person.
† See the chapter on this subject by B. Olatunji Oloruntimehin.

Lieutenant-Colonel Gallieni. The new commander had grown wiser since his days as an impetuous young diplomat. He could now appreciate the value of maintaining good relations with the Tukulors, for Ahmadu's friendship would greatly facilitate the suppression of Mahmadu Lamine's rebellion and the reimposition of French control over the Senegal–Niger valley. Accordingly, Gallieni allowed the Sultan to resume his purchases of gunpowder and then proposed a new treaty confirming the pledge not to invade Ahmadu's territories in return for the establishment of a nominal French protectorate over his empire. Ahmadu accepted these terms without hesitation and affixed his seal to the treaty in May 1887. Relations between the two sides remained cordial throughout the following year.[8]

By the end of Gallieni's second campaign in 1888, it seemed that the bases for a lasting Franco–Tukulor entente had been laid. Weakened by dissensions which Gallieni's secret agents assiduously fomented, the Tukulor armies in Kaarta no longer posed a serious threat to French security. Indeed, Gallieni now considered it positively advantageous to keep Ahmadu at Nioro and therefore stepped up his military aid to the Beledugu Bambaras. The commander at least was convinced that Ahmadu could gradually be turned into a French puppet, entirely dependent on his European protectors. But it was not to be; by 1888 the fate of the Tukulor empire had been surely if indirectly sealed. Hitherto, the empire's chief defence against European attack had been the complications which beset the French occupation of the Senegal–Niger valley. The complete failure of railway construction to keep pace with the military advance left the Sudan without an effective network of supply. The scandalous mismanagement of the railway and the astronomic rise in Sudanese expenditure provoked such opposition in the French Parliament that the whole future of the colony was at one point thrown into question. Costly military expeditions against Samori and Mahmadu Lamine made it all the more desirable to avoid conflict with the Tukulors. But Gallieni's campaigns completely transformed the situation. By 1888 a new treaty had been signed with Samori, and Mahmadu Lamine had been defeated and killed. The forts had been provisioned and their garrisons relieved. Roads had been repaired, and the railway had at last reached Bafoulabé. Parliamentary opposition was no longer a factor to be reckoned with. Although Gallieni himself wished to maintain the alliance with the Tukulors until Ahmadu's death enabled the French to take his empire without a fight, the very success of his efforts made the empire's immediate destruction possible.

The aggressiveness of the French military command made it inevitable. Gallieni's successor, Major Louis Archinard, did not share his belief in the value of co-operation with Ahmadu. In February 1889, without orders and for reasons which had little to do with the situation in the Sudan, Archinard stormed the isolated Tukulor fortress of Koundian. It was a more difficult operation than the commander might have expected. Although the town's garrison was only 300 strong, the Tukulors were expecting an attack and had prepared for it by removing all the thatching from the roofs in order to prevent the spread of fire. Koundian's double walls of masonry stood up well to the fire of Archinard's 80 mm mountain-guns; it took eight hours for the breach to be made. The Tukulors also stood firm under the bombardment, met the French assault with sustained musket-fire and then conducted a desperate house-to-house resistance until the last man fell. But the outcome was never in doubt. The preliminary shelling had decimated the defenders, and the French were able to occupy the town with only light casualties.

For Archinard, Koundian was but the first campaign in the total destruction of the Tukulor empire. His next and more important objective was Segu. Returning to Paris in the summer, he pressed the Colonial Department to authorise an early expedition against the Tukulor capital, and in February 1890 he received permission to march. The commander was determined to take no chances; he had begun to prepare for the campaign a year before and had even persuaded Paris to give him two 95 mm field-guns with 100 of the latest melinite shells. These were sound precautions, for Segu's massive earthwork fortifications proved as sturdy as the walls of Koundian. But the assault itself posed no problems. Madani, Ahmadu's son and viceroy, had placed his *talibés* on the banks of the Niger to oppose the French crossing and was caught in the open by the preliminary bombardment. Concerted artillery fire prevented the defenders from regaining the walls and soon created panic in their ranks. Unable to rally his troops, Madani abandoned the struggle and fled north, eventually making his way to Nioro. Although the walls of Segu had been breached, the French were able to enter the city through its gates.

The capture of Segu, however, did not satisfy Archinard. Anxious to forestall any counter-offensive by Ahmadu and to clear the way to Nioro for his Bambara allies in Beledugu, he too moved north— against the fortress of Ouossébougou on the eastern frontier of Kaarta. Because water was scarce, he took only 300 regular troops and a section of 80 mm mountain-guns with him, although he could rely on the support of several thousand Bambara auxiliaries. Even with their help it was a risky venture. Ouossébougou's garrison, composed of Muslim Bambaras who had remained loyal to Ahmadu and therefore expected no quarter from Archinard's auxiliaries, resolved to fight to the last. Although the town's earthworks were much less solid than those of Segu, the defenders partially filled the breach, and with the help of fires deliberately started to increase confusion they managed to hold off the first assault. In the end, Archinard had to open a second breach at right angles to the first in order to launch a two-pronged attack against the inner redoubt. The two-day battle cost him dearly. Of the twenty-seven Europeans on the expedition, two were killed and eight wounded, four of them seriously. Thirteen *tirailleurs* were killed and seventy-six wounded. Casualties among the Bambara auxiliaries who bore the brunt of the final assault were probably higher, and among Ouossébougou's garrison much higher still. Six hundred bodies were found in the fortress when the French entered it. To round off his successful campaign, Archinard then returned to the Upper Senegal and marched north against Koniakary, the capital of Diambouku. Choosing to meet the French in open country where the element of surprise and the possibilities of escape were greater, the Tukulors made their stand along the Krikou river, using its steep banks for cover. But they were easily dislodged. Koniakary itself, despite its strong walls, was not defended and was occupied without opposition.

Having witnessed the utter collapse of his diplomatic strategy, Ahmadu finally took up arms. He had wanted to attack the French after the loss of Koundian but was unable to raise enough troops. After the loss of Segu, he threw caution aside and sent what men he had into battle. In June the Tukulors attacked the railway at Talaari and skirmished all along the Kayes–Bafoulabé line. During one particularly heavy engagement, the French lost forty-three killed and wounded out of a force of 125. In September, when the French columns had been disbanded and the annual floods had isolated Koniakary, Ahmadu tried to retake the town. But the fortress had been left well provisioned, and the Tukulors were easily beaten off. The Sultan now had no option but to prepare for Archinard's inevitable assault on Nioro. He did so with some care. The Tukulor forces in Kaarta were divided into four sections. The Guénar and Toro regiments and the garrison of Diambouku under the Sultan's brother Bassiru, a total force of some 5,000, were sent to block the French advance from the south. The Irlabé regiment, based on Diala, also guarded the southern flank. The refugees from Segu under

Madani guarded the eastern approaches against a Bambara attack from Beledugu. The main concentration, led by the *sofa* general Bafi and the deposed king of Djollof, Ali Buri, remained with the Sultan at Nioro. But these dispositions failed to slow the French advance. As soon as Archinard returned to the Sudan, he reformed his expeditionary column and set off against Nioro. On 23 December Bassiru's forces tried to engage the French at Niogoméra but were dispersed by the 80mm and the 95 mm guns. A week later the main Tukulor formation was defeated in the marshes just north of Nioro. Once more, the fortress itself was left undefended, and Archinard entered it on New Year's Day 1891. By now, Ahmadu had had enough; but Ali Buri persuaded him to make one final effort, and on 3 January the Tukulors made their last stand near the village of Youri. Ali Buri marshalled the defenders, placing some of them under cover in a dry river-bed while others tried to form square in the French style. All of them fought with the courage of desperate men, but again the issue was not in doubt. Those who charged the French square or stood their ground were mown down by the *tirailleurs;* those who broke were ridden down by the *spahis.* The battle soon became a rout, and by the end of the day the Tukulor armies had virtually ceased to exist; their losses during the campaign totalled more than 3,000 killed and captured. Abandoning the un-equal contest, Ahmadu and a small band of retainers fled east across the desert to Masina.

There the Sultan gained a short breathing space. Since the death of Tijani in 1887, Masina had been ruled by one of Ahmadu's brothers, Muniru, who had fought against him with Muntaga and had later become a protégé of the French. Muniru, however, was detested by his *talibés,* and Ahmadu was easily able to depose him. Meanwhile, the resumption of the campaign against Samori and the suppression of a major rebellion in the newly conquered province of Segu kept the French fully occupied in the south. But Ahmadu's days were numbered. In 1892 his nemesis returned to the Sudan, completed the restoration of order in Segu and then invaded Masina. Archinard's first objective was Jenné, the most important trading town on the Upper Niger. He hoped that its merchants would surrender without a fight, but the latter, reaffirming their loyalty to Ahmadu, refused to open the gates. In order not to slow down his column, the commander had left his heavy 95 mm guns at Segu, and he again found it difficult to make a breach with his 80s. Despite an all-night bombardment with fragmentation shells, moreover, the town's inhabitants and military garrison were still able to resist the assault.

The amount of ammunition expended and the casualties on both sides testified to the ferocity of the engagement. Archinard's cannons fired 560 rounds and the *tirailleurs* spent 40,000 cartridges. The French lost fourteen dead and fifty-seven wounded; at least 500 of the defenders were killed. Archinard then moved to Mopti on the Niger and sent for the 95s. As soon as they arrived, he set off for Ahmadu's new capital at Bandiagara. The Sultan, vowing never again to flee, sent his troops to meet the French along Bandiagara's natural line of defence, the rocky escarpment of Kori-Kori. The Tukulors prepared their positions carefully, building low fire walls to supplement the cover afforded by the rocks, but to no avail. The long-range fire of the French artillery soon demoralised them, and even Ali Buri refused to take part in the final battle. On 28 April the *tirailleurs* advanced along the narrow but badly defended paths up the rocks and soon occupied the high ground, driving the Tukulors back without much of a struggle. On the following day, Archinard occupied Bandiagara, and on 4 May he installed Aguibu, now a loyal collaborator, as Sultan of Masina. Ahmadu led what remained of his following into the Niger Bend and eventually sought refuge in the empire of Sokoto. The conquest of the Tukulor empire was complete.

Clearly, the most striking features of Tukulor resistance to French expansion were its ineffectiveness and the haphazard fashion in which it was conducted. The empire's contact with the French spanned a period of some forty years, yet for most of this time it offered no military resistance whatsoever. Only during the initial phase of Umari expansion and the last stages of the French conquest were the two sides openly at war with each other. The effectiveness of military resistance also tended to decline. French battles with Umar were hard-fought affairs; sixteen men were killed and sixty-three wounded during the defence of Médine, thirty-nine killed and ninety-seven wounded during the capture of Guémou. By comparison, the losses inflicted by Ahmadu's forces were negligible. The whole conquest of Kaarta cost Archinard five dead and fifty-three wounded, the capture of Koniakary two dead and ten wounded, Koundian one dead and three wounded, Segu no casualties at all. When his enemies defended their fortresses the commander's casualties were of course much higher, but so too were those of the defenders. In strictly military terms, Ahmadu's resistance never approached that of Samori. Even in the territories of the Tukulor empire, the most serious opposition was put up by the Bambaras who turned against their French allies when the latter's intention to replace the Tukulors as masters of the Sudan became clear. The rebellions in Segu after 1890 caused the French far more trouble than Ahmadu's attempts to defend himself. The capture of the rebel town of Diéna in 1891 cost Archinard 120 casualties and had a considerable political impact in Paris. [9]

The reasons for the ineffectiveness of Tukulor military resistance are fairly obvious. In Africa the vast economic and technological resources of a modern European state could always be translated, when necessary, into an overwhelming military superiority. The Tukulors were hopelessly outgunned. Their motley collection of muskets and obsolete rifles were no match for French artillery and the latest repeaters. The stone walls of their imposing fortresses provided some protection, but all of them were breached in the end. After 1890, the Tukulors did not even enjoy a significant advantage in numbers. French military success depended to a large extent upon the use of African troops recruited and trained on the spot. Local recruitment was relatively cheap and enabled the French to place large armies in the field. Seven hundred and fifty troops took part in the expedition against Segu, 700 in the campaign for Kaarta, 900 in the invasion of Masina. In addition, the French could draw on a horde of irregular auxiliaries provided by their African allies. These auxiliaries raised the fighting strength of the Segu column to 2,200. Another 1,300 accompanied the expedition against Nioro, and 3,000 marched with the *tirailleurs* to Ouossébougou. In none of his campaigns against the Tukulors was Archinard heavily outnumbered. The disparity in the quality of the two armies was still more marked. The *tirailleurs* were by far the most effective military force in the Western Sudan. They were well trained, well armed, reasonably disciplined, and led by European officers and N.C.O.s who were among the most seasoned practitioners of colonial warfare in the world. Ahmadu's regiments no longer possessed the religious fervour which had inspired the original *jihadis*. Years of petty bickering and inconclusive campaigns against rebellious subjects had sapped their determination and undermined their morale. They fought bravely out of desperation at the end; but without the weapons, the training or the discipline, they never stood a chance.

Contacts with the French did have some effect on Tukulor tactics. From the siege of Médine they learned the futility of attacking well fortified European positions, and they remembered the lesson until they attempted to retake Koniakary. The capture of Koundian taught them the dangers of defending their fortresses against artillery fire and made their decision to face the French on open ground understandable if ineffective. But the Tukulors never mastered the techniques of guerilla warfare which Samori employed with such devastating effect, and it is doubtful whether they could have done so. The empire did not possess the necessary support, active or passive, voluntary or coerced, of the mass of the population. When Archinard attacked Segu, the province was already rent by rebellion and completely isolated from Kaarta; and Segu itself was coming under Bambara attack. After its capture, the Tukulors were only too glad to leave the area and so escape massacre at the hands of their former subjects. The Samorian empire possessed an elaborate military organisation with effective central control, a high degree of mobility, and with it the readiness to surrender ground in order to avoid the set-piece engagements where the full superiority of French fire-power could be brought to bear. The Tukulors lacked the central organisation and were too dependent on the revenues extracted from their subject territories to copy Samori's mass migrations and scorched earth tactics. Theirs was an established territorial empire which could not be lightly abandoned and had in the end to be defended.

French military superiority, however, does not provide the whole answer; the military imbalance between the two sides was not always as great as it was during the final stage of the conquest. Political factors were equally important. Ultimately, Tukulor military resistance was ineffective because Ahmadu never intended to resist the French by military means. For more than twenty years his policy was based on diplomacy and aimed at the conclusion of a *modus vivendi* with his aggressive European neighbours. This was his objective in 1866, in 1874, in 1880 and even in 1887, long after the futility of diplomatic negotiations with the French had become apparent. During this period he made no attempt to conclude anti-European alliances with other African powers in the Western Sudan. Although the French always suspected him of plotting with Abdul Bubakar, the most powerful Tukulor leader in Futa, relations between the two do not seem to have been particularly close or cordial. On the other hand, the Sultan tacitly supported the French in their early campaigns against Samori and actively assisted their operations against Mahmadu Lamine. Only after the outbreak of war did his policy change. By 1890 he had formed alliances with Abdul Bubakar and Ali Buri, and most probably with Samori as well.* One of his sons and one of his cousins joined the *imam* after the fall of Segu and later

* According to the local French commanders, Samori had made overtures for a defensive alliance against the French after his return from Sikasso, and Ahmadu had replied favourably. By January 1890 the two were supposed to have confirmed their friendship by exchanging prisoners.

commanded regiments in his army. Having reached Masina, Ahmadu made further attempts to unite against the French with Samori and Tiéba of Sikasso, and he supported the rebellion of his former Bambara subjects in Segu. But his new diplomacy was doomed to fail. By then he had allowed the French to determine the timing and the conditions of the war, and this was absolutely fatal.

Why military resistance did not figure more prominently in Tukulor policy is thus a more interesting and important question. Clearly, the clash of opposing religions and cultures did not automatically make for violent conflict; nor is religion the only factor to be considered. The response of an African state to the challenge of European penetration at a given point in time, it has been aptly pointed out, was generally determined by the socio-political nature and military strength of the state at that particular time. Empires on the 'upswing', territorially expansive, militarily strong, drawing their dynamic force from a militant religious mission or a policy of conquest fundamentally incompatible with the extension of European control, had a greater capacity and incentive to resist than did settled empires which had passed their apogee and had begun to decline.[10] The history of Tukulor responses to the French bears this analysis out. When Umar first ran up against them, he was the head of a dynamic and powerful state which had the political as well as religious incentive and the military capacity to dispute their claims to the Senegal. Once his losses and the diversion of his advance had lessened his political incentive and weakened his military capacity to maintain his opposition, religious scruples did not prevent him from negotiating a truce.

After the death of Umar, the importance of the religious factor both in the empire and in its relations with the French tended to decline. Unable to maintain his father's religious authority, Ahmadu had to base his power on more secular foundations. As his rule grew more secular, so his need to oppose the French on purely religious grounds diminished. By 1887 he could risk compromising his religious prestige by accepting the 'aid and protection' of a European power. More importantly, the progressive disintegration and growing instability of his empire weakened the Sultan's capacity to resist. He had to combat French expansion indirectly by diplomacy or by imposing embargoes on trade. No matter how grave the French threat to his empire became, the risks of a military confrontation always seemed graver still.

The weaknesses of the Tukulor empire, on the other hand, strengthened its incentive to co-operate with the French. Traders, townsmen and officials all had an interest in maintaining peace and good commercial relations with a strong European power. Accordingly, many influential figures in the Tukulor leadership, including Samba N'Diaye and Ahmadu's chief councillor, Seydou Djelia, favoured an alliance. Overriding all other considerations was the Sultan's desire for European military support against his African enemies. Ahmadu's most pressing concern was to prevent the complete break-up of his empire through Tukulor factional strife or Bambara rebellion. The French may have represented a still more serious danger to his security, but theirs was a long-term threat before the 1890s, and Ahmadu had little leisure for long-term planning. The possibility of an alliance with the French may have been remote, but the Sultan's other options were hardly more realistic. He might have tried to reunify his followers and revive their enthusiasm by proclaiming an anti-European *jihad*; but he had no reason to believe that the *talibés* would respond to his call. He might have sought an earlier alliance with Samori, but there was a tradition of ill-will between the two empires which could not easily be forgotten. The possibility of an alliance with the Bambaras was scarcely worth considering. Ahmadu based the survival of his empire on the negotiation of a settlement with the French because he had no other choice. It was a hopeless and fatally miscalculated decision, but it was not an incomprehensible one.

There is one final point to be made. Ahmadu's policy of co-operation failed because the French had no intention of letting it succeed. Once the establishment of a political dominion over the Western Sudan had become an objective of French African policy, all hope of a lasting accommodation with the Tukulors vanished. At best, the policy-makers in Paris and a few enlightened officers might have allowed the Sultan to live out his days as a French client; the military commanders who controlled the execution of policy would not even countenance this much. From the start, the destruction of the Tukulor empire was the goal which they pursued, directly when they could, indirectly through support for the Bambaras when they had to. As soon as the conditions were ripe, they launched their decisive assault, and nothing Ahmadu might have done would have altered their decision. But if the outbreak of war made Ahmadu's policies over the past twenty years quite meaningless, it did present him with two clear options: to surrender unconditionally or to resist. Faced with these alternatives, he chose to fight and save his honour if not his empire. It was not much of a choice, but it was a real one. Like his brother Aguibu, he might have tried to settle for a comfortable old age. That he did not merits him some consideration as a leader of African resistance to European imperialism.

NOTES

1 J. M. Abun Nasr, *The Tijaniyya, a Sufi Order in the Modern World*, London, 1965, p. 108, claims that Umar was appointed *muqaddam* rather than *khalifa,* but African accounts refer to him as *khalifa.*

2 Faidherbe to Minister of Marine and Colonies, 19 July 1857, Section Outre-Mer des Archives Nationales [SOMAN], Senegal I 43/a.

3 Whether Umar's declaration amounted to the proclamation of a *jihad*, however, is doubtful. The term *jizya,* the special tribute paid by non-Muslims to a Muslim ruler, was also used to describe the duties on trade which the French already paid to local rulers. The substance of Umar's letter was an appeal to the Muslims of St. Louis not to assist the French in any way or to live under French rule.

4 Most accounts claim that he assumed the title in 1873, but Abun-Nasr's research has shown that he did so five years earlier.

5 This information is contained in Valière to M.M.C., 20 July 1874, cited in Y. Saint Martin, 'Les relations diplomatiques entre la France et l'empire toucouleur de 1860 à 1887' *Bulletin de l'Institut Français de l'Afrique Noire,* série B, vol. xxvii, 1965, p. 193.

6 For a fuller discussion of the significance of these developments in French policy, see C. W. Newbury and A. S. Kanya-Forstner, 'French Policy and the Origins of the Scramble for West Africa', *Journal of African History,* X, 1969.

7 Ahmadu to Brière de l'Isle, n.d. [received 12 May 1881], SOMAN Senegal IV 73/c.

8 Ahmadu's relations with Gallieni can be followed in: Gallieni to Ahmadu, 28 November 1886; Ahmadu to Gallieni, 7 January 1887: Gallieni to Ahmadu, 6 February 1887; Ahmadu to Gallieni, 4 March 1887; Gallieni to Ahmadu, 5 April 1887, SOMAN Senegal IV 88/b.

9 Under-Secretary of State for Colonies to Governor of Senegal, 11 March 1891, SOMAN Senegal I 91/b: '*Affaire Diana [sic] . . . impressionne vivement et défavorablement gouvernement et opinion publique . . . Opinion redoute prolongation indéfinie état guerre Soudan. Dites Archinard que ma confiance en lui est absolue mais il est indispensable que je puisse rassurer opinion et gouvernement.*'

10 These views are advanced in R. E. Robinson and J. Gallagher, 'The Partition of Africa', *The New Cambridge Modern History,* vol. XI, pp. 617–20. Where the present writer differs from them is in their assessment of the nature and strength of the Tukulor empire under Ahmadu.

SUGGESTIONS FOR FURTHER READING

Much has been written about the career of Umar and various aspects of the Tukulor empire. The most important African accounts are:

M. A. Tyam, *La Vie d'el Hadj Omar,* tr. H. Gaden, Mémoires de l'Institut d'Ethnologie, no. 21, Paris, 1935.

J. Salenc (tr.), 'La vie d'el Hadj Omar', *Bulletin du Comité des Etudes Historiques et Scientifiques de l'Afrique Occidentale Française,* vol. I, 1918.

M. Delafosse (ed.), 'Traditions historiques et légendaires du Soudan occidental', *Afrique Française, Renseignements Coloniaux,* 1913.

Contemporary accounts by Europeans provide valuable sources of information. The most useful are:

F. Carrère et P. Holle, *De la Sénégambie française,* Paris, 1855.

E. Mage, *Voyage dans le Soudan occidental,* Paris, 1868.

J. S. Gallieni, *Voyage au Soudan français (Haut-Sénégal et pays de Ségou) 1879–1881,* Paris, 1885.

J. S. Gallieni, *Deux campagnes au Soudan français, 1886–1888,* Paris, 1891.

P. Soleillet, *Voyage à Ségou, 1878–1879,* ed. G. Gravier, Paris, 1887.

For the doctrines of the Tijaniyya and the religious basis of the Umari *jihad,* see:

J. M. Abun-Nasr, *The Tijaniyya, a Sufi Order in the Modern World,* London, 1965.

J. R. Willis, 'Jihad fi sabil Allah—its Doctrinal Basis in Islam and some Aspects of its Evolution in Nineteenth-Century West Africa', *Journal of African History,* vol. VIII, 1967.

There is information about Umar's early career in:

J. H. Ba and J. Daget, *L'empire peul du Macina,* Paris, 1962.

O. Houdas (tr.), *Tarikh Sokoto,* Publications de l'Ecole des Langues Orientales Vivantes, 4th series, vol. XX, Paris, 1901.

On the empire's military strength, see:

Y. Saint-Martin, 'L'artillerie d'El Hadj Omar et d'Ahmadou', *Bulletin de l'Institut Français d'Afrique Noire,* série B, vol. xxvii, 1965.

On the significance of anti-Tukulor resistance, see:

B. O. Oloruntimehin, 'Resistance Movements in the Tukulor Empire', *Cahiers d'études africaines,* no. 29, 1968.

On the last days of the empire, see:

B. Mademba, 'La dernière étape d'un conquérant', *Bulletin du Comité des Etudes Historiques et Scientifiques de l'Afrique Occidentale Française,* vol. III, 1921.

J. Emily, 'La fin d'Ahmadou Sheicou', *Communications de l'Académie des Sciences Coloniales,* vol. VIII, 1926–7.

On the Sultan's brother Aguibu, see:

A. de Loppinot, 'Souvenirs d'Aguibou', *Bulletin du Comité des Etudes Historiques et Scientifiques de l'Afrique Occidentale Française,* vol. II, 1919.

Y. Saint-Martin, 'Un fils d'El Hadj Omar: Aguibou, roi du Dinguiray et du Macina (1843?–1907)', *Cahiers d'études africaines,* no. 29, 1968.

Tukulor relations with the French are discussed in:

J. D. Hargreaves, 'The Tokolor Empire of Ségou and its Relations with the French', *Boston University Papers on African History,* vol. II, Boston, 1966.

Y. Saint-Martin, 'Les relations diplomatiques entre la France et l'empire toucouleur de 1860 à 1887', *Bulletin de l'Institut Français d'Afrique Noire,* série B, vol. xxvii, 1965.

and most fully in:

Y. Saint-Martin, *L'Empire toucouleur et la France, un demi-siècle de relations diplomatiques (1846–1893)* Dakar, 1967.

The best-known work on the French conquest is:

J. Méniaud, *Les pionniers du Soudan, avant, avec et après Archinard,* 2 vols., Paris, 1931.

Franco–Tukulor relations are discussed in the wider context of French African policy in:

A. S. Kanya-Forstner, *The Conquest of the Western Sudan: A study in French Military Imperialism,* Cambridge, 1969.

Senegambia–Mahmadou Lamine

The movement with which we are concerned in this chapter took place in the Senegambia region from mid-1885 to the end of 1887. The most important figure in it was Mahmadou Lamine, who led the Sarrakole in the struggle to rid the area of French and Tukulor political authority and occupation. In the process of trying to achieve this, he created a state which at its greatest spread over Bambuk, Bondu, Guoy, Khasso and the emirates of Diafounou and Guidimaka in the Kaarta section of the Tukulor empire.

It was from among the Sarrakole population of these places that Lamine quickly built up an immense mass following and a fighting force which represented the only common serious threat to the existence of French and Tukulor imperial interests in the area in the nineteenth century. The situation created by Lamine's movement was dangerous enough for the two imperial rivals to forget their rivalry for the moment, and join in a military alliance. Even with the combined efforts of the two powers it still took about two years of continual fighting to destroy the movement.

The significance of Lamine's movement lies not only in the fact that it was another example of military resistance to European occupation but also in the fact that it involved the masses of a politically alert and articulate people. In this sense it represents an early prototype of the anti-colonial mass movements of the twentieth century.

For at least thirty years before the emergence of Lamine, Kaarta

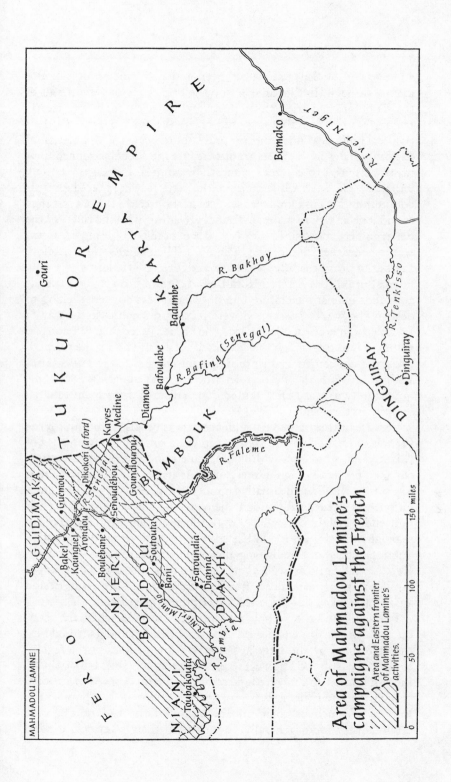

Area of Mahmadou Lamine's campaigns against the French

Area and Eastern frontier of Mahmadou Lamine's activities.

0   50   100   150 miles

and parts of the Senegambia had been under the rule of the Tukulor empire of Segu. In the same period the French, as imperial rivals of the Tukulor, had tried through several devices—including treaty-making with favourably disposed chiefs—at first to establish their political influence and authority, and later to effect the occupation of the other states in the Senegambia. At first the French confined their major activities to commerce and their political influence was only indirectly felt. For a while their political actions were geared towards countermining Tukulor expansionism in the area. In the process they found it necessary to maintain friendly relations with the rulers of the Senegambian states since they lacked the means of fighting continual wars against the Tukulor and their allies. Their agents were therefore at pains to prove that they were first and foremost traders whose only interest in politics derived from their desire to protect their friends and allies against the empire-building Tukulor who were seeking to destroy the weaker states and were placing difficulties in the way of French commerce. In other words, the French based their relations on common interests which they assumed they shared with the rulers of the states concerned against the Tukulor empire. For the rulers also, association with the French provided a convenient and welcome opportunity to ward off Tukulor imperialism and maintain internal security in their states.

Because of this mutual dependence, it was usually sufficient for the French to maintain their presence in the area by signing treaties of alliance and protection with willing chiefs and thereafter leave such chiefs to protect French interests in their states. To enable the chiefs to do this, the French usually supplied them with arms and ammunition and occasionally aided them in waging wars against their unfriendly neighbours. This was, for example, how the French maintained their position in Khasso where they were in alliance with Juku Sambala of Medine against the latter's relation and rival, Kartum Sambala, as well as in the pro-Tukulor district of Logo. Similarly, they maintained Bubakar Saada in power over Bondu against the wishes of large sections of the population.

For as long as the French concentrated on trade, which they conducted from their factories on the River Senegal and its tributaries, they remained by and large at peace with the peoples of the region. It must be stressed, however, that their involvement in politics, though limited and mostly indirect, caused irritation and occasional trouble between themselves and some sections of the population. But in as much as their imperialist ambitions had not become obvious they were generally able to hold their positions, expand their activities and even encourage and direct the hostility of the people of the area against the Tukulor.

But from 1876 onwards, beginning with the governorship of Brière de l'Isle, the French became gradually, but very clearly, imperialistic and aggressively expansionist in their activities. Under Governor Brière de l'Isle the policy of minimum, indirect involvement in politics changed to one of direct military intervention and control. Alleging threats to French commercial and political interests, Brière de l'Isle began the new era of territorial acquisition through the military with the sack of Sabousire, the capital of Logo and the subjugation of the rest of the state in 1878.[1] The Logo episode was followed in 1879 with the establishment of the the the Upper Senegal–Niger High Command with responsibility for the expansion of the French sphere of influence. A railroad to link the Senegal with the Niger was launched in 1880. In that year also, starting with the Gallieni mission, political missions and military campaigns commanded by officers of the Marine Corps of the French Army annually set out to expand the areas of French political influence and authority. At first the political missions and military campaigns operated ostensibly only against the Tukulor empire and Samori Ture as well as loyalists of these in the Senegambia.[2] But it soon became clear that the French were determined to be masters over all—foes and friends alike. In the pursuit of their objectives, the French conscripted labour and men from the neighbouring territories to meet the needs of building their railroad and swell the ranks of their military forces.

However, once it became clear that the French were reversing the old basis of their relations with the states of the Senegambia and were now pursuing the objectives of military conquest and political domination the people were quick in showing their resentment and, in some cases, outright hostility. For example, the Sarrakole population in the various states soon began to resist their forceful recruitment into the labour force needed for the railway project and the military forces. Although the Sarrakole had for long served the French community in several capacities—for example as marine men ('laptots') and carriers of trade between St. Louis and other French trading stations and the rest of the Sudan[3]—they guarded their independence bravely and jealously. They would work with the French only out of their own free choice. Hence, according to Colonel Henri Frey, they resisted on many occasions the French attempt to recruit their people for forced labour as porters in the army or as labourers on the railway project, pointing out to French officers in many villages that the Sarrakole were not French captives.

This spirit of independence was demonstrated by the people of Bakel against Captain Zimmermann in July 1874, and in December 1880, apparently as a reprisal for the misconduct of the French officers on a topographic mission in the area, the Sarrakole population of Goutioube village attacked some members of the mission under Captain Saillenfest. Similar incidents were said to have taken place in the Sarrakole villages of Segala, Lanel and Tombokane. In the latter place, on 9 December 1880, Colonel Borgnis-Desbordes had to threaten to destroy the village if the people persisted in their refusal to provide him with guides and porters. Indeed hostility towards French penetration and attempts at occupation continued to be shown until 1885. For instance in 1881 the Sarrakole population of the area between Bakel and Kayes constantly raided French convoys, depriving them of their cattle and other animals which they treated as booty taken from the enemy. Their refusal to provide service for the French in their penetration of the Western Sudan continued till November 1885 when even in spite of the offer of some remuneration the Sarrakole refused to work for the postal services of the French.[4]

It is against this background of widespread Sarrakole hostility to the French that one has to consider the movement led by Mahmadou Lamine. In effect when he emerged as a religious and political leader in 1885 his people, the Sarrakole, had already established a tradition of resistance against, first the Tukulor rulers and since 1879, against the French who were making a bid to establish their political authority in the Western Sudan. Given the prevailing circumstances in the Sarrakole areas of the Senegambia, Lamine's general background and experience made him admirably suited to the role of leader which he was soon to play.

Lamine (also known as Muhammād Al-Amīn Demba Debassi) must have been born between 1835 and 1840 in the village of Goundiourou (or Koundiourou)[5] in the Kaniaga province of Khasso some eight kilometres (about five miles) south of Kayes, lying between the latter town and Medine. His father was a marabout (a religious leader) who not only taught the religion of Islam but also served as a judge in several places in Khasso. Goundiourou is reputed to have been a great religious centre where many marabouts resided, and has even been referred to as an holy city (' . . . *la ville sainte*').[6] Lamine himself had his religious education under his father as well as in several other centres of learning in the Senegambia, particularly Futa Toro which since the eleventh century, in the days of Tekrur, had had the reputation for being the nerve-centre of religious evangelisation and revivalism in the Senegambia. He grew up as a tall, robust man, highly intelligent and enjoyed a considerable reputation for piety and courage. From available evidence, it appears that he left on the pilgrimage between 1868 and 1869, returning home only in 1885. In the interval, he had spent seven years in Mecca and other places, such as Constantinople, and another seven years (1878–85) as a prisoner of Ahmadu, the Tukulor ruler at Segu. He spent the rest of the period on his travels. Before he returned home, he had already become renowned for his sanctity, his ability to perform miracles and his great qualities of leadership.[7]

On the political plane, Lamine had also acquired considerable experience and knowledge. As a youth, he must have witnessed the beginnings of Umar's Tukulor empire and the Franco–Tukulor struggle for the control of the Senegambia which came to a climax between 1857 and 1860, beginning with the siege of Medine.[8] In these events, his people, the Sarrakole, had been among the peoples who, in collaboration with the French, fought against Tukulor imperialism in Khasso and other parts of the Senegambia. The memory of this early resistance to Tukulor rule must have been revived and reinforced by the harsh treatment he received at the hands of the Tukulor ruler who detained him for seven years at Segu. When he regained his freedom in 1885, he left for home with an unrelenting resolution to replace the Tukulor empire with a revived Sarrakole one.[9] This determination was clearly in line with the traditions of his people, and more, it was in tune with the current situation in which the Sarrakole found themselves having to resist the penetration of the French, their erstwhile allies against the Tukulor. As part of his development, Lamine must have acquired a good deal of sophistication deriving from his wide travels and long period of training abroad.

Given this background, it would appear that the movement led by Lamine was not just a negative reaction to French occupation but was in essence an expression of Sarrakole nationalism. It seems clear also that the movement was inspired by the ideas of Islam, perhaps Sanusiyya in particular, regarding the undesirability of the rule of infidels (non-Muslims) over Muslims and the need to restore Islam to its pure primitive form.

The idea that Lamine's movement was an expression of Sarrakole nationalism derives partly from the fact that it came as a climax to a long period of Sarrakole resistance to alien rule. The resistance was still going on against both the French and the Tukulor at the time Lamine arrived in Khasso in 1885. Apart from the cases of resistance to French penetration already mentioned, Sarrakole resistance had also been taking place against Tukulor rule in the Guidimaka (Diomboko) and Diafounou emirates of Kaarta on the left bank of the Senegal. Like the other subjects in Kaarta the Sarrakole populations of these two emirates had consistently resisted the Tukulor since the latter conquered the area. From 1872 to 1877 both areas were involved in prolonged resistance against the Tukulor, and, occasionally during the period, they even co-ordinated their resistance efforts. For instance, the Diafounou resistance leaders who had captured their Tukulor emir, Nuru, even aided the war efforts of Moriba, the Chief of Sero, against the Tukulor emir of Diomboko, Basiru, between 1875 and 1877. In the latter year, Moriba was given refuge in Diafounou after he had been defeated in Diomboko.[10] Lamine's movement was in a sense a continuation of the general Sarrakole tradition of resistance against alien rule. In his encounters with the French, his following was mainly Sarrakole and his programme as well as the spontaneity with which it was embraced by the Sarrakole populations of the Senegambia and the two emirates of Kaarta[11] show that the factor of ethnic solidarity in the movement was strong. It is not being suggested, however, that the sense of affinity which the Sarrakole shared was co-extensive with the desire for a unified political state. The latter was no doubt Lamine's idea.

It is clear that Lamine's movement derived part of its inspiration from Islam. What is in doubt is the precise nature of the Islamic influence in it. Practically all the people involved in the movement were Muslims. But so also were the rulers of the Tukulor empire to whom, like the French, the movement was opposed. Theoretically, all Muslims were supposed to belong to the same spiritual community *(Umma)* and to be united against unbelievers. But the reality since the emergence of the Tukulor empire had been that Muslims had been divided according to their conflicting ethnic, social and political interests. But the Islamic factor in Lamine's movement appears to have been more than just the result of this negative effect of the rise of the Tukulor empire.

When he arrived in Khasso in 1885, he declared his intention to launch a *jihād* and immediately embarked upon a tour of preaching and conversion in the Senegambia. For a people who were already practising Muslims, the need for conversion to Islam seems difficult to understand, and this is the more so in relation to populations under the Tukulor regime—an Islamic theocracy. Apart from his desire to recruit a personal following, Lamine's activities appear more meaningful if one assumes that he belonged to a different

Islamic brotherhood from the Qadiriyya and Tijaniyya—the two brotherhoods embraced in his area of operation. It seems probable that he was a Sanusi. This suggestion is based on indirect evidence of the existence of Sanusiyya influences, or even adherents, among the Sarrakole of the Senegambia as well as the identity of Lamine's ideas and practices with those of the Sanusiyya movement. It is claimed that the Muslims in the Sarrakole villages of Kounguel, Lanel and Dramane practised their religion and taught Islamic doctrines and socio-political ideas that were closely identical with those of the Sanusiyya. Moreover, there is evidence of relations between Sanusiyya centres in Fez, Tripolitania and Cyrenaica and the Muslims in Senegambia. The people of these places also showed that they were unusually knowledgeable about Lamine's movement and its varied fortunes.[12]

It is not easy to distinguish between the Sanusi and the other brotherhoods especially as the original founder made it clear that membership of another order was not inconsistent with adherence to his own society. This latter point must have made it easy for Lamine to recruit converts among those already in the Qadiriyya and Tijaniyya. It is claimed that the Sanusi were perhaps more ascetic and more insistent on realising the idea that no Muslim should live in any region where non-Muslims ruled. Like the original Sanusi, the Sarrakole in the Senegambia regarded tobacco and coffee, among other things as taboo.[13] What was of particular relevance and appeal to the situation in which Lamine and his followers found themselves in the Senegambia was the idea and actual experience of the Sanusi in militantly resisting European penetration in Tripolitania, Cyrenaica and Tunisia.[14] According to the Sanusi, the resistance to the French and the Tukulor could be justified as a search for freedom from non-Muslim authority and a nominally independent Islamic state. This idea complements the nationalist element in the movement.

The creation of the Lamine state

In 1884 Sultan Ahmadu had left his capital, Segu, for Kaarta to suppress the rebellion which his half-brother, Muhammad Muntaga, was leading against his authority there. Lamine soon took advantage of the absence of Ahmadu to escape from his detention. On his way home, he reached the French fort at Bamako on 1 June 1885. At this time it was already known that he was planning to launch a *jihād* with a view to founding a Sarrakole empire.[15]

On arrival at Goundiourou in Khasso in July 1885 Lamine

pursued his objective resolutely, but tactfully. First, while working out his plans, he hastened to assure the French of his friendship and good neighbourliness. He got in touch at once with Sambala, King of Medine, who, since 1855, had been a constant friend and ally of the French against the Tukulor. Sambala, for his part, assured the French of the peaceful intentions and disposition of Lamine.[16] With these assurances, he was able to hide his real intentions from the French and was therefore able to go about prosecuting his plans unsuspected. In any case, he had arrived during the wet and hot season of the year when French personnel and troops were usually reduced to the minimum because most of them had gone on leave to escape the deleterious effect of the climate on their health.

Having already acquired a reputation for piety and good qualities of leadership, Lamine soon built up around himself a corps of devoted disciples. With these disciples he embarked on a tour of evangelisation and recruitment in Khasso, Gadiaka, Guoy, Bondu and Bambuk. He also sent emissaries to other areas. He soon acquired the prestige of a Kāhlifā, and even a *Mahdi,* who had come to liberate his people. In many places, people submitted to his authority and he quickly laid the foundations of his empire. He announced his plans to wage a holy war and started to develop the nucleus of his army. In the meantime, he had tried to ensure good relations between himself and his neighbours, especially the rulers of Futa Toro and Bondu. He established contact with Abdul Bubakar, the Almamy of Bosséia and Futa Toro, inviting him to join in prosecuting the holy war which he was planning. Although the latter did not join him, he treated him as a good neighbour. Like Al-hajj 'Umar before him, Lamine made direct contacts with the French officers in a bid to divert their attention from the real issues. He told them he was planning to wage war on the inhabitants of Guidimaka and of Tenda (Gambia) and was soliciting their help, especially with the supply of arms. As a further guarantee of his good intentions, he offered to send a mission to the French Governor at St. Louis. All that Lamine was trying to do by making these moves was to deceive the French into thinking that he was only concerned with the Gambia, where at the worst he would only be a menace to the British, and Guidimaka where he would be a problem for their rivals, the Tukulor. He succeeded in deceiving the French[17] and therefore had the opportunity of building up his army with French arms, and embarking upon his state-building without having to come into conflict with them too soon.

By the end of the year, Lamine had only been able to assemble a standing army of about 250 men, all stationed at his village, Goundiourou.[18] But in fact his position was much stronger than the impression that the small size of his army might give. In the first place he enjoyed great popularity and respect among an overwhelming majority of the Sarrakole population. Indeed he had become a charismatic figure for most of them in the Senegambia and in the Kaarta section of the Tukulor empire. As has been stated earlier, in most of these places the Sarrakole were currently involved in resistance against both the French and the Tukulor and they had virtually accepted him as their leader against these enemies. Indeed when he appealed to the people to join in his projected war, the response was enthusiastic and people came *en masse* from all parts of the Senegambia as well as Guidimaka and Diafounou. At that time, the French misunderstood the significance of what was happening thinking that the mass movement initiated by Lamine had been motivated by a desire to pillage a few British factories in the Gambia for booty.[19]

The fact that he possessed considerable strength was soon further proved by the events which took place between December 1885 and February 1886. Soon after Ahmadu had suppressed the rebellion against him in Kaarta, it became clear that he was planning a military campaign against the Sarrakole in Guidimaka and Diafounou. In these two areas the Sarrakole quickly accepted Lamine as their ruler. Diafounou accepted Lamine's son, Soybou (or Souiabou), as its governor, while people came in large numbers from Guidimaka to join his army. In this way, by December 1885, Lamine had incorporated the two emirates of Kaarta in his nascent state.

Secondly, in Bondu, Bubakar Saada, the Almamy, died on 18 December 1885. He had been maintained on the throne by the French, although the vast majority of his people resented the French presence and had little affection for him.[20] There seems little doubt that the loyalty of the vast majority of the Bondunké had gone to Lamine even before the death of Saada. Following Saada's death the French, in an attempt to protect their interests in Bondu, quickly imposed another of their protégés, Umar Penda, as successor in place of the more popular and rightful candidate, Usman Gassi. The dispute over the succession caused considerable bitterness and internal division in the state. The masses rejected the French protégé and collaborated with Lamine in his bid to establish his own authority over Bondu. After the French had instigated Umar Penda to reject Lamine's call to surrender, the latter mobilised his forces and marched on Bondu capturing the village of Dianweli, and later Boulebane, the capital, without having to fire even a shot. He did not have to fight because the masses had accepted his authority and had already abandoned the French-backed Almamy and the rest of the ruling family. In the circumstance, the latter were in no position to offer any resistance and they just had to flee in disgrace before Lamine finally entered Boulebane. A few days later, Lamine occupied Senoudebou, where the French had established a post, and had himself installed as ruler.[21]

After his successes in Bondu, Diafounou and Guidimaka, the Sarrakole populations of Bambuk and the various areas of Khasso, notably Logo, accepted his authority. In Logo the chief and people of Sabousire, the capital, were accused of collaborating with Lamine, giving him every assistance in material and men.[22] Thus, between December 1885 and February 1886, Lamine had rapidly built up the core of his state.

Although he was building his state at the expense of the French and the Tukulor, none of these was in a strong military position to tackle him effectively. As has been noted, Ahmadu had been engaged in suppressing an armed rebellion in Kaarta since 1884 and was not yet sufficiently strong to embark on new military adventures against Lamine. As for the French, the forces at their disposal in the Senegambia hardly sufficed to police their commercial establishments in the area, let alone fight a full-scale war with Lamine. The funds available to the colonial authorities were limited and the Governor of Senegal had standing instructions since 1884 not to engage in any military encounter the cost of which he could not provide from his budget. To make matters worse, Lamine's operations had taken place precisely when most of the troops in the Senegambia had been committed to fighting Samori Ture and this meant that their posts in the Senegal valley were only scantily protected. All these, coupled with the hostility and rivalry between the two, rendered Lamine strong *vis-à-vis* the French and the Tukulor. To be able to face up to the threat posed by Lamine, the French had to stop their military engagement against Samori, quickly arrange a diplomatic settlement and deploy available forces to the Senegal valley.[23]

Having done this, the French were for the first time able to engage Lamine in battle in March 1886. But they were at that stage not yet an effective deterrent to Lamine's state-building enterprises. He occupied the villages around the French post at Bakel in March, and in April he occupied the state of Guoy.[24] At this stage the position of the French had become critical and it had become clear that they would not be able to maintain their position in the Senegambia, unless they were able to defeat Lamine militarily. Henceforth we shall be concerned with Lamine's military resistance to French penetration and occupation.

The Franco–Lamine military struggle

The opposing armies: Lamine's army was made up largely of volunteers. His strength lay not so much in the numbers of his regular forces, but rather in the fact that he was leading what was really a mass movement. His army was not made up of professionally trained men, but of civilians, fanatical devotees who had come from many different walks of life. This fact is significant because it conditioned the outlook, organisation and tactics of his forces. It was difficult to know the exact strength of the forces since successes often led to a sudden rise in the number of adherents while set-backs in the fortunes of the movement could lead to temporary withdrawal by some of the less fanatical elements. This situation probably accounts for the variations in the estimates of his forces which are contained in various sources. These estimates range from 3,000 to 12,000. It is reasonable to suggest that the constant elements in his army probably never exceeded 3,000 to 4,000.[25]

It must also be pointed out that Lamine was not just fighting the French but also their allies who were Africans like himself. Over the previous fifty years before the rise of Lamine, economic and political interest-groups, for whom the French presence was beneficial and had indeed become essential, had arisen in various parts of the Senegambia. Among the political interests were 'protected' rulers like Bubakar Saada and Umar Penda in Bondu and Juku Sambala of Medine in Khasso. The economic interests were made up mainly of the traders and merchants *(traitants* and *negociants)* doing their business mainly with the French commercial houses on the Senegal between St. Louis and the Upper Senegal–Niger region. Although in terms of number, these elements constituted a minority they were nevertheless important as people with special interests to protect. They were members of the same community as the pro-Lamine elements; but during the period of stress they had to protect their interests, and therefore, support the French. In any case they were treated as fifth columnists by Lamine's men and fought alongside the French as enemies. Whenever this happened, as in the siege of Bakel and Boulebane, the movement took on the character of a civil war. In the tumultuous situation created by such a siege, it was always difficult to estimate the exact strength of the forces of Lamine. In a general uprising, there seems no doubt that some people would be drawn to action not because of their concern for the issues at stake but by their desire to loot. When one is given an estimate based on an impression of the number of the people, including the rag-tag elements, involved in the movement, all of whom were taken to be pro-Lamine elements by disdainful French officers, any figure between 10,000 and 12,000 is mentioned.[26]

On the other hand, not all those with French connections necessarily defended the French cause. There was, for example, a fairly large body of people (estimated at between 12,000 and 15,000) in the Senegambia who had served the various French interests in St. Louis and other parts of the Senegal colony before the outbreak of Lamine's movement. Many of these had served as sailors, soldiers, boatsmen, drivers and in various other trades in which they had acquired considerable expertise. Some of them had retired from French service and some deserted to serve the Sarrakole cause under the leadership of Lamine. This group represented an invaluable asset to Lamine's movement. They had become familiar with the French way of life, had acquired some technical skill which would be useful in war, and since they were often not easily distinguishable from pro-French elements with a similar background, they could have access to sources of information which would be of help to Lamine. The main motivation of this group of people seems to have been the desire to defend their cultural nation against French imperialism.

In view of the nature of his movement, it is difficult to imagine how Lamine could have subjected his forces to any European-type military discipline and organisation. The organisation and operation of the army followed the tradition in many African societies according to which every physically fit adult male was a potential soldier, there being no professional soldiery. Neither Lamine nor any of his immediate lieutenants was known to have had any experience of organising and fighting in an army built on the European model. In terms of supply, Lamine had limited access to European arms and ammunition bought from French traders and agents on the Senegal, or seized during battle. Some Sarrakole who were resident in St. Louis also served as secret agents for the supply of arms and ammunition to Lamine's men. It is suggested that he got quite a number of his weapons from British 'factories' in the Gambia through the Sarrakole elements in that colony.[27] Although European arms and ammunition were of immense value, there seems no doubt that supplies from private sources constituted the major source of the weapons used in the Lamine movement.[28] These weapons comprised mainly outmoded Europeans guns and, by the standard of European military technology at the time, crude instruments like poisoned bows and arrows and spears which depended for their effectiveness on having the enemy at close range.

The French army had as its core officers and men drawn from the Marine Corps *(infanterie* and *artillerie de la marine)* of the French national army. While the leadership of the army came from this group, the bulk of the fighting force came from the Senegalese native infantry known as the *Tirailleurs Sénégalais.* The *Tirailleurs* were constituted into a standing force by General Louis Faidherbe in 1857. Before then, Africans who had fought in French colonial wars had done so as volunteers; but henceforth they were trained and treated as regular soldiers. At first, the recruits were mainly from the colony of Senegal but at the time of the French encounter with Lamine, the *tirailleurs* had become Senegalese only in name as they were made up principally of Bambara and other ethnic groups from the Sudan. These elements were peculiarly suited to the imperial interests of the French as they were mostly people from Tukulor subject groups; or else they were former slaves of some chiefs in the Senegambia who, from 1848 onwards, had been liberated by the French as a reprisal against their masters whom the French had found unfriendly. The *tirailleurs* were therefore men with a sense of dedication to the French whom they saw as protectors against their oppressors. They were also encouraged by the French to make soldiery their career. They were generally well trained and well armed and, from the beginning, deserving ones among them were given commands as junior officers and N.C.O.s. In 1857, for example, Paule Holle, a Mulatto from St. Louis, commanded French operations during the siege of Medine and one native officer, Alioun Sal, took part as second-lieutenant *(Sous-lieutenant)* in the campaigns against Al-hajj 'Umar in the Senegambia. African and European troops were mixed in the French campaigns from the start. At the beginning, European elements in the rank and file were greater in number. For instance, of the regular soldiers who were sent from St. Louis to reinforce French forces in the Senegambia in August 1857, there were 200 French infantry and seventy artillery men to 100 African infantry-men. On that occasion there were also 100 European volunteers from St. Louis.[29] Before the end of the century, however, the African elements had become predominant in the French army in the Sudan, although the commanders and the other officers were, in the majority, people who held their commissions direct from the

French army. But the success of the French army depended mainly on the *tirailleurs* who, being Africans, were accustomed to the local conditions and were able to withstand the effects of the climate. They were for all practical purposes the section of the army that could undertake the serious fighting in the inhospitable wet and hot season of the year, called by the French the *hivernage*. For a long time, the high mortality rate among the Europeans prevented their use on a large scale.[30] The French further stiffened the devotion of the *tirailleurs* by freely distributing to them women captives or 'liberated' slaves, referred to euphemistically as *épouses libres*.

While on campaigns, the French forces relied for their auxiliary services on conscripted labour from among the local population. People were usually conscripted to serve as porters and guides and when the populations were resentful and hostile to the practice, the French resorted to tapping the so-called Freed Slaves Homes *(Villages de liberté)* at will.[31]

Unlike Lamine's forces, the French had at their disposal a compact well-disciplined, professional army which rarely exceeded 4,000 men at any time.[32] The French army also had a regular supply of more modern and superior weapons to those of the forces of Lamine. They had both heavy and light arms. Of the former they had several types of cannons: for example, they had models 4 *(Canons de 4)*, 65 mm and 80 mm *(de montagne)*, the last being particularly effective for breaking down fortresses *(tatas)*. The infantrymen, mainly drawn from the *tirailleurs*, were armed with repeater rifles *(fusils à tir rapide)* models 1874 and later 1884 (Kropatschek). A cavalry detachment made up of the European elements used mules for transportation.[33] This is in contrast to the cavalry of Lamine's forces which had horses at its disposal for this purpose.

From the above it is evident that, as a fighting force, the French army was better than Lamine's in terms of equipment and training; and that Lamine's strong point lay in the fact that he was leading a mass movement and fighting largely among a friendly population, a situation which the French army, professional in outlook and attached to fighting pitched battles according to well-worked-out strategies and battle formations, would find difficult to deal with.

In the war against the French, Lamine employed mainly guerilla tactics. Both sides on different occasions employed surprise attacks on each other. On a few occasions the French managed to force Lamine to fight pitched battles. Needless to say, with their better equipment and tighter organisation, the French almost invariably won such battles. By contrast, Lamine's men usually won when they took on the French by storm, or in guerilla operations. Occasionally, however, the French had to use a large number of volunteers locally recruited, and since these were untrained militarily, they had to operate more or less like Lamine's forces. When the French forces, like Lamine's, were made up of local recruits the struggle necessarily took the form of civil war in which street fighting and surprise raids, rather than organised battles, featured. Both sides employed spies.

The war was not limited to military encounters alone. Diplomatic manœuvres and propaganda formed a significant aspect of the struggle. In the following passage, an attempt will be made to illustrate the use and effects of the different tactics mentioned so far.

At the outbreak of hostilities both the French and Lamine tried to win the support, or at least the benevolent neutrality, of some of the rulers in the Senegambia. As already mentioned, this was the essence of Lamine's friendly overtures to Bubakər Saada of Bondu and Abdul Bubakar of Futa Toro, as well as the French, at the beginning of the movement. At that time, although Lamine could not get these two chiefs directly involved on his side, he was able to launch his movement without any fear of hostility from them and the French. The French engaged in diplomacy primarily to extricate themselves from their position of military and political weakness. The inadequacy of the forces at their disposal has been noted. But their position was made worse by the fact that they were operating along an over-extended line of communication and in the midst of unfriendly states. They had, since 1876, been fighting against the Senegambian states of Futa Toro, Joloff and others, and since 1883, intermittently, against Samori Ture. At the same time, their relations with the Tukulor empire were delicate and fraught with the danger of an outbreak of armed conflict. All these put the French in a state of isolation in and around their posts. Without correcting their relations with their erstwhile hostile neighbours by, at least, settling their old problems, they risked being attacked from all sides and being consumed in the process. It was to avoid such a situation that the French quickly arranged a diplomatic settlement with Samori in 1886 and made overtures to Abdul Bubakar of Futa Toro with a view to enlisting his support in their fight with Lamine. The quickness with which they got their protégé, Umar Penda, installed in succession to Bubakar Saada was motivated by their long-standing policy of protecting their interests in the neighbouring states through such dependent rulers. Once installed and protected against more legiti- mate and popular candidates, such rulers could be relied upon by the French to fight their wars for them. The struggle between Umar

Penda and Lamine at the beginning of the campaigns can be seen as an example.

Military encounters: As a prelude to the military confrontation between the French and Lamine, the former took measures to reinforce the garrisons in their posts in the Senegal valley, particularly Bakel which appeared to be exposed to the danger of attack from Lamine's men who were then still operating in Bondu. Two companies of the *tirailleurs* were sent to Bakel from Kayes by Lieutenant-Colonel Frey. The first company received orders to leave Kayes on 5 February 1886 while the second had its orders on the 15th. These reinforcements brought the number of troops in Bakel to 250, a force which was considered strong enough to defend and maintain order in Bakel and surrounding villages while awaiting the arrival of more troops. Early in March, Lieutenant-Colonel Frey attempted to force Lamine to stop his activities by taking his family and attendants as hostages. He ordered the commandant of the French post at Kayes, battalion commander Major Houry, to order the second company of the *tirailleurs,* while on its way through Medine to Bakel, to call at Goundiourou and take as hostages Lamine's wives and relatives, and raid his treasury. Colonel Frey enjoined complete secrecy over the plan in order to assure success.

The raid on Lamine's compound at Goundiourou was carried out on 13 March by the second company of the *tirailleurs* under the command of Captain Ferrat, assisted by Lieutenant Rodot and Second-Lieutenant Samba Maram. The raid took place at dawn while the inhabitants were still asleep. The people were taken by surprise but nevertheless they still put up some resistance and even killed one of the invading soldiers. The company, however, accomplished its mission taking thirty-four people—Lamine's wives, children and relatives—as prisoners and looting his treasury and other belongings.[34] While all these preliminary military preparations were going on, Colonel Frey continued his efforts to get Abdul Bubakar engaged in military action against Lamine.

The first military confrontation took place on the 14 March at Kounguel. Before then, Lamine's troops had been campaigning in Bondu where they had conquered most of the villages. The total force at his command at this time has been estimated at 4,000. Out of this, he withdrew about 1,500 from Bondu in time to render ineffective the French military build-up at Bakel. His men arrived at Kounguel, some six kilometres (about four miles) from Bakel, around the same time as the last of the reinforcements of *tirailleurs* reached

Bakel after raiding his place at Goundiourou. There seems no doubt that the appropriate timing of the arrival of his troops was due to his having received good intelligence reports from his spies about the plans and movements of the French. Indeed, the French accused their interpreter at Bakel, Alpha Sega, of giving him intelligence reports on them. He was also charged with deliberately misleading the guides employed by the French forces about the true position of Lamine's men.[35]

French forces at the battle of Kounguel numbered about 600, while Lamine's were estimated at 1,500. The advanced group sent out by the French comprised a company of sixty-six *tirailleurs* under the command of Captain Jolly, assisted by Second-Lieutenants Laty and Toumané; and a section under Sergeant Féméland. The section later joined the company at Gouianiam Kolé, mid-way between Bakel and Kounguel. In all, the advanced group numbered eighty-seven. But in addition there were auxiliaries made up of twenty-four native carriers for the ammunition and other baggage. The advanced group was armed with a cannon *(de 4 de Montagne)* and repeater rifles. The bigger force, numbering between 500 and 600, followed under the command of Captain Lefranc. The force was made up of both regular *tirailleurs* and volunteers.

But Lamine did not give the French any chance to succeed in their plans. His men took the advance party of the French force by surprise, approaching as near as forty yards before the latter were aware of their presence. The French were given no chance to draw up their troops in any systematic fashion and they were left with no alternative but to fight Lamine's men in close combat. The situation was particularly suited to the latter who needed close combat to be effective against their enemies in view of the preponderance of bows and arrows, as well as poisoned spears, among their weapons. The battle began as early as five o'clock in the morning and within four hours French forces had been routed by Lamine. The French troops had to flee in disorder, pursued and attacked from the rear by Lamine's men. Neither was their situation improved when Captain Lefranc, commanding the main body of troops and volunteers, joined in the engagement. The French lost quantities of weapons including the cannon which they never had a chance to use. They also lost the two boats which the section under Sergeant Féméland had used to carry supplies for the troops. The French reported the loss of ten killed, made up of seven privates, Sergeant Ciré Boubakar and Corporals Abd el-Raman and Richard. Thirty-six were reported wounded, over half seriously. Among the wounded were two

French officers, two N.C.O.s *(sous-officiers)*, one French, one African, as well as the N.C.O. of the cavalry. Worse still, the telegraph line between Bakel and Matam was cut by Lamine's men who thereby disrupted the French communications system in the area. Bakel itself was also blockaded.

With victory won, Lamine's forces were rapidly increased by the addition of new Sarrakole volunteers from surrounding villages, especially from Diafounou and Guidimaka. The situation was critical as it became clear that the French were not in a position to reverse the situation in their own favour. As the Governor of Senegal informed Paris, it was absolutely impossible to send reinforcements from St. Louis which had none to spare: and even if these had been available the communications problem was such that they could still not have been sent. At that time of the year, the waters were at a low level and the River Senegal was therefore unnavigable for the boats which could have taken the troops to Kayes or any of the posts. In the circumstances, the Governor emphasised, the only hope lay in the overtures being made to Adbul Bubakar succeeding, and in the latter agreeing to engage Lamine.[36]

Lamine used his victory at Kounguel to advantage. As news of it spread, more and more people came to join his forces. Lamine spent the latter part of March consolidating his position and massing his forces around Bakel which he planned to take by siege. As for the French, Colonel Frey tried to cope with the situation by giving way quickly to Samori and diverting all the troops hitherto engaged in the war against the latter to Kayes from where they were redistributed to Bakel and other posts. At Bakel the French had some 200 soldiers armed with repeater rifles and about 1,100 volunteers. The latter were made up of African merchants and traders, mainly from St. Louis, and numbered about 250; friendly elements among the Sarrakole; about 300 Bondunké made up largely of followers of the ousted royal family under the command of Usman Gassi; about 200 Bambara volunteers and about 200 Tukulor from various parts of the Senegambia. In addition, the French could count on the sympathy of about 4,000 refugees who had come to Bakel from several different areas in the wake of Lamine's campaigns.[37]

The battle for Bakel took place in the first few days of April. It began with an encounter at the village of Guéry-M'Palé in the neighbourhood of Bakel on 1 April. Here, Lamine's forces were beaten back by French forces already stationed there under the command of Lieutenant Laty. On the 2nd, the inhabitants of the village of Mody-N'Kané deserted their village after burning it and moved *en masse* to join Lamine. Thereafter, Lamine reorganised his forces, dividing them into three corps and took over their command personally. The preparations took place near Tuabo, a village only three kilometres away from Bakel. From there on the 4th a two-pronged attack was directed against Bakel through Guéry-M'Palé and Mody-N'Kané. The contingents which passed through Guéry-M'Palé failed to break through the cordon of French troops; but those which passed through Mody-N'Kané routed the French forces on their way to Bakel. There the French fort was defended with cannons although the French depended mainly on volunteers for its defence. The attempt to recall troops from the neighbourhood to defend the town merely made it easier for Lamine's forces, pursuing hard the withdrawing French forces, to enter Bakel from other directions. Both the French and Lamine had support in Bakel and the situation created by the clash between the two forces was one of civil war. The fighting was done in the streets with the French fort and warehouses, as well as the shops of their African supporters, raided. In the confusion that inevitably followed, it must have been difficult to distinguish between the supporters of both sides as bands of people ran helter-skelter from street to street. Furthermore, organised fighting in which the French could have used their superior weapons to advantage was impossible. Similarly, the use of heavy weapons like cannons could only have been to the disadvantage of both foes and friends in such close fighting. Weapons like bows and arrows and spears were perhaps more suitable and this must have given Lamine some advantage over the French. Nevertheless, Lamine's men were repulsed from the town.

After the fight in Bakel, a large number of regular soldiers and volunteers were found to have been killed or maimed. According to the reports of the French officers on the incident, Lamine lost about 300 men killed while the French side lost twenty-five killed and about 100 incapacitated. But this report must be taken with caution since it must have been extremely difficult to specify correctly which of the corpses of volunteers in the streets were anti- or pro-French. The only ones whose allegiance could be ascertained with any certainty were those of the merchants and traders who had regular dealings with the French and one is not surprised to find in Frey's report specific names of those who had been killed in this group.

Lamine later withdrew his men to Tuabo and the other villages around Bakel. From these places, the blockade against Bakel was maintained between 5 and 10 April. As part of the offensive against Bakel, Lamine's men destroyed the telegraphic connection between

Bakel and Kayes. Apparently in their panic, the French officers at
Bakel arrested their interpreter, Alpha Sega, whom they had earlier
on accused of collaborating with Lamine, and shot him on the pretext
that he had been an accomplice in Lamine's raid on Bakel.[38]

After the fighting at Bakel, the French feared that Lamine would
return for another attack. In readiness for such an eventuality, they
re organised the defence arrangements at the post and other places at
Bakel. In the meantime, Colonel Frey, as supreme commander,
ordered that troops who had just been released from the war against
Samori should move to Kayes, the headquarters of the Upper
Senegal–Niger territory as well as commercial headquarters for the
French in the area. His plan was, at all costs, to avoid the experience
of Bakel being repeated at Kayes. He declared a state of emergency
and personally took over the command of all French military
operations. But Lamine did not strike back as expected. He appears
to have realised that he had very little chance of winning any encounter against any of the garrisoned towns where the French were
strongest. Rather than do any such thing, he resorted to sporadic
guerilla attacks against French positions around the two areas.
He appears to have concentrated on Bakel between the 5th and 10th
and thereafter to have extended his activities to Kayes. During this
period, Lamine seems to have been operating from bases in Diafounou and Guidimaka—areas over which the French had no control.
While Lamine maintained his hit and run, surprise attacks, the
French were particularly vulnerable. As the situation was becoming
desperate, Colonel Frey decided to carry the campaign against
Lamine into Guidimaka.

The Guidimaka phase of the war began from the middle of April
and continued without either side winning any decisive victory until
about 24 May. At the outset, Frey's forces comprised cavalry,
artillery and infantrymen of about 140 Europeans and 380 *tirailleurs*
and *spahis*. But he soon lost most of his men in battle or because of
the hot, inhospitable weather which was particularly ruinous to the
European troops. The French forces suffered partly because they
could not cope with Lamine's guerilla tactics. As the war dragged on,
Frey became desperate and resorted to sheer vandalism. Early in
May, concerned by the ineffectiveness of his troops so far, Frey set a
great part of Guidimaka on fire, and informed the Governor of
Senegal of his action saying in part: '. . . *Ainsi que je vous en ai rendu
compte j'ai brulé la plus grande partie du Guidimaka . . .*'[39] Since Colonel
Frey had introduced this element into the war, albeit in desperation, Lamine soon took his cue from him and within a few days the

reprisals came against the French. Lamine's men, in retaliation, set the French post at Senoudebou, which they had occupied, on fire, and it soon became clear that fire was a mutually destructive weapon to use. The Governor of Senegal, who saw the wider implications of Frey's action even for Franco–Tukulor relations, quickly warned him against such operations.[40]

By June 1886, at the end of the 1885–6 campaign, it had become clear that the French had lost their grip on the situation. Although they had actually not been routed, their forces had been depleted by war and disease. For example, of the 100 infantrymen constituting the 39th company of the Marine, only four were fit to continue fighting; all the cannons had been ruined. Moreover, of the 1,000 men who formed the expeditionary corps, only about half were left to continue the fight, the rest having been killed or incapacitated. Of these, eight officers and 210 soldiers were said to have died of fatigue, fifty-five killed or wounded in battle and 140 hospitalised for other reasons.[41]

On the other hand, Lamine appeared to be going strong. The performances of his forces in the encounters against the French had been impressive. What they lacked in terms of coherence they compensated for by the psychological strength deriving from their fanatical religious sense of mission and the idea that they were protecting their people against foreign invaders. In addition, whereas the French had to withdraw the bulk of their troops at the end of June to escape the deleterious climate, Lamine's men were in a position to continue the fight as before since they were used to the climate. From June to October when most of the French forces were away, Lamine was free from any major threat to his position. He used the period to recover lost ground, reorganise his forces and establish a new headquarters at Dianna in the Upper Gambia region.

At Dianna he built a fortress from which he directed his military operations and propaganda throughout the neighbouring territories. For instance, from Dianna he sent his disciples to the surrounding districts of Tiali, Nieri, Gamou and Ferlo to preach to and convert the people. The people responded favourably, putting themselves under his authority. So also did the people of Badon and Niocolo in the Gambia region willingly accept his authority. Even those areas like Bambuk which did not peacefully surrender to his authority had to do so after they had been conquered militarily. In July Lamine again invaded Senoudebou and burnt down the French post there. He also went to Bondu with about 3,000 men to reconquer the capital Boulebane and killed the new almamy, Umar Penda, in the process. To ensure that the whole region fully submitted to his authority, he returned to attack Senoudebou once more on 23 September. On that occasion, his men were halted by a garrison of *tirailleurs* under Second-Lieutenant Yaro-Comba. Soybou, Lamine's son, also strengthened his control over Diafounou. Thus it is clear that in the three months when the French were unable to keep an effective force in the Senegambia Lamine seized the opportunity to rebuild and expand his empire.[42]

The only response the French were able to give was to protect their posts on the Senegal river with garrisons of *tirailleurs* and to continue their efforts to secure collaboration with Abdul Bubakar whose military assistance and prestige they wanted to use against Lamine. For this purpose, they pressured Bubakar unsuccessfully throughout July and August.[43] As Lamine's position became stronger so the French position became more precarious. To arrest the undesirable development and salvage their commercial and other interests in the Senegambia, the French Ministry of Marine and Colonies made urgent arrangements to deal more effectively with Lamine. As part of the new measures, Lieutenant-Colonel J. S. Gallieni was appointed the new supreme commander in place of Colonel Frey. Colonel Gallieni, whose appointment had been announced in August, arrived at his headquarters, Kayes, in October 1886.

Gallieni's assignment was to defeat Lamine, using both diplomatic and military means. He was to try, through diplomacy, to limit French military engagement to Lamine, making sure that all other thorny problems in the area were either settled or shelved for the meantime. He was to do this by working for at least a *détente* in French relations with the Senegambian states, some of which had been at war with the French for several years, and for a treaty of co-operation or even protectorate with Samori. It was hoped that, by clever manœuvring on the part of the French, Samori and the rulers of the Senegambian states would at least refrain from attacking the French while they would be busy fighting Lamine. In relation to the Tukulor, the Lamine episode provided an ideal opportunity for resuming diplomatic negotiations which had become impossible since the French failed to ratify the treaty of Nango in 1881. But more than this, since Lamine posed a threat to both parties, it became easier for Gallieni to approach the Tukulor with the idea of converting their relations, hitherto dictated by the competitiveness of their interests, into a working alliance against a common enemy. The new French disposition represented by Gallieni was also acceptable to

Ahmadu of the Tukulor empire who found it convenient for tackling the internal problems of his state.

Gallieni had no problem in getting Ahmadu to collaborate with the French in fighting against Lamine. In any case he was eager to dislodge Lamine's son, Soybou, from Diafounou and Guidimaka. Therefore, militarily, collaboration began almost immediately after Gallieni's arrival. The other plan of getting Ahmadu to sign a treaty of protection establishing French authority over his state also materialised eventually in the treaty of Gouri of 12 May 1887, which was signed after protracted manœuvrings.[44]

To Ahmadu, the situation in Guidimaka and Diafounou, where Tukulor subjects had accepted Lamine's son, Soybou, as governor, was nothing but an insurrection which had to be ended as quickly as possible. Thus Ahmadu's own self-interest in fighting Lamine coincided with Gallieni's desire for collaboration. By November 1886, Ahmadu had begun his campaigns to dislodge Soybou from Gouri, headquarters of Diafounou. In that month, Tukulor forces had been assembled at Kerani, south-east of Koniakari, from where they began the march against Soybou under the command of Bafi, one of Ahmadu's army leaders. In the war which lasted for about six months, both sides used *sofas* and cavalrymen. Details of the battles are not now available to the writer; but it is known that apart from the open encounters in the field, the war was also fought through sieges. For example, as early as February 1887 Ahmadu's men had put Gouri, where Soybou himself was directing the military operations, under siege.[45] It was after a prolonged period of siege that the Tukulor were able to defeat Soybou's men in April 1887.

Siege as a method of fighting was effective against Soybou's men mainly because of the co-ordination of effort between Gallieni and Ahmadu. On assumption of command, Gallieni had established his base camp at Arondu at the confluence of the rivers Senegal and Faleme. He had also established a cordon of troops linking the French posts on the Senegal to police the river banks on the side of Diafounou and Guidimaka and prevent any movements from the Sarrakole population of the area to join or collaborate with the main body of Lamine's army in the Senegambia. This ensured that at the time when Ahmadu was laying siege to Gouri, Lamine's forces had been cut into two, each side besieged by those unusual allies—the French and the Tukulor. Without any possibility of effective co-ordination of efforts with, or even supplies of arms and ammunition from, the main army under his father at Dianna, it would have been quite understandable if Soybou had given up the struggle at Gouri after some three months' heroic resistance.

However, even after his defeat at Gouri, Soybou did not give up. Rather he tried with his men to rejoin the main body of troops under his father at Dianna. It was in the process of doing this that he was caught trying to cross the River Senegal at the village of Dikokori, a short distance from Gallieni's camp at Arondu. Here a detachment of French troops under the command of Lieutenant Reichemberg forcefully stopped and arrested him after he and his men had put up a brilliant struggle. After his arrest, Soybou was 'court-martialled', charged with directing the siege against Bakel, and with burning the surrounding villages. Two Bakel traders were brought to bear witness against him and, as might be expected, he was declared guilty. Throughout the mock trial, Soybou remained unruffled and displayed a heroic defiance of the French. Facing death calmly, as one with a strong sense of mission, he sent his thanks to Lieutenant-Colonel Gallieni for having him shot rather than treating him to a mean death.[46]

The Soybou episode in the war demonstrates the usefulness of the Franco–Tukulor alliance against Lamine. Both had co-operated to ensure the success of the siege against Soybou in Diafounou and when the latter had escaped the Tukulor forces the French troops on the Senegal river had fought him to a halt and later had him shot. For the French, the suppression of Soybou was of great significance since it left them free to concentrate their attention on the campaigns in the Senegambia.

At this time, Lamine himself was still based at Dianna in Upper Gambia from where he had established control over the two banks of the Faleme as well as Bambuk.

In a determined attempt to crush him, Gallieni had personally directed an expedition against him in December 1886. From his base at Arondu, he organised his troops into three columns, two of which marched simultaneously against Lamine's base at Dianna. The two columns engaged in the campaign were commanded by Gallieni himself and Major Vallière respectively. The third column was to perform security duties at the base after the departure of the other two.

Gallieni's column comprised Captain Fortin as Chief of Staff, and Lieutenant Bonacorsi of the Marine artillery; a platoon of *spahi* as cavalry, under Lieutenant Guérin; infantrymen made up of 250 *tirailleurs* from the 3rd and 8th companies commanded by Captain Robert, Lieutenant Renard, and Second-Lieutenant Maubert; as well as a platoon of Marine men under Second-Lieutenants Pichon and

Lefort. The artillery comprised a section with cannons of 80mm *(de montagne)* and one of 65 mm; seventy-five gunners and two officers as well as half a company of workmates *(courriers d'artillerie)*. To provide other services there was a detachment of native army engineers; an ambulance and one doctor—Dr. de Tréglodé. The second column under Major Vallière was similar in composition; but was based at Diamou. The combined columns made up a total of about 1,400 men.

The two columns began the march on Dianna on 12 December 1886. The first moved through Senoudebou while the second went across Bambuk. Lamine's men knew only of the column under Major Vallière and they engaged it in battle at Saroundian, east of Dianna on the 24th. Lamine's men lost the battle mainly because Major Vallière's column had the services of cannons and other superior weapons. In the night Lieutenant-Colonel Gallieni's men converged with those of Vallière and marched jointly on Dianna on the 25th. Before they reached Dianna, however, Lamine had evacuated his men. Gallieni nevertheless had the place shelled and set ablaze. Beyond this, however, little was achieved as Lamine and his men had withdrawn deep into the Gambia.[47] French forces returned to base in January 1887.

The expedition against Dianna was the most significant move against Lamine in the 1886–7 dry season. Gallieni won the battle, but it was a Pyrrhic victory. Lamine had his fortress destroyed by heavy fire-power; but he was still strong enough to continue fighting effectively. Indeed, it soon became clear that he still controlled the situation in the Senegambia. At the end of the season, it was apparent that his only setback had been the loss of the emirates of Guidimaka and Diafounou, along with his son. He had been unable to break through the French lines to aid Soybou, and this accounted for the latter's defeat and death. However, as in 1886, Lamine took advantage of the hot and rain-soaked months of June to September to reorganise his forces for renewed fighting against the French. In spite of the sporadic fighting against men of the *tirailleurs* during these months, he appeared to still have under his command a force of about 3,000.[48]

Gallieni returned to Kayes for the 1887–8 dry season only to find that Lamine had regained some lost ground and had recruited more forces. For instance, he had regained control of Niani, Sandougou and parts of Saloum. Fresh military expeditions were directed against him from October to December 1887. During the period however, it became clear that he was avoiding pitched battles and mainly using guerilla tactics. To cope with the situation the French had to rely on volunteers from the various states who were familiar with the communications of the area. They were drilled in the use of rifles and machine-guns and generally left to pursue Lamine while the latter engaged in his hit and run tactics. Where possible the French regular forces engaged him in pitched battles. It was through a combination of regular military encounters and the use of volunteers in pursuit that Lamine's movement was finally brought down in December 1887.

The last battle which Lamine fought was that of Toubakouta in December 1887. Gallieni later claimed that at this battle the French forces used 200 cannon balls and 30,000 gunshots in less than an hour.[49] Thus it is clear that the victory at Toubakouta was due to the overpowering might of French weapons. But even then Lamine escaped with part of his forces, pursued by groups of volunteers fighting on the French side. He must have been caught and killed, or found dead, by one of these groups. It is not clear whether he was actually killed and, if so, how. There were conflicting claims[50] on these points from groups that were eager to take the credit for killing the man who had for three years made the French presence a dangerous and precarious affair.

The defeat of the movement and death of Lamine marked the end of the Sarrakole nationalist movement in the Senegambia. Before his death, Lamine had been able to create a state and struggle against the French and the Tukulor empire for over two years building upon the widespread resentment of the Sarrakole against alien rule. During the period, he sustained the movement through the use of guerilla tactics in his wars against the French. But he was defeated nonetheless partly because the French and Tukulor allied for the occasion and pooled their resources against him. The defeat of Soybou and the fact that the French were able to direct their energies solely against Lamine resulted from the Franco-Tukulor alliance. On the military side, the French used superior weapons which were particularly effective as soon as Lamine fought from fortifications as at Dianna. Against his fortress at Dianna, all the French forces had to do was to shell with their cannons from a distance thus destroying Lamine's strong position with little damage to their own. It is also important to record the role of indigenous volunteers who supplemented French military efforts with their own knowledge of the terrain and possessed the ability and aptitude to match Lamine's strategy where the formal military tactics of the French proved inadequate.

NOTES

1 See B. Olatunji Oloruntimehin, *The Segu Tukulor Empire 1848–1893*, unpublished Ph.D. Thesis, University of Ibadan, 1966, pp. 281–310, for an analysis of the Logo episode.

2 The reference here, apart from the Logo episode, is to the treaty-making expeditions among the Bambara of Beledugu, the sack of Mourgula in 1883 and the initial clashes of French forces under Colonel Borgnis-Desbordes against Samori's *sofas* in 1883.

3 Lieutenant August L. C. Gatelet, *Histoire de la Conquête du Soudan français 1878–1899*, Paris et Nancy, Berger-Levrault & Cie, Editeurs, 1901, p. 5.

4 For the Zimmermann incident see Daniel Nyambarza, 'Le marabout El Hadj Lamine d'après les archives françaises' in *Cahiers D'Etudes Africaines*, 33, vol. IX, No. 1, 1969 pp. 124–45, esp. pp. 134–5:
See Colonel Henri Frey, *Campagne dans le Haut Sénégal et dans le Haut Niger (1885–1886)*, Paris, Librairie Plon, 1888, pp. 245–9.

5 Charles Monteil, 'Le site de Goundiourou' in *Bulletin du Comité, d'Etudes Historiques et Scientifiques de l'Afrique Occidentale Française* 1928, p. 649.

6 Monteil, *op. cit.*, p. 652.

7 Frey, *op. cit.*, pp. 250, 252, 254–60; August Gatelet, *op. cit.*, pp. 67–8. Gatelet claims that Lamine left on his pilgrimage in 1873 and puts the duration of his detention at Segu at six years.

8 See B. Olatunji Oloruntimehin, 'Muhammad Lamine in Franco–Tukulor Relations 1885–1887' in *Journal of the Historical Society of Nigeria*, vol. IV, No. 3, December 1968, p. 380. For a suggestion that he had taken part in some of 'Umar's wars in 1857, see Daniel Nyambarza, *op. cit.*, p. 125. This suggestion should be taken with caution, however. The author knows of 'Umar Lamine who took part in 'Umar's revolution and was Emir of Guomoukoura in Kaarta.

9 See Frey, *op. cit.*, p. 263. The idea of reviving the Sarrakole empire refers to the ancient Mali empire of the Soninke, an alternative name for Sarrakole.

10 Archives du Sénégal, Fonds de L' A.O.F., Dakar (A.S.A.O.F.) 15 G 110/1 (327), 'Le Commandant du Poste à Monsieur le Gouverneur du Sénégal et Dépendances' Médine, 25 January 1876; 15 G 111/1 (5), 'Le Commandant du Poste de Médine à Monsieur le Gouverneur ...', Médine, 9 March 1877; Archives Nationales, Section, d'Outre-Mer (Rue Oudinot, Paris) (A.N.S.O.M.). In Sénégal I, 6/C, 'Brière de l'Isle, Gouverneur du Sénégal à Monsieur le Ministre de la Marine et des Colonies', St. Louis, 22 July 1876.

11 See Frey, *op. cit.*, p. 231, where it is reported that '. . . *A sa voix, les populations Sarrakholaises accoururent en masse se ranger sous ses ordres . . .*', also pp. 272–3 for Lamine's appeal to Sarrakole sense of nationalism; also Gatelet, *op. cit.*, p. 104, where his death is reported in the following terms: '. . . *Sa mort met fin à la resistance des Sarracolets . . .*'

12 See Frey, *op. cit.,* pp. 243–5.

13 *Ibid.,* pp. 243–4.

14 For a brief survey of the history and ideas of the Sanusiyya see: D. S. Margoliouth, 'Sanusi' in James Hastings (ed.), *Encyclopaedia of Religion and Ethics,* vol. XI, Edinburgh, T. & T. Clark, 1920, pp. 194–6; Cl. Huart, 'Al-Sanusi' in *The Encyclopaedia of Islam,* 4, S–Z, Leyden and London, 1934, pp. 154–5.

15 Institut des Sciences Humaines, Bamako, (I.S.H.), IE/6 'Poste de Bammako, Journal du Fort', 1 June 1885; P. Legendre, *La Conquête de la France Africaine,* P. Paclot et Cⁱᵉ Editeurs, Paris, n.d., p. 91.

16 Frey, *op. cit.,* p. 264.

17 A.S.A.O.F., ID 79/21, 'Le Commandant Supérieur p.i. du Haut-Sénégal à Monsieur le Gouverneur du Sénégal et Dépendances', Kayes, September 1885. That the French were deceived is clear from the evidence of the Governor of Senegal who in his report to Paris stated as follows: '*Mamadou Lamine nous a trompés par ses protestations de dévouement à notre cause, de haine contre nos enemis . . .*' See A.N.S.O.M. In Sénégal I, 99(b) 'Le Gouverneur du Sénégal et dépendances à Monsieur le Ministre de la Marine et des Colonies', St. Louis, 28 March 1886.

18 A.N.S.O.M., In Sénégal IV, 84b, 'Confidentielle—Le Lieutenant-Colonel Commandant Supérieur du Haut Sénégal à Monsieur le Gouverneur du Sénégal . . .' Kayes, 20 December 1885.

19 Frey, *op. cit.,* p. 271.

20 Frey, *op. cit.,* p. 268, describes Bubakar Saada as being '*. . . peu aimé, il est vrai, de ses sujets . . .*'

21 A.N.S.O.M., In Sénégal IV, 85(a), 'Résumé des opérations militaires contre le Marabout Lamine d'après le rapport du Colonel Frey . . . 1885–1886'; Frey, *op. cit.,* pp. 270–2.

22 A.N.S.O.M., In Sénégal IV, 84(a), 'Note pour Servir à la rédaction des Instructions au Colonel Commandant Supérieur du Haut—Sénégal—B. Desbordes. . . .' Paris, 10 September 1886; In Sénégal IV 84(b) 'Télégramme, Commandant Supérieur à Gouverneur, St. Louis, 28 February 1886; Frey, *op. cit.,* pp. 272–6.

23 See B. Olatunji Oloruntimehin, 'The Treaty of Niagassola 1886: An Episode in Franco–Samori Relations in the era of the Scramble' in *Journal of the Historical Society of Nigeria,* vol. IV, No. 4, pp. 601–13, June 1969; Also Oloruntimehin, 'Muhammad Lamine in Franco–Tukulor Relations . . .' pp. 382–3.

24 A.N.S.O.M., In Sénégal IV, 84(b) 'Commandant Supérieur à Gouverneur, St. Louis', 18 April 1886.

25 For similar estimates of his army at particular battles see A.N.S.O.M., In Sénégal I, 99(b) 'Le Gouverneur du Sénégal . . . à Monsieur le Ministre . . .' St. Louis, 28 March 1886; Gatelet, *op. cit.,* p. 94.

26 See, for example, Frey, *op. cit.,* pp. 315–16.

27 Nyambarza, *op. cit.,* pp. 144–5. Gatelet, *op. cit.,* p. 94.

28 Frey, *op. cit.,* p. 316 fn.
29 Le Général Faidherbe, *Le Sénégal: La France dans l'Afrique Occidentale,* Paris, Librairie Hachette et Cⁱᵉ, 1889, esp. pp. 198–200.
30 See Frey, *op. cit.,* pp. 314 and 421; and p. 417 for an example of campaigns in which more African soldiers than French ones were involved. In the battle of Guémou, against Umar's forces, on 28 October 1859, the French column comprised 760 African soldiers to 320 Europeans.
31 See Denise Bouche, 'Les Villages de liberté en A.O.F.' I, in *Bulletin de l'Institut Francais d'Afrique Noire, Sér,* B., XI, 1949, pp. 526–40, esp. p. 529.
32 See A. S. Kanya-Forstner, *The Conquest of the Western Sudan: A Study in Military Imperialism,* Cambridge University Press, 1969, p. 10.
33 See Gatelet, *op. cit.,* pp. 99–100, also Frey, *op. cit.,* p. 295.
34 Frey, *op cit.,* pp. 280–6.
35 *Ibid.,* pp. 288–9.
36 A.N.S.O.M., In Sénégal I, 99(b) 'Le Gouverneur du Sénégal et dépendances à Monsieur le Ministre de la Marine et des Colonies', St. Louis, 28 March 1886; Frey, *op. cit.,* pp. 289–92; Gatelet, *op. cit.,* pp. 77–9.
37 Frey, *op. cit.,* pp. 294–5; Gatelet, *op. cit.,* p. 80.
38 A.N.S.O.M., In Sénégal IV, 84(b) Télégramme: 'Commandant Supérieur à Gouverneur, St. Louis', 18 April 1886; See also Frey, *op. cit.,* pp. 292–9, especially pp. 297–9 for a list of pro-French merchants killed; Gatelet, *op. cit.,* pp. 80–1.
39 A.N.S.O.M., In Sénégal 84(b) Télégramme: 'Commandant Supérieur, à Gouverneur, St. Louis', Colonne, 10 May 1886.
40 A.N.S.O.M., In Sénégal IV, 84(b) Télégramme: 'Commandant Supérieur à Gouverneur St. Louis', Colonne, 13 May 1886; The Governor's telegram is contained in Sénégal IV, 84b. 'Gouverneur à Commandant Supérieur, Haut Fleuve', St. Louis, 18 May 1886.
41 Gatelet, *op. cit.,* p. 93 fn.
42 A.S.A.O.F., ID 90 'Rapports du Lieutenant-Colonel Gallieni . . . pendant la campagne 1886–87', pp. 1–3; Archives du Ministère des Affaires Etrangères (M.A.E.), In Mémoires et Documents: Afrique 85 'Le Sous-Sécretaire d'Etat au Ministère de la Marine et des colonies à Monsieur le Gouverneur du Sénégal', Paris, 20 October 1886; Gatelet, *op. cit.,* p. 94; Frey, *op. cit.,* pp. 442–3.
43 A.N.S.O.M., In Sénégal I, 99(b). 'Télégramme, Commandant Supérieur à Gouverneur, St. Louis', Kayes, 26 July 1886; also Sénégal I, 99(b), 'Le Gouverneur du Sénégal et dépendances à Monsieur le Ministre de la Marine . . .' St. Louis, 12 August 1886.
44 See Oloruntimehin, 'Muhammad Lamine in Franco–Tukulor Relations . . .' for an analysis of the treaty of Gouri.
45 A.N.S.O.M., In Sénégal IV, 87(b), 'Le Lieutenant-Colonel. Gallieni à Monsieur le Gouverneur du Sénégal et dépendances à St. Louis',

Kayes, 2 December 1886; *ibid.,* for 'Télégramme du Commandant Supérieur du Soudan français', 20 February 1887.

46 J. S. Gallieni, *Deux Campagnes au Soudan français 1866–1888* (Paris, Librairie Hachette et Cⁱᵉ, 1891) pp. 179 ff.

47 Gatelet, *op. cit.,* pp. 97–101.

48 A.S.A.O.F., In 15 G 76/2, 'A sa grandeur le Sultan Chef des Croyants à Nioro de la part de son ami le Commandant Monségur à Kayes', Kayes, 10 August 1887.

49 A.S.A.O.F., In 15 G 76/2, 'Le Lieutenant-Colonel Gallieni, Commandant Supérieur . . . au Sultan Ahmadou', Camp du Galougo, 25 December 1887.

50 See for instance, Gallieni, *ibid.;* A.N.S.O.M., In Sénégal, I, 99(b), 'Télégramme, Capitaine Commandant Poste Nioro à Gouverneur', Nioro, 15 December 1887; Gatelet, *op. cit.,* p. 113, all of which are contradictory.

YVES PERSON
Translation by Joan White

Guinea–Samori

After more than half a century of colonial activity and a complete overthrow of the traditional structures of African society one might expect the earlier periods of the country's history to be judged with at least a minimum of objective detachment. Far from it: the case of Samori shows that this is not so.

In the course of his long career this formidable adversary won the respect and admiration of his enemies, the French officers of the Marine Corps, even if they did on occasion misrepresent his actions and motives the better to influence public opinion in France. He was less fortunate with colonial historians at the beginning of the century, most of them almost totally preoccupied with justifying the French imperial order. In this period Samori was cast in the role of villain and he found himself presented to the world as a cruel sadist dripping with blood. General Duboc's book *Samori le Sanglant* did not appear until 1947 and marks the end of this period of basic misrepresentation.

The new forces of African nationalism adopted him eagerly. When in 1949 E. Deloncle celebrated what he called 'the fiftieth anniversary of a liberation' in the colonialist weekly *Climats* he aroused an energetic response in support of the 'African Vercingetorix' from Fily-Dabo Sissoko. The discussion still goes on and when the venerable *Bulletin du Comité de l'Afrique Française* published its farewell number in 1960 it saw fit to print an article by G. Joseph violently attacking the historians of the new African republics who had the sauce to try to rehabilitate this criminal.

There was, of course, the other side of the coin: alongside the 'black legend' was a sort of hagiography where every awkward incident in his career was passed over in silence and the drama of his last days presented in the most lurid light. His arrest at Gelemu in 1898 was interpreted as the fruit of treason and his death in exile in far-away Ogowe was seen as the result of poison from the hands of his jailers.

Honours and indignities alike come from a common source. Samori arouses the highest passions because more than any other leader in pre-colonial Africa he symbolises heroic and determined resistance to the European conqueror. Over seventeen years separate his first contact with the French in August 1881 and his arrest in September 1898. Fighting was by no means constant during this period, but no other confrontation between colonised and coloniser had ever lasted so long without the former surrendering his liberty. Samori's field of action happened to coincide with that of the French Marine Corps, the infantry body specially created for fighting in the colonies, possibly one of the best instruments of conquest ever used by any country. Their frank admiration for Samori always served to enhance their own reputation and it is certain that no other enemy had ever shown such skill and tenacity in the field.

Samori escaped from the oblivion of his earlier days by virtue of his role as war-leader. He was a Muslim, but it is significant that this fact is scarcely ever mentioned: indeed, his adversaries—who exploited every possible complaint they could—hardly ever accused him of fanaticism. He does not appear in the same light as El Hadj Omar and his heirs: the religious element was slight in the campaign led by this ruthless but admirable fighter. This statement demands some qualification, of course, but by and large it corresponds fairly well to the truth of the matter.

The preceding view of Samori does not coincide completely with the historical character presented by Malinke tradition. He had already been politically active for a good twenty years when he received Lieutenant Alakamessa and it is quite wrong to see him only as an adversary of the French. The activities of El Hadj Omar were known to France: they took place more or less within earshot of the French colony in Senegal. Samori was different: they had never even heard of him before 1878. He had built a purely African empire and he had built it in response to an internal crisis in his own country, not for the simple purpose of resisting the French. Indeed, they were the least part of his worries at that time—he never thought for a moment that they would play a major part in Africa. However, the construction of his empire demanded a military enterprise of unprecedented size and it is for this reason, primarily, that it is right to see Samori as a military leader first and foremost. It is by studying his relations with the problem of war that the nature and significance of his undertaking can be properly appreciated.

1 Samori and the Dyula revolution

Samori came from the Milo valley on the northern border of Konyan, a land of lofty mountains and high plateaus which serves as counter-fort to the north flank of the famous Guinea Highlands. It is an enclave of savanna lands, much affected by Sudanese influences and perched high up on cliffs which plunge down into the heart of the damp rain-forests of Dyani (Saint-Paul) and Sassandra. The rivers which rise in this watershed are affluents of the Niger (Milo, Dyon, Sankarani) and run to the north; since the sixteenth century, this area has been the homeland of the Konyanke, a tribe of pagan warriors of Malinke stock. Contacts with coastal settlements in the Monrovia area and in particular the proximity of the kola producers (forest peoples speaking Mande, like the Toma, Guerzé and the Dan, and, more to the east, the Guro) brought a very powerful minority group of Muslim Dyula into the country at an early date. These traders lived in the great commercial centres of the pre-forest zone on the edge of the vast solid stretch of forest which separates the inland regions from the Gulf of Guinea; they had similar establish-ments in the markets which had sprung up all along the trade routes going up towards the north. The trade in kola, a product which is mainly consumed along the Niger but which keeps very badly, demanded the establishment of a complicated network of commercial transactions and transport facilities to get the product to the Sudan area with the minimum delay. Ever since the Middle Ages this region had also taken slaves from the forest and had sent back in return salt from the Sahara, cloth, cattle and goods made in the Magrab. The eighteenth century saw this trade extended to include products of European manufacture (cloth, ironmongery and an increasing amount of firearms); these goods were originally imported from the Côte des Rivières (Sierra Leone and the Republic of Guinea) by the Dyula city of Kankan. Sea salt also came along this route and the trading contacts thus established brought the region out of its isolation to a certain extent.

In spite of religious differences, these traders belonged to the same cultural background as the original pagan inhabitants and this meant

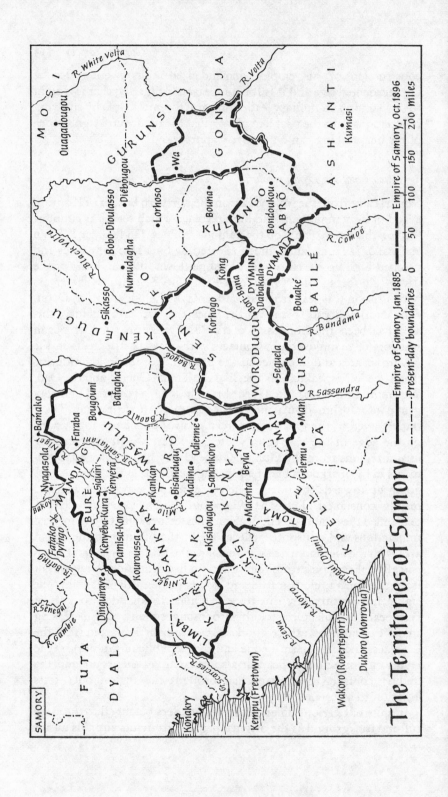

The Territories of Samory

————— Empire of Samory, Jan. 1885
━━━━ Empire of Samory, Oct. 1896
–·–·–· Present-day boundaries

0   50   100   150   200 miles

SAMORY

MOSI
R. White Volta
OUAGADOUGOU

GURUNSI
Diébougou
Bobo-Dioulasso
Wa
GONDJA
R. Volta
ASHANTI
Kumasi

Lorhoso
Bouna
KULANGO
Bondoukou
ABRO
DYAMALA
R. Comoé

R. Black Volta
Numudagha
Sikasso
SENUFO
Kong
Bori-Bana
DYIMINI
Dabakala
BAULÉ
Bouaké

KENEDUGU
Korhogo
WORODUGU
Séguéla
GURO
R. Bandama

R. Bagoé
R. Sassandra
MAN
Man
DÃ

Bamako
Nyagasola
Batagha
Bougouni
R. Baoulé
MANDING
Faraba
TORO
Odienne
KONYA
Gbélemu
KPELLE

R. Niger
BURÉ
Siguiri
Kényéba-Kura
R. Sankarani
Bisandugu
Madina
Sanankoro
Beyla
Macenta
TOMA
S. Paul (Diani)

Bakoy
Fatako
Dyingo
Damisa-Koro
Kankan
Kisidougou
Kouroussa
SANKARAN
R. Milo
KISI
R. Morro

R. Bafing
Dinguiraye
R. Niger
R. Niandan
KURANKO
R. Sewa
R. Senegal
FUTA
DYALÕ
R. Gambie
LIMBA
R. Scarcies

Konakry
Kempu (Freetown)
Wakoro (Robertsport)
Dukoro (Monrovia)

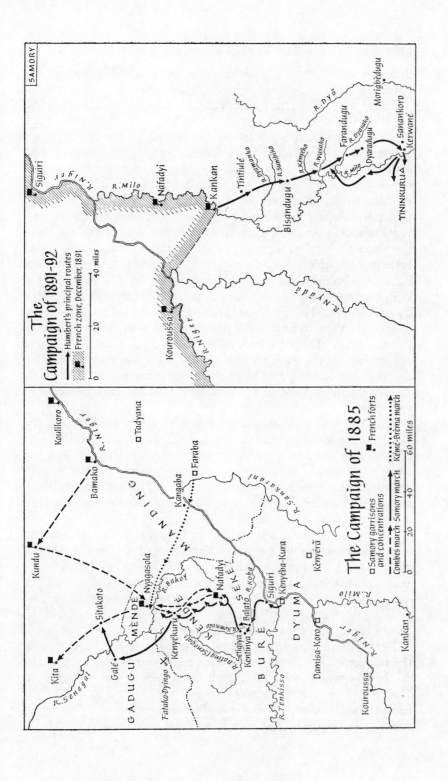

The Campaign of 1891-92

→ Humbert's principal routes

▨ French zone, December, 1891

0   20   40 miles

R. Niger

Siguiri

R. Milo

Nafadyi

Kankan

Tintiulé

Kourroussa

R. Niger

R. Nyadi

Bisandugu

R. Dyamanko

R. Sumbiko

R. Kenyeko

R. Wasaka

R. Dyö

Farandugu

R. Dyassao

Morigbedugu

Dyaradugu

Sanankoro
Kerwané

R. Milo

TININKURLA

The Campaign of 1885

■ French forts

□ Samory garrisons
and concentrations

▬ ▬ Combes' march   ▬▬▬ Samory march

∙∙∙∙∙∙ Kémé-Bréma march

0   20   40   60 miles

Koulikoro

R. Niger

Bamako

□ Tadyana

Kundu

Kangaba

□ Faraba

Sitakoto

MANDING

R. Bakoy

Nyagasola

Kita

R. Senegal

Galé

MÉNDÉ

GADUGU

Fatako-Dyingo ×

Kenyékuru

SÉKÉ

Nafadyi

R. Koba

R. Bafing (Senegal)

K. Kummodo

Seligiya

Balato

Kentinya

Siguiri

Kenyéba-Kura

BURÉ

R. Tenkisso

Damisa-Koro

DYUMA

□ Kényérá

R. Milo

Kouroussa

R. Niger

Kankan

that the two groups lived together in reasonably satisfactory harmony.

The Dyula were perfectly content with their favourable economic situation and entertained no thought of holy war: they were happy to leave all political activities to the old pagan families *(tuntigi)*. These in turn were settled in a hierarchical society based on two classes *(horon* or free men and *dyon* or slaves *)* and a system of artisan castes *(nyamakala)*—these were, for instance, blacksmiths *(numun)* or *dyèli* and so on. They lived on the agricultural crops they produced themselves, working mainly with the hoe and growing manioc and yams as well as cereal products like millet, maize and rice. In spite of the proximity of the forest, the mountain climate made some stock-breeding possible; it was mostly in the hands of the Malinke-influenced Foula who had settled down with the Konyanke on the high plateau. The political unit was the *kafu* (assembly), dominated by one of the ruling families, usually from the Kamara clan in the Konya, for they claimed kinship with the semi-mythical conqueror Feren-Kaman. The *kafu* were often referred to as *nyamaana* (from the Arabic *jema'a)* even though this word could also be used to describe the Konyan as a whole. The country was unusual in its structure and in spite of its basic divisions inspired tremendous patriotism.

The *kafu* was a military unit as well as a political one and the Konyanke had a reputation for belligerence. For the last two centuries they had been nibbling away at the Toma lands along the route to the sea, to the south of their own country, and had been in constant conflict with the Kuranko, another Malinke branch living along their western frontier—and all this without neglecting their many civil wars.

Their political leader was the *Masa,* a somewhat holy person whose title recalls the one borne by the Emperors of medieval Mali, but when a crisis occurred he could appoint a *Keletigi,* or 'war-leader', who would take charge of military matters. It was his task to mobilise the men within the framework of four age groups or *Kari;* the youngest were given both the great collective undertakings and the most difficult and dangerous military expeditions.

They were not particularly well armed, for at the beginning of the nineteenth century firearms were reserved for hunters, and the art of war was usually lacking in both variety and imagination. Fighting in open country was rare and battles were usually of the hand-to-hand variety or else dwindled into interminable sieges of enemy strong-points. Each settlement was surrounded by a wall, usually a *dyin* of rectilinear outline though it might sometimes be a chevron-shaped *tanta;* their traditional weapons could very rarely overcome these obstacles. Though horses were well able to live in the Konyan climate, they were not used in battle and were kept for chiefs and notables to ride in special processions.

The *kafu* or *nyamaana* showed characteristics which set them on the borderline between chieftainships and small states; sometimes they served as a basis for warrior hegemonies, but these were usually very short-lived and never gave rise to stable superstructures.

This general atmosphere of warrior activity provided a means for the Dyula to acquire large numbers of captives for export, the demand for these having increased steadily ever since the route to the Côte des Rivières had been opened in the early eighteenth century. At the same time, the place of traders in this society began to grow in importance, for the local chiefs, like the big merchants and the religious leaders, needed an increasingly large amount of imported goods. Finally, the use of firearms as weapons of war spread to the tribes and each political unit was obliged to furnish itself with as many as it could. Without them they were in grave danger. It seems as though the process of social differentiation began to develop more quickly than ever with this increase in long-distance trade, though society itself remained basically unchanged.

It is clear, therefore, that the crisis under consideration came at a time and in an atmosphere peculiarly favourable to it, but the impulse which released it came from the outside.

Greater in numbers, infinitely richer, better placed than anyone else for acquiring firearms, the Dyula began to consider abandoning their traditional reserve; it took some time before they settled their minds to the idea of war and it is inevitable that the example of other Muslims must have had something to do with this. The holy wars of the Fulani in the Sudan, especially that of Masina which dates from 1818, had made a tremendous impression on the travelling traders who went around the banks of the Niger, but the Dyula had little in common with these nomad cattle-breeders. The great metropolis of Kankan had more influence on them, but Kankan was to sit firmly inside a strictly pacific policy until its alliance with the Omar Tijanniya in mid-century.

It was, however, from Kankan that the human catalyst eventually came: this was the marabout Mori-Ulé Sisé. He had studied for a long time with the Dyakhanke, the Muslim Manding minority in the Fouta-Djallon, and there can be no doubt that his ideas of a holy war came from close observance of the victorious Fulani aristocracy.

It was clear that Kankan was not yet ready for projects of this kind, so Mori-Ulé Sisé went with a student friend to start a community of his own in the south, well apart from the local pagans and in the desert area which lies between the Konya and the Toro. This was early in the 1830s: it was not long before Madina became more of a town than a simple settlement and it was packed with adventurers from all over the Manding world. Mori-Ulé employed large numbers of elephant-hunters and used the ivory to buy guns and even a few horses. When he felt ready (in about 1835) he proclaimed a holy war and easily conquered the local *kafu*. Taking the title of Faama, he organised a small centralised kingdom, Moriulédugu, the first that had ever existed in the region.

The state was built on a very simple structure and was never divided up into separate territorial areas of government. Its vassal states were controlled by small troops of armed men commanded by *dugukunnasigi*.

The true originality of the state rested in its army which was concentrated in the capital. Mori-Ulé abandoned the idea of enlisting men in age groups and divided them up without reference to their origins in *sé* (feet) of ten men and *bolo* (arms) of 100 to 200 men. He armed as many as possible with guns and provided horses for most of the leaders. He developed plans for the speedy reduction of fortified encampments so as to shorten sieges as much as possible.

The inspiration for this political and military revolution was undoubtedly of northern origin, even if many of those who contributed to its success were born in the southern territories. The local well-established Dyula played no part in it at all.

There were repercussions very soon. Further to the east, a Turè family—merchants and weavers who lived around Odienne in the Nafana, a great kingdom organised in the eighteenth century by a Bambara group from Segou, the Dyarasuba—followed Mori-Ulé's example. One of the Turè, Vakaba Turè, learnt the art of fighting with Mori-Ulé, but killed the latter whilst defending his pagan kinsmen. He overthrew the Dyarasuba and set himself at the head of their kingdom, converting it to Islam under the name of Kabasarana.

His reconciliation with the Sisé was followed by his alliance with the sons of the dead leader, Sérè-Burlay (Abdulay Sisé) and later Sérè-Brèma (Ibraima Sisé), all working together to re-establish the power of the Moriulédugu. They followed this by moving against the Upper Konya and the Milo valley which were successfully conquered between 1850 and 1860 in spite of strong resistance and several uprisings.

Mori-Ulé had been pious and probably fanatical as well: his plan had been the destruction of the existing social order and the forcible conversion of the local populace. His sons appreciated the difficulties of this rather more than their father had and their course was therefore considerably modified. They showed much less religious zeal and sought their allies among those they had conquered, though they were as ruthless as their father in their methods of government. Their subjects were forced to pay a crushing tribute which went by the misleading name of tithe *(dyaka,* from the Arabic *zakat).*

A curious thing happened all along the Milo soon afterwards. Just as Vakaba had fought for his pagan kinsmen in the east, a Dyula lineage that had long been settled on the Milo—the Bèrèté—allied with the local pagans, the Konaté, to fight against the invaders even though they and the latter were linked by religion. They were conquered twice and their small hegemony never became very important, but they were better fighters than the pagans and caused the Sisé a great deal of trouble.

This event foreshadowed Samori's enterprise which was to loom so greatly in the history of West Africa that many of his precursors in the same field were totally forgotten. The proud but archaic Konyan animists found themselves facing a mortal danger in the shape of a superior military power. If they were to offer proper resistance, they would have to make the most far-reaching changes in their own society, changes which only some native-born son could achieve, one sworn to defend and not to destroy. But it had to be someone who had managed to escape the rigidity of pagan traditionalism; only one type of person could possibly fulfil this role—a Dyula from the Konya.

Samori met these conditions remarkably well: he came from a family of Turè who had given up trade and re-adopted paganism via marriage with Kamara families. He was born in about 1830 and had already returned to trade and the religion of his ancestors when his mother was captured by the Sisé, probably in 1853. He then spent some five years with them, learning the art of war, before he went to live among the Bèrèté; he was soon at odds with them and had to flee, spending the rainy season of 1861 in hiding in the Gbe mountains.

This was a time when the power of the Bèrèté seemed to wane whilst that of the Sisé increased and spread all over the country. Samori offered his military skill to his Kamara 'uncles' after two famous palavers, one in Dyala in 1861 and another in Sanankoro in 1862. He was appointed Keletigi and was given the right of mobilising the *kari* as well as the means of organising a small permanent troop of warriors. He appointed friends, relations and soldiers of fortune, all personally devoted to him, gave them arms and trained them in the ways he had learned in Madina. His authority was soon acknowledged over a wide area from the Milo to the Dyon. His former masters were naturally somewhat anxious when they saw his gradual rise to power, but one of Samori's greatest talents was his ability to avoid any uncertain combats, skilfully dividing his enemies and disposing of them one after the other. He managed to effect a reconciliation with the Sisé by helping them fight and conquer the Bèrèté in 1865. He still felt unable to do battle with Sérè-Brèma and in order to avoid open conflict with him withdrew for a year to the forest region in the Toma. In the following year the Sisé were deflected from the south by the great Wasulu wars and Samori re-took his Milo territory where he spent the next three years relatively peacefully (1867–70).

He made good use of this break. Up to then his army had been modelled entirely on that of the Sisé, but now he planned some changes. His contacts with the Dyula allowed him to buy large numbers of guns and even a certain number of horses. He subjected his troops to rigid discipline and adopted the warrior title of Faama, which indicated that he had his eye on total sovereignty.

By 1870, he was ready to make his appearance, but he was still numerically inferior to the Sisé. This was less important than might appear and his political acumen more than made up for it. Some shrewd concessions persuaded Sérè-Brèma to let him attack and crush the Toro pagans led by Nanténen-Famudu (1871–4). He moved his headquarters to Bisandugu, an area which had barely recovered from conquest, to show that he was no longer his 'uncles'' man: from then onwards he was the leader of a revolution of his own. Without either rejecting his pagan connections with the Konya or giving Islam a more considerable place in his plans, he declared that he was determined to defend trade from the extortions of local chiefs and to open up the trading routes. This made an instant appeal to the Dyula network and everywhere these traders began to prepare for his arrival with the intention of helping in the organisa-tion of the new empire.

His next move was an alliance with the Muslims in Kankan, helping them break the pagan blockade which was bringing the great city to ruin, and when this was achieved he went a step further and acquired the great tracks of territory which stretched along the Niger from the frontiers of the Fouta-Djallon to the Burè goldfields

(1875–9). This conquest provided him with the means of building a powerful army and in 1880 he turned to attack the Sisé and Kankan who resisted in extended order. In a few months he destroyed his last rivals and incorporated their troops into his old army. During the rainy season of 1881, when he had set up his headquarters at Gbèlèba in the south (where he was joined by the Turè from Odienne), he found himself the leader of the largest empire that the Malinke in the south had ever known. All those individual movements usually listed together as the Dyula revolution had been more or less forced to join him by circumstances and served to strengthen his army and support his plans.

What he needed now was a unifying principle and he found one in the cause of Islam, partly under the influence of his Kankan supporters. In 1884, after eliminating a pagan rival in the upper Konyan, Saghadyigi Kamara, he renounced the old title of Faama and took that of Almami, inspired by the Fouta-Djallon. In 1886 and 1887 he went a step further, proclaiming a total theocracy and demanding the conversion of his subjects, though with a little compromise here and there. The ease with which he abandoned this great plan when the 1888 catastrophe exposed his misjudgements proves that Islam was always a means to an end as far as he was concerned. The new empire was basically a military organisation, built for the regeneration of Malinke society and for the better integration of the Dyula, and to understand Samori properly, this fact must be appreciated.

The military institutions that Samori set up should be studied in some detail before we see them in direct confrontation with the French, a confrontation which was to have a very profound effect on their every feature.

2 The old army

Samori's army grew out of the Sisé's and for a long time he copied their methods exactly. He recruited men from every sphere. Around a nucleus of friends and supporters, including a fair proportion of men from artisan castes *(nyamakala)* and Dyula, he built up a force of warriors captured during his wars, giving them their freedom in return for service. A third element was based on levies of young men which he obliged conquered territories to provide as part of their ritual submission (i.e. 'drinking *dègè*', a mixture of flour and sour milk). Others were mobilised every year to fight in campaigns of limited duration.

The army soon took on a quasi-national character because it

achieved a very remarkable homogeneity. Most of its members were from different tribes of the Manding group and it was only after 1893 far to the east that other ethnic groups, mainly Senufo and Kulango, came to play an important part.

This Dyula army differed fundamentally from the old Malinke militia, which were levies based on the framework of the *kari* and used during the empire period only in exceptional circumstances (invasions, the 1888 revolt) and then only for a general levy of all able-bodied men. Instead of being grouped by class or by village, men were divided up arbitrarily in more or less standardised units. These units were permanent and their members did not return home after every battle, so they were soon linked by very strong feelings of friendship and loyalty. These feelings extended to their leaders, and in turn the leaders felt the same loyalties to the *kèlètigi* commanding the armies, and finally to the Almami himself.

This was essentially an infantry army, even though its members bore the paradoxical name of *sofa* ('horse father'). In the old *kafu* permanent troops had been drawn from the Masa's servants who acted as grooms to their horses and the name *sofa* still persisted. The military traditions of the south demanded that chiefs should be mounted whenever they could, but there were no cavalry troops comparable to those which dominated the Sudan. Samori was keenly aware of the impact of mounted men on foot-soldiers as well as of their importance in winning victories and he was anxious to organise troops of his own. Moreover, he was desperately in need of a change of tactics if he were to capture the territory further down the Niger. There were bands of cavalry in his army by 1881, at the siege of Kankan, and their number increased steadily up to the great crisis of 1888. Afterwards, when Samori completely altered his military methods, he diminished their part in the army in favour of an infantry based on European models.

Even during this short but glorious seven years the cavalry played only a minor role. It never comprised more than 3,000 men, whilst the conqueror's army reached a total of 30,000 to 35,000 during the Sikasso war (1887–8).

Even before the 1888 crisis there were developments in the way Samori's men were armed. Apart from the individual European weapons which were the personal property of the combatants, Samori provided them with guns and he took great care that every man in the army had one. Up to 1875 or 1876 these were guns obtained from traders, easily repaired by local blacksmiths who also made the ammunition for them. But when he reached the borders of the Fouta-Djallon he took care to import more modern weapons from Sierra Leone. This was a time when arms manufacture in Europe was developing very rapidly from the technical point of view and Samori set himself to study and understand the rapid succession of different models. For instance, he distributed a number of Chassepot rifles among his men but soon noticed their defects—the big cardboard cartridge was heavy and soon rotted in the humidity. From 1885 he systematically replaced these weapons with Gras rifles which had a light-weight metal cartridge and Kropatscheks which were really Gras repeaters (known as *data,* ten mouths). In his last years he was interested in the Lebel rifles, but could never obtain them in sufficient numbers. A technical reason obliged him to stay faithful to the Gras and Kropatschek guns: he had managed to build up groups of workmen who were able to copy these rifles extremely well so it was obviously sensible to go on using them. Constant changes in the rifles meant, of course, that it would have been difficult for these village craftsmen to keep up with developments and the work in any case could not go beyond a certain level of precision.

Moreover, the spread of quick-firing rifles (which does not necessarily mean repeating rifles) was very slow at first. As late as 1888 Samori had only a few hundred of these and it was only in anticipation of the conflict with France that he began to buy them in increasing numbers. In the end he had about 6,000 modern weapons at his disposal in 1893 when he retreated towards the east, and this total, which was never to be repeated, lasted him until his defeat. At first these precious weapons were reserved for the very best fighters, that is for the cavalry and especially the sovereign's personal body-guard. Before 1888 the latter was the only section of the army to have a uniform inspired by that of the French riflemen: blue clothing with red belt and tarboosh.

These weapons were paid for by money from the sale of the gold and ivory Samori's country produced and also—indirectly—by the sale of slaves who were used in the transactions which brought horses from the Sahel and the Mossi territory. The 'black legend' suggests that Samori sold his own subjects to meet his financial requirements. In fact these slaves were exclusively rebels and prisoners of war. A total of 2,800 to 3,000 per year were sold in this way, that is the equivalent of a four-hundredth of the population of the empire.

In the period preceding 1888 Samori was content to bring his art of war to perfection, radically altering what he had learnt from the

Sisé. The *sofa* were organised into permanent units of ten to twenty men, known as *sé* (feet) or *kulu* (heaps), commanded by one of the *kuntigi* (chiefs) usually on foot. Ten *sé* formed a *bolo* (arm) commanded by a *bolokuntigi* with a small mounted general staff which included military griots wearing panther skin adornments.

The *bolo* was the main striking force and each one had a tremendous feeling of team loyalty. The horsemen *(sotigi)* rode alongside in bands about fifty strong, called *sèrè*.

No permanent formations came between the *bolo* and the army proper, or *kèlè*. Larger or smaller groups of *bolo* might act as small garrisons for difficult spots, or else be formed into columns for campaigns of minor importance. They were then placed under the command of one of their own chiefs or else of an army leader's right-hand man, often a griot, and this commander was called the *sofa-kuntigi* (leader of the *sofa*).

The army itself deserves special mention. The administrative reforms which Samori introduced were closely connected with the army, for they were basically concerned with the way the conquered territories were ruled and on them depended the efficient running of the empire. The Sisé had been quite content to establish their own *dugukunnasigi* in the conquered *kafu* and *nyamaana,* but this system proved inefficient where the territory was more than 60–100 miles across. Samori had been forced to improvise to keep his immense areas of conquered land under control. The new system he devised seems to have been prompted by similar ones used by the Toucouleurs: he decided to divide his territory into a central nucleus, the *Foroba* ('great field': collective fields belonging to villages and, by extension, state property) and a number of military governments which were never more than five in number. Each of these existed within very strictly defined limits and was the domain of an army *(kèlè)* whose commander *(kèlètigi)* was appointed or dismissed at will by Samori. In the first phase of his career (from 1878 when the army of Damisa-Koro was created on the lower Niger to 1888, the year of the great revolt), he appointed either brothers or men whom he particularly trusted. Later on, he was more inclined to appoint his sons as titular chiefs but backed them with tried and trusted warriors. The *kèlètigi* was not just a plain soldier. In the area granted to him, he had the same powers as Samori, with the obvious reservations. He was supported by a state apparatus similar to that of the central government and was responsible for all economic and political activities. In principle, the territory governed was supposed to provide recruits and victualling for the occupying army. Naturally, the ruler reserved the right to even things out where there was disproportionate income of any kind, but this was the only way in which he intervened directly in local affairs.

A war of conquest could not be undertaken without his agreement, but the suppression of revolts and frontier skirmishes fell within the province of the *kèlètigi* alone. Various sources suggest that the latter probably had an average of 5,000 men at their disposal. This figure was not to be exceeded till after 1895, when the army of Sarankènyi-Mori totalled 8,000.

It was difficult to feed more than this in the course of campaigning and it was only in exceptional circumstances such as in 1885 and 1887 that several *kèlè* were gathered: this posed very serious transport problems.

It might be supposed that Samori was taking grave risks by allowing such wide powers to be assumed by men of real ambition and in areas of considerable size. Indeed, his son Managbè-Mamadi, leader of the eastern army in Bafagha (the Bougouni district), was to try to break away in due course in 1889, but this attempt was extremely ill-advised and was a ridiculous failure. It was in fact the only one of its kind. What really happened was that the Almami always packed the local councils with his own supporters, often appointed his *bilakoro* (see below) or men from his body-guard as leaders of the *bolo* and everywhere he appointed a superb network of *karamogho,* or schoolmasters, who kept him constantly informed of what was happening.

More than this, all the local governments together barely surpassed in size the nucleus of the empire, the Foroba, which Samori kept firmly in his own hands. This territory supported a large reserve army of 8,000 to 10,000 men and had an extremely fine weapon supply. It kept the name Foroba and whenever the occasion arose would send detachments to help any *kèlètigi* in difficulty. Its forces were led by his brother Manigbè-Mori, who had no territory of any kind under his control and who was killed at Sikasso in 1888. After his death there was no general leader for the whole Foroba and its last detachments were directly controlled by the Almami.

In addition, he had his special corps of men—the body-guard, for instance, which never left him—and his sons' guard which after the heroic battle at Dabadugu in September 1891 was to be remodelled on a European basis and which showed the most outstanding team spirit (the *Dabadugu-Bolo*).

These units were officered by former *bilakoro* (young lads); these were young captives whom Samori had brought up from their earliest youth. They were completely devoted to him and were trained to a peak of great physical and mental perfection.

In spite of its use of modern weapons, this army was always built on traditional lines. It was capable of extremely swift changes of location and never lost its attachment to the old-established tactics like surprise attacks on fortified strong points. If necessary the attacking forces would build wooden campaign fortifications and would settle down to virtually interminable sieges. Their discipline and energy were unequalled, but their firing power was disorganised and their aim uncertain: they could not offer much sustained resistance to a detachment trained in European-type tactics, like the French riflemen, and the lack of artillery made their inferiority overwhelming.

Within the framework of the old Africa the astonishing rise of Samori revealed a tactician whose strategic skill was without equal. But the relative mediocrity of his means of action was to leave him powerless in the face of adversaries whose genius was nil, but whose techniques of modern warfare were unequalled on the continent.

3 The French threat (1881–91)

This chapter cannot give a full account of the interminable conflict which dragged on between Samori and the French; the most that one can do is indicate the general course of events and describe some of the particularly significant episodes.

Within the general setting of French colonial imperialism the conquest of the French Sudan is an exceptional case on account of the autonomy enjoyed by the officers of the Marine Corps who were responsible for its government from 1880 onwards. Until the arrival of the new civil governor, Grodet, in December 1893, political measures and the general rhythm of military expansion were matters decided on the spot, the government in Paris being quite content to approve and ratify matters already decided. As the colony grew, it provided its own support and the annual mobilisation of former riflemen supplied the army's commanders with substantial bodies of men from 1893 onwards.

The French depended less and less on the resources of either Metropolitan France or Senegal and every dry season saw them moving further and further into the immensity of the great savannas with their accompaniment of family groups, herds of cattle and bands of captives.

The Niger was the line they followed for their gradual penetration, then they moved through the curve of the river and finally set their sights on Chad. The original projects for linking up with the Gulf of Guinea colonies had to be postponed in the face of natural obstacles, but eventually they struggled through to Dahomey and the Fouta-Djallon in 1896 and to the Ivory Coast in 1898.

The march towards the Niger, led by Colonel Borgnis-Desbordes in the period 1881 to 1883, was aimed not at Samori, hardly known at that time, but at the Toucouleur empire whose power much impressed the French and whose Muslim associations reminded them of their conquest of Algeria.

The first contact in February 1882 was therefore more by accident than design. During the previous rainy season, Samori had been visited at Gbèlèba by Lieutenant Alakamessa, who had come from Kita to order him to keep away from Kènyéran, a large market in the Fyé valley. Since this town had given shelter to refugees from Kankan, and at the same time effectively barred Samori from the Manding and the Bambara, he refused to consider the request. He moved in to besiege it in November and as Borgnis-Desbordes intended to concentrate on the capture of Bamako that year they should never have come up against each other. But it so happened that yellow fever broke out in Senegal and it was impossible to send appropriate reinforcements. Borgnis-Desborde therefore received orders not to go beyond Kita, and instead he took it into his head to form a light column of men and move in to relieve Kènyéran. This was to prove most ill-advised. On 22 February he surprised Samori's army, which had just captured the town, but he was forced to retreat with great precipitation. As far as the Africans were concerned, they saw this as a defeat for the French.

This foolish and fruitless raid beyond the Niger was harshly criticised, but it served a useful purpose for Samori in that he had an opportunity to see the extraordinary firing power of the white soldiers. This did not suggest to him that he should instantly capitulate, but henceforward he imposed the strictest reserve on his men.

It was against his will that two battles were fought in the following year—on 2 and 12 April, at Wèyanko, close to Bamako. Whilst Samori was besieging Saghadyigi on Mount Gbankundo in the south, his brother Kémé-Brèma, leader of the northern army, was instructed to occupy Bamako. The French got there before him: Kémé-Brèma was unwilling to admit this to his brother and thinking that he would have no difficulty in driving out an enemy small in numbers and sick into the bargain—and ill-received by the local inhabitants—he moved in to the attack. In spite of his numerical superiority and the bravery of his men, his first victory on 2 April was followed by a decisive defeat ten days later. Thus, Samori's counsels of prudence in the face of the French were proved correct.

The following months saw the beginning of the duel which was to bring Samori face to face with Tyèba of Sikasso, the Faama of Kénédugu. The proximity of the French forts at Kita and Bamako left Samori in no doubt as to the wisdom of keeping well within a strict defensive position.

The lull in Samori's relations with the French might well have lasted a little longer if the French officers had not grown impatient with their orders to mark time until communications between Senegal and Bamako had improved. Being ill-prepared for an attack on Segou, but ever anxious for a fight on any possible occasion, they turned their eyes to that tempting territory Burè, the land of gold.

This was why Major Combes, the temporary commanding officer, pursued the small garrisons settled in by Samori on the banks of the Niger instead of simply occupying Nyagasola and revictualling Bamako as he had been told to do. In March 1885, leaving Captain Louvel's company garrisoning Nafadyi in the Séké, he assumed that the campaign was over and went peacefully back towards Senegal in May.

The events which followed have been greatly magnified by colonial historians and they do indeed deserve the closest attention, for they reveal the nature of the two opposing sides.

In spite of being poised to attack Sikasso, Samori realised that he could in no way give up his hold on the wealthy territory of Burè which had paid him a tribute in gold ever since 1878; to accept the French provocation without any reply was to damage his prestige very profoundly. The answer he gave his new adversaries was shattering and revealed his outstanding genius for strategy.

Kémé-Brèma was fighting near Sikasso, so he was brought back and ordered to establish his army on the Niger upstream from Bamako; Samori took the Foroba army towards Siguiri which marked the confluence of the Niger and the Tenkiso and his brother Masara-Mamadi moved to join him with the army from the north-west, the Damisa-Koro army.

This was the pincer movement which was to crush the French in the Séké. The garrison felt strongly that something was afoot in spite of the persistently hostile silence of the local population and in

May Louvel decided to evacuate Nafadyi. A furious order from Combes made him go back again.

On 27 May Samori's army, whose presence was already suspected by Louvel, suddenly crossed the Tenkiso and started to destroy the villages which had supported the French. After a few skirmishes Lieutenant Bonnard was nearly overcome on the 31st in the forest corridor of Kommodo. A swift hand-to-hand battle led by Louvel saved Bonnard and his men from certain death and the French troops managed to get back to Nafadyi where they were instantly besieged by Samori: there was no water and they were short of provisions.

All seemed lost and this is what Combes thought when he heard the news at Kundu on 3 June. His irresponsible actions had put his comrades in danger and he decided to go and die with them. He joined up with Péroz at Nyagasola on 6 June and they marched together in a light column towards Nafadyi. By an extraordinary chance they got there by the 10th without meeting any of Samori's army. The retreat which they instantly organised was extremely arduous, for the swift-moving *sofa* kept ahead of the French troops and occupied every obstacle they came to so that constant bloody combats were necessary along every step of the way.

The worst was yet to come. The French did not know that so far they had encountered only one side of the pincers. Kémé-Brèma had crossed the Niger downstream and whilst Combes moved steadily southwards, this second army had settled down before the fort at Nyagasola and had strongly fortified the forest corridor of Kokoro. When Combes got this far with his exhausted men on 14 June he found the track closed whilst the great army of the Foroba and Masara-Mamadi pressed at his rear. Samori assumed that his skilful manœuvre would utterly crush the French column.

But once again the enemy's guns deprived him of victory. At the cost of a terrible assault the French managed to storm the palisades around the Kokoro and took refuge behind the walls of the fort. From a superior position up the hill Samori saw the strong stone building with some astonishment and decided to suspend operations for the time being. An assault he launched a few weeks later was a terrible defeat for him.

Samori was forced to acknowledge his impotence. Between 31 May and 15 June he had lost at least 900 men, whilst the French had had two killed and twenty-nine seriously wounded. Several of his best commanders had been hurt, including Masara-Mamadi, who was to die from his wounds several months later. The enemy's weakness in numbers and strategic skill was compensated for by his firing power. As the threat from Sikasso grew ever stronger in the east, Samori concluded that it would be wise to bring to an end the conflict with France, a conflict which threatened the very existence of his empire.

His enemies did not appreciate his decision immediately, for the rainy season had started and the small French garrisons shut themselves up for the time being in the forts at Kita and Nyagasola. In the latter Péroz was still more or less under siege, whilst patrols of *sofa* worked their way right up to the gates of Bafoulabé almost without striking a single blow. There was tremendous panic in Senegal and this spread swiftly to Paris, so much so that the Government decided to make an unusual effort to help the colony, in spite of its general unpopularity, simply for the honour of the flag.

Colonel Frey accepted this mission of sacrifice in spite of the fact that he believed the French should pull out of the Sudan—though only after inflicting a crushing defeat on the enemy. This pleasure was denied him, for most of Samori's army had already withdrawn towards Sikasso. In spite of routing a rearguard in Fatako-Dyingo on 18 January 1886, his encircling movements were a failure and he realised that it was impossible to fight without crossing the river. There was no question of going so far, for at that very moment the uprising led by Mamadu Lamin* threatened Bakel on the upper Senegal.

Frey decided to come to terms with an enemy who in fact asked for nothing better. Captain Tournier and Lieutenant Péroz went to Samori's headquarters at Kenyeba-Kura where they signed a peace and trade treaty on 28 March 1886. The Almami promised to recall his men on to the right bank, but preserved his political rights over the Burè and the Manding of Kangaba. His favourite son, Dyaulé-Karamogho, aged seventeen or eighteen, was to accompany the mission on its return to France and visit the authorities in Paris.

The boy stayed in France throughout August and September, visited President Grévy and General Boulanger and was greatly impressed by the military power of the whites. The journey had no political consequences, however. The colonialist party found the treaty unacceptable on two counts: it maintained some of Samori's rights on the left bank and it failed to include a protectorate clause and thereby left the country open to other colonial powers.

As Colonel Gallieni, the new commander, was committed to the reduction of Mamadu Lamin, a diplomatic mission was entrusted to Captain Péroz, who went to Bisandugu where he persuaded Samori—

* See preceding chapter.

not without difficulty—to sign an amendment on 25 March 1887. Samori ceded the left bank and the French promised not to build a fort there 'before some time'. Without realising how much he was compromising his liberty, Samori also accepted the basic idea of a French protectorate.

He was under the impression that he had signed an alliance which left him free to follow his own internal politics and he hoped to receive at least moral support against Sikasso which he had decided to crush without further delay. If he succeeded he would no longer be caught between two opposing powers; the sweep of Niger would lie open before him right up to the Mossi frontier and he would be able to speak to the French with greater authority. There was no more question of fighting them unless this became absolutely necessary, for Samori had a very accurate estimate of his own powers.

In April 1887 he set off to attack Sikasso and found the obstacle more difficult than he had anticipated. The siege, which lasted till the end of August 1888, was a succession of partial successes and bloody reverses. The accounts given by Captain Binger and Major Festing who visited the Almami at this time vouch for the basic accuracy of the oral tradition here, but their information must be used with care. For instance, Binger says he saw only 6,000 warriors before Sikasso because of the rainy season and a general breakdown in supplies. In fact, there were at least double this number and the defeat that followed was all the more stunning on that account.

This tragic succession of misfortunes shook Samori's prestige at an unfortunate moment for him: his subjects were already disturbed at the crushing burden of the war and his religious impositions made them extremely discontented. The French did the rest. Interpreting Péroz's promises in his own way, Gallieni marched on Siguiri where he started building a fort on 23 January 1888. His agents went on to rouse the tribes on the right bank against Samori. In a very short time a vast insurrection spread almost all over the empire, excluding the Milo valley and Kankan and the regions of Odienne and Bougouni. Cut off from the rear, Samori was obliged to raise the siege without even being sure of saving his army. He left Sikasso almost alone on 28 August, with the intention of attacking the most dangerous insurgents, the Wasulu, who closed the route to Bisandugu.

Gallieni's political manœuvring may not impress by its honesty at this stage, but it was certainly far from inconsistent. Like the rest of his companions, the colonel could not accept the presence of strong native commands within the framework of the French colonial system. They could only lead to trouble, especially if they were

Muslim, and always disturbed the establishment of the French system of direct administration and the policy of cultural levelling. In any case, it was clear that Samori would never surrender and his sudden swerve towards theocracy made him even more suspect than a few years earlier. So it was better for France if he disappeared—and the sooner the better, whatever the means.

Towards the end of 1888 the French thought they were in a winning position and began to prepare themselves for taking over the lands held by the Almami as soon as his fall was properly confirmed. They were soon proved to be very wrong indeed. Not everyone had abandoned the Almami, for Samori, with all his faults, was still the living embodiment of the hopes and aspirations of much of the Malinke world. He set up a provisional capital at Nyako on the Sankarani and from here he launched the methodical crushing of this totally anarchic and uncontrolled rebellion.

Major Archinard, a young officer who greatly admired Borgnis-Desbordes, had replaced Gallieni as commander in the Sudan and was quick to see the opportunities this unexpected situation provided. In spite of his small number of troops he decided to take advantage of Samori's difficulties to spread over as much of his territories as possible so that he could force Samori to integrate himself completely into the French colonial system. This would leave him free, he hoped, to attack and destroy the Toucouleur empire, which would be his main objective. As for Samori, he could wait: the French would deal with him in the fullness of time. On 21 February 1889 Lieutenant Bonnardot went to Nyako and obtained the cession of the left bank of the Niger right up to the source, as well as a promise that the Almami would come to Siguiri to see Archinard.

Unfortunately, at the very same moment, rebels who had fled into French-held territory launched a series of raids deep into the area behind the river without any opposition from the French. Samori interpreted this as a lack of good faith on the part of his partners and refused to leave Nyako. Archinard was furious and decided to intimidate him. He went up the left bank of the river with a small column, storming Dugura to humiliate the Almami's supporters, and after occupying Kouroussa on 17 April pushed onwards to the borders of the Fouta-Djallon.

On his way back he was astonished to hear that Samori was actually returning him the treaty from Nyako. Instead of reproaching himself for his own brutality and lack of psychology, he lost his temper and stormed back to France with the intention of settling Samori's account at the first opportunity.

But the Almami still felt himself bound by the Treaty of Bisandugu and had no intention of breaking with the French, though his confidence in them was henceforth absolutely nil. He saw only too clearly that he had only two options: either to submit to them completely, that is to abandon his life's work, or fight a last conclusive and probably hopeless battle with them. He chose the second, but he was still not ready to do battle on a proper scale and he needed time to prepare. First he had to put down the Great Revolt and then he could re-open the road to Freetown where the British would sell him arms.

The insurgents went on fighting in some areas up to June 1890, but as early as February that year, Bilali, the new leader of the western army, made contact with the outposts of Sierra Leone. On 23 May 1890 Samori met the travelling commissioner, Mr. Garrett, at Bisandugu where he signed a treaty recognising a British Protectorate in the hope of avoiding a direct clash with the French in the Sudan. It was a vain attempt, for the 1889 and 1890 agreements confirmed that he had passed his territories over to French control. However, the British in Sierra Leone were willing to start trading relations with him once again and for the next three years the Almami bought modern weapons in increasing quantities from Freetown— some of his suppliers were of French nationality. The operation was financed by requisitioning gold from the women in his country and by mobilising a regular army of hunters to bring in enough ivory to make the purchase of guns possible. All the local blacksmiths were organised into bigger and more efficient units.

The Dyula empire prepared for the last fight.

4 The great confrontation

The empire Samori won back again was ravaged and terribly depopulated, but there was more at stake than its speedy reconstruction. First of all, Samori had to reorganise the army on completely new lines so that they would be prepared to meet the ordeal ahead of them.

There was not much hope of conducting the aggressive kind of war that Samori was used to: everything had to be defensive in concept, but not the usual sort of defensive measure which meant shutting themselves up in some strong point and sitting there till the enemy grew tired and went away. The white man's artillery could shatter any fortification it chose and this sort of siege was tantamount to a death warrant.

Samori's intelligence system was efficient and he was not slow to appreciate that the enemy's weak point was the heaviness of his convoys and the relative slowness of his men. Contrary to established tradition, he decided to attack in open country, making short sharp raids on the enemy columns. But if he wanted to keep them from the heart of the empire, he needed more than guerilla warfare and to this end he made an immense effort to prepare efficient earthworks along the way, cutting back the banks of the river channels to make the fords difficult of access, building palisades and even dry stone walls to help defend the passes and the forest corridors.

It was obvious, of course, that his troops could never hope to occupy permanent positions and he had to make the most of their mobility if he was to avoid serious losses. The widespread use of more modern rifles gave them a firing power ten times stronger than ever before and brought a proportional reduction in his effective fighting force with their porterage trains. Combes had faced 15,000 men before Nyagasola, Humbert was to fight no more than 2,500 and the siege of Kong in 1898 was to be conducted by only 2,000 *sofa*. One could still find great bands of fighting men armed with the old guns, but they were used for fighting African opponents who lacked the powers of proper resistance.

The change-over from old-fashioned to modern weapons would have been of little use, though, if it had not been accompanied by corresponding reforms in discipline. In point of fact Samori decided as early as 1888 to organise units trained in the European way as speedily as possible, and for this reason he made a point of welcoming any soldiers, deserters or otherwise, who came from the British and French armies and who would be useful in training his warrior bands. They were joined by a good number of prisoners and some of them seem to have been motivated by a very genuine African patriotism.

Companies were formed in this way, usually comprising 150 men, or half as many again as a unit of riflemen, though the number sometimes rose to 200. The training they were given made certain that their firing power was very effective, which came as a great surprise to Péroz in 1892. They were able to fire in volleys, manœuvring in response to bugle calls of considerable unorthodoxy; this new army managed to retain a fair degree of the mobility which distinguished the old *sofa* and was able to scatter and re-form very quickly. Its effective was always small in number, however, and seems never to have gone beyond twenty or so companies, with about half the men armed with modern guns.

Samori never relaxed in his efforts to organise this army and it came to its peak of perfection in the east after 1895. The great confrontation with the French took place before it was able to show what it was really capable of doing and although it showed itself to be reasonably effective, it was too limited in its powers to shift the balance in Samori's favour.

Ségou was captured in March 1890 and Archinard decided to finish off Samori before he passed his command over to his brother officer, Lieutenant-Colonel Humbert. When he returned to Bamako in March 1891 after sweeping the Toucouleurs from their last positions in the Sahel he made a surprise attack towards the Upper Niger, occupied Kankan in flames on 7 April and sent a reconnaissance party to burn Bisandugu whilst he himself went down with blackwater fever.

Tactically, this was a surprise for Samori, who had expected to be attacked at some time, though not until after the rains. In any event, the raid did not weaken the Almami at all and the empire did not collapse quietly as Archinard expected. On the contrary, the affair came as a useful warning to Samori who now had all the time in the world to mobilise his resources in view of the clash to come after the rains and afterwards Humbert was to see the raid as the source of his misfortunes.

The 1891–2 campaign was to produce the major clash between the two antagonists—from both their points of view. Humbert wanted to strike right at the heart of the empire in order to provoke a major battle and so destroy Samori and the Almami, who by now felt his men to be better armed, hoped that his new army would be able to stand firm. Throughout the rainy season it had harassed the French garrison in Kankan and had even been extremely successful on 3 September at the battle of Dabadugu.

Meanwhile, the worst attack of epizootic disease of the century wiped out the cattle in the Sudan and it was an exceedingly heavy convoy which left Kankan on 6 January 1892: Humbert led 1,300 fighting men and 3,000 porters towards the Milo. They soon clashed with Samori's men, barely more in number than the French riflemen (about 2,500), but the Almami's chosen troops, fighting like demons, clung fiercely to every defensive point on the way. Samori was in personal command and in most of these fights showed his immense tactical skill, particularly on 24 January at Farandugu where he managed to change front when the French unexpectedly got around his stone fortifications.

But Humbert forced his way through. Forts were built at Bisandugu which was occupied on 9 January and at the twin villages of Sanankoro and, Kérwané taken on 26 January. On 14 February Samori's arsenal on the top of the cliffs at Tininkuru was taken by storm.

The French were now deep inside the empire, but they found themselves in a wilderness, for the Almami had ordered all the local population to leave as the enemy approached, taking all foodstuffs with them and destroying all their villages. To get supplies to the new forts the French had to set up a proper shuttle service between them and Kankan and had to fight every inch of the way there and back. Weeks passed and still Humbert could find no way out of this agonising and futile impasse. Finally, he decided to retreat on 9 April, leaving his new garrisons in a state of siege: Kérwané was to stay cut off from the rest of the world for nearly seven months.

Humbert was furious and deeply discouraged, determined never to set foot in the Sudan again. He admitted that he had been defeated—which was evident to everyone—but laid the responsibility at Archinard's feet. Accordingly, Archinard asked to be sent back to the Sudan.

There was really no need for such a drama, for by now, it was clear that Samori had played and lost. He had tried to stop the French with his finest troops, surely the best that the colonising army had ever encountered in West Africa. The *sofa* had managed to restrict the movements of the whites almost completely, but they had not been able to repulse them and even less to conquer them. Their relative success had been obtained at the most frightful cost: their fantastic feats of skill and bravery had ended in death for many of their number. The French had taken few prisoners and over a thousand men had died on the Almami's side, for a total of a mere hundred French soldiers wounded.

The Almami had lost several of his bravest and best companions and in February 1892 he seems to have taken a major decision. He had just fought the battle he had been preparing for ever since 1888 and in conditions which were perfect for him: his weaknesses were all too obvious. It was pointless to continue the fight and since there was no question of surrender, there was only one course open to him—to withdraw and find some distant region where the whites would leave him in peace for a time. The execution of Sérè-Brèma which took place just about now in a retired spot takes on a symbolic value: the Almami was ready to leave his fatherland and the society which had given birth to the Dyula revolution. A realistic assessment of the situation forced him to be accommodating, but at the same time he could not surrender—so he withdrew quietly in the face of French superiority and left them to pursue their conquests in another direction. But by doing this, he broke with the atmosphere he was born to and his military empire was transferred to an exotic world which robbed it of its *raison d'être*. The fighting force he had built no longer served to build a new world, but hung fire, an end in itself and nothing more.

5 The years of reprieve

The military power of Samori's army was still considerable and indeed it increased steadily up to the final crash. It had some years of military conquest before it, but it was never again to fight European opponents apart from the odd short and fierce conflict: Samori had no desire to remind France of his existence.

Colonial historians have presented the campaign led by Combes under the ægis of Archinard between December 1892 to May 1893 as a glorious epic struggle. Its territorial achievements were important: France occupied all the western part of the former Dyula empire and reached the borders of Sierra Leone as well as the fringes of the great forest. But there was no major battle, for Samori systematically avoided any encounter and his army was still fighting splendidly at the battle of Morigbèdugu in April.

Samori was still pursuing his scorched-earth policy and he began to speed up the evacuation of his people towards the east where the army of Amara-Dyèli had opened the way to Bandama and Comoé for him. In December 1893 he was surprised by Colonel Eugène Bonnier at Koloni where he was putting down a Bambara insurrection. His losses in the subsequent fight were fairly small. At this point he recalled his son Dyaulé-Karamogho who still occupied the Upper Konya and the road to Monrovia in the south (January 1894). He had been cut off from Freetown since the year before and this new withdrawal meant that he lost his last source of modern weapons. From now until his final collapse he was able to buy only a very small number.

Moving quickly towards the south-east through what is now the hinterland of the Ivory Coast, the Almami hoped he would avoid any pursuit by the French in the Sudan. As they had just been placed under the orders of a civil governor, Grodet, he tried to open new negotiations, but without success. The final break came in December 1894 and all contact between Samori and the French ceased for the time being. They were even convinced by a rumour that the Almami had died. They turned their attention to the conquest of the area contained within the great sweep of the Niger and did not come upon Samori's army again until August 1896 when they were in the Gurunsi territory trying to link up with Dahomey and hem the British inside the Gold Coast.

Samori wanted to avoid contact with the whites at all cost, but this could be achieved only if they would leave him in peace in his place of refuge, that was in the open savannas which back on to the forest from Sassandra to the Volta. But his presence here meant that he hindered French projects for a link between the Ivory Coast and the Sudan and he was soon faced with the prospect of battle. At the beginning of 1895 he found himself up against the Monteil column which was travelling from Bassam through the Baulé country with the intention of pushing him back towards the west and occupying Kong. Thanks to a decisive superiority in numbers and a brilliant flash of tactical skill, Samori stood his ground from 2 to 18 March in a series of hard conflicts ranging over the pre-forest savannas of Dyimini and Dyammala.

Samori seemed to be clear of danger now and his men easily conquered the Abron kingdom with the centre of Bondoukou (July 1895) and moved on to take western Gondja (January 1896). The next year was calm and peaceful and he spent it organising his new domain and strengthening his army; he was lucky enough to get several consignments of horses through his vassals in Kong and their kinsmen in Gwiriko (Bobo-Dioulasso).

His territory, unfortunately for his peace of mind, lay right across the British expansion route, for they had just taken Kumasi and were anxious to move on towards the Mossi in the hope of getting there before the French. Samori was disappointed in his old trading partners, for they had refused to supply him with guns, quoting the Brussels act of 1890. They were foolish enough to complicate their refusal by asking him to cede Bouna, also sought by the French. He did not think much of their military prowess, but even so wished to avoid fighting them and it was much against his will that his eastern army led by his son Sarankènyi-Mori destroyed Henderson's column at Dokita and Wa between 29 March and 5 April 1897.

Samori's empire now found itself resting on very shaky foundations, a situation which was hardly improved by the betrayal of Kong. He marched on this town and destroyed it on 18 May, sweeping on to the gates of Bobo in July (the siege of Numudagha). Here he came up against the outposts of Diebougou and Lorhoso which

Commandant Caudrelier had just set up to the west of the Black Volta.

Samori was caught between the two great colonial powers and once again he showed his great political genius. As the French did not appear overtly hostile, he offered to cede Bouna to them, hoping thereby to set them against the British and avoid the storm a little longer. This skilful move was turned to catastrophe by the stupidity of Sarankènyi-Mori. A column led by Captain Braulot which was marching with an escort of *sofas* was massacred in a surprise attack within sight of the Kulango capital on 20 August 1897.

This sealed Samori's fate, for the French army could not ignore him for much longer. A last brief reprieve came from the tense Franco–British rivalry on the Volta, the Niger and the Nile.

The fighting started up again on the Comoé, quite by accident, when Lieutenant Demars occupied Kong against all his instructions on 25 January 1898. He was instantly besieged by 2,000 men from Sarankènyi-Mori's army, armed with two cannons captured at Wa, and the siege lasted till the end of May, a bitter test of endurance for the French troops.

Samori thought that the moment had come for his last great stand and planned to entrench himself in the tata of Bori-Bana which he had built in a very isolated spot on the Bandama west of Katiola. But on 1 May 1898 the French took Sikasso by storm and when he heard that this fortress, the strongest in the western Sudan, had fallen he realised that his plan could only lead to certain death.

He therefore decided to join his allies in the Toma country, deep inside Liberia. At the beginning of June 1898 he pulled out of his eastern territories in a matter of weeks and concentrated his entire army, together with a huge throng of 100,000 civilians, on the narrow Bafinko plain on the borders of the Dan and the Mau countries (between Man and Touba, Ivory Coast). According to Lartigue, he then had 12,000 fighting men, 4,000 of whom had modern rifles; 2,000 of them were mounted. It was here on 20 July, at Owé, that he won a brilliant victory over Commandant de Lartigue who had rashly attacked him.

Then came Samori's last mistake: he decided to move westwards across the forest-clad Dan mountains in the middle of the rainy season. The victorious army was instantly overtaken by famine and his troops disappeared almost overnight. He had not many men with him when he was surprised at Gélému on 29 September by a reconnaissance party led by Gouraud.

When he was captured he had already begun to work out a treaty with the enemy and had more or less been promised permission to withdraw to his native Konya. Even so, he was deported to Ndjolé in Gabon where he died of pneumonia on 2 June 1900.

Conclusion

Samori wanted to build an empire to meet the crisis which shook the Manding world and he would never have succeeded if he had not found immense popular support among his compatriots. The revolt of 1888 cannot conceal the fact that he was seen as a national leader by the Malinke in the south. The French forces constantly under-estimated his popularity and this brought them a large number of setbacks.

The empire was built on a military basis; it was formed by force of arms and held together by the army. Without the army it would almost certainly have collapsed in 1888, which was what Gallieni hoped, and it would never have been rebuilt in the east, far from its natural foundations, if the army had not held together.

Samori could never have forged this marvellous instrument, never have bonded together so many disparate elements, without his extra-ordinarily attractive personality, for he had the gift of inspiring the most fanatical devotion. He knew exactly what his men wanted and what their difficulties were and it was because he took care to satisfy them that their loyalty never faltered. Where the wounded were concerned, every possible effort was made to save them; the dead were buried decently and the maimed were given jobs to help them live in reasonable comfort.

His warriors' love for him was also founded on a proper basis of confidence: they were convinced that he would lead them to victory and as early as 1883 Borgnis-Desbordes acknowledged his military genius. Archinard was wrong to contradict him and to say that Péroz's admiration for Samori was sheer naïvety.

We have seen how Samori was able to take all the traditional resources of the African leader, adapt them to his needs and even on occasion completely transform them to meet some new require-ment. He bowed to the social and technical customs of his back-ground, but at the same time he had an instinctive feeling for terrain and a rapidity of reflex which Humbert much admired: 'As soon as Samori heard that we had left Kankan, he knew that he had to concentrate his men around the outpost as quickly as possible if he was to offer proper resistance. . . . The choice of the Sombiko and Dyamanko channels as lines of defence, the swift wheeling movements of his troops show a very real understanding of the art of war.' (*Rapport,* p. 109.) Like all truly creative imaginations, his was always open to the lessons of experience. In 1892, when the frontal defence of the river channels proved too costly, he moved his men up to the heights overlooking the tracks which allowed him to delay Humbert with the minimum loss of men.

Apart from this genius for tactics, Samori's greatness lay in his talent for strategy, inextricably linked to the building of an empire and a skilled diplomacy which allowed him to elude the colonial grasp for quite some time. His awareness of a political end, transcending all his military aims, alone gave him the audacity to mobilise all the forces of the empire, craftsmen and traders included, within the framework of a coherent policy. He never swerved from his objectives, though he always fought to win them for the lowest possible price. He did all he could—and more—to go around them, to lay siege to them and to sap their resistance so that a direct confrontation—which never deterred him—would happen only as a last resort.

The rules of the game were irreversibly broken by the white men whose technical superiority made his finest strategic schemes totally sterile. The Almami was as always quick to react, treating with the enemy and trying to modernise his army. The great defeat at Sikasso left him a mere step away from disaster and he instantly determined the outlines of a new policy which he was to follow right to the very end: avoid every possible fight with the white men, but never, never accept surrender.

His military undertakings have all the sadness of wasted efforts. In the space of a mere twenty-five years, he made the most profound changes in the art of war as fought in his country, turning from the old Konya warrior bands to the new Dyula army, and from this to companies specially trained to fight the white men. These changes were possible only through the mobilisation of all the resources of the empire and no other African ruler would ever have dared to attempt this.

His great work was condemned from the start, for neither his energy nor his farsightedness, nor even the fierce love he inspired in his men could make up for the technical insufficiency which doomed Africa to colonisation.

SELECT BIBLIOGRAPHY

My thesis, which appeared at the end of 1969, contains a detailed study of sources.

Most works dealing with Samori are concerned only with his struggles with the French, which does not necessarily mean that they treat them seriously.

Some of the old standard works are worth re-reading, e.g. Péroz, *Au Soudan Français,* Paris, 1889, and *Au Niger,* Paris, 1895: Péroz has a vivid imagination and must therefore be read with care, but he is intelligent and understanding. His 1887 report appears in Gallieni: *Deux campagnes au Soudan,* Paris, 1891.

Among modern writers who have covered the subject, the least mediocre is Delafosse, *Afrique occidentale française,* in Hanotaux *Histoire des Colonies Françaises* Paris, 1931.

The best account of military operations is to be found in Gâtelet, *Histoire de la conquête du Soudan français,* Paris, 1901. There are, however, quite a number of mistakes in it.

L'Histoire militaire de l'A.O.F., Paris, 1931, is exceedingly weak on the subject of Samori.

General Duboc's books, *L'épopée coloniale en Afrique occidentale,* Paris, 1938, and *Samory le sanglant,* Paris, 1947, present no special interest. General Ingold's *Samory sanglant et magnifique,* Paris, 1961, must be considered a literary more than a historical work.

Some isolated events have been treated very soundly, for instance:

H. Labouret, 'Les bandes de Samory dans la Haute Côte d'Ivoire' in *Renseignements coloniaux (Bulletin du Comité de l'Afrique française),* Paris, 1925.

H. Labouret, *Monteil, explorateur et soldat,* Paris, 1937. (Kong column in 1895).

J. Méniaud, *Les pionniers du Soudan,* Paris, 1931. Outstanding work in spite of a tendency to idolise Archinard.

J. Méniaud, *Sikasso ou l'histoire dramatique d'un royaume noir au XIXe siècle,* Paris, 1935. The French attack is studied in detail, but Samori's siege is treated briefly.

Y. Person, 'L'aventure de Paorèkèrè et le drame de Waima' in *Cahiers d'Etudes africaines,* Paris, no. 19 (1965) and 20 (1965). (Sierra Leone border in 1893.)

There is one very fine work on the subject of military organisation: Martin Legassick, 'Forearms, horses and Samorian army administration', (*Journal of African History,* VII, 1, 1966).

I have published the following works as preparatory studies for my thesis:

Y. Person, 'Les ancêtres de Samori' in *Cahiers d'Etudes africaines*, Paris, no. 13 (1963). English translation in McEwan, *Africa from early times to 1800*, O.U.P., 1967.

Y. Person, 'La Jeunesse de Samori' in *Revue française d'Histoire d'Outre Mer*, Paris, 1962.

Y. Person, 'Samori et la Sierra Leone' in *Cahiers d'Etudes africaines*, Paris no. 25, 1967.

There is an overall account of his career in my essay 'Samori, and resistance to the French', in Rotberg and Mazrui, *Black Protest*, Oxford, 1970.

For Samori's links with Islam:
Y. Person, 'Samori and Islam', in R. Willis (ed.) *Studies in the History of Islam in West Africa*, London, to be published in 1970.

DAVID ROSS

Dahomey

In the years immediately preceding the French Conquest the West
African kingdom of Dahomey occupied the southern third of what
is today the republic of Dahomey. The eastern boundary of the state
followed the course of the River Ouémé while the western boundary
lay along the River Cuffo. The northern frontier ran between the two
rivers, beyond the northern centre of Atcheribé, while on the coast
Dahomey's territory stretched from just east of Grande Popo to a
little east of Cotonou. The core of the kingdom lay on the interior
plateau surrounding the capital, Abomey. This plateau was separated
from the coast by a broad swamp, the Lama, which was difficult to
cross even in the dry season. The easiest route from Abomey to the
coast was not by direct overland trek but via the River Ouémé.

Dahomey had emerged in the seventeenth century and had developed as the rulers of Abomey extended their sway over the princi-
palities of the plateau. In the second decade of the eighteenth
century Dahomey conquered Allada and Whydah, the two kingdoms
which lay to the south of the plateau, between the Lama and the
coast. After the conquest the Dahomans gradually built up a
provincial administrative system through which they governed
Allada and Whydah. In the nineteenth century the Dahomans
expanded eastwards and set up similar administrations over the
districts of Cotonou and Agony. The inhabitants of all these territories spoke the same language and shared many of the same
traditions as the people of the plateau and long before the end of the

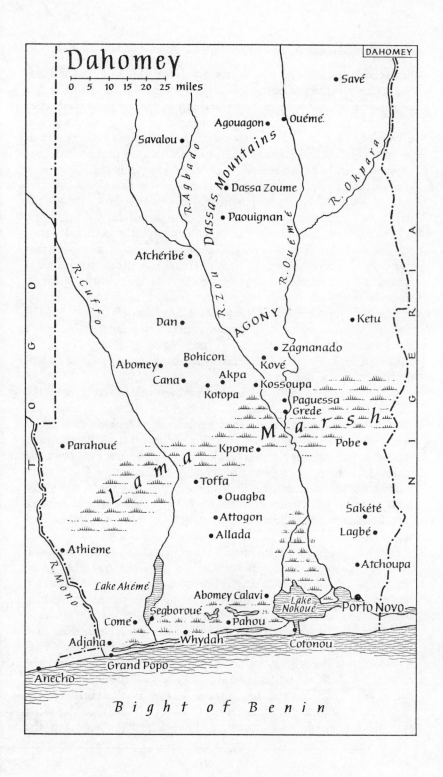

Dahomey

0 5 10 15 20 25 miles

Savé

Agouagon   Ouémé.

Savalou

Dassas Mountains

Dassa Zoume

Paouignan

R. Agbado

R. Okpara

Atchéribé

R. Zou

R. Ouémé

AGONY

Dan

Ketu

Zagnanado

Abomey   Bohicon   Kové

Cana   Akpa   Kossoupa

Kotopa   Paguessa

Grede

M   a   r   s   h

Parahoué   Kpome   Pobe

L   a   m   a

Toffa

Ouagba   Sakété

Attogon   Lagbé

Allada

Athieme   Atchoupa

R. Cuffo

R. Mono

T   O   G   O

N   I   G   E   R   I   A

Lake Ahémé

Abomey Calavi

Segboroué   *Lake Nokoué*

Comé   Pahou   Porto Novo

Adjaha   Whydah   Cotonou

Grand Popo

Anecho

B i g h t   o f   B e n i n

nineteenth century the whole area had been welded into one state.

To the Fon, the people of Dahomey, their state was not only a a territorial unit, it was also a spiritual entity. The notion of Dahomey as a semi-sacred concept had developed as the state grew and expanded. Out of the various triumphs and vicissitudes of their history, the Fon had evolved an ethos by which the preservation, the expansion and the glorification of their kingdom had become a sacred trust, passed on from generation to generation. Dahomey had become a spiritual force which incorporated all the Fon people—the living, the dead and even the unborn. The sacred duty of the living was to perform the various rites which ensured the perpetuation of the Fon world and to pass on to their descendants, intact, the kingdom which they themselves had inherited from their ancestors. It was this determination which gave the Fon people the spirit to resist attempts to modify their institutions or seize their territory.

The development of Dahomey had been closely related to the growth of trade with the Europeans, and by the nineteenth century both the upkeep of the elaborate, expensive court in Abomey and of the proportionally large Fon army were, to a large degree, dependent on the profits of that trade.

Before the 1840s trade had been almost entirely in slaves: after the 1860s it was largely in palm oil. By the 1880s the new trade was carried on mainly, although not exclusively, through two major ports. The older of these, Whydah, which lay on the coastal lagoon at nearly the mid-point of the Dahoman sea-board, had been the major Dahoman slave-exporting centre. Its economic importance had, however, declined after the ending of the slave trade, and Cotonou, which lay between the sea and Lake Nokoué in the extreme east, had emerged as the most important Dahoman palm-oil exporting port.

Much of the palm oil produced on the plantations of the Dahoman interior was sent via the River Ouémé to Cotonou. This river, since it provided the only easy route from the coast to the plateau, had always been of great strategic importance. In the second half of the nineteenth century it gained economic importance as well. That so many vital interests were centred on a vulnerable border area posed something of a political problem for the Fon; they had, however, by the 1870s, resolved this difficulty by bringing the district more closely under central supervision. Dahoman control of the eastern marches was made more secure by the creation of a new administrative unit centred on Cotonou. Control of the other side of the border was maintained by loosely supervising the affairs of the petty state of Porto Novo—a kingdom which had been tributary to Dahomey since the 1820s. Fon interests in the Cotonou–Ouémé–Porto Novo area at the end of the 1870s seemed well guarded and perfectly safe.[1]

In the 1870s Franco–Dahoman contacts were mainly confined to trading matters and were, on the whole, fairly amicable.[2] During the 1880s, however, tension started to mount as the French began to demand that the port of Cotonou be handed over to them. The French claimed, and the Fon denied, that the town had been ceded to them in trading treaties made in 1868 and 1878. In fact the clauses concerning Cotonou, in these treaties, had been forged by French merchants.

Franco–Dahoman hostility was aggravated by the fact that Porto Novo became involved in the dispute. In the early 1880s this kingdom had obtained French protection and in 1888, relying on the security afforded by this new relationship, had repudiated Dahoman suzerainty. By 1889, in fact, French activities were rapidly undermining Dahoman political influence in an area of the utmost economic and strategic importance.

In November 1889 the French sent the Lieutenant Governor of the Rivières du Sud, Dr. Jean Bayol, a fanatical, and often impetuous, advocate of French overseas expansion, to the Slave Coast to try to settle the problems of the area in a manner favourable to France. The Lieutenant Governor travelled to Abomey in November 1889 and in an interview with Prince Kondo, the Vi-Daho or Crown Prince, demanded that Dahomey should immediately fulfil her treaty obligations and hand over Cotonou. Kondo replied that Dahomey had never ceded Cotonou and had no intention whatsoever of doing so. Bayol, realising that further negotiations were pointless, on the 22 February 1890 ordered that Cotonou should be occupied and that its Fon administrators should be placed under arrest. His excuse for this, that the Fon were planning to attack French installations and were already holding a group of Whydah merchants prisoner, was totally unjustified. Bayol's action meant that the dispute between France and Dahomey had erupted into war.[3]

The Fon national leader at this critical juncture was King Behanzin, the former Vi-Daho Kondo, who had succeeded to the throne in December 1889. The new king was not as powerful as former rulers had been; a series of political crises had weakened the Dahoman monarchy and by 1890 the King was only one, albeit the most important, of a number of powerful leaders. The diminished political status of the monarch, however, made no difference to the determination of the Fon to defend Dahomey's territorial integrity. As soon as the seizure of Cotonou became known the machinery for mobilising the Dahoman army went into operation.

The Fon army in 1890 was a complicated organisation whose composition faithfully reflected the manner in which the force had developed as Dahomey grew. In theory all free men were liable to military service; in practice the men of the 'older' areas had a more important role in the armed forces than did those from areas which had been incorporated at a later date. A general levy was only undertaken before a major campaign; routine duties were undertaken by the 2,000 to 3,000 men who were levied on the Aboman plateau. These men were raised, like the levies from other parts of the country, by the chiefs bringing in their family and followers to serve in the army. On the plateau region most of the soldiers belonged to contingents raised either by the great dignitaries or by the King. They were therefore the groups most dedicated to, and most involved in, the concept of 'Dahomey'.

By the end of the nineteenth century these soldiers appear to have been in arms all the year round. They not only always took part in the annual campaign, but were also involved in the nearly continuous round of court ceremonial in Abomey. In the 1880s, moreover, about half of their total number were stationed semi-permanently in the province of Agony, where they had the duty of keeping watch on what was, at that time, the most vulnerable and dangerous Dahoman frontier. Possibly soldiers from the capital and its immediate hinterland, who could live at home and take part in the normal life of their community, undertook more of the routine military duties in Abomey than did their comrades from further afield; it may be too that these soldiers from beyond Abomey worked on a rota system whereby only a percentage of their number had to be in the capital at a given time.[4] Nevertheless by the 1880s it does appear that there were always a large number of soldiers from the plateau under arms, and that even if these units were not always fully staffed they were always in existence and could, in an emergency, be quickly brought up to their full quota. In fact, as a result of the nearly continuous Yoruba wars of the second half of the nineteenth century, the levies from the plateau had taken on the most important characteristics of a regular army.[5]

By the 1880s a substantial part of the Dahoman army was made up of female soldiers—the famous Amazons. In the eighteenth century the Dahoman Kings had, in emergencies, enlisted some of their wives as soldiers. It was, however, only in the early nineteenth century

'The white man brings his cannon to the bush' — Hausa artillerymen moving guns across the Pra in the 1874 campaign

Sultan Ahmadou, ruler of
the Tukulor empire

A Tukulor
cavalryman

Mahmadou Lamine's forces attack a French square at Kagnibé:
this demonstrates clearly the differences in weapons used by
African and French armies

Dignity even at the point of death: the execution of Soybou,
son of Mahmadou Lamine. 'Remercie le Colonel de me tuer avec
ses fusils et de ne pas me rendre indigne du séjour d'Allah'

The Almami Samory

The French Military Mission received by the Almami Samory

General Dodds, the Franco-Senegalese
conqueror of Dahomey

An Amazon warrior: the Amazons were
among the mainstay of the Dahomeyan army

Behanzin, King of Dahomey, shortly after his surrender to the French

Bai Bureh shortly after his capture

Nana Olomu in exile
c. 1896

Ilorin cavalry charging the British square on the eve of the
conquest of the Ilorin by the British

A survivor of the Fulani-British wars

Brevet-Major Cunningham

Lieutenant J. A. Burdon

Major A. J. Arnold

that the system became institutionalised. The Amazons became a permanent part of the royal forces as a result of the fact that after a dynastic revolution in 1818 the usurping monarch, King Gezo (1818–58), felt his position to be so insecure that he created from amongst the women of his palace a permanent body of soldiers who would defend him in any civil conflict. At this time the Amazons' personal loyalty to the ruler was assured by the fact that only young non-Dahoman captive girls were selected as members of the corps. After Gezo's death, however, this selection policy broke down and Amazon officers were recruited even from the important Dahoman families. They were therefore as heavily involved in Dahoman politics as were their male counterparts.

In the last decades of the nineteenth century the Amazons no longer satisfactorily fulfilled their role as the monarch's civil guard. They had, however, developed into one of the most important units in the Dahoman army. They probably first became involved in Dahomey's foreign wars in the 1840s, when the first of the major Fon wars with the Egba necessitated the employment of every available soldier. The Amazons soon became the most warlike, and the most feared, of all the Dahoman troops. It was they who bore the brunt of the fighting in a number of the most important of the nineteenth-century Dahoman wars. It was they who tended to suffer most severely when the Fon either won a Phyrric victory or sustained a costly defeat. During the most desperately fought of all Fon wars, the struggle against the French, their losses were so severe that as a fighting force they were completely destroyed.

These female soldiers had all the privileges of important royal wives: they lived in the royal palaces; they had their food prepared for them; anyone who met them on the roads had to make way for them. They had also to obey the regulations which governed the lives of the King's wives. The most onerous of these was that, although they obviously could only enjoy the favours of their royal spouse infrequently, they were forbidden any relations with other men. Any deviation from this rule was punishable by death. No doubt this enforced state of chastity does a good deal towards explaining their ferocity.

During the course of the nineteenth century, then, there had evolved in Dahomey two military organisations, the regular male group and the Amazon corps, which taken together can reasonably be called a 'standing' army. They in fact formed an élite body whose equipping and maintenance depended on the profits of overseas trade. It was this standing army which operated alone in under-

taking the obligatory annual campaign,[6] in fulfilling routine ceremonial tasks and in undertaking the duty of guarding vulnerable
frontiers.

When a major campaign was contemplated the traditional concept
of a levy of the whole free male population was put into operation
and a call was sent out for a general mobilisation. In the areas of
Dahomey which had a fully organised provincial administration,
Whydah, Cotonou, Allada, and Agony, the levy was conducted by
the provincial governor—the Yeovogun of Whydah, the Yeovogun
of Cotonou, the Apologun of Allada and the Fiogbé of Agony.
These governors, who did not go to war themselves, were responsible both for raising the men of their provinces and for dispatching
them to rendezvous with the other levies. The contingents from the
south (Whydah, Cotonou and Allada) met at Allada and then
proceeded to Cana where they joined the men from the north.
Men from areas beyond the plateau not under a regular provincial
administration seem to have been dispatched by their local authorites
directly to the King in Cana.

At a local level, recruitment appears to have been undertaken in a
similar manner throughout the kingdom. When the call went out,
the local authorities brought their followers either to the provincial
or central rendezvous. Recruitment in the 'older' areas of Dahomey
was different, in that the 'local authorites' tended to be the highest
dignitaries in the land, while their followers, in the period immediately before the French wars, were permanently in arms. The loyalty
of the men of the plateau to the ideal of Dahomey could be relied
upon absolutely; that of the men from some of the other provinces
may have been somewhat more suspect; the levies from Agony, an
area which was only finally incorporated into Dahomey in the 1880s,
had a reputation for running away from battle. All of the contingents
raised by general levy seem to have been placed under the control of
the leaders of the royal army, and all of them became part of an
organisation which was simply an extension of that army.

Before the eighteenth- and nineteenth-century expansion of the
kingdom the Dahoman military high command seems to have
consisted of the Abomey civilian dignitaries operating in a military
capacity—as each great chief in peacetime had civilian responsi-
bilities, so in time of war he had military duties. The military
hierarchy nevertheless did not exactly duplicate the civilian order; an
extraneous element was present in that the Gaou, a chief who had no
civilian duties, was commander-in-chief of the army and on campaign held a position superior even to that of the King. Presumably

matters were thus arranged so that failure in war should not discredit the bureaucrat-officers and make it difficult for them to fulfil their civilian duties.

With the growth and development of Dahomey, the system of command underwent a series of modifications which tended to further separate the conduct of military and civil affairs. The position of the King, and perhaps other of the leading state dignitaries, underwent something of a change. After the reign of King Tegbessou (1740–74) the monarch, although he continued to accompany the army on campaign, did not take part in the actual fighting. The Megan and the Mehou, the most important men in the kingdom after the monarch, probably also ceased to fight. The business of governing Dahomey had become too complex to permit that the most important Fon leaders should risk their lives in battle. It seems more than likely that as the forces raised on the plateau developed into a standing army, substitutes fulfilled the active military duties of the greatest chiefs.

The tendency to specialisation was increased by the creation of provincial administrations which brought into being a group of high administrative officials, the provincial governors, who had nothing to do with war at all. On the other hand the development of the Amazon force and the creation, in the reign of the usurper Gezo, of princely deputies to all the great chiefs,* greatly increased the number of chiefs concerned only with war. This increasing specialisation of function did not however lead to the growth of military cliques or a loss of civilian control over the army. The preliminary decisions, where and when to attack, were taken by the whole Fon political class, including the military chiefs, when assembled in Abomey for the great festivals—the Dahoman customs. Later tactical decisions were taken, it seems, by the King, together with the military chiefs and bureaucrat-officers who went on campaign. Leadership in the field was all that was delegated to the military chiefs.

The Fon army was traditionally viewed as an arc formation divided into right and left wings—the officers and divisions of the right wing ranking higher than those of the left; this conception was similar to that existing in civilian affairs where an official who stood at the right hand of the King was superior to one who stood at the left. The Dahoman army campaigned and fought in four groups formed by dividing both right and left wings into two parts. The Megan, as chief dignitary on the right hand of the King, was in

* The creation of these deputies was necessitated by the growing power of the royal family.

charge of the right wing of the male army, and in theory, although probably not in practice, was the leader of the right division of the right wing in battle. The leader of the left division of the right wing, the Gaou, was the Megan's subordinate but was nevertheless in battle commander-in-chief of the army as a whole. On the left wing the position of officer in charge and leader of the left division was occupied by the Mehou. The leader of the right division of the left wing in battle, and second in command in the field to the Gaou, was the Kposu. These two officers were of course the two leading military chiefs.

The four divisions which made up the male army were each divided into a series of units which, with respect to accoutrements at least, had often more in common with sections of the other divisions than with each other. Presumably these units were either the contingents, or subdivisions of the contingents, out of which the army was formed. It may be, indeed, that the division into right and left, which characterised the higher echelons of state, was reproduced down the chain of command and that each group was divided into right and left in relationship to the chief who raised it. If this was the case, the division must have ended at the level of the Aoungan, the war-chiefs of the villages, who acted as the lowest ranking of the officers, and who commanded the men of their locality. At any rate, every Aoungan must have known his place in the division.

The organisation of the Amazon force exactly duplicated that of the male, the she-Megan, an official known as the Gundeme, was in charge of the right wing, while the she-Mehou, the Yewa, was in charge of the left wing; it remains doubtful if these personages even accompanied the army on campaign. In battle the left division of the Amazon right was led by the she-Gaou, the Khetungan, and the right wing of the Amazon left by the she-Kposu, the Akpadume. Since there were only four divisions in the Dahoman military formation, the Amazon force, rather than functioning as a unit on its own, must on campaign have been split up, with each of its four groups fighting alongside the equivalent male body to form one major division. Only the veteran Amazon group which formed the King's body-guard and remained with him during a battle, two miles behind the front, seems to have remained outside this formation.

Long before embarking on a campaign the Fon undertook a series of elaborate ritual preparations including the sending out of spy-magicians, and the consultation of the oracles.[7] These completed, and war decided on, the army left Cana and marched towards its objective. The majority of the soldiers of the standing army carried, in 1889, as their most important weapon, a flint-lock rifle or carbine. Some detachments, however, instead bore 'nursey rhyme' blunder-busses or bows and arrows. Besides these arms, soldiers of the standing army always carried short swords to be used in close fighting. In 1891, after a series of arms deals with the Germans, at least half of the flint-lock rifles used by the soldiers of the standing army appear to have been replaced by rapid-firing rifles, while bows and arrows were dispensed with altogether. In terms of equipment the Fon in the latter half of the nineteenth century appear to have fallen behind their enemies the Yoruba, many of whom in the early 1880s possessed rapid-firing guns.*

The monarch provided the standing army with weapons and ammunition. The provincial troops had to supply their own arms and consequently their weapons were often of an inferior type—on occasion indeed some of them appear to have wielded only machetes. After 1891, however, most of these provincial soldiers seem to have been provided with flint-lock rifles—presumably those no longer required by the standing army.

The various guns used by the Dahomans were all imported; many of them were, however, repaired and reconditioned by local blacksmiths—who also produced swords and ammunition. Powder, like guns, was always imported. Ammunition was, however, only occasionally brought in from abroad; normally it consisted of bolts of bar-iron. The only large purchase of European ammunition seems to have been made in 1891 when the Fon were re-equipping their army after the first French attack.†

The Fon soldier had to carry his own food as well as his own arms and ammunition. Normally he carried just enough to last a fortnight: on a lengthy campaign the army had, of necessity, to live off the land. During a long seige, or a protracted confrontation, crops would be both planted and harvested. If the campaign were waged in or near Dahomey food could often be bought from the local inhabitants or brought to the front line from the interior.

The Dahoman army marched towards its objective in its formal four-division formation. It is probable, although by no means certain, that it also fought in this formation. If it did so, the divisions must, at various times, have been grouped together to form different combinations. In an attack on the Yoruba city of Abeokuta, in 1851, the Dahomans fought in two sections; in another attack on that

* See Robert Smith's chapter on Ijebu.
† On this re-equipping of the army see p. 158.

city in 1864 they fought in three bodies. Unfortunately, since the French were never able to distinguish a pattern underlying the flux created by battle conditions, it is impossible to determine how the Fon operated during their last campaign. Presumably their four-division structure was sufficiently flexible to allow them to produce a combination appropriate to the situation in which they found themselves.

No matter in what way the army as a whole operated, individual units always fought in the same fashion. When a section was advancing to the attack, groups of soldiers would rush to the front, discharge their weapons and retire—thus making way for their comrades to fire. This procedure was necessitated by the fact that the flint-lock rifles and carbines, used by the Fon, took at least three minutes to load. Even after they had bought nearly 2,000 rapid-firing rifles in 1891 they appear to have continued to operate in the same manner. The Dahoman battle line therefore appeared to be in a constant state of ebb and flow. When in battle the Dahomans, in order to avoid recoil, usually fired their weapons either from the hip or from at arm's length—this procedure hardly mattered to those soldiers who wielded blunderbusses, but it must have severely limited the accuracy of those who used rifles.

In spite of the fact that the core of the Dahoman army, the 'standing' army, was almost always under arms, the Fon seem to have had no concept of rigorous battle training. Even a last-minute attempt, in 1891, to get a German trader, an ex-soldier, to demonstrate European techniques and drill was a complete failure. The energy of the warriors of the standing army, when not on campaign, was devoted to the undoubtedly complicated round of court ceremonial. Even demonstrations of attacking techniques employed against recalcitrant villages appear to have been more in the nature of ritual and ceremonial than examples of parade-ground training sessions.[8] There appears, in fact, to have been no attempt either to drill or to train in the best use of weapons. As a result, if its attacks did not succeed, or if it was itself taken by surprise, the Dahoman army tended to fall into confusion.

Most of the annual Fon pre-conquest wars were minor affairs undertaken by the standing army alone; such operations were a combination of punitive expedition and slave raid and took the form of surprise dawn attacks on border towns and villages.[9] The Dahoman procedure during a typical raid was to surround a town under the cover of darkness and then, at daybreak, to force an entry. The army's main aim was not to kill, but to capture as many people as possible. The Fon did not often, in the course of these raids, encounter any really serious resistance—the majority of the population, when the alarm was given, usually seem to have managed to flee into the bush. After the Dahomans had departed with their prisoners they usually returned to rebuild their village; more often than not they would secure their political future by acknowledging Dahoman suzerainty. This was certainly not all-out warfare. Only in areas where the Dahoman vied with some other major power for sovereignty did real devastation take place.

In the fifty years before the French conquest even the full-scale wars undertaken by the Fon tended to follow the pattern of the punitive raid. Although the wars were sometimes long, the actual campaigns fought by the Fon tended to be short. The most important of these wars culminated in desperate attacks on two large Yoruba towns—on Abeokuta in 1851 and 1864, and on Ketu in 1883 and 1885. The Fon conducted each of these operations as large scale punitive raids. The attacks on Abeokuta ended in disaster, basically because such tactics were useless against a distant, populous, determinedly defended city. In dealing with Ketu the Fon were more successful; Ketu, although ancient, was fairly small and had become isolated in the turbulent politics of nineteenth-century Yorubaland. Even so, the Fon were only able to sack the town in 1883 because the main part of the Ketu army was on campaign elsewhere. They were, moreover, able to destroy finally their weakened enemy in 1885 only after a protracted seige and a treacherous promise of peace.[10]

For the Fon, the main feature of a major war, even in the latter part of the nineteenth century, remained an attack on a city. In fact, the Dahomans always appear to have avoided fighting pitched battles—presumably because their tradition of accretive town-taking did not prepare them for such conflicts. At any rate in the fifty years before the outbreak of war with France they were only involved in four major pitched battles. None of these were of their own making; all of them occurred when they were either advancing to, or retreating from, an attack on a city. They were decisively defeated in all of them.

In spite of the development of the standing army and in spite of the increase in the number of specialised war-chiefs, the Dahoman army appears to have remained, late in the nineteenth century, what it had been from its formation—an instrument for conquering and controlling border towns. It was a machine well suited to the political conditions of the eighteenth century when Dahomey formed part of the Oyo empire. It was still adequate in the early nineteenth century when the break-up of the Oyo empire enabled the Fon to extend their sway over many of the areas formerly protected by that empire. It was, however, unable to deal effectively with the armies of Oyo's large Yoruba successor states—states which seem to have inherited the basic Oyo military system.[11] Possibly the trouble was that, as a result of their town-taking tradition, Fon tactics provided for only one major attack. If that was beaten off, the Fon force became disorganised, had difficulty in re-grouping, and thus easily fell victim to a counter-attack.

In 1889, then, the Fon possessed a military system which was remarkable in its time and place for both its composition and methods of recruitment; that a state the size of Dahomey could in peacetime maintain a standing army of about 4,000 warriors, half of whom were women, and in an emergency field about 12,000 warriors, was no mean administrative achievement. Nevertheless Dahoman tactical organisation does not seem to have developed to a corresponding degree of sophistication. In the latter half of the nineteenth century the Fon were at a considerable disadvantage when dealing with the militarily more versatile Yoruba. They were at an even greater disadvantage when they had to face the disciplined army fielded by the French.[12]

When 360 French soldiers seized Cotonou on 22 February 1890 the Fon immediately tried to recapture the town. They where so determined that the French should not for long remain in control of Dahoman territory, that they did not take the time to assemble their whole army before counter-attacking. Instead on the 23rd, the day after the occupation of the port, the troops levied in the province of Cotonou hurled themselves against the hastily raised French defences. On 1 March a contingent consisting of the troops raised south of the Lama attacked. The standing army, which must have moved quickly, threw itself against the town three days later. In spite of the fact that in this last attack the Dahomans took the small French garrison by surprise, in what might be described as a classic exercise in Dahoman battle tactics, a dawn attack, the Fon found that they were quite unable to retake Cotonou.

Fon losses were considerable, especially in the third attack when they left 127 dead (including the she-Gaou) inside the French lines. After this final repulse the Fon moved a large section of their army to the Porto Novo area, where they concentrated upon raiding and destroying palm-oil plantations—presumably in the hope that economic pressure would force the French to sue for peace.

Bayol now wished to go on to occupy the whole Dahoman coastline and declared that the French would not encounter serious opposition if they did so. The French cabinet, however, did not accept the Lieutenant Governor's assurances on this score and ordered that French troops should advance no further. The ministers' reason for this decision was the knowledge that, although minor skirmishing would not affect their Parliamentary majority, involvement in a major campaign might. The Cabinet determined to take no risks and on 1 April recalled Jean Bayol. His successor was ordered to obtain an honourable peace as soon as possible. The French were determined to hold Cotonou, but for the time being were going to take no further aggressive action.

In spite of the change in French policy the fighting did not cease immediately. On 20 April a French force, operating in the hinterland of Porto Novo, encountered a Fon raiding party near the village of Atchoupa. Battle was joined and the Dahomans were driven from the field. Whether the Fon were forced to retreat, or whether they simply conducted a strategic withdrawal, remains a matter for conjecture. The French at any rate claimed a major victory.

Although the so-called battle of Atchoupa was the last military engagement of this war, peace-making was delayed until October. This was partly because of the obstructionist attitude of certain colonial officials, but also because a section of the Fon leadership, headed by the Yeovagun of Whydah, refused to accept any settlement which involved the loss of Cotonou. Behanzin was more realistic and when a well-liked Whydah missionary, Father Dorgère, was sent to Abomey with peace proposals, the King foiled a plot to ensure the outright rejection of the French offer. After long, hard negotiations a peace settlement was finally signed on 3 October.

By the terms of the settlement the French possession of Cotonou was recognised. It was accepted that the French flag was to fly there, that the French would levy customs and that French troops should garrison the town. The French had, however, to make an annual payment of 20,000 francs to the Fon, as compensation for their loss of revenue from the Cotonou customs. Dahoman pride was further placated by permission being given for the displaced Dahoman authorities to return to the town to look after the affairs of the Fon inhabitants. The Dahomans were thus able to claim that the people of Cotonou were still ruled by the Dahomans and were therefore not really alienated from the Fon state. This consideration was probably paramount when they agreed to make peace.[13]

As a result of the French Government's refusal to undertake a full-scale colonial war, the first Franco–Dahoman clash ended without Dahomey having been decisively defeated. Nevertheless the Fon army had proved unable to reoccupy one of Dahomey's own towns, even when it had taken the small defending garrison by surprise in a dawn attack. In retrospect, it is abundantly clear that if the Fon could not retake Cotonou under these favourable circumstances they could not hope to withstand a serious French attack.

At the beginning of their campaign, as the haphazard nature of their attacks on Cotonou showed, the Fon had thought that the expulsion of the French would be an easy matter. This fits in with later rueful admissions that they thought of the Europeans as traders, or sailors, who would not, or could not, fight. This illusion was destroyed by the events of the 1890 war when it was realised that the French were exceptionally powerful adversaries. The defeats of the 1890 war did not, however, produce a peace at any price movement. The only group in the Fon leadership which had deviated from the general line was one which refused to make peace at all. The realisation that the French were powerful adversaries did not alter the obligation to guard and preserve Dahomey. Indeed, in order better to protect their country, the Fon set about equipping their army with more efficient weapons. Between January 1891 and August 1892 they bought 1,700 rapid-firing rifles, six Krupp cannon of various bore, five machine-guns, 400,000 assorted cartridges and a large quantity of shell.[14] These they bought from German firms trading at Whydah. It is more than likely that they bought other armaments from Germans operating in Lome.

The Frenchmen favouring colonial expansion had not wished to end the war with Dahomey in October 1890, and, after the conclusion of peace, worked, in Parliament, to obtain support for its resumption. By November 1891 they had succeeded in converting a majority of the deputies to the view that a war against Dahomey was essential.[15] An excuse for resuming hostilities presented itself on 27 March (1892) when the Resident of Porto Novo was fired on by a body of Fon soldiers while he was making a trip up the River Ouémé in the gun boat *Topaz*. Since the vessel was well within Dahoman territory at the time, it is hardly surprising that a group of worried Fon soldiers, on their own initiative, fired on the boat. The Resident sent an alarmist report to Paris, stating that he feared the Fon were massing for an attack on French territory. Although he soon afterwards admitted that he had been mistaken, the French Government made the trivial *Topaz* incident their *casus belli*.[16]

Action was taken quickly. On 12 and 13 April Parliament voted credits of three million francs to be used for a war against Dahomey.

On 21 April it was decided to place the conduct of the war in the hands of the Ministry of Marine and to put Colonel Dodds, commander of the troops in Senegal, in command in Dahomey.

Dodds, who was himself a Senegalese of part African descent,* arrived in Cotonou on 20 May, bearing instructions to inflict upon the Fon a defeat severe enough to ensure that they would negotiate seriously with France; in other words, to reduce Dahomey to obedience. The Colonel advised that a severe blow to Dahomey could best be effected by a march on Abomey: he recommended that such an attack be made by way of the River Ouémé. The Government accepted Dodd's proposals and agreed to despatch to the Slave Coast the troops he considered necessary for such a campaign.

The French spent three months in assembling a 2,000-strong expeditionary force, and making Porto Novo into a suitable base for launching an attack on Dahomey. By the end of September everything was ready and Dodds proceeded to move his men by boat up the River Ouémé as far as Gbedé. In spite of the fact that the French tried to confuse the issue by sending, at the same time, a small force to operate in the Grande Popo area, the Fon realised immediately that an attack on Abomey was about to begin; they had known for generations that their capital was vulnerable from the coast only by way of the Ouémé. The whole Fon army, which until then had been divided into three parts, so as to be better able to guard the coast, was reunited and stationed on the direct route between the river and Abomey.

On 4 October the French began to march overland towards Abomey. They advanced via Paguessa, Kossoupa, Akpa and Kotopa and occupied Cana on 6 November. In little over a month the Dahoman army had been completely destroyed and the French were poised ready to occupy Abomey. On almost every day of that terrible month the Dahomans had tried to halt the progress of the invading column; in spite of the ferocity with which they fought, and, in spite of innumerable acts of personal bravery, they found that they could not stop the inexorable advance. They had no means whatsoever of dealing adequately with the sort of campaign waged by the French; their notion of warfare as a sporadic activity, culminating in a raid or a seige, left them completely unprepared for

* Alfred-Amedée Dodds (1842–1922). The son of a local administrator whose family originated in the Gambia, Dodds was born in St. Louis. Between 1871 and 1891 he gained considerable experience of colonial campaigning in Senegal and Indo–China.

the purposeful, steady, month-long advance of the well-equipped, well-disciplined French force.

The Fon found that their traditional approach, the surprise dawn attack, in this war employed against the various French camps, was even less successful than it had been against the Yoruba cities; French sentries were too well organised to be taken by surprise, while French fire-power was too concentrated and well directed for the Fon to get anywhere near the enemy lines. Dahoman attempts to use their natural advantage of manœuvre in the bush, both to harry and to strike unexpectedly at the invading column, had no better success. Fon defensive stands at natural and man-made hazards along the route, were also a total failure. A French bayonet charge, it was found, could drive the Fon from any defensive position— whether in a village, in dense bush or in hastily prepared trenches.

The French marched forward in a 'square' formation. They thus protected their more vulnerable sections and prevented any one unit being cut off from the main body. When moving through un-known country with unreliable guides this last consideration was of great importance—it was, in fact, more than likely that an isolated French unit could have been overwhelmed by the sheer weight of Fon numbers. Besides making sure that they would be neither divided nor taken by surprise, the invaders also, by building defensive staging posts and clearing roads to the Ouémé, made certain that their supply routes would not be interrupted.

The Fon lost numerous soldiers in every one of their attempts to halt the French; their practice of removing their dead from the field, however, prevented the French from assessing accurately even the number of soldiers who died on the battleground. There is, besides, no way of knowing how many died of wounds or of disease. It is certain, nevertheless, that losses in the ranks of the standing army were very heavy indeed; the Amazon corps was destroyed as a fighting force, while the male body suffered only slightly less severely. Casualties amongst the other troops were moreover by no means negligible. A contemporary French observer-administrator, whose estimates seem reasonable, worked out that about 2,000 Fon soldiers were killed while more than 3,000 were wounded.[17] The French lost ten officers and sixty-seven men.

Heavy casualties were not the only drain on Dahoman resources. During the second half of the campaign the army was dangerously short of provisions and the soldiers were on the verge of starvation. In a lengthy campaign the Fon normally relied on either being able to grow food or on being able to bring it from the interior. During this last campaign the steady French advance prevented the Dahomans from settling down to cultivate the soil. The Fon were, moreover, unable to collect food in the provinces which were unaffected by the French attack. This was because the successful French advance into the heartland of Dahomey had sparked off a revolt among the Yoruba slaves working on the Fon palm-oil plantations. These Yoruba seized the opportunity presented by the French invasion to rise against their former masters. Their sole object, it appears, was to get back to their homelands while they had the chance; on their way, however, they wreaked vengeance on their former captors, and, the Fon later claimed, during their passage through the country, did more damage and caused more distress than did the invading French army. The disorganisation they caused certainly prevented any food being sent to the army.

Losses in dead and wounded deprived the Dahomans of many of their most loyal soldiers; others were forced to return to their homes either to seek food or to protect their villages against marauding bands of ex-slaves. Those who remained in the field were weakened by hunger and many of them fell victim to an outbreak of smallpox— a disease which had on many previous occasions ravaged the Dahoman army. Altogether it is hardly surprising that the casualty stricken, semi-starving, disease-ridden, demoralised force began to fall to pieces even before the French occupied Cana. In the final battle Behanzin was, it seems, in order to make up his army's diminished numbers, forced to recruit into its ranks criminals from the jails of Abomey. Even this last desperate gamble was of no avail. The Dahomans were defeated yet again. After the occupation of Cana it became obvious that what was left of the army could no longer put up even a token resistance.

The French victory represented a triumph of order, discipline and planning. This is not to say that French weapons were not of a higher calibre than those used by the Fon. They were both better and more numerous. Nevertheless it remains true that the Fon did not make effective use of the powerful weapons they had brought from the Germans in 1891; bullets from their rapid-firing rifles tended to speed high over the heads of the French troops, while shells from their cannons and howitzers, although accurately aimed, under the direction of two Whydah mulattos,* more often than not, failed to explode.

* These were not the only non-Dahomans involved in the Fon campaign. The French captured, and summarily executed, four Europeans, three Belgians and a German. These were claimed to be engineers, may have been traders, but were probably instructors.

The Fon showed themselves both courageous and persistent, but they lacked the disciplined organisation, which might have enabled them either to have stood against the French, or, at least to have retired in good order. Even with six times as many soldiers as the French, the Fon were never able to advance to the attack through the steady hail of French bullets; neither were they themselves capable of keeping up an equally continuous fire when the French moved against them. They could never, moreover, stand firm when confronted by the undoubtedly terrifying spectacle of a disciplined bayonet charge. Only if they had caught the invading force off-guard, would they in fact have had any chance of destroying it. The superb leadership of Colonel Dodds, who made certain that his force was never taken by surprise, never divided and, above all, never cut off from its base, ensured that no such eventuality transpired.[18]

With his army crushed and his country the prey of marauding bands of ex-slaves, Behanzin had little choice but to sue for peace. It was the only way to save anything of Dahomey. The King therefore sent messengers to Dodds, offering to open negotiations. Behanzin seems to have anticipated that Dahomey would have to cede her coastal provinces and would have to pay tribute to France. Probably it was expected that Dahomey's relationship with France would be similar to Dahomey's eighteenth-century links with Oyo. At that time Dahomey had been allowed to continue functioning as a state, but had had to pay annual tribute and acknowledge Oyo suzerainty.

Dodds told the messengers that to obtain peace, the Fon would have to hand over to the French both a large sum of money and all the arms which they had bought from the Germans. The Fon, thinking, presumably, that this was simply a token demand, agreed, and as an indication that they were willing to submit, handed over a number of their weapons. In all probability, they would have found it impossible, at that time, to gather together all their guns. They certainly had no cash with which to make an immediate money payment. The Dahoman leaders seem to have considered that their gesture made their state tributary to France.

The French, of course, had no idea of demanding tribute and simply wanted to deprive the Fon of an opportunity of again taking up arms against them. When it proved that their demands were not going to be met in full, the French resumed their march on Abomey. They entered the capital on 18 November 1892: Behanzin and his followers, after having first burned large sections of the royal enclosures, fled northwards.

With Abomey occupied, the expeditionary force was thought to have completed its task. The French expected that having lost his capital, Behanzin would submit to any demands they might choose to make. If he did not submit unconditionally they hoped that the Fon would rise against him and put in his place someone with whom they could deal more easily. Behanzin, however, declined to submit and the Fon showed no intentions of replacing him. In the vain hope that it might encourage the Dahomans to depose their king and submit to the French, Dodds, on 3 December issued a Proclamation deposing Behanzin. What the French could not admit was that it was not only the King but the whole Dahoman people who were committed to resistance.

Illness amongst the troops and the impossibility of using the Ouémé route to Abomey in the dry season made the French wish to end operations as quickly as possible. Dodds, now promoted to the rank of general, left Abomey for Porto Novo on 30 November. The Abomey expeditionary force was dissolved on 1 December and only four posts manned by French troops were left north of the Lama. The French were in fact still convinced that if they waited long enough the Fon would be bound to submit unconditionally.

Once they had withdrawn the greater part of their forces from the plateau, the French proceeded to occupy the lands of the old kingdoms of Whydah and Allada. Bereft of their fighting men and surrounded by French troops, the peoples of these territories made no attempt to resist. The Fon realised that it was impossible to preserve these lands and concentrated on maintaining Dahomey north of the Lama.

After the capture of Abomey, Behanzin and his followers withdrew to Atcheribé in the northernmost part of Dahomey. Once established there, the King began to reorganise his shattered forces. Atcheribé was in fact a fine base for the fugitive king, since it was far from any French post and had nevertheless a loyal Fon population. It had another advantage in that food supplies could easily be brought there from the fertile province of Agony.

The shattered Fon army gradually reassembled at Atcheribé, and Behanzin, by March 1893, was able to count on the support of 2,000 armed men. A start was even made on the recruitment of young girls to take the place of the fallen Amazons. Dahoman control was gradually reasserted over most of the Abomey plateau and armed bands of Fon warriors began to patrol regularly even the territory around the French posts. The resurgence of Dahoman power was so marked that the officers commanding the French posts began to fear that they might even be prevented from communicating with the French forces in the south.

These fears were, however, unfounded; the Fon took good care not to antagonise the French; in spite of the collapse of the Cana negotiations the Fon still appear to have hoped that, in return for an acknowledgement of their suzerainty and the payment of tribute, the French would retire south of the Lama and leave the Fon state in the north to its own devices. The withdrawal of the greater part of the French force from the interior must have encouraged this hope.

The Dahoman desire to be left in peace to rebuild their state was reflected in a series of peace negotiations undertaken in April 1893. During these the Fon again indicated that they were willing to cede the area south of the Lama, to accept a French protectorate and to hand over all their arms and ammunition. They would not, however, agree that Behanzin be deposed. The person of the King symbolised Dahomey itself; to accept that he be deposed would have been to agree that Dahomey not only became tributary to France but ceased to function as an independent entity at all. This the Fon were not yet ready to concede.

The Dahoman refusal to accept French terms unconditionally and the persistence of Fon organisation convinced the French that another expedition would have to be undertaken against Dahomey. General Dodds, who had left the Slave Coast on 23 April 1893, returned on 30 August with instructions to see to the final pacification of the country. A new expeditionary force was formed and in September it was divided into three parts. The main body advanced through the heartland of Dahomey, while the other two sections, in order to prevent Behanzin escaping into English or German territory, operated on Dahomey's frontiers.

The Fon knew that they could not fight off another attack and continued to attempt to make peace. On 3 November, Fon messengers arrived in the French camp offering to hand over all their remaining arms and ammunition provided the King's title was respected. Dodds took no notice of what the messengers said and told them that if the Fon leaders wanted peace they would have to give themselves up. The French were now convinced that the only way to prevent a resurgence of Dahoman opposition was to take all the Fon leaders into custody. The Fon naturally understood the French demand in terms of their own traditions and seem to have thought that the French, as the price of peace, wanted a number of Fon dignitaries to be handed over for sacrifice. The Dahomans seem to have made up their minds that they would have to agree to this and on 6 and 8 November a number of Fon leaders gave themselves up.

The French now concentrated all their attention on the capture of Behanzin himself. They realised that the King's hold on the imagination of his people was so strong that they would never be able to control the country while he was at large. By 20 December, French forces had effectively occupied the whole of Northern Dahomey. Behanzin was unable to escape through the French lines to English or German territory and was reduced to the position of a fugitive fleeing, with an escort of only four or five men, from village to village. Time after time the King only avoided capture by the narrowest of margins; on each occasion he owed his escape to the loyalty of the people of the countryside. During this protracted man-hunt Behanzin was, in fact, fed, protected, sheltered and encouraged by the common people, whose fidelity frustrated all the efforts of the French to lay hands on his person. Behanzin's epic flight provides indeed, a saga as heroic and romantic as do the wanderings of the Young Pretender through the Scottish Highlands after Culloden.

While Behanzin was at large, the French took into their custody the majority of the Fon dignitaries. On finding that their lives were spared, and that they were well treated, these leaders seem to have begun to see some hope for the future. They began to believe that General Dodds was sincere when he proclaimed that France would be magnanimous and would change none of the institutions of the country.

As long as their king, the symbol of their nation, remained at liberty, the Fon seem to have felt that 'Dahomey', as a spiritual entity, continued to exist. It was, however, fairly obvious that Behanzin could not hold out for ever. The captive Fon leaders, seeing their country completely helpless and totally overrun by French troops, seem to have begun to see that further passive resistance was futile, and to think that perhaps something of Dahomey's heritage might be preserved by co-operation with the invader. The time for resistance was over; the period of collaboration had begun.

General Dodds was, by the beginning of 1894, determined to establish a puppet king who would rule Northern Dahomey under French supervision. He therefore began to take soundings amongst the captive Fon leaders as to which Dahoman dignitary would make a suitable replacement for Behanzin. The Fon leaders decided to co-operate with the General—probably because they hoped that, having appointed a new king, the French would at last withdraw south of the Lama and exert only some sort of remote control over the Abomey area.

On the advice of a number of members of the royal family, principal amongst whom was Prince Topa, the former Mehou, Dodds chose Prince Goutchile, a brother of Behanzin, as the next King of Dahomey. This prince, the former Gaou, was then designated king by the unanimous choice of the captive dignitaries. The French declared that they had ascertained that Goutchile should have become king in 1889 and that he had only been deprived of the crown by the intrigues of the war-mongering Behanzin. This was, of course, merely window-dressing.[19]

Whether or not Behanzin himself approved of these manœuvres remains something of a mystery. One authority considers that Behanzin concluded a blood pact with Goutchile and authorised him, at least temporarily, to take his place; it is certainly true that both men were still at large when the decision to crown Goutchile was taken. On the other hand, Prince Topa, Dodd's principal Fon adviser, had, before 1889, been Behanzin's principal dynastic rival, and may have taken this opportunity of settling old scores. One of the other princes has, moreover, recorded that although the captive dignitaries were told at the time that Behanzin approved of the election of Goutchile, they discovered soon afterwards that he did not. At any rate, whatever the background intrigues, the Fon leaders do seem to have felt that they would in future have to collaborate with France and that a new king, who had come to power with French support, would have more chance than Behanzin of preserving Dahoman traditions.[20]

After Goutchile had been chosen as king, Topa brought him to Dodds, and on 15 January the new king was presented to the people under the new name of Agoli-Agbo. On the 25th the King informed the General that he knew where Behanzin was hiding. A detachment of troops was then sent to the ex-king's place of concealment and Behanzin was persuaded to give himself up.

On 29 January Agoli-Agbo signed a treaty of protection with France. The kingdom of Dahomey was shorn of all territory south of the Lama, and the King, it was agreed, was to reign over the remainder with the guidance of a French Resident.[21] If the Fon had accepted a new king in the hope that the French would leave them to look after their own affairs, they were disappointed. French interference in Fon affairs, in fact, became progressively greater, until in 1900 the pretence of maintaining the Fon monarchy was abandoned.[22] Even the ghost of the Fon kingdom had finally been removed. The memory of the Fon kingdom was, however, kept alive in that in 1894 their conquerors gave the name Dahomey to their new colony.

ABBREVIATIONS USED IN NOTES

M.A.E.   Archives of Ministère des Affaires Etrangeres, Paris.
M.M.C.   Archives of Ministère de la Marine et des Colonies, in custody of Ministere de la France d'Outre mer, Paris.
E.D.   Études Dahoméénnes.

NOTES

1 For the eighteenth- and nineteenth-century history of Dahomey, see I. Akinjogbin, *Dahomey and its Neighbours 1708–1818,* Cambridge, 1967, and D. Ross, *The Autonomous Kingdom of Dahomey 1818–94.* Ph.D. London, 1967. Deductions about the role of the Dahoman army in the nineteenth century are based on the development of the Fon state as outlined in the latter work.

2 On the nineteenth-century trade and diplomatic background, see J. D. Hargreaves, *Prelude to the Partition of West Africa,* London, 1963, pp. 110–20 and pp. 201–14.

3 D. Ross, *op. cit.,* pp. 308–30. C. W. Newbury, *The Western Slave Coast and Its Rulers,* Oxford, 1961, pp. 128–9.

4 This at least is the impression given by a French observer. M.M.C. Dahomey III, 1 B. Bayol to Etienne, Porto Novo, 11 January 1890. Reproduced in part in J. Bayol. 'Les forces militaires du Dahomey, in *Revue Scientifique,* vol. XLIX, Paris, 1892.

5 The question of whether or not Dahomey had a standing army is one which has given rise to some controversy. A number of slaver authors claimed that Dahomey had, in the eighteenth century, a 'standing' or 'regular' army. While it seems clear however that the Kingdom's leaders all, in both the eighteenth and nineteenth centuries, mentioned an armed following, it also seems clear that the great majority of these followers were, for most of the year, engaged in non-military activities. The nineteenth-century visitors to Dahomey who made a detailed study of the Kingdom's institutions concluded that Dahomey did not in fact have a standing army, i.e. did not have a body of trained military men who always remained together and who were throughout the year ready to act as a military force.

W. J. Argyle, the only authority who seems to have studied both the eighteenth- and nineteenth-century literature, has concluded that Dahomey did not have a standing army, *The Fon of Dahomey* (Oxford 1966), pp. 81–9. I. A. Akinjogbin, on the other hand, in his account of eighteenth-century Dahomey, seems to have taken the works of the eighteenth-century slavers at their face value (*op. cit.*, p. 38). R. C. C. Law, in his study, 'Horses, firearms, and political power in pre-colonial West Africa', *Past and Present*, No. 72 (1976), p. 127, fn 81) seems to have done the same.

6 That the annual campaign was 'obligatory' is convincingly argued in W. J. Argyle, *op. cit.*, pp. 80–9.

7 W. J. Argyle, *op. cit.*, p. 83.

8 F. E. Forbes, *Dahomey and the Dahomans*, London, 1851, vol. II, pp. 122–7.

9 W. J. Argyle suggests that the elaborate precautions which the Fon took to avoid giving their intended victim advance warning of an impending attack may have been motivated by calculations of 'super-natural advantage'. W. J. Argyle, *op. cit.*, pp. 83–4.

10 European documentary sources indicate that Ketu was sacked in 1883 and destroyed in 1885. Works based on oral tradition give various other dates.

11 J. F. Ade Ajayi and R. Smith, *Yoruba Warfare in the 19th Century*, Cambridge, 1964, p. 13.

12 There is a great deal of tangled information on the Fon army in both published and unpublished sources. M.M.C. Dahomey V 6a and 10a. General Dodd's Reports on the Campaigns of 1892–3 and 1893–4. M.M.C. Dahomey III 2 Colonel Audeoud's Military Report, February 1891. Reproduced in *E.D.* IX pp. 115–19. Lieutenant Governor Bayol's Military Report, see p. 8 f.n.l. E. Dunglas. Articles in *E.D.*, vol. I, 1948, vol. II, 1949, vols. XIX and XX, 1957, vol. XXI, 1958. R. F. Burton, *A Mission to Gelele King of Dahomey*, London 1864, vol, I. pp. 200–30 and vol. II, pp. 63–85. R. F. Burton, *Abeokuta and the Cameroons Mountains*, vol. I, pp. 118–26. A. le Herissé, *L'ancient royaume du Dahomey*, Paris, 1911, pp. 58–72. M. J. Herskovits, *Dahomey: An Ancient West African Kingdom*, New York, 1938, vol. II, pp. 70–101. A. J. Skertchly, *Dahomey as It Is*, London, 1874, pp. 443–8.

13 M.M.C. Dahomey V 2a Commander Terrillon's Journal 7 February to 7 April 1890. J. Bayol, 'L'Attaque de Cotonou', *Révue Bleu*, Paris, 1892. M.A.E. Afrique, 126, Lieutenant-Colonel Terrillon to Governor of Senegal, Cotonou 26 and 31 March 1890. M.M.C. Dahomey I 3D Vice Admiral Cuverville to Marine 5 October 1890. A. de Salinis, *Le Protectorat Français sur la Côte des Esclaves*, Paris, 1908.
E.D. IX p. 101, Arrangement between France and Dahomey 3 October 1890.

14 A. L. D'Albeca, *La France au Dahomey*, Paris, 1895, Annex I p. 216. They purchased the following types of rifle: 300 Peabodys; 133 Winchesters; 648 Chassepots; 200 Albinis; 240 Sniders; 200 Spencers.

15 On the development of French Imperialism and its effect on Dahomey, see H. Brunschwig, *Mythes et Realités de L'Imperialisme Colonial Français 1871–1914*, Paris, 1960, London, 1966. M. Blanchard, 'Français

et Anglais au Niger, 1890–1898', *Le Monde Français,* 1948. F. Berge, 'Le Sous Sécretariat et les Sous Secretaires d'Etat aux Colonies,' *Revue d'Histoire d'Outre-Mer,* 1960. V. Campion-Vincent, 'L'Image du Dahomey dans la Presse Française (1870–95); Les Sacrifices Humaines.' *Cahiers d'Etudes Africaines,* No. 25, vol. VII, 1967.

16 M.M.C. Dahomey I 6D, Ballot to Ballay, Porto Novo 8 April 1892. M.M.C. Dahomey I 5A. Ballot to Under Secretary, Porto Novo 22 April and 8 May 1892.

17 A. L. D'Albeca, *op. cit.,* p. 103. E. Dunglas, working partly from oral sources, more than doubled these figures. Four thousand dead and more than eight thousand wounded would have put the whole army out of action. This does not seem to have been the case. *E.D.* XXI p. 82.

18 M.M.C. Dahomey V 6A, Dodds, Report on the Campaign of 1892–3. A. le Herissé, *op. cit.,* pp. 338–47. E. Dunglas, 'Contribution à l'Histoire du Moyen-Dahomey'. *E.D.:* vol. XXI, 1958. E. E. Aublet, *La Guerre au Dahomey 1888–93,* Paris, 1894. A. de Salinis, *La Marine au Dahomey,* Paris, 1911. J. de Riols, *La Guerre de Dahomey 1889–94,* Paris, 1893.

19 M.M.C. Dahomey V 10a, Dodds Report on the Campaign of 1893–4. M.M.C. Dahomey V 8a, Lambinet to Marine, Negotiations with Behanzin, March to May 1893. A. Le Herissé, *op. cit.,* pp. 347–52. E. Dunglas, 'Contribution à l'histoire du Moyen–Dahomey'. *E.D.,* vol., XIX, 1958. E. E. Aublet, *La Conquête du Dahomey,* Paris, 1895.

20 Information on Agoli-Agbo's accession can be found in the following: M.M.C. Dahomey V 10A, Dodds' report on the Campaign of 1893–4. A. Le Herissé, *op. cit.,* pp. 351–2. P. Hazoume, *Le Pacte de Sang au Dahomey,* Paris, 1937, pp. 36–8.

21 The events of the Conquest are recounted in two works by R. Corn-evin: *Histoire du Dahomey,* Paris, 1962, pp. 315–64 and 'Les Divers Episodes de la Lutte Contra la Royaume, d'Abomey' (1887–94) *Revue Français d'Histoire d'Outre-Mer,* vol. XLVII, 1960.

22 C. W. Newbury, 'A note on the Abomey Protectorate, *Africa,* vol. XXIV No. 2, April 1959.

ROBERT SMITH

Nigeria–Ijebu

Southern Yorubaland in the late nineteenth century

The attack launched from the British colony of Lagos against the capital of the Ijebu in May 1892 began the last phase in the long, often hesitant, expansion of that colony, opening the way to the rapid extension of British rule over the Yoruba country which soon became the Lagos Protectorate and in 1906 was merged with the former kingdom of Benin and territories to the east of the Niger in the Protectorate of Southern Nigeria. As a major event in the political history of Nigeria, the expedition has been examined in a number of studies which provide the background for the present attempt to assess the military aspects of this Anglo–Ijebu 'war'. To the British, the determined resistance of the Ijebu to the invasion came as a shock which forced them to revise their unflattering preconceptions of their adversaries and subjects-to-be, while for the Ijebu, and indeed for the Yoruba and Nigerians as a whole, the very fact of their resistance was, and perhaps still is, 'of great psychological significance'.[1]

Despite their common language (with its many dialects) and cultural affinities, the Yoruba were at this time still divided among a dozen or more major kingdoms, within which every town ruled by an oba was a kingdom in itself. Under the stress of internal disorder and attack from without by the warriors of the Hausa-Fulani jihad early in the century, Oyo, the largest and northernmost kingdom, had collapsed; although a new capital, also called Oyo, had been established on the edge of the southern forests, much of its former territory was ruled now by the military town and metropolis of Ibadan under the nominal suzerainty of the oba of Oyo, the Alafin. On the south-east was the small but ancient kingdom of Ife, revered as the centre from which, according to tradition, the Yoruba people and their rulers had all come—indeed, it has been said that the word 'Ife' would more properly be applied to the people of all the kingdoms than 'Yoruba', a word which originally described only the subjects of the Alafin. Eastwards from Ife lay the Ijesa, Ekiti and Owo kingdoms, the last marching with Benin. West of Oyo was Ketu, periodically ravaged and conquered by its Dahomean neighbours, while the south of the country was divided between the Egbado, Awori, Egba, Ijebu and Ondo.

The kingdom of the Ijebu[2] was of considerable antiquity and size. It was mentioned in a Portuguese description of the coast written in the early sixteenth century and the list of its principal kings, the Awujale, refers to forty-eight reigns. It extended from the river Ogun, which enters the lagoon to the north of Lagos, on the south-west, to the river Oni some seventy miles to the east, and from its boundary with the Egba and Ibadan on the north to the coast, a distance of some forty to fifty miles. For the most part this was a rolling countryside covered by high tropical forest, far denser then than today, and containing numerous fair-sized towns and very many villages. By contrast, the coastal region was a desolate, sparsely-inhabited wasteland of swamp and sand-dune, forming a long, narrow island which shut off the lagoon from the Atlantic. The capital was the centrally placed town of Ijebu Ode, the seat of the Awujale. Other important towns, also ruled by oba, were Ijebu Ife in the east and Ijebu Igbo and Ago Iwoye in the north. The western part of the kingdom was the land of the Ijebu Remo, a people who acknowledged the paramountcy of the Awujale at Ijebu Ode but in practice maintained a good deal of independence, especially during the nineteenth-century wars. Their capital was at Sagamu, a town founded only in 1872 when thirteen older towns decided to amalgamate for greater security. Among other Yoruba the Ijebu had the reputation of being a proud people, hostile to strangers;[3] they were also known as exceptionally keen traders, dealing primarily in slaves and textiles. Today their country seems to be the richest and most populous part of Nigeria's Western State, and its capital and other towns are distinguished by their many well-built 'storey' houses and Brazilian-style mansions.

The British presence in southern Yorubaland dated from the last days of 1851 when a naval force, after a fiercely contested landing

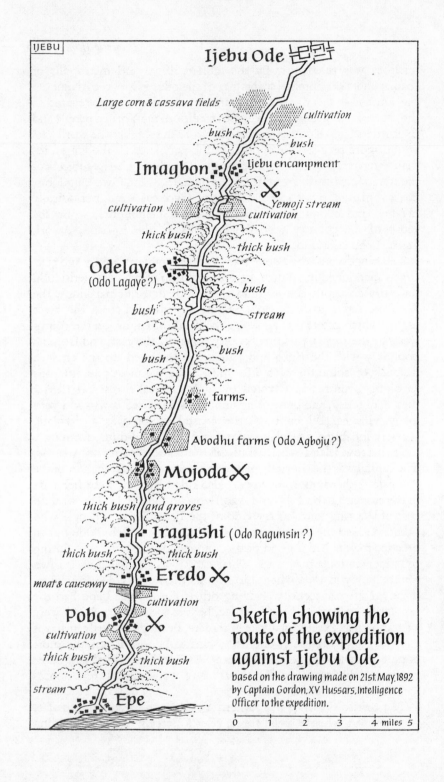

Ijebu Ode

Large corn & cassava fields

cultivation

bush

bush

Imagbon   Ijebu encampment

Yemoji stream

cultivation   cultivation

thick bush

thick bush

Odelaye
(Odo Lagaye?)

bush

bush   stream

bush

bush

farms.

Abodhu farms (Odo Agboju?)

Mojoda

thick bush and groves

Iragushi (Odo Ragunsin?)

thick bush   thick bush

Eredo

moat & causeway

cultivation

Pobo

cultivation

thick bush   thick bush

stream   Epe

Sketch showing the route of the expedition against Ijebu Ode

based on the drawing made on 21st May, 1892 by Captain Gordon, XV Hussars, Intelligence Officer to the expedition.

0   1   2   3   4 miles 5

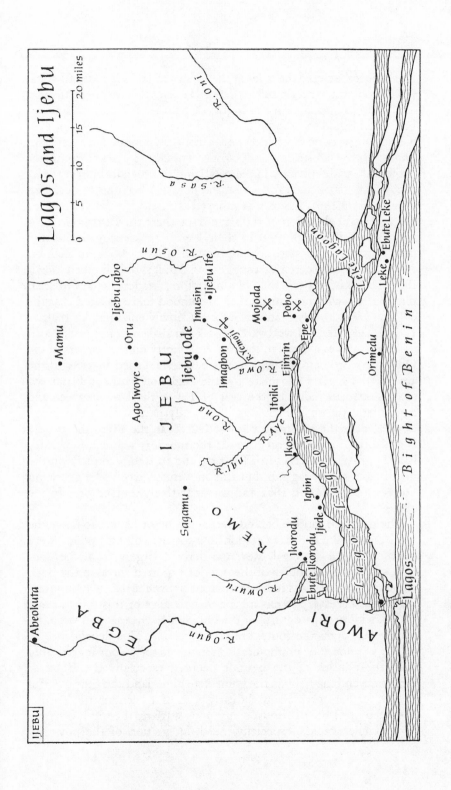

Lagos and Ijebu

IJEBU

20 miles
15
10
5
0

R. Oni

R. Sasa

R. Osun

Mamu

Ijebu Igbo

Oru

Ago Iwoye

I J E B U

Jjebu Ode

Imusin

Ijebu Ife

R. Yemoji

Imagbon

R. Owa

Mojoda

Pobo

Ejinrin

Epe

Lekki Lagoon

Leke

Ebute Leke

Orimedu

Bight of Benin

R. Ona

Itoiki

R. Aye

Ikosi

R. Ibu

R E M O

Sagamu

Igbin

Ijede

R. Oli

Ikorodu
Ebute Ikorodu

R. Owuru

E G B A

Abeokuta

R. Ogun

A W O R I

Lagos

from the sea, evicted the ruler of the small coastal kingdom of Lagos, Oba Kosoko, and reinstated his deposed uncle Akitoye on the throne. The British consulate for the Bights of Benin and Biafra, which had been established in 1849 with its headquarters on the island of Fernando Po, was now divided and a consul appointed to reside in Lagos with two main, and closely connected, tasks: to foster 'legitimate trade' (mainly in palm-oil) and to prevent the recrudescence of the slave trade for which the port had been notorious. Ten years later, in 1861, Lagos was annexed as a British colony. But after the successful abolition of the slave trade there the British Government showed little interest in their Yoruba possession during the next thirty years, despite the importance of its harbour; indeed, on several occasions there was a suggestion that it should be abandoned. But the activities of the administrators, traders and Christian missionaries who now made their livelihood there ensured that the colony was not only retained but even slowly enlarged, so that by 1890 it had extended westwards to take in Badagry (and briefly also Cotonou) and eastwards to the Itsekiri country on the borders of the Oil Rivers Protectorate which had been established in 1885 in the area of the former consulate for the Bight of Biafra; this narrow coastal strip included to the east of Lagos the land between the lagoon and the sea which was historically part of the Ijebu kingdom.[4] Under the administration of Glover in the 1860s the colony had also begun to extend towards the interior, acquiring territory in the Egbado hinterland of Badagry and in Remo country on the north bank of the lagoon, but this movement received a check on Glover's departure in 1872 and was tentatively revived only in the 1880s.

The principal motive behind the expansion of Lagos, so far as the local officials immediately responsible for the colony's policy were concerned, was financial. Revenue derived largely from the dues imposed on the products of the interior exported through the port, and if the territory was to be prosperous or even merely self-supporting it was necessary to ensure the maintenance of this transit trade from a wide area by control of the coastline to the east and west and by keeping open the routes from the interior. This dependence of Lagos on trade and communications involved the colony inextricably with the politics of the interior peoples, especially the Egba of Abeokuta and the Ijebu in the immediate hinterland and the powerful Ibadan further north. From the early years of the century the Yoruba had been in a state of almost continuous warfare, the result of many and complex causes, especially the disintegration of the powerful

Oyo kingdom and the attacks of the Hausa-Fulani from the north and the Dahomeans from the west. In 1886, as a result of initiatives by the Lagos authorities backed by the Christian missionaries, a peace settlement had been achieved over most of the country. But this was precarious and old animosities still smouldered. From the point of view of the colony the main issue now was the enmity towards the Ibadan of the Egba and Ijebu, whose alliance dated from mid-century. This enmity had led on many occasions to the closing by the allies of the 'roads' (really bush paths and tracks)[5] and rivers by which the Ibadan obtained their supplies, including guns and powder, from the coast and exported their own produce. Such action by the Egba and Ijebu caused an immediate drop in trade and a general increase in prices at Lagos. Thus most officials and traders there, both European and Lagosian, tended to sympathise with the Ibadan and to support them as far as they could; a third influential element, the missionary party, many of whom had seen in the Egba the hope for Christian progress in the interior, also pressed for the opening of the roads in the interests of evangelisation and 'legitimate trade'. But even when the roads were open, trade and travel were still subject to many vexations. Both the Ijebu and the Egba imposed tolls on all goods entering or leaving their countries, and regulated the trade in other ways. The Ijebu, in particular, insisted that foreign traders should do business only in their frontier markets established for this purpose: Ejinrin on the lagoon, where the Lagos trade centred, and Oru north of the capital, where the Ibadan dealt. They refused all requests for the removal of these restrictions and kept a strict check on all strangers on their roads.

The genesis of the war: 1889–March 1892

The Lagos requests to the Ijebu for direct trade can be traced, as Ayantuga has shown, as far back as 1859 when the British merchant (and later acting consul) McCoskry made the first recorded visit by a European to Ijebu Ode.[6] But the conclusion of the international agreements of the 1880s which 'partitioned' Africa, and in particular the agreement of 1889 by which the French and British governments settled their rivalries in West Africa by defining their spheres of interest, created a new situation. Commercial interests, expressed now not only through the traders of Lagos but also by the powerful Chambers of Commerce in England, began to press more vigorously than before for the opening of the routes through Yorubaland to direct trade and for an end to the intermittent blocking of trade in accordance with the shifts of war and politics in the interior. Though the Egba were at least equally to blame for these hindrances, it was the Ijebu who came to be seen as the principal obstacle to the achievement of British objectives, an assessment for which the Christian missionaries may bear the greatest responsibility[7] but which was enthusiastically supported by the local officials; Millson, the Assistant Colonial Secretary, reporting on a tour of the interior in 1890, wrote that 'The difficulties put in the way of the realisation of [this] prosperity alike for Lagos and the land of the Yoruba lie solely at the doors of the king and people of Jebu . . .'.[8]

In May 1891 Denton, the Acting Governor of Lagos, insisted on visiting Ijebu Ode for a discussion of trading matters. On arrival he asked that the roads should be opened to free and direct trade, and accompanied his request by an offer of financial compensation for the abolition of tolls. But the Ijebu maintained that trade should continue to be channelled through Ejinrin and Oru; they reinforced their stand by rejecting the customary presents which their visitor had offered and refusing him permission to pass through their territory to Abeokuta. Their action provided the British with the pretext they needed. The 'insult' to Denton was reported to the Colonial Office and in November, two months after the arrival of the energetic new governor, Carter, instructions reached Lagos from Whitehall that a full apology should be required from the Ijebu and that a treaty should then be made with them to secure 'free and unmolested' passage through their land for 'all traders and other persons'; if these conditions were refused, measures to ensure compliance were to be taken.[9]

Faced by a thirty-day ultimatum brought from Lagos to the Awujale by the Acting Inspector-General of Police in the colony, the Ijebu at last agreed to open negotiations. Their delegation arrived in Lagos in January 1892. After they had made apologies for their treatment of Denton they were told by Carter that their 'practice of compelling all produce to be sold in their own markets at their own price . . . was not the English idea of open roads'; '. . . the Queen did not want to take over an inch of their territory', but if they did not open the roads force would be used against them. They were next presented with an agreement providing for free trade in and passage through their country, and after pleading that they 'did not understand book' they allowed it to be signed on their behalf by two Ijebu residents of Lagos.

The validity of a treaty arrived at under these circumstances is doubtful,[10] but in any case it can hardly be held ever to have entered into operation. In February trouble broke out between the Ijebu and a party of Ibadan carriers sent by an Anglican missionary to collect the loads which he had left at Itoiki, an Ijebu port on the lagoon, on his way from Lagos to Ibadan. Both sides reacted strongly. The missionaries protested to the Lagos administration who passed on their reports to Whitehall, while at the end of the month the Ijebu and their allies, the Egba, again closed the roads, causing an almost immediate rise in the price of palm oil in England. Knutsford, the Colonial Secretary, was now 'worn down' (as Aderibigbe puts it)[11] by Carter's despatches about the iniquities of the Ijebu and Egba, by pressure from trading interests in England, and by the advice of his officials in the Colonial Office. On 18 March he telegraphed to Lagos his approval of decisive action being taken against the Ijebu, adding that this could be expected also to produce 'a good impression on the Egba'.[12]

The approach of war: April–May 1892

Preparations for mounting an expedition against Ijebu Ode were rapidly under way. Yet agreement on this step did not imply that the authorities in London and Lagos were of the same mind about the objectives of their action. The Colonial Office drew Carter's attention to a statement by the Secretary of State in the House of Commons that Her Majesty's Government had no intention of establishing a protectorate over the Ijebu, which would only be done 'on the special and earnest request of the people themselves'.[13] The politicians in London were adhering to the line that their only aim was to secure the opening of the roads. The administrators in Lagos showed more realism, and the Governor and his Executive Council were now pressing for the establishment of an Ijebu protectorate as the only means of ensuring uninterrupted trade.[14] Meanwhile there seems to have been no attempt to conceal either the military preparations or their immediate objective, and the colony at large was openly debating the issue. Among the traders, African and European, there was almost unanimous support for the administration's policy (of the Europeans only John Holt preferred the adoption of more peaceable measures).[15] The local press and official reports both suggest that this support was widespread among the population. A correspondent in the *Lagos Weekly Record*, signing himself 'K'Irede', asked 'how long must Christianity, Civilisation, and Commerce be hindered from having each its own scope and progress?' and 'were we in the hands of any other

European power, say France or Germany . . . where would our brethren the Egbas and Jebus have been?' On the other hand there was a small but vociferous element in the town which expressed sympathy with the Ijebu and opposition to the approaching 'trade war'; a leader of this group was the Anglican priest of Breadfruit Church, the Rev. James Johnson, described by Carter on a later occasion as a 'mischievous patriot'.[16]

The official view in Lagos was that the Ijebu would not put up much resistance. Carter had told the Colonial Office that he did not 'anticipate any difficulty from a military point of view' and he contrasted the 'pusillanimous Jebu' with the 'warlike Ibadans', adding that an important section of the Ijebu, the Remo, were anxious to escape from the yoke of Ijebu Ode and were well disposed towards his own government. He thought that the march to Ijebu Ode would not take more than two days and that the expedition would be absent from Lagos not longer than ten days.[17] His optimism, which in part reflected the pro-Ibadan sentiments of the colony, also stemmed from the desire to persuade the authorities in London to sanction military action. But in planning the expedition the Governor made a more cautious appraisal. Previous encounters over the last forty years between British or British-led forces and the southern Yoruba had shown that an invasion might meet stiff opposition,[18] and the forested terrain would be heavy going, especially after the beginning of the rains, usually in late April or May.

The force immediately available to the Lagos Government consisted only of the local Constabulary, the 'Lagos Hausa', whose numbers Carter had recently raised from 250 to 500.[19] Of these only some 150 could be spared to take part in the expedition, and the Colonial Office agreed with the Governor that reinforcements were needed. These were to consist of, first, an equal number of constables from the Gold Coast—the 'Gold Coast Hausas'[20]—and secondly a company from the West India Regiment stationed in Sierra Leone,[21] the Colonial Office having thought it 'safer that some regular forces should be engaged'. Permission was then obtained to add a number of Ibadan 'war boys' who had volunteered their help and who were to be used as either troops or carriers. The commander of this mixed force of Africans and West Indians was to be the Inspector-General of the Gold Coast Police, Colonel F. C. Scott, C.B., a veteran who had fought against the Ashanti eighteen years before[22] and was senior to Major Stanley, the Inspector-General in Lagos (in the event the latter was unable to accompany the expedition, being 'prostrated with gout'). In addition to the four officers already attached to these forces, seven Special Service officers from England were seconded to the expedition, one a cavalryman, another a gunner, and the rest infantry of the line.

The armament of the force was as heterogeneous as its composition. The Gold Coast constables were equipped with Martini-Henry rifles whereas their Lagos counterparts had Sniders.[23] The West Indians seem still to have been using Martini-Henry's rather than the Lee-Metfords now issued to regular British units.[24] The Ibadan auxiliaries were armed with 'trade guns', the majority of these being presumably the flint-lock muskets known on the coast as 'Dane guns', although a few may have had Sniders provided by their chiefs. The expedition was also allotted three seven-pounder guns,[25] one Maxim machine-gun,[26] two Nordenfelt machine-guns,[27] and three rocket troughs.[28]

Meanwhile the authorities at Ijebu Ode were well-apprised of the preparations at Lagos and were determined to defend their independence. There was a considerable Ijebu element in the population of Lagos and no shortage of agents there ready to report home on developments. But by no means all these Ijebu expatriates were in sympathy with the policy of defiance, and in April a delegation from this latter party visited the Awujale to counsel a more conciliatory attitude. The Ijebu responded only to the extent of promising to send another delegation to Lagos within thirty days.[29] Their confidence in their ability to repel any invasion was such that about the same time they turned down an offer of direct military aid from the Egba, adding (according to Johnson)[30] that if they could not drive back the invaders within three months they would then be glad to receive such help. The Egba meantime maintained their blockade on the river Ogun and the roads to Lagos, and refused to receive an emissary sent by Carter.

It is not clear at what point the Ijebu fully realised the aggressive intentions of the Lagos Government and began to put their forces on a war footing.[31] But the assembly of an army did not occasion elaborate or unfamiliar procedures for them. In theory every able-bodied man in the Yoruba kingdoms was required in time of war to serve in the army of his town,[32] but during the nineteenth-century wars an approximation to standing armies came to be widely adopted. These were based on the household retainers of the war chiefs of a town, known as their 'war boys' *(omo ogun)*. The Ijebu army which was mobilised in 1892 seems to have consisted almost entirely of such semi-regular troops. It was also a wholly infantry army—as a forest people the Ijebu seem never to have developed a cavalry arm, though horses were in use in their kingdom[33]—and the majority of the troops must have had battle experience during the internal wars which had for so long plagued Yorubaland. Though a Yoruba army did not wear uniform, most of the Ijebu soldiers probably wore above their wide trousers *(sokoto)* the padded, many-pocketed war jackets, *(ewu ogun)* hung about with charms, (and similar to those worn by hunters), while the chiefs would be distinguished by their *bante* or war aprons. At close quarters mutual recognition was assured by the Ijebu facial scarifications, usually three vertical and three curved horizontal lines.

The size of the army which encountered the Lagos force in the main battle on the Yemoji was estimated by their opponents at between 7,000 and 10,000 men.[34] With the exception of detachments possibly provided by the towns of Ijebu Ife and Imusin, this army had been raised from the capital and its immediate environs. Though in the event of a general threat to the whole country the Awujale could look to the other Ijebu oba for reinforcements to his own army, he seems not to have called for these in 1892. The Remo would have been unlikely to respond. There was also some fear of attack by the Ibadan on a 'second front'; Johnson recounts that the Governor of Lagos had written to ask the Ibadan authorities for such support and that the letter had been intercepted by the Ijebu, and though there is no confirmation of this story from other sources, the possibility of Ibadan intervention was taken seriously enough for the Awujale to ask the Ago Iwoye that their army should keep a special watch on the northern borders.[35] The Iwoye also believe that the Ijebu Ode expected great spoils from the European invaders, who 'had gold and silver in their bellies', and so wanted to 'monopolise' the war— which may explain the rejection of Egba help. Finally, internal discord deprived the Ijebu of the services of two notable warriors and their followers. The first was Ogunsegun of Ijebu Igbo, who had taken part in numerous wars in the time of Awujale Afidipote but who since the exile of that king in 1882–3 had been conducting his own intermittent hostilities against Afidipote's successors. The second absentee was Kuku, the Seriki of Ijebu Ode,[36] a Moslem and the master of many war boys; he had been expelled from the capital in 1883 for selling munitions to the Ibadan and after living for some years in Ibadan had now moved to the sanctuary *(ibi asala)* of Ijebu Ife.[37]

The command of the army devolved upon the Ologun, or war chiefs. These were members of the Parakoyi, described by Ayantuga as the 'war committee' of the Pampa, the last of the three great councils which, with the Awujale, made up the government of the capital. The head of the Ologun was traditionally known as the Oloriogun, although the alternative title of Balogun, borrowed from Ibadan, had come into use during the century.[38] In 1892 this office had been held for many years by Onafowokan, an elderly man formerly of great influence who had acted as regent during the interregnum in the kingship between the exile of Afidipote and the installation of his successor Aboki in 1886. It is not clear to what extent Onafowokan was responsible for the organisation of this last undertaking by an Ijebu army, but it seems that he was overshadowed by younger subordinates among whom the most prominent was Akala, from the Porogun ward, and most informants agreed that he was not present at any of the engagements of the war.

Precise information about the weapons of the Ijebu forces can no longer be obtained, but it is possible that all the warriors were equipped with some kind of firearm. From early in the century Ijebu traders, profiting from their contact with Europeans at the coast, had been able to obtain muskets, and the Ijebu had used these on a large scale in the Owu war about 1820, at a time when firearms were scarce among other Yoruba. Just as they had been foremost in obtaining muskets, so they had also pioneered (with the Egba) the use in their wars of the greatly superior breech-loading rifles which were available on the coast from about 1870, and many, perhaps most, of their warriors in 1892 were armed with Sniders. Apart from the riflemen, the rest of the army must have carried Dane guns (unrifled muzzle-loaders, or muskets, which were usually flint-locks), firing shot or slugs and also half-inch bolts of iron of which four could be discharged at a time. After the battle of the Yemoji a large quantity of ammunition (presumably ball cartridges) for the Sniders was found in the Ijebu camp, with gunpowder in barrels marked with the name of Régis Ainé, the Marseilles traders with a branch at Palma (Orimedu) between the lagoon and the sea. In addition to their firearms, most warriors probably also carried swords or cutlasses as auxiliary weapons for close fighting, but in the event these cannot have been used in this war.

Despite their long acquaintance with firearms, the Ijebu (like other Yoruba) never evolved any drill for their efficient handling, and after the introduction of rifles they continued to load and fire these weapons from a standing rather than a prone position, sacrificing a major advantage of the breech-loader over the muzzle-loader. Moreover, it is unlikely that they were using the recently-introduced smokeless cartridges in their rifles,[39] while the Dane guns were packed with banana fibre as wadding, greatly increasing the smoke from the discharge. Thus, neither protection nor concealment could be hoped for in any defensive position, however well-chosen.

Despite the fact that the Ijebu are reported as having used 'cannon *(akba)*; that is, small bronze pivot guns' for the defence of their towns in the early years of the century,[40] they apparently brought no artillery into the field. Nor had they obtained any form of machine-gun, a surprising improvidence, especially if the report is true that their neighbours and allies the Ijesa were using a Gatling against the Ibadan in the Kiriji war during the early 1880s.[41]

The campaign opens: 12 May—15 May 1892

In Lagos the military operations were being delayed by the late arrival of the West Indian troops who had been sent on an expedition into the interior of Sierra Leone.[42] When at last they landed on 9 May only forty-seven of the 100 other ranks were fit for duty, and by now the rainy season was beginning. But the seven Special Service officers, as well as the Gold Coast constables, had arrived on 20 April and were busy exercising the other members of the force in bush fighting at Ikoyi and enjoying local hospitality. On 10 May Carter held an inspection of the combined force on the race-course, at which he professed himself particularly impressed by the Ibadan fighting contingent. On the same day he issued his instructions to Colonel Scott. In these he wrote that:

> The main object of the Expedition is to compel the Jebus to permit a free passage through their country to all persons whether Native or European from the Interior to the Lagoon and vice versa and in fact to open all roads and waterways passing through their Country, to legitimate Commerce.' To attain this, Scott was 'to proceed to Ijebu Ode, and occupy the place, by peaceable means if practicable but if not by force.'

The instructions stipulated that the expedition should proceed by water to Epe whence there was believed to be a reasonably good road to the Ijebu capital.[43]

The choice of Epe as starting-point had been made by the Governor after a reconnaissance of the north shore of the lagoon by two officers on 23 April. The usual and shortest route to Ijebu Ode from Lagos was via Itoiki, west of Epe along the lagoon, but Itoiki had the disadvantage of being approached by a narrow creek which would provide good opportunities for an ambush. At Epe a large element in the population was Lagosian rather than Ijebu in origin, having settled there during Oba Kosoko's exile in the town, and so was likely to be well disposed towards the expedition. Finally, the road from Epe to Ijebu Ode was known to pass through comparatively well-cultivated country where the defenders would find less cover than on the other route.

At daybreak on 12 May, in heavy rain but 'amidst much enthusiasm', as the local newspaper reported, the expedition began to embark. It consisted of the commander, Colonel Scott, thirteen European officers (including police officers), four local police officers (two being Lagosian and two Gold Coast 'Hausas'), and 458 rank and file made up of sixty-seven regular other ranks of the West India Regiment, 148 Gold Coast and 143 Lagos 'Hausa' constables, and 100 Ibadan warriors under Chief Toyan. This fighting force was accompanied by the Acting Colonial Surgeon as Chief Medical Officer and a Surgeon-Captain from the West India Regiment, by 350 carriers, increased by later recruitment at Epe and Leke to 536,[44] by twenty-seven guides and interpreters, and finally by the proprietor and editor of the *Lagos Weekly Record,* John Payne Jackson, as Special Correspondent,[45] the total expedition numbering some 1,042.[46] Their transport consisted of the government steam yacht *Margaret* with six large canoes and six covered lighters towed by steam launches.

Embarkation was completed at about 10.30 a.m. and an hour later the expedition was under way. Progress up the lagoon was slow, but during the night the flotilla arrived off Epe and disembarkation began there at daybreak. The northern, or Ijebu, half of the town was found to have been deserted, but the inhabitants of the lagoon-side, of Lagos descent and mostly Moslems, proved as friendly as had been expected and under the leadership of Braimo Eddo co-operated with the expedition. Headquarters were set up in the compound of an accommodating resident named Gani, and the whole town was occupied by the troops. On 14 and 15 May a party engaged in recruiting more carriers at Leke on the further side of the lagoon (during which the *Margaret* went aground), and reconnaissance patrols from the Ibadan reported the desertion of the neighbouring villages and took a few prisoners. At 7.30 on the morning of 16 May the force of 463 Officers and men and 566 non-combatants set out on its march to Ijebu Ode, leaving a rearguard at Epe of one officer and twelve men of the West India Regiment.

By now the Ijebu were prepared to meet the invaders. They seem to have had no intention of basing their defence on the capital itself, though it was surrounded by the usual fortifications of a Yoruba town, consisting here (as the invaders later observed) of a mud wall some three to four feet high, an outer ditch over six feet deep and ten feet wide, and a zone of thick uncultivated bush—conditions similar to those which had, for example, enabled the Egba to hold Abeokuta against fierce Dahomean attacks during the latter part of the century.[47] Instead, the army was first concentrated some miles to the south-west of the capital on the road to Itoiki whence the Lagos force was expected. When the landing at Epe was learnt, they were re-deployed along the south-eastern approaches.[48] The main plan now was to deny to the enemy the crossing of the river Yemoji (whose waters were regarded by all Ijebu as sacred) where it met the track from Epe about six miles from the capital, but advanced detachments took up positions well to the south of this strong point.

The first encounters: 16 May–18 May 1892

From the waterside at Epe the land rises sharply to a bluff above the town, and thence the road to Ijebu Ode, some twenty miles to the north, runs across rolling country intersected by many small rivers and streams. The Lagos force began their march by breasting this slope, on which the compounds of the northern half of the town were built. A little further on they crossed the Otiyan stream and were then encompassed by dense forest. The narrow path forced them to keep to single file, so that the column stretched for nearly two miles, and was so worn on either side that the troops had to adopt a 'straddling position' in marching. In this way they were able to cover only some one and a half miles in the hour.

In the van as scouts were the Ibadan, accompanied by Captain the Honourable A. S. Hardinge, one of the officers sent out from England, with whom as interpreter and aide was Abraham Claude Willoughby, the twenty-nine-year-old former Deputy Registrar for the Lagos Government at Leke who belonged to a Lagos family of Ibadan descent and who had recently been appointed an Assistant Superintendent in the Lagos Constabulary.[49] The advance guard was provided by thirty men of this constabulary under Captain Bower, with two of the three machine-guns and one rocket trough under Lieutenant Lawrie. Colonel Scott and his staff came next, accompanied by an escort of thirty Gold Coast constables under the command of Lieutenant Davies of the Grenadier Guards (a Special Service officer who four months later was to publish the clearest account of the expedition). Then came the main body with the rest of the guns and the reserve ammunition, and stretcher parties, and driving thirty-three head of cattle as part of the provisions for the troops. The carriers presumably marched next, with the rearguard following on with the one machine-gun allotted to them. The Lagos and Gold Coast constables provided the main body and the rearguard, apparently each of about the same strength, on alternate days.[50]

After a march of three to four hours, during which they noticed a number of deserted hamlets on their route, the expedition reached the village of Pobo or Poka.[51] Here the first action of the campaign was fought. An advanced detachment of Ijebu had taken up positions in the surrounding bush and now received the invaders with a volley of fire. The Ibadan and the constables at the head of the column, reinforced by one seven-pounder gun, returned the fire and must at the same time have deployed into the bush in accordance with the tactics laid down for such engagements[52] and practised at Lagos. But having inflicted casualties, the Ijebu soon withdrew, falling back towards the hamlet of Naforija, about three-quarters of a mile to the north. They were followed by the Lagos force and another exchange of fire took place here before the Ijebu again broke off the engagement.

Eight of the Lagos force had been wounded[53] in this short but sharp battle, and although it was still only early afternoon the commander decided to halt his advance and camp for the night in the empty houses of Pobo. Of the casualties, seven were Ibadan warriors and the other a carrier. Their wounds had all been inflicted by slugs or buckshot, and only in one case were serious; this last was an Ibadan who died a few days later in Ijebu Ode. The extent of casualties among the Ijebu remained unknown.

The following morning, 17 May, the expedition made an early start, first burning the houses of Pobo where they had spent the night and then moving off along the track northwards. On their right was Naforija whence they had driven off the Ijebu the previous day. A few hundred yards further north they crossed the great earthwork known as the Eredo which encircles the kingdom of Ijebu Ode, and which Captain Gordon, the expedition's Intelligence Officer, marked on his sketch map as 'Moat and Causeway'. A village to the right of the path, also known as Eredo ('Eridu' in the staff diary and on the map) was shelled but proved to be already deserted. Then, shortly before 8 a.m., as the column wound its way between hills covered by dense forest, it came under heavy fire from the defenders.

The Ijebu position here, at a place known then as Pasida, lying probably to the west of the present main road near the village of Odo Ragunsin, was a strong one, well covered and commanding the leading ranks of the invaders. The latter were led, as on the previous day, by the Ibadan under Hardinge and their own chief and the two companies of constables under Captains Gordon and Bower. Despite the Ijebu fire they continued to press slowly forward on the line of advance, while the rest of the column were led by Captain Owen on a flanking movement and Lawrie manœuvred his guns into position. The whole weight of the Lagos fire was then brought to bear on the Ijebu, who had made no counter-move to outflank the expedition, and after a short time the defenders were forced to withdraw from the cover of the forest across neighbouring farmland where they provided a target for artillery as well as rifle fire. The Lagos force was now able (as Davies wrote) 'to make full use of the superior range of their weapons'. After enduring an hour of this fire in their new positions, the Ijebu again began to retreat. The Ibadan and the constables joined in pursuit, but as they did so, Willoughby, 'venturing too far', Johnson says, received a fatal wound; according to tradition in his family this was delivered by a bowman shooting from a tree with poisoned arrows, but it seems more likely to have been caused by gunshot.[54] Hardinge was also wounded here, although only slightly.

Willoughby's death brought the pursuit to a halt.[55] The Lagos troops spent the rest of the day and that night in the deserted compounds of a nearby village, either Majoda or Odo Ragunsin.[56] The wounded were cared for and Willoughby was buried near to the place where he had fallen. At about 4 p.m. a few Ijebu, led by a chief in a red cap, made a sortie from the bush but were driven back by 'a few rounds from the Maxim gun and a seven-pounder shell', leaving the chief and several others dead.[57] A quiet night followed.

On 18 May Scott again got his men on the march at first light. Throughout the morning nothing was seen of the enemy but reports were brought in that the Ijebu army was preparing to stand not far away, and the villages on the route had all been abandoned. A little to the north of Majoda the column crossed the cultivated land marked on the sketch map as the 'Abodhu Farms', which must be Odo Agboju, and after some two hours they reached a point said to be half-way between Epe and Ijebu Ode (depressing intelligence for the expedition which had hoped to reach the Ijebu capital in three days at the most). At about 10.30 a.m. they crossed a river and soon after midday occupied a village described as 'Odelaye'—almost certainly this was Odo Lagaye—where they encamped.[58]

In his report Scott estimated the day's march at eight miles, and by his calculations the expedition had now covered some twenty-one miles. This compares with a distance measured on the modern metalled road between Epe and Odo Lagaye of only eleven miles, and though Scott's calculations may have exaggerated the distances marched (as his Intelligence Officer's map also suggests) the discrepancy illustrates the tortuous nature of the bush paths of southern Yorubaland, winding round fallen trees and marshy ground and from hamlet to hamlet. An average of seven miles a day was not slow on such a path and in a tropical climate. Moreover, from Pobo onwards it had been clear that the Ijebu, far from capitulating at the entrance of the expedition into their country as had been anticipated in Lagos, were determined to contest the invasion to the utmost and their attacks might be expected at any point along the route.

The battle of the Yemoji: 19 May 1892

The small river Yemoji flows south-west to the river Owa which in turn enters the lagoon about half a mile to the east of Ejinrin, and was crossed by the track from Epe at a point some five miles in a direct line from Ijebu Ode. Here the river, running through a 'steep and narrow ravine', broadened out into a 'little lake' about forty yards in width with marshy banks; a ford led through the western side to connect the two ends of the track while on the east was a 'grassy island'. Although it was still early in the wet season there had been a heavy fall of rain on the previous afternoon and even at the ford the water was waist-deep. From the Epe direction 'a hollow and rugged path' dropped down the side of the heavily-wooded slope, crossed a small tributary stream, and then reached the ford some 300 to 400 yards beyond. On either side of the lake the river narrowed and ran through dense bush.[59]

At this formidable spot in the Gothic gloom of their forests the Ijebu had resolved to defend their capital. (Today the landscape has been tamed and changed: a metalled road crosses the Yemoji by a concrete bridge, the forest has been thinned by cultivation, and a small waterworks has been built above the little lake which has become a swimming pool.) The main body of the Ijebu army was concealed in good firing positions on the steep and wooded slopes of the further side of the river, 'divided' (as the report in the London *Times* put it) 'into battalions and led by their various chiefs', while a large detachment, estimated at about 700 men, was posted forward of the river to cover the enemy's approach. The ford itself had been deepened and obstructed by the Ijebu who threw 'snags' (presumably boulders) into the water as well as adding charms or 'medicine', while the thick bush both screened the movements of the defenders and made it impossible for the Lagos to deploy as soon as they came under fire and so bring their superior fire-power to bear.

Soon after beginning their march on the morning of 19 May the Lagos encountered scattered firing from the hills on their left, probably meant as a signal to the main Ijebu army to the north. About an hour after leaving their camp, they reached the crest of the hill above the Yemoji valley (a point from which today an extensive view stretching beyond Ijebu Ode is obtained, but which in 1892 must have been buried within high forest). The Gold Coast constables were in the van with the Ibadan, and the column still extended, by Scott's estimation, to nearly two miles. As they descended the slope, on a path which must have been slippery with mud, the Ibadan suddenly checked, averring that they could 'smell' the enemy ahead, and began to sound their drums and look to their war charms. A few minutes later, as the column rounded a bend in the path, the Ijebu opened fire. It was now 7.15 a.m., and a hard battle lasting nearly three hours lay ahead.

Continuing their slow advance down the 'hollow path', the Lagos force crossed the tributary stream flowing to the Yemoji. At this point the Ijebu fire, from positions commanding (it seemed) the whole length of the column, became intense, and a number of Lagos men were hit. This hindered movement on the path and pinned down the invaders for about thirty minutes as they tried to make an effective return of fire against an invisible foe. At last the leading members of the column emerged on a patch of level and more open ground bordering the river, where they were able to spread out into open formation to minimise the effect of the heavy fire coming from the main body of the defenders on the opposite side of the valley. The battle of the Yemoji was now at its crisis. If the Ijebu could hold the invaders on the further bank of the river for that morning and continue to inflict casualties, they would save their kingdom, while for the Lagos expedition, greatly outnumbered and exposed to a galling fire, there was no way left for any flanking movement and no choice but to force a passage of the river.

The Lagos were now deployed into three columns, with the two companies of constables on the flanks and the West Indians in the centre and (apparently) to the rear. As they came up to the river, Lawrie—who had accompanied the leading rifles—succeeded in bringing his Maxim to bear on the enemy ahead, sweeping the opposite bank with fire. Under this cover Owen and Gordon led the Hausa into the water, but immediately Owen was hit and the troops wavered and held back.[60] At this crucial point, the fifty-eight-year-old Colonel Scott (in the account given to Johnson) sprang into the waist-deep water and 'thundered out—Second West, advance!'.[61]

The West Indians, under Major Madden, responded and entered the river, steadily wading towards the opposite bank, under fire and 'stumbling on the snags' but still going at the enemy.[62] Meanwhile, the seven-pounders and rockets had been positioned, and as the rest of the force followed on through the ford they fired over their heads so that to the defenders the trees seemed to burst into flame and the Ibadan acclaimed Scott as *adana sun igbo,* 'he who sets the forest ablaze'.

By 8.30 a.m. the main body of the Lagos force had crossed the river, 'every man and every gun being engaged' as Davies says, and now their superior fire-power began to tell against the superior numbers of the defence. The Maxim had played a big part in the river crossing, and though Lawrie had been slightly wounded in the action, the machine-guns accompanied the troops across the river, followed by the seven-pounders (one of which was shouldered over by Colley-Green, a Lagosian Assistant Superintendent of Police). The Ijebu continued to dispute every turn of the path which they lined on either side, but the bush here, though still dense, was comparatively low so that the Lagos guns and rocket troughs could be brought into effective action from the path. In the rear heavy firing caused some concern for the safety of the long line of carriers and their loads, but the rearguard held its own. Then, as the main body fought its way up the slope on the further side of the river, the Ijebu fire began to slacken. By about 9.45 the defence was breaking and the Ijebu began to withdraw. But their withdrawal was no rout, and it was about 11 a.m. before the main Lagos force, after shelling the village of Imagbon half a mile ahead, completed the ascent of the further side of the valley and occupied the deserted village and the adjacent camp of the Ijebu army.[63]

The losses among the Ijebu had been severe, amounting to seventeen chiefs and some 1,000 warriors killed[64] and many more wounded. Among the dead or dying was the Ologun Akala of Porogun, who had been conspicuous for his courage and who in the absence of the Oloriogun was foremost among the war chiefs on the field. There seems to have been no thought among the survivors of making any further stand, and having turned their backs to the enemy, they hastened towards Ijebu Ode. As they went, they learnt that Kuku had placed himself with his war boys from Ijebu Ife between them and the capital, and fear spread that the Seriki would bar their retreat. But Kuku, who had taken his stand where the track from Ilese joined the Epe-Ijebu Ode road about a mile to the north-west of Imagbon, was content to laugh at his unhappy compatriots and made no attempt to impede them as they passed by.

The figure of casualties in the Lagos force presents a difficulty since there is a serious discrepancy among the authorities. According to the staff diary of the expedition, losses in the battle of the Yemoji amounted to only five killed and three officers and thirty other ranks wounded. Davies, however, puts the number of those killed at fifty-six, with thirty wounded including the three officers.[65] His figure seems much the more likely and may be accepted as applying to the whole force, while it seems reasonable to assume that the staff diary, written perhaps an hour or so after the action, refers only to immediately ascertainable casualties among the regular troops and constables.

Though the Lagos force had now occupied what was evidently the main camp of the Ijebu army, with the clothes of the warriors still in the huts and their cattle in the enclosure, the plight of their enemy was not yet realised and it was expected that the next day would bring further fighting. Late in the afternoon a white flag was seen planted beside the path to Ijebu Ode, but Scott feared a trap and this only increased his vigilance. The rest of the day, therefore, the expedition rested at Imagbon and prepared for whatever lay ahead.[66]

Aftermath and reckoning

The Ijebu army carried back to their capital the news of their defeat. Their Sniders, and even their ancestral gods in whom they had reposed their greatest faith, had failed them, and they were to make no further resistance, either behind the walls of Ijebu Ode or in their forests. As they passed through the town and melted into the country beyond, most of the citizens followed them.[67] The next morning, as the Lagos force, after burning the camp at Imagbon, resumed their advance along a path strewn with the debris of the defeated army and churned into deep mud, six emissaries from the Awujale met them, bearing a flag of truce and asking for peace. As they passed down the column to see Colonel Scott, Davies noted that 'No one could help being struck with the fine bearing and apparent indifference of these men'. Scott sent back two of the emissaries with his demand for the surrender of the capital and retained the rest as hostages. The advance then continued, and at 11.30 a.m. the troops entered Ijebu Ode. But for the King himself and a few elderly followers the town seemed deserted. A defensive position was taken up, and some looting occurred. Less than an hour later, the troops encountered an old man staggering towards them, complaining that one of the constables had entered his compound and taken away the leopard skin on which he was sitting. This proved to be the Oloriogun Onafowokan, the nominal commader of the Ijebu army. His leopard skin was restored to him and orders given that he should not be molested. Meanwhile Scott sharply questioned and upbraided the Awujale, who, so he told Carter, 'appears to have no authority over his people and throws himself on Your Excellency's mercy'. Three days later Scott dispatched a flying column northwards under Captain Owen (recovered from his wound) to ensure the opening of the roads between Ibadan and the Ijebu kingdom.

Back in Lagos, Sir Gilbert Carter had been waiting impatiently for news, a prey to alarming rumours (which in the week after the expedition's departure had caused the inhabitants of Ebute Metta on the mainland to flock into the town for safety). At last on 24 May Scott's despatch, written two days before, reached the Governor, and after sending the news to the Colonial Secretary, Carter himself set out for Ijebu Ode. At Epe he received word that owing to the 'foulness of the road' he should travel via Itoiki where an escort under Gordon awaited him, and on the afternoon of 26 May he arrived in Ijebu Ode by this route. The countryside was quiet and the town still almost completely deserted, the troops posted in a strong position round the royal compound. The Awujale was being 'very properly kept under the supervision of the sentries'; he was a weak man, Carter decided, old but not decrepit nor wanting in sense. Within a few days the inhabitants began to return, and with them a number of Hausa (or Hausa-speaking) slaves who were quickly enlisted into the Lagos Constabulary. The most important of the new arrivals was Kuku, who soon profited from the situation to recover and to increase his influence in the capital. Owen's opening of the road to the north and destruction of the toll-gate[68] had rapid effect, and by 30 May the first party of Ibadan traders had appeared and a market was established. The Governor's political and military dispositions were equally rapid: a column consisting of forty-three men of the West India Regiment, fifty-seven constables and the Ibadan warriors was sent under Madden's command on a march through Remo country to open the roads westwards, reaching Sagamu on 1 June and returning to Lagos via Ikorodu on 4 June. A small detachment of constables was sent to Itoiki, and later another to Epe, while at Ijebu Ode itself a garrison of 140 constables was established.

On 31 May Carter left for Lagos accompanied by Scott and the rest of the force, the Governor being particularly anxious that the Special Service officers (other than Bower who remained in Ijebu Ode)[69] should leave by steamer on 6 June to relieve the colony of the expense of their maintenance.[70] The Governor and his party disembarked at the Marina on 1 June; the crowd gave them an ovation which

(Jackson wrote) the officers received 'with commendable (and, we suppose, military) equanimity'. There was a dinner-party at Government House, the Special Service officers left on schedule, and on 6 June Carter sent off his recommendations for the award of a campaign medal (for which he, his secretary and Mr. Jackson all at first proved eligible), adding that Colonel Scott (soon to become a Knight Commander of St. Michael and St. George) had told him that 'there was no such severe fighting during the whole of the Ashanti campaign as that of Magbon'.[71]

Scott's acknowledgement of the determination of the Ijebu army raises an important question. The resistance encountered by the Lagos expedition had been unexpectedly strong, so much so as to lead to recriminations: Carter believed 'the Government to have been misled by certain disloyal and interested persons in Lagos'[72] and *The Times* correspondent wrote that 'The false and malicious reports given to the Lagos authorities by certain black traders that the Jebus had no intention of fighting and possessed no arms were fortunately unheeded'. But given their numerical superiority of at least ten to one, how did the Ijebu come to suffer such complete military defeat? There is force in the usual answer that the expedition had superior armament. The support of the machine-guns and the seven-pounders was especially valuable—the rockets were frightening but not otherwise very effective. 'This is one of the first big expeditions in which the Maxim gun has been really tried', wrote *The Times*. 'It worked well and did good service', and Burns refers to the Ijebu as being 'shelled out of their positions' on the Yemoji.[73] But these weapons could not be brought into use in the early stages of an engagement in the bush when it was the rifles which counted, and here the defenders, many of them armed with Sniders and well concealed, had an advantage which they failed to press home.

This points to a further reason for the Ijebu defeat: their lack of tactical skill and initiative. From this aspect, though they may have been their equal and more in courage and determination, they were far surpassed by the Ashanti whose aim in forest fighting was to work round the flanks of an enemy and then attack from all sides. The vulnerability of Scott's column from the time it left Epe presented an opportunity which was never taken since the Ijebu had apparently but one concept of defensive warfare: to stand and fight in a chosen position until they were either victorious or driven off by weight of fire. Allied to this tactical conservatism was an equally inadequate strategy which envisaged the war as concerning only the protection of the capital; it is perhaps permissible to speculate how serious a problem would have been created for Scott and the Lagos

Government had the Ijebu sent an army to occupy Epe and Itoiki in the rear of the expedition.

The casualties incurred by the Lagos force had been comparatively heavy, amounting to 9·35 per cent of the total fighting strength according to the staff diary, while Davies put it at over 11 per cent. It remains impossible even to reach an approximation of the casualties among the non-combatants, but these are unlikely to have been numerous.[74] Despite this, and whatever the opinion of the troops who marched and fought from Epe to the Yemoji, the victory had been cheaply won. Financially, the cost was absurdly small by comparison with the achievement, amounting (at the official figure) to a mere £4,631 8s. 1d.[75] Apart from its 'extraordinary cheapness' (in the phrase of Hamilton at the Colonial Office), the expedition was remarkable in other ways more interesting to the military. It demonstrated the value of a strongly built water-cooled machine-gun, the Maxim,[76] especially against an enemy unprovided with this weapon. It had also shown the potential value of locally raised African troops when well trained and led. Hamilton's comment was typical; after rather unfairly disparaging the West Indians who had been 'carefully placed in the rear of the column where they had not much to do' (he had only read the official account of the Yemoji battle), he goes on:

> The Houssa are by no means perfect, but when they are properly drilled and disciplined, a long way in front of any native forces they are likely to be in collision with, and after the Jebu affair their prestige will be higher than ever . . . if you want to get men to take the place of regular troops you must get them from the Mohammedan tribes of the interior . . . and the Governors of the West African colonies should turn their attention to this.[77]

Politically and economically, the results of the expedition were even more gratifying to the British and their supporters. In the first place the immediate objective of opening the roads through Ijebu country was achieved with all the anticipated benefits to the trade both of Lagos and of the 'interior people', especially the Ibadan. Seeing this, and fearful for their own prosperity and independence in the new situation, the Egba within a few months made their peace with the colony and opened their roads and waterways to direct trade. But the political consequences of the defeat of the old order in Ijebuland went much further. In Johnson's phrase, 'The taking of Ijebu Ode sent a shock of surprise and alarm through the land';[78] apart from a few minor incidents, such as that at Oyo in 1895, the Yoruba made no further resistance to the extension of British influence, and then of British rule, over their kingdoms. After Carter's treaty-making trek in 1893, the whole of Yorubaland, except for Ilorin and, nominally, Egbaland, became a protectorate attached to the colony of Lagos. Wide territories and a large population were thus added to the fast-growing empire of the British, without occasioning the least disturbance to the national life or economy of Great Britain. The imperial idea was approaching its apogee, and with it that complacency which was to be challenged by the Boers within a decade.

For the Ijebu, May 1892 was the beginning of a new world. To them had fallen the honourable duty of defending their country against foreign invasion, and in this they were in the van of all the Yoruba. Their determination, their long tradition of independence, their wealth and trading connections, all fitted them for this role. But their army, numerous, comparatively well organised, equipped with many modern rifles and plenty of ammunition, and imbued with a deep faith in the efficacy of their gods and government, suffered a shattering defeat at the hands of a mixed and numerically far inferior force, but one which was well officered and trained, practised in the use of its weapons and supported by a tiny but well-handled artillery. The old order of the Ijebu collapsed, and enthusiastically the new was embraced. Probably the most important of the new influences to which the Ijebu now opened their country and their hearts was Christianity; in this they saw, as Ayandele writes, 'the secret of the white man's power'.[79] But the Christian missionaries were not only the agents of spiritual change; they also brought about an educational renaissance, and for the Ijebu this was the vital issue. It was this which enabled them to assert their influence in the politics and trade of the new protectorate, and sixty years later in the new Nigeria. In this new order the sacrifice and courage of the warriors at Pobo, Majoda and on the Yemoji sometimes seem forgotten, and yet, for good or ill, they continue to nourish that sense of political and spiritual identity which binds the Ijebu everywhere.[80]

Postscript: since the first publication of this book, E. A. Oroge's unpublished PhD thesis, *The Institution of Slavery in Yorubaland with Particular Reference to the Nineteenth Century* (Birmingham 1971), has become available. Oroge considers that Governor Carter's ambition to spread 'Civilization' and in particular to put an end to the large-scale holding of domestic slaves by the Ijebu was an important motive in the undertaking of the 1892 expedition. Many such slaves were in fact liberated in Ijebuland during and immediately after the expedition (Oroge, pp. 362–6).

NOTES

1 A. B. Aderibigbe, 'The Ijebu Expedition, 1892: An Episode in the British Penetration of Nigeria Reconsidered', T. O. Ranger (ed.), *Historians in Tropical Africa: Proceedings of the Leverhulme Inter-Collegiate History Conference,* Salisbury, Rhodesia, 1962, p. 3.

2 A description of Ijebu in the early nineteenth century by Osifekunde, a native of Makun in south-eastern Ijebu, was published in 1845 by D'Avezac-Macaya and has been reprinted in translation, edited by P. C. Lloyd, in P. D. Curtin (ed.), *Africa Remembered,* Wisconsin, 1967, pp. 217–88. For an introduction to Ijebu history, see Robert Smith, *Kingdoms of the Yoruba,* second edition, London, 1976, chapter VI. O. O. Ayantuga, 'Ijebu and its Neighbours, 1851–1914', thesis presented for the degree of Doctor of Philosophy, University of London, 1965, gives an account of Ijebu institutions (though saying little about the army). For a brief ethnographic description, see P. C. Lloyd, *Yoruba Land Law,* Oxford, 1962, pp. 136–50.

3 Two Yoruba aphorisms *(owe)* illustrate these characteristics: *Ijebu Ode ajeji ko wo; bi ajeji ba wo laro, won a fi sebo lale* ('Ijebu Ode, a town forbidden to strangers; if a stranger enters it in the morning, he is sure to be made a sacrifice in the evening'); *a f'Ijebu a f'Oyinbo, aiye dede eru ni* ('except for the Ijebu and the white man, all the world are slaves'). The second is quoted from S. Johnson, *The History of the Yorubas,* Lagos, 1921, p. 610.

4 Osifekunde, in Curtin, *Africa Remembered,* pp. 241–2, describes this area as within the Ijebu kingdom. The population today is mixed, mainly Ijebu and Awori.

5 In the semi-savannah country of northern Yorubaland, these 'roads' could be quite wide and respectable highways, 'not at all inferior to a drive round a gentleman's park in England' as the Landers noted (*The Niger Journal,* ed. R. Hallett, London, 1965, entry for 26 April 1830). In the heavily forested south, however, they were narrow, tortuous and impeded. Carter, describing his visit to Ondo in 1892, wrote of the road from Mahin to Ilesa as so narrow that a hammock could seldom be used. Fallen trees were frequent and rarely cleared away, so that the distance between two points was often doubled. (CO 147/84, Carter to Knutsford, 14 March 1892.)

6 FO 84/1088, Campbell to Malmesbury, 22 March 1859; Lodder to Malmesbury, 7 May 1859. McCoskry certainly visited Ijebu Ode in April or May 1859 and may have paid an earlier visit in March. But there is a tradition in Ijebu Ode that long previously Portuguese merchants had visited and even resided in the town.

7 See E. A. Ayandele, *The Missionary Impact on Modern Nigeria, 1842–1914,* London, 1966, pp. 54–68. He shows that in 1892 'the European traders were more anxious about the Egba than about the Ijebu routes'.

8 CO 879/33 of 14 February 1890, quoted by Ayantuga, *Ijebu and its Neighbours,* p. 255.

9 CO 879/36, 428, Knutsford to Carter, quoted by Ayantuga, *Ijebu and its Neighbours*, p. 267. There is some disagreement between Ayantuga and Ayandele about the respective roles of Carter and his predecessor Moloney. Ayantuga maintains (p. 267) that Carter 'did not initiate the policy of coercion. All he did was to implement the programme suggested by Moloney and accepted by Knutsford.' Ayandele describes Moloney as 'a man determined on a pacific policy' (*The Missionary Impact*, p. 36) by contrast with Carter who, as 'a firm believer in the forward policy', came to Lagos 'with the preconceived plan of smashing the Ijebu and Egba if they continued to close their routes' (p. 60). Johnson, a contemporary observer of all this, seems to share the second view of Moloney (*History*, pp. 613–14).

10 The point is made by Aderibigbe, 'The Ijebu Expedition', pp. 271–2, and Ayantuga, *Ijebu and its Neighbours*, pp. 270–5.

11 'The Ijebu Expedition', p. 274.

12 CO 147/84, Knutsford to Carter, cited by Ayantuga, *Ijebu and its Neighbours*, p. 281.

13 CO 147/85, Knutsford to Carter, 13 May 1892.

14 CO 147/85, Carter to Knutsford (telegram and dispatch), 5 May 1892.

15 Ayantuga, *Ijebu and its Neighbours*, p. 279.

16 See the letters from 'A Native', answered by leading articles and other correspondents, in the *Lagos Weekly Record (LWR)* for May and June 1892 (the K'Irede letter is in the issue of 14 May 1892). James Johnson was a repatriate, born in Freetown of an Ijesa father and an Ijebu mother. For some years he was a member of the Legislative Council in Lagos and in 1900 he was consecrated bishop.

17 CO 147/84, Carter to Knutsford, 22 March 1892 and 20 April 1892; CO 147/85, Carter to Knutsford, 5 May 1892.

18 See Sir A. Burns, *History of Nigeria*, London, 1955, pp. 118–22, for the attacks on Lagos in 1851; Burns, pp. 128–9 and Ayantuga, *Ijebu and its Neighbours*, pp. 76–7, 120–3, for the attacks on Epe in 1853 (against Kosoko) and 1863 (against Possu); Johnson, *History*, p. 360, and Burns, pp. 131–2, for the 'Courtyard War' *(Ogun Agbala)* at Ikorodu in 1865.

19 The Lagos Constabulary descended from a force raised in 1863 by Glover, Harbour Master and later Administrator of the colony, who recruited them from runaway slaves. For the increase in numbers, see Geary, *Nigeria under British Rule*, London 1927, p. 50. Though known as 'Hausas', a large proportion were either Yoruba or non-Hausa (though usually Hausa-speaking) peoples of northern Nigeria.

20 The Gold Coast Constabulary descended from the remnants of the Lagos Hausa who took part in the Ashanti expedition of 1873–4 and later garrisoned Elmina.

21 It is usually assumed, for example by Johnson, *History*, pp. 619, 621, that these troops were from the 2nd battalion of the West India Regiment, but F. J. Davies, 'The Expedition against the Jebus',

The United Service Magazine, 1892, p. 631, describes them as from the 1st battalion. Caulfield, *One Hundred Years History of the 2nd Battalion, West India Regiment,* London, 1899, p. 197, confirms that the 2nd battalion returned from West Africa to the West Indies in 1892, being replaced by the 1st battalion.

22 Francis Cunningham Scott (1834–1902) was commissioned into the 42nd Highland Regiment (the Black Watch) in 1852 and served in the Crimean War, the Indian Mutiny and the Ashanti War of 1874 before becoming Inspector-General of the Gold Coast Constabulary in 1891. He was later to command the Ashanti Expedition of 1895–6. He was created K.C.M.G. in 1892 and K.C.B. in 1896 (*Who Was Who 1897–1916,* London, 1935).

23 Neither rifle had a true magazine at this time, so were not repeaters. Both were breech-loaders, the main difference being that the Martini-Henry was loaded by pressure on a breech on top of the barrel while the Snider had a side-opening breech.

24 The Martini-Henry had been adopted by the British army in 1871 and replaced in 1888 by the .303 Lee-Metford repeating rifle with a box magazine. Davies, 'Expedition', p. 633, reports that the West Indians carried seventy rounds of Martini-Henry ammunition per man.

25 These had brass barrels and were of the 'RML' (rifle-muzzle-loading) type. They were normally mounted on a two-wheeled carriage but could be dismounted and carried on the shoulder—as on this expedition. A friction tube was inserted into a touch hole on the barrel and the gun was fired by a lanyard.

26 All Maxims after 1890 were Maxim-Nordenfelts. This was probably the Maxim-Nordenfelt .45 single barrel gun of *c.* 1887, mounted on a tripod, said to be the first water-cooled gun produced. It was belt-fed and capable of firing 2,000 rounds in three minutes.

27 This was probably the model produced about 1887 with three .303 barrels. It could be dismounted from its carriage in action. An earlier model had a single .303 barrel and was mounted on a tripod.

28 Probably Hales rockets (with a rotary action) rather than Congreve rockets (with a stick action). Rockets were usually mounted on carriages and fired from elevated launchers like ladders, but they could also be fired from the trough alone, the method adopted by this expedition.

29 Ayantuga, *Ijebu and its Neighbours,* pp. 282–3. The Lagos delegation was led by J. P. Haastrup, a prominent Lagosian related to the Owa of Ijesa but with a title from Ijebu Remo.

30 *History,* p. 618.

31 Ayantuga, *Ijebu and its Neighbours,* p. 283, considers that mobilisation did not take place until news was received that the Lagos force had embarked.

32 Exceptionally, there seems to have existed in Ijebu Ode at the beginning of the century, and presumably in earlier times, a small standing force, the *omodogwa,* which in war was the nucleus of an expanded

army based on the usual militia. This is described by Osifekunde in Curtin, *Africa Remembered,* pp. 286–7, but there is now no recollection of such a force and it does not seem to have been in existence in 1892.

33 In other Yoruba states, for example Ibadan and Abeokuta, chiefs and their entourages were usually mounted, and Ibadan had inherited a cavalry tradition from Oyo. For the earlier use of horses in Ijebu (where they were 'only numerous in the province of Idoko'), see Osifekunde in Curtin, *Africa Remembered,* p. 287.

34 On capturing Imagbon, Scott estimated the force which had been encamped there at between 7,000 and 8,000 (CO 147/85), while Jackson concluded on the same evidence that a force of 10,000 had occupied the camp (*LWR,* 28th May 1892). Davies, 'Expedition', p. 639, writes: 'At the very least 5,000 men must have occupied the camp the night before the battle; probably they had numbered 6,000 to 7,000 but it was estimated by wounded Jebus at 10,000.'

35 *Johnson, History,* p. 622, alleges that the Governor's letter was found with other stolen mail in the palace at Ijebu Ode after the capture of the town. But this is not mentioned in official or other sources.

36 Ayantuga, *Ijebu and its Neighbours,* p. 55, describes the Seriki as second-in-command to the Balogun (or Oloriogun). The title (for which see Johnson, *History,* p. 133) usually implied the leader of the youthful warriors of a town. Ijebu Ode informants insist that in Kuku's case it was self-conferred. It derives from the Hausa word for 'king' and in Ijebu was probably copied from Ibadan.

37 Osifekunde in Curtin, *Africa Remembered,* pp. 285–6, mentions these places of sanctuary for criminals and other refugees in Ijebuland. Examples from Oyo and Ketu are found in Johnson, *History,* p. 57, and Parrinder, *The Story of Ketu,* Ibadan 1956, p. 35. Lloyd's footnote 171 in Curtin implies that the Yoruba concept of sanctuary applied only to certain compounds within towns, but it seems that in some cases, including Ijebu Ife, the whole town constituted a sanctuary (*ibi asala*).

38 Another borrowing from Oyo in the late nineteenth century was the civil title of 'Bale' for a village head, the usual Ijebu title being 'Olori ilu'. Ijebu informants had not heard of the three titles given for army commanders ('Oloukongbon', 'Ade chegou', and 'Ade kola') by Osifekunde in Curtin, *Africa Remembered,* p. 286, and suggested that they might be family names. They said that until quite late in the nineteenth century the Ijebu Ode army had been commanded by the Olisa, the leading chief of the Ilamuren, corresponding to the Basorun at Oyo who also commanded the army of that kingdom's capital.

39 Smokeless rifle powder was invented in 1885 by Vielle, and from then 'the old terror of a visible foe had given way to the sensation of advancing on an invisible foe' (J. F. C. Fuller, *The Conduct of War,* London 1961, p. 140), adding to the advantages of the defence.

40 Osifekunde in Curtin, *Africa Remembered,* p. 287.

41 Johnson, *History,* p. 490.
42 The description of the campaign in this and the two following sections is based mainly on: (i) Scott's report of 22 May 1892, enclosed in Carter's despatch 176 of 25 May 1892 to Knutsford (CO 147/85); (ii) the staff diary of the expedition, presumably kept by Captain Larymore, Scott's staff officer, enclosed in Carter's despatch 182 of 3 June 1892 (CO 147/85); (iii) Davies's account in the *United Service Magazine;* (iv) The *Lagos Weekly Record (LWR)* for May and June, 1892 (a slightly altered version of the account in the *Record* for 21 May 1892, 28 May 1892, and 18 June 1892 is contained in J. B. Losi, *History of Lagos,* Lagos 1914, pp. 58–76). (i) and (ii) are rather laconic but well-supplemented by (iii). Jackson, in the *LWR,* is graphic but unreliable in detail. Other sources are: (v) Johnson, *History,* pp. 618–22, and (vi) the London *Times* of 26 July 1892, p. 8. Johnson's informant was 'an officer who took an active part in the fight', presumably on the Lagos side.
43 CO 147/85, Carter to Knutsford, 14 May 1892.
44 The *LWR* referred on 21 May 1892 to 'the insufficiency of carriers supplied by the Lagos Government' to the expedition. In the next issue (28 May) a correction appeared by Alvan Millson, the Acting Colonial Secretary, affirming that the Government had placed no restriction on the number of carriers and had promptly approved and executed every requisition.
45 For J. P. Jackson, see L. C. Gwam, *Great Nigerians,* Lagos (n.d.: 1967?), pp. 41–4. It is unfortunate that Jackson seems to have taken no camera or photographer with him. According to the *LWR* of 15 May 1892, 'Mr. Photographer Holm was present with his camera' when the West India company landed at the Marina from Sierra Leone.
46 Accounts of the size and composition of the expedition vary. Davies's list ('Expedition', p. 634) is clearest and probably most dependable. He divides the force as follows: (i) Colonel Scott and three staff officers; (ii) Lieutenant Lawrie, in charge of the guns (the gunners being included with the constables); (iii) Major Madden and fifty-five other ranks of the West India Regiment (plus one officer and twelve other ranks left at Epe); (iv) four officers with thirteen N.C.O.s and 132 other ranks of the Lagos Constabulary; (v) two officers with 150 other ranks of the Gold Coast Constabulary; (vi) one officer with 100 Ibadan warriors; (vii) one transport officer; (viii) two medical officers; (ix) 536 carriers; (x) twenty-seven guides, interpreters, etc.
47 A plan of Ijebu Ode showing the walls, pierced by six gates and five 'wickets', is annexed to Carter's despatch 182 of 3 June 1892 (CO 147/85). The *LWR* reported that the four major gates had 'double walls' and were 'loopholed for purposes of defence' (11 June 1892).
48 Johnson, *History,* p. 619, writes that the Ijebu army first took up a position at 'the Eluju grassfields not far from the town of Ibefun',

which is about nine miles south-west of Ijebu Ode and four miles north of Itoiki. An informant in Ijebu Ode described the army's first position as being at Imodi Ijasi, also on the Itoiki road but only some six miles south-west of the capital. Perhaps resistance was planned at both these points. Other informants denied that the choice of the Epe road came as a surprise, since spies in Lagos relayed prompt information about the enemy's intentions as well as his movements.

49 For the Willoughby family, see J. H. Kopytoff, *A Preface to Modern Nigeria: the 'Sierra Leonians' in Yoruba,* Wisconsin, 1965, pp. 300–1. Willoughby's grandparents were liberated slaves who in 1845 had returned (as 'repatriates' or 'emigrants') from the settlement at Sierra Leone to their native country.

50 This order of march is based on Davies, 'Expedition', p. 635. Davies does not mention the position of the seven-pounders on the march, but these were certainly kept well forward.

51 All the sources refer to this village as 'Pobo'. The name now only applies to the market area of the village of Poka. Scott describes Pobo as seven miles from Epe, whereas by the modern road it is barely four.

52 Tactics for bush fighting, designed to prevent envelopment by a numerically superior force, called for deployment on either side of a centre file remaining on the path being followed, the wings firing to their respective flanks on a usually unseen enemy. These tactics were based on Wolseley's instructions for his 1874 Ashanti campaign. 'Fighting in the bush is very much like fighting in the twilight', Wolseley had written. Haywood and Clark, *The History of the Royal West Africa Frontier Forces,* Aldershot, 1964, Part II, Appendix II, describe a similar method evolved in southern Nigeria in the 1920s called 'browning the bush' or 'burning powder'. There was no satisfactory alternative to these ammunition wasting tactics (a point which escaped the amateur critics of Nigerian operations in the civil war of 1967–70.

53 Scott's report in CO 147/85. Davies, 'Expedition', p. 636, says that there were nine casualties at Pobo.

54 The return of casualties annexed to Scott's report attributed all the wounds incurred to gunshot.

55 Tradition among his descendants relates that Willoughby's death was followed immediately by a darkening of the sky and tremendous rain. The informant quoted in this connection a proverb: *ogun a fi ase gba ojo,* 'war gathers the rain in a sieve', that is, war—unlike the Danaidae—performs wonders. Severe sudden storms are common in the climate of Yorubaland, but according to Davies, 'Expedition', p. 637, the only rain which fell during the expedition was on the afternoon of the next day, 18 May.

56 There are contradictory accounts of the movements, engagements and casualties of 17 May. The intelligence map indicates two battle sites at Eredo and Majoda. Scott treats the battle as a single engage-

ment, taking place just outside (presumably to the south of) Majoda, and says that the troops spent the night in that village. The *LWR* (28 May 1892) gives to the site of the first and main engagement the name Pasida or Kpasida, which is unrecognised in the area today, and says that the troops bivouacked at Iragusi, which must be Ode Ragunsin, nearly two miles south of Majoda. Johnson, *History*, p. 620, places the battle still further south at 'Erebo' (Eredo). It seems clear that the battlefield was somewhere between Eredo in the south and Majoda to the north, and probable that the first position of the Ijebu was slightly north of Eredo and the second to the north of Odo Ragunsin. There is a tradition that Willoughby's grave is in the bush on the eastern side of Odo Ragunsin, opposite St. Peter's School there. It should be noted that the Federal Survey map errs in showing the main road running north through Ibonwon; the present route is via Majoda. Davies, 'Expedition', p. 636 gives the casualties, on this day as two killed and nine wounded, whereas the *LWR* (28 May 1892) writes of only one killed and four wounded.

57 Only Davies, 'Expedition', p. 637, mentions this sortie.

58 Scott's report names the village where the column bivouacked on 18 May as 'Layon', which sounds like Odo Layanra, but this is only about two and a half miles from Majoda. The staff diary has 'Odalaye' for the halting place and Gordon's map shows it as 'Odeleye'. The *LWR* says that the night was spent at Majoda, which is clearly wrong.

59 The description of the battlefield as it was in 1892 derives from Scott's report, the staff diary, Davies's 'Expedition', the *LWR*, and Carter's account in his dispatch to Ripon of 17 August 1892 (CO 147/86). Gordon's map shows the tributary stream and Carter appends a sketch showing the lake and its grassy island. It seems probable that in 1892 the path ran to the east of the modern road through the hamlet of Oke Ako.

60 Carter writes that it was the Gold Coast constables who hesitated when ordered into the river; Johnson, *History*, p. 621, that it was the Lagos force. Scott, the staff diary, and Davies, 'Expedition', are silent about the episode.

61 See note 21. Either Scott made an understandable slip of the tongue in referring to the 2nd West India battalion, so recently replaced, or Johnson (or his informant) erred in his account.

62 The decisive action of the West Indians here is described by Johnson, *History*, and by Jackson in the *LWR*. It is not mentioned in the other sources, though Scott did couple the West Indians with his praise of the Hausa for having 'behaved in a most efficient manner' on the Yemoji.

63 Davies, 'Expedition', p. 639, gives the time of the occupation of Imagbon as 10.15 a.m., the *LWR* as 11, and the staff diary, probably referring to the entry into the village of the carriers and rearguard, as 1 p.m.

64 This figure of Ijebu dead is taken from the staff diary. According to Ayantuga, *Ijebu and its Neighbours,* p. 287, n. 1, the late Chief Ogunade, who as a boy of sixteen had served the Ijebu army, estimated the dead at about 700. Davies, 'Expedition', p. 640, wrote that 'we were told afterwards that nearly all the principal chiefs had been killed or wounded, and that there was not a household in the Jebu Ode [*sic*] but what had to mourn the loss of at least one of its members'.

65 'Expedition', p. 640.

66 The *LWR* differs from the other sources in describing the Lagos camp on 19/20 May as being at 'Ligbosi', which cannot now be traced.

67 Some members of the army are remembered as remaining many years at Ago Iwoye after taking refuge there.

68 The toll-gate was at Mamu, about ten miles north of Oru and subject to Ago Iwoye.

69 R. L. Bower was later the first Resident at Ibadan.

70 The officers sent out from England received special service pay at a guinea a day with local allowances, and a Colonial Office official minuted: 'These gentlemen will be pretty well off' (CO 147/88).

71 CO 147/85, Carter to Knutsford, 6 June 1892. An Army Order of 1 September 1892 granted a medal of the same pattern as for the Ashanti War to imperial and colonial forces for operations against the Ijebu between 12 and 25 May 1892. A special silver medal was awarded by Queen Victoria to Sergeant Bakari Kemberi of the Lagos Constabulary. The previous month a D.S.O. had been awarded to Major Madden and brevet majorities to Captains Owen and Hardinge.

72 CO 147/85, Carter to Knutsford, 6 June 1892.

73 *History,* p. 205.

74 The different casualty figures are extremely hard to reconcile. Scott had reported the total casualties of the expedition as four killed and forty-two wounded (CO 147/85, Carter's telegram of 24 May 1892). In view of the high casualties on the Yemoji alone, this must refer only to the West Indians and the constables. 9·35 per cent of a fighting force of 463 comes to forty-three whereas eleven per cent comes to fifty-one.

75 CO 147/86, Carter to Ripon, 12 October 1892. The biggest items were £937 17s. 6d. for carriers, messengers, and clerks, £882 7s. 4d. for transport, and £608 13s 6d. for the pay due to the Gold Coast constables. No account was taken of the pay due to the West Indians or the Lagos constables. Pay and presents for the 100 Ibadan volunteers amounted to £229 17s. 6d. Carter's original estimate for the cost of the expedition had been £3,000.

76 The British development of quick-firing weapons had lagged behind that of the French who used their Montigny machine-gun in the war of 1870.

77 CO 147/86, minutes by W. A. Hamilton on Carter to Ripon, 12 October 1892.

78 *History*, p. 623.
79 *The Missionary Impact,* p. 68.
80 The writer expresses his gratitude to all those who assisted him, especially His Highness the Awujale and other chiefs of Ijebuland, and to Dr. O. O. Ayantuga and Mr. R. C. C. Law who read the chapter in draft and made valuable suggestions. His thanks are due also to the authorities of the University of Lagos for a research grant in the 1967–8 academic year.

SOURCES AND REFERENCES

I. *Primary Sources*

(a) *Oral tradition*
Visits were made to Ijebu Ode and district in February and March 1968 in order to collect and check oral tradition about the war and to identify the battlefields. The principal persons interviewed were: at Ijebu Ode, H.H. the Awujale and the Olotufore (Chief O. Odutola, a local historian, born in 1883); at Ijebu Ife, H.H. the Ajalorun and the Balufe; at Ijebu Igbo, H.H. the Orimolusi and Mr. S. A. Solu (a descendant of Ogunsegun the Seriki); at Ago Iwoye, H.H. the Ebumawe; at Imagbon, the Bale (or Olori ilu, to use the proper Ijebu term) and Mr. Israel Osunlalu (born about 1883); at Poka, the Bale (Mr. Sanni); at Majoda, the Bale and Mr. A. O. Sanwo. Information was also obtained from the late Mr. A. C. Willoughby, M.B.E., of Yaba, Lagos (posthumous son of Assistant Superintendent A. C. Willoughby).

(b) *Official papers*
British Government papers, Public Record Office, London:
CO 147/84, 1892
CO 147/85, 1892
CO 147/86, 1892
CO 147/88, 1892

(c) *Newspapers*
Lagos Weekly Record (LWR), May and June 1892
The Times (London), 26 July 1892

(d) *Maps*
Federal Survey maps, Nigeria, 1964: Sheet 280, Ijebu Ode, NW, NE, SW, SE. 1:50,000

(e) *Collections of weapons*
Examples of the artillery (including rockets), machine-guns and rifles used by the Ijebu expedition were seen at the Rotunda Museum, Woolwich Barracks, by courtesy of the curator, Mr. A. J. T. Dalkin. The Nigerian Museum in Lagos has a number of Yoruba weapons, mostly not on display.

A small collection of weapons was started a few years ago in the museum
of the University of Ife. Chief Odedina of Ijebu Ode preserves a Dane gun
(without its stock) which he believes to have been used by his grandfather
in the battle on the Yemoji.

II. *Secondary Sources*

(a) *Published sources*

Aderibigbe, A. B. (1962), 'The Ijebu Expedition 1892: An Episode in the
British Penetration of Nigeria Reconsidered', in Ranger (1962).

Ajayi, J. F. A. and Smith, R. (1964), *Yoruba Warfare in the Nineteenth
Century,* Cambridge.

Ayandele, E. A. (1963–4), 'An Assessment of James Johnson and his
Place in Nigerian History, 1847–1914', *Journal of the Historical Society of
Nigeria,* II, 4; III, 1.

Ayandele, E. A. (1966), *The Missionary Impact on Modern Nigeria, 1842–
1914,* London.

Burns, Sir A. (1955 edition), *History of Nigeria,* London.

Crowder, M. (1966 edition), *The Story of Nigeria,* London.

Curtin, P. D. (ed.) (1967), *Africa Remembered,* Wisconsin.

Davies, F. J. (1892), 'The Expedition against the Jebus', *The United
Service Magazine,* September.

Geary, W. N. M. (1927), *Nigeria under British Rule,* London.

Gwam, L. C. (n.d.: 1967?), *Great Nigerians,* Lagos.

Haywood, A. and Clarke, F. A. S. (1964), *The History of the Royal West
African Frontier Force,* Aldershot.

Johnson, S. (1921), *The History of the Yorubas,* Lagos.

Kopytoff, J. H. (1965), *A Preface to Modern Nigeria: the Sierra Leonians in
Yoruba, 1830–1890,* Wisconsin.

Lloyd, P. C. (1962), *Yoruba Land Law,* Oxford.

Lloyd, P. C. (ed.) (1967), 'Osifekunde of Ijebu', in Curtin (1967).

Losi, J. B. (1914), *History of Lagos,* Lagos.

Ranger, T. O. (ed.) (1962), *Historians in Tropical Africa: Proceedings of the
Leverhulme Inter-Collegiate History Conference,* Salisbury, Rhodesia.

Smith, R. (1967), 'Yoruba Armament', *Journal of African History,* VIII, 1.

Smith, R. (1969; second edition 1976), *Kingdoms of the Yoruba,* London.

Smith, R. (1976), *Warfare and Diplomacy in Pre-Colonial West Africa,*
London.

(b) *Unpublished source*

Ayantuga, O. O. (1965), *Ijebu and its Neighbours, 1851–1914.* Thesis
presented for the degree of Doctor of Philosophy, University of
London.

OBARO IKIME

Nigeria–Ebrohimi

The myth that the European penetration of the African continent was remarkably easy and peaceful has been satisfactorily exploded. However, the study of the exact nature of African resistance to this penetration is by no means complete. As is well known, African resistance took various forms. Some groups mounted military resistance, others preferred more subtle means such as diplomacy. One area where African resistance ultimately led to military confrontation was the Itsekiri country in the western delta of the Niger.

The Itsekiri, a coastal people, had been in contact with Europeans since the sixteenth century. First they had traded with the Portuguese, the first Europeans to reach West Africa, in pepper, ivory, cloth and a little palm oil. Then like other West African peoples, they had become involved with the overseas slave trade. The era of the slave trade was one of comparative prosperity for the Itsekiri. Economic progress influenced political developments, and it is reasonable to assume that the emergence of the Itsekiri kingdom as a well-knit political entity was largely due to their participation in the slave trade. The same was true for the states of the eastern delta of the Niger.[1]

The Itsekiri kingdom as it emerged did not grow into a large one territorially. In fact until about the beginning of the second decade of the nineteenth century, it consisted mainly of the capital, Ode Itsekiri, and a few villages built very close by. The Olu, as the Itsekiri call their ruler, governed the kingdom with the advice of a council of state made up of *ojoye,* the titled 'nobles' of the land. In the villages, the elders, headed by the founder or sometimes by a priest, maintained law and order, arbitrating and settling disputes. The authority of the Olu and his council was, of course, supreme.[2]

The nature of the slave trade in this as in many other parts of Africa is a subject that requires a great deal of further study. It is impossible in the present state of our knowledge to make categorical statements as to the actual organisation of the trade. We are equally uncertain about the volume of the trade even at its height. A few facts, however, are known for certain with regard to the Itsekiri and the slave trade. The bulk of the slaves they sold to the Europeans came from the hinterland peoples—the Urhobo, the Kwale and the Bini. Yoruba slaves also found their way to the Itsekiri through the creeks which link Itsekiri land with the Ondo province. There exists no tradition of any large scale wars mounted by the Itsekiri against the hinterland peoples for the purpose of obtaining slaves for sale to Europeans. Habitual criminals were disposed of by various hinterland peoples as slaves; prisoners taken during inter-clan fights were sold as slaves; the unwary traveller or wandering child were occasionally enslaved.[3] In the Benin teritories the Oba (King), from time to time, had a large number of slaves for sale as a result of the many wars fought by the Bini during the period of expansion of that empire. The total number of slaves obtained from all of these sources, however, was much smaller than that obtained in the eastern delta. Writing in the eighteenth century, Jean Barbot claimed that the Itsekiri country could not at the time supply more than 500 slaves a year even though these were of excellent quality.[4] In 1769 it took Captain Landolphe three months to find a cargo of 360 slaves at a time when he enjoyed a virtual monopoly of the trade.[5] It is important to stress the fact that the Itsekiri did not wage wars against their neighbours in order to obtain slaves. They did not grow into a military people like the Asante or the Dahomey. At no time did the Itsekiri possess a state navy. Generally speaking, therefore, it can be claimed that the Itsekiri kingdom was never really organised for large-scale war.

That is not to say, however, that the Itsekiri were completely ignorant about war or the weapons of war. They acquired firearms at an early stage since these were some of the earliest articles of trade brought into West Africa by the Europeans. Once again it is not certain what use the Itsekiri made of these firearms. They must have used them for trade themselves. The Olu and leading traders probably kept a store of these as a token of wealth. These arms certainly did not inspire the formation of a state army or navy, but by the eighteenth century the Itsekiri already possessed what came to be known as war canoes—canoes fitted with cannon and paddled by slaves. These canoes probably made occasional forays along the waterways that abound in these parts and may have obtained a few slaves as a consequence. They may also have been used occasionally against the Ijo, another neighbouring people who occupy some of the more inclement parts of the delta. Some of these Ijo are known to have sallied forth from the creeks from time to time and to have preyed on Itsekiri canoes and even European vessels. There are traditions of Itsekiri–Ijo 'wars' in the nineteenth century. It is probable that similar wars took place at an earlier date.[6]

A much clearer picture of Itsekiri history emerges in the nine-teenth century. The century began for the Itsekiri, as indeed for other Niger delta and West African peoples, with the problems posed by the British determination to suppress the overseas slave trade. The Itsekiri, like other peoples in West Africa, found it difficult to give up a trade which had become their economic main-stay. Despite the British anti-slave trade squadron, the Itsekiri continued to trade in slaves until the early twenties of the nineteenth century. But slave-traders were afraid to come into their territory because the difficulty of navigating the bar of the River orcaFdos left them little chance for escape in the event of a chase by ships of the British squadron. The records indicate that very few skaves were being sold in this area in the 1830s.[7]

In view of the above circumstances, the Itsekiri had to turn their attention quickly to the trade in palm oil. Fortunately the Urhobo hinterland abounded in oil-palm trees and the Urhobo were, and remain, good at producing oil from their fruit. Captain John Adams noted that by the 1820s there were already large quantities of palm oil for sale in the Itsekiri country. Unfortunately for the Itsekiri, European firms did not visit their territory as much as they did the eastern delta. The result was that there was not much competition for Itsekiri oil and its price was therefore low.[8] On the whole the first half of the nineteenth century constituted a period of near depres-sion for Itsekiri trade.

One consequence of the abolition of the Atlantic slave trade (and the loss of wealth which went with it), and the slow progress in the palm-oil trade, was the collapse of the Itsekiri monarchy. In the days of the slave trade not only did the Olu receive the 'comey' or customs duties and other 'gifts' from European traders anchoring in Itsekiri 'territorial waters', but he was himself a large trader. The abolition of the slave trade hit him hard because it virtually put an end to 'revenue' derived from 'comey', since only a few ships now called in at the Forcados river. The palm-oil trade which replaced the trade in slaves required much greater capital outlay. The palm-oil trader had to have a large fleet of canoes. This meant a large labour corps to man these canoes. The trader had to have men in the producing areas of the hinterland to organise the buying of the oil. As competition for the palm-oil trade increased, so it became necessary to have war canoes to convoy the trade canoes. Back in Itsekiri land, the successful trader had to be seen to be successful if he was to continue to get 'trust' (credit) from the European traders.

The Olu found things difficult in the new situation. Perhaps what made it really impossible for him to remain a wealthy trader in his own right was the fact that the trade of the Itsekiri country moved from the River Forcados, on the banks of which the capital town of Ode Itsekiri is sited, to the Benin river. European ships preferred the anchorage of the latter river to the former. As a consequence both the leading traders of the day and aspiring traders moved out of the area near the capital to the Benin river. The towns of Batere, Jakpa and later Ebrohimi were founded by leading Itsekiri traders.[9] The Olu, on the other hand, could not leave his seat of government. As there was no tax levied on the Itsekiri people themselves, the sources of revenue left to the Olu were extremely slim. Things were not made any better by the fact that the Olu at the time, Akengbuwa I, was not particularly beloved of his people. His rule is remembered for its harshness and demonstrations of ingratitude to loyal supporters. The monarchy, bereft of wealth and so of effective political power, tottered on until 1848 when Akengbuwa I died. His two sons and most likely successors, Omateye and Ejo, followed him to the grave within a few months. The royal family failed to produce a candidate sufficiently wealthy and powerful to win the respect of the Itsekiri people. Indeed the royal slaves, many of whom were traders in their own right, seized power in the capital. Yet no man of slave origin, however wealthy, could, by Itsekiri law and custom, occupy the throne. The ultimate outcome was that Akengbuwa's death ushered in an interregnum which lasted until 1936.[10]

Even before Akengbuwa's death real wealth, and with it influence, in the society, was slipping from the palace to the men who were facing the challenge posed by the trade in palm oil more adequately than the Olu could. Some of these men like Oritsetsaninomi,[11] Yonwuren and Numa were themselves connected with the royal family. Others like Idibofun, Idiare and Olomu were descended from the Ologbotsere family, the second most important to the royal family in Itsekiri land. In any case birth, which tended to determine the role which an Itsekiri played in society,[12] had suddenly lost a great deal of its importance. Wealth and with it power acquired from the new trade in palm oil became the surest qualification for wielding influence in the society. Hence this period is sometimes referred to as the age of the new men. The rise of these new men was the other major consequence of the suppression of the overseas slave trade. It was accompanied by a new competitive spirit among leading traders which sometimes led to war and lasting family feuds.

The development of the palm-oil trade was marked by the establishment of trading stations, called factories, by various European firms. By the 1850s the firms of Horsfall and Harrison and Co. were already established along the Benin river. Others joined them in the 1860s. Most of these firms maintained resident agents in their factories. The relations between these firms and the Itsekiri form an interesting chapter of Itsekiri history in the nineteenth century. Indeed it was to protect the lives and property of these European, mainly British, traders that the British government began to appoint consuls for the Bights of Benin and Biafra as from 1849. The persistent interference of these British consuls in the internal affairs of the delta states became a commonplace of their nineteenth-century history. John Beecroft, the first consul, visited Itsekiri land and bombarded an Itsekiri village in 1851 because the Itsekiri were alleged to have attacked a European factory. Later consuls did likewise. The result was deep mistrust between leading Itsekiri traders and the Super-Cargoes as the European traders were called.[13]

In the absence of an Olu, the only centrally recognised authority among the Itsekiri was an officer-styled Governor of the River. Originally the *Gofine,* as the Itsekiri called him, was the Olu's collector of customs as well as his chief trading agent. In the interregnum the Governor's status became greatly enhanced. It now devolved on him not only to collect the 'comey' and share it among the leading Itsekiri families, but also to protect Itsekiri trading interests against the European traders. The European traders for their part saw in the Governor an officer of state whom they held responsible for protecting their own lives and property against Itsekiri 'depredations' in the age of the palm-oil ruffians. These two conceptions of the duties of the Governor were often incompatible.

Whatever the peculiar difficulties imposed on the office of the Governor of the River by the circumstances of the interregnum, there can be no doubt that the incumbent was always in a very influential position in society. The European traders courted his custom since he was always a leading trader in his own right. The Itsekiri looked up to him as a leader. It was this realisation of the importance of the office that led to the practice that developed whereby the Governor was chosen in turn from the royal family and that of the Ologbotsere. During the interregnum the following people held the office: Idiare (Ologbotsere family), Tsanomi (royal family), Olomu (Ologbotsere family), Nana Olomu (again Ologbotsere family). The election of Nana Olomu as Governor in succession to his father in 1883 broke the established pattern and won for Nana the hatred of the royal family group led at the time first by Numa and then by Numa's son, Dogho.[14] This hatred was an important factor in deciding the role played by Dogho and his henchmen during the Ebrohimi expedition.

It was not for nothing that Nana was chosen Governor despite the fact that it was the turn of the royal group to provide the candidate. Nana's father, Olomu, who died in 1883, was acknowledged by all the European merchants as the most wealthy and powerful Itsekiri of the time. Indeed in 1870 the British consul advocated the appointment of Olomu as Governor, but the Itsekiri elders chose Tsanomi instead. It was not till 1879 that Olomu became Governor.[15] Olomu's wealth was the result of his ability as a trader. He was clearly the leading Itsekiri trader. His main spheres of trade were the Ethiope and Warri rivers. His marriage alliances with various Urhobo families and his friendship with leading men in various Urhobo clans made him the most sought-after Itsekiri customer. Wealth and power went together in that age. His labour corps made up of slaves as well as freeborn of little means numbered over 1,000. He had a large fleet of trade canoes protected by a fleet of war canoes. He was thus the most wealthy and the most powerful man in Itsekiri land at the time he became Governor. His governorship merely enhanced this wealth and this power. When he died his son Nana succeeded to his father's wealth and power. In view of this he became Itsekiri land's most powerful man just like his father. His election as Governor was a recognition of this fact, for it was feared that if someone else were made Governor he would be unable to control Nana.

If Nana was wealthy in 1883, he became wealthier in the years that followed. He was an even more astute trader than his father. He won the friendship of some of the Urhobo clans that had not loved his father. He stationed his trading boys all over the lands of the Urhobo clans along the Ethiope and Warri rivers. By a judicious mixture of friendships, marriage alliances, gifts and, occasionally, force, he established a virtual monopoly over the trade of the Ethiope and Warri rivers. Fellow Itsekiri traders fretted at this monopoly. European merchants were angry that he was in a position to refuse 'trust' from them and, as Governor, to impose a trade boycott as he did in 1886. Less successful Itsekiri traders together with European traders put in their place by Nana united in hatred and intrigue against one of the most colourful, intelligent, resourceful and successful merchant princes of West Africa in the nineteenth century.

The Ebrohimi expedition which the British launched against Nana in 1894 arose out of a familiar pattern of events in the history of West Africa in the age of the Scramble and Partition. In 1884, soon after he became Governor of the River, Nana headed the Itsekiri leaders in signing a treaty of 'protection' with the British consul, Edward Hyde Hewitt. The provisions of the treaty were the familiar ones. Article I extended the protection of the Queen of Great Britain to the Itsekiri at the 'request of the chiefs and people of Jakri'. Article II forbade the Itsekiri to enter into agreements and treaties with foreign nations without the sanction of the British Government. Article V bade the Itsekiri seek the advice of British consular officers in matters to do with the administration of justice and the development of the natural resources of the country. These and some other provisions of the treaty the Itsekiri accepted. But Nana and the Itsekiri elders with him refused to accept two clauses of the treaty—clauses VI and VII. Clause VI stated: 'The subjects and citizens of all countries may freely carry on trade in every part of the territories of kings and chiefs parties hereto, and may have houses and factories therein.' Article VII provided for the operation of missionaries in the Itsekiri country. The Itsekiri were polygamous. They feared that Christianity would hit at this cherished way of life. It was as middlemen that the Itsekiri made their wealth and if the European traders were allowed to trade wherever they wished, they might penetrate into the Urhobo hinterland and so undermine the Itsekiri position there.

As a consequence of Itsekiri opposition to these two clauses, the treaty was concluded thus: 'This Treaty shall come into operation, so far as may be practicable, from the date of its signature, except as regards Articles VI and VII which are to be left for negotiation on a future occasion'.[16]

In 1889 Nana led the Itsekiri in another negotiation with the British. In that year Major Claude Macdonald had been sent out to the Oil Rivers Protectorate, of which Itsekiri land formed a part by virtue of the 1884 treaty, to find out from the chiefs and people whether they would accept rule by a chartered company or prefer rule by the British Crown. At that time the Royal Niger Company was operating in the Forcados river area and causing the Itsekiri a great deal of annoyance by preventing them from gaining access to some of their traditional markets. Naturally the Itsekiri voted against rule by a company that was in itself a trade rival. In opting for rule by the British Crown, however, the Itsekiri again made an important reservation. They were prepared to accept 'Queen's Government' provided that this did not interfere with their keeping of slaves. The palm-oil trade as organised by the Itsekiri required a large labour force. This force was made up largely of domestic slaves. The Itsekiri insisted that nothing should be done to undermine their labour force.[17]

Up to the time of the Macdonald mission discussed above there had not been established any effective British rule over the Itsekiri or for that matter any part of the Niger delta. Nana therefore continued to enjoy his pre-eminent position as leader of the Itsekiri people and the wealthiest and most powerful figure for miles around. In 1886 he imposed a trade boycott because the British traders were offering an unacceptable price for palm oil. He was later made by the British consul to allow trade to be resumed.[18]

In 1891, however, following the Macdonald mission two years earlier, the Niger Coast Protectorate was formally inaugurated. Major (now Sir) Claude Macdonald himself was appointed Commissioner and Consul-General. For the first time two British consuls were stationed in Itsekiri territory—one at Warri and the other by the Benin river. Nana's troubles began soon after this. Because Nana was the most successful and powerful trader and had the largest labour force, virtually every disturbance in the area was ascribed to him. He was accused of organising midnight raids on markets to drive off his rivals. He was accused of raiding the Urhobo for slaves. He was even accused of setting the Urhobo against the British Government of the Niger Coast Protectorate. If trade was bad Nana was said to be responsible: his boys were preventing the Urhobo from trading.[19]

These and many allied accusations can be explained in two ways. First there was the chagrin and hatred of other Itsekiri traders, led first by Numa and then by his son Dogho as from 1892, who found that Nana's organisation and contacts in the hinterland left them little room for manœuvre as traders. Closely allied with this was the irritation of the European traders who cried out, not against the middleman system as such, but against an over-mighty middleman who was sufficiently powerful and resourceful to dictate his own terms. Secondly there was the whole question of British imperial ambitions in West Africa. Up till now Britain had been rather undecided about the acquisition of colonies, but by the 1890s French and German activities in various parts of Africa as well as her own enlightened self-interest had decided her to make good her claims to territories in Africa. The British officers stationed in the Itsekiri country soon found that for most of the people in the area Nana represented the only authority they knew or respected outside their local chiefs and village elders. The power and influence of Nana thus represented an obstacle to the acceptance of British rule. It was to remove this obstacle that the Ebrohimi expedition was mounted against Nana in 1894. The charges of causing a breach of the peace, of breaking his treaty obligations and of engaging in the slave trade later levied against him were no more than plausible excuses.

Before describing the actual expedition, however, a word about Nana's previous war experiences. Earlier it was stated that the Itsekiri had neither a state army nor a state navy. There was thus no formal military or naval training. As traders, however, the leading Itsekiri men had to be capable of defending themselves against attacks by rival groups as well as attacks by Ijo pirates. Especially in the nineteenth century, the leading traders had war canoes fitted with cannon. Olomu is reputed to have had many of these, so also had Nana. We have it on Macdonald's testimony that when Nana arrived for a meeting with him in 1891 he arrived in a war canoe 'paddled by upwards of one hundred slaves, with four or five similar canoes in attendance'. Neither Nana nor Olomu reached the top of their profession without making enemies. These enemies did not flinch from war.

Nana was brought up the hard way in his father's trade and war canoes. Olomu himself is reputed to have fought seven wars in his time—thrice against the Urhobo, once against the Ijo and thrice against his fellow Itsekiri men. The wars against the Urhobo arose from Olomu's trading activities in the hinterland. The Urhobo had few firearms but they were apt to be recalcitrant or difficult on occasions. The Abraka people, for example, demanded that Olomu and other Itsekiri traders should pay a 'comey' equivalent to one third the value of their trade. The Igun people sheltered slaves who had run away from Olomu's town of Ebrohimi, while an Okpe warrior sought to obstruct the passage of Olomu's canoes up the Ethiope. Each of these people suffered defeat at the hands of Olomu. Nana as a boy and then as a young man was probably involved in some of these wars. But they were all small scale affairs, involving no more than Olomu marching in with a following of slaves armed with rifles or other guns against Urhobo people much less well armed. There were no pitched battles; consequently Olomu's men did not have to possess any experience in tactical drill or skilled fighting manœuvres.

The wars against the Itsekiri and the Ijo were 'naval' affairs.[20] No detailed information is available. The canoes of the opposing sides flying the flags of their owners sallied forth on the rivers. The aim was to sink the canoe of the enemy through cannon fire. The sinking of the canoes was regarded as all the victory needed, but even this required a certain skill in shooting and manœuvring on the water. On the other hand a war canoe on the open river was a fairly sizable target except that it was a moving target all the time. It is difficult to say whether Olomu's victories in these encounters were the result of the remarkable marksmanship of his cannon shooters or that of sheer numbers both of canoes and cannons. Nana himself definitely took part in these wars and Neville claims that it was the daring and bravery which Nana displayed in these wars that led his father to single him out as sole successor instead of the usual practice whereby the father's property was shared amongst his children.[21] One thing, however, is clear: all the wars were local, single day affairs which did not require any massive military build-up, or entail the management of supply lines or call for constant reinforcements. The war against the British, however, was to be very different. In that sense Nana was ill-prepared for the kind of war that was forced upon him in 1894.

If the wars discussed above failed to provide Nana with the kind of naval and military experience that could serve him to advantage during the Ebrohimi expedition, he nevertheless had one strong point which all but defeated the British onslaught. This was the position of his town, Ebrohimi. Earlier it was said that the mid-nineteenth century witnessed the founding of new settlements by leading Itsekiri traders. Jakpa was one of these new settlements. Olomu, Nana's father, moved to Jakpa in the interest of his trade. Nana himself was born in Jakpa. Some time in the second half of the nineteenth century, Olomu became dissatisfied with Jakpa from the point of view of his commercial needs. The settlement was getting rather crowded and expansion was difficult especially for a trader like Olomu whose slaves and other 'staff' were increasing rapidly in numbers. Ebrohimi was founded as a result of Olomu's decision to branch out on his own in the interest of his trade. With him went his entire family, slaves, and others who desired to throw in their lot with him.[22]

From the point of view of defence, the site of Ebrohimi could not have been better chosen. The town was built smack in the middle of a dense mangrove swamp. The land on which the building was done was actually reclaimed through the dumping of clay and sand brought from other areas of the Itsekiri country. Only a narrow creek off the Benin river led up to Ebrohimi. There was no way of reaching it by land except by cutting a path through a dense and extremely soggy mangrove swamp.[23] One cannot be sure why Olomu chose such a site but it is clear that his phenomenal success as a trader had made enemies for him, and he consequently sought a site which could be easily defended in the event of an attack. In the wars to which reference has been made it would have been easy for his canoes to withdraw to the Ebrohimi creek (if one may so name it) and dare the enemy to follow. Nana was to find the siting of Ebrohimi his greatest asset in the fight against the British.

The crisis which led to war began to take shape in the closing months of 1893. Henry Lionel Gallwey, Vice-Consul Benin river, undertook a tour of parts of the hinterland in November 1893. According to his reports, he discovered that Nana's 'boys' resident in the Urhobo areas he visited had been turning the Urhobo against the British Government of the Niger Coast Protectorate. What was perhaps even more irritating to Gallwey was the discovery that Nana's influence in the hinterland was so strong that it constituted a definite challenge to the British. Gallwey wrote to Nana at the beginning of December 1893, reporting his observations, warning Nana to expect full punishment for the actions of his boys and informing him that the subsidy of £200 which the government had been paying to him in lieu of 'comey' since the institution of customs duties in 1891 would be stopped forthwith. Gallwey also accused Nana and his boys of 'injuring' the trade of the Benin river and Warri districts. A full report, Gallwey said, was being sent to the Consul-General, Sir Claude Macdonald.[24]

It was no doubt as a result of Gallwey's report that Macdonald wrote to Nana in April 1894 informing him that as the British Government was already well established in the area, Nana was no longer to regard himself as Governor of the River and so head of the Itsekiri people, but only as head of his own family. If Nana was caught meddling in other peoples' affairs or intimidating them, whether this be inside or outside Ebrohimi, the Consul-General would take 'very serious notice' of the fact.[25] Macdonald's letter was a letter of deposition. Yet the Itsekiri elders who had elected Nana in 1884 had not been consulted. Nana did not, however, intend to give up his position without a struggle.

The struggle which Nana had in mind in April 1894 was probably not one involving military confrontation. He probably hoped, by demonstrating to the British that the charges against him and his boys were false, that he could work out a *modus vivendi* with the British which would leave him in the position he had occupied since his father's death in 1883. Such hopes were soon dashed. On 21 June 1894, Ralph Moor, the acting Consul-General, arrived on the Benin river. According to him reports had reached him to the effect that affairs in the Benin river districts were 'unsettled' as a consequence of Nana's men seizing some Urhobo people in the neighbourhood of Abraka.[26] Moor wrote to Nana requesting him to report to the vice-consulate to discuss the situation.[27] Nana replied that there had been three recent deaths in his family and that his brother was even then seriously ill. He found it impossible to travel in the circumstances but would send his trusted messenger, Tonwe, to represent him at any discussions the consul might wish to hold.[28] Moor wrote back refusing to deal with an intermediary and urging Nana to attend a meeting to discuss 'matters of great importance'. Again Nana replied in the same vein as his earlier letter.[29] Moor's reference to unspecified 'matters of great importance' had probably filled Nana with great suspicion about the intentions of the British Government.

Nana's suspicions, apart from any rumours he might have heard from sources close to the vice-consulate, sprang from the Jaja episode of 1887. Jaja, King of Opobo, had in that year fallen foul of Acting Consul Harry Johnston, in much the same way as Nana had now fallen foul of the British. In what appeared to be a final effort at reaching a settlement, Johnston invited Jaja on board the gun boat HMS *Goshawk* for 'an exchange of views'. Jaja suspected that this might be a trap. He therefore sought, and indeed obtained, assurances of a safe conduct. Once on board, however, Jaja was given an ultimatum. He either had to allow British traders to exploit the hinterland of Opobo or face a bombardment of Opobo. If he did not wish to have his town bombarded, and would not allow British traders to penetrate into his hinterland, then he would be deported. Jaja was completely at the mercy of Johnston. True Johnston did say he could go back on shore, but this was followed by the warning that if he did, Opobo would be bombarded as soon as he landed on shore.[30] Jaja had no choice really. He submitted to deportation. The perfidy of Johnston on this occasion was not lost on the men and

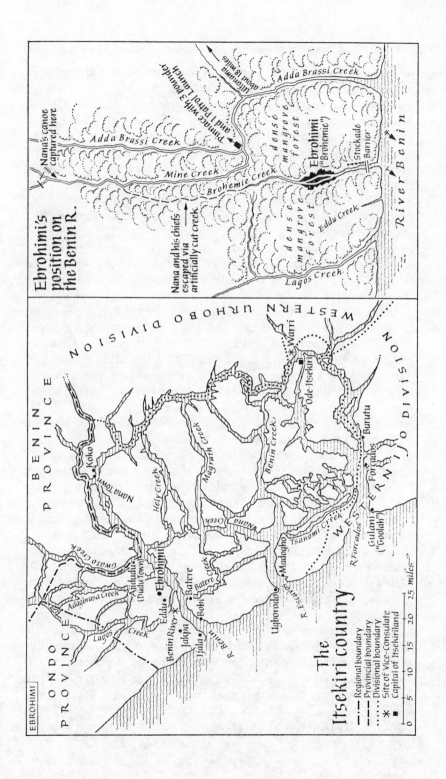

EBROHIMI

Ebrohimi's position on the Benin R.

Nana's canoe captured here

Adda Brassi Creek

Mine Creek

Pinnace with 3 boats and 1 Patrol Launch

Ultimatum about 18 miles

Adda Brassi Creek

Brohemie Creek

dense mangrove forest

Ebrohimi ("Brohemie")

Stockade

Barrier

River Benin

dense mangrove forest

Eddu Creek

Nana and his chiefs escaped via artificially cut creek

dense mangrove forest

Lagos Creek

The Itsekiri country

BENIN PROVINCE

ONDO PROVINCE

WESTERN URHOBO DIVISION

WESTERN

ERNIJO DIVISION

Gwaio Creek

Adagbrasa Creek

Aliadudu (Dudu Town)

Ebrohimi

Eddu

Lagos Creek

Benin River

Jakpa

Ijala

Bobi

Batere

Batere Creek

Koko

Nana Town

Hely Creek

Magrath Creek

Benin Creek

Nana Creek

Sokoto

Madagho

Ugborodo

R. Benin

Tsanomi Creek

R. Essravos

R. Forcados

Warri

Ode-Itsekiri

Burutu

Forcados

Gulani ("Goolah")

Regional boundary
Provincial boundary
Divisional boundary
Site of Vice-Consulate
Capital of Itsekiriland

0   5   10   15   20   25 miles

rulers of the coastal states. Nana must have seen Moor's invitation in 1894 as an attempt at re-enacting the events of 1887.

Moor would not deal with messengers. He wrote another letter to Nana asking him to give instructions to his 'boys' in the Abraka area to desist from disturbing the peace and trade of that district. Nana was also ordered to recall Ologun, the head slave in charge of his trade in Eku, since the latter was alleged to be terrorising that area. Nana was given two weeks to carry out these instructions. He was warned that if he failed to do so no canoes belonging to him or his people would be allowed on the River Ethiope. Nana replied immediately. He apologised for his inability to attend the suggested meeting. He would send word to Abraka as Moor suggested; he would (and did) recall Ologun, though he pleaded that Ologun be later allowed to go to Eku to collect outstanding debts to the tune of two hundred puncheons of oil.[31]

At the end of two weeks, Ralph Moor again steamed to the Benin river. He brought with him one officer and twenty men of the Niger Coast Protectorate Force to strengthen the contingent of one officer and fifty men stationed in the district. This was the beginning of what was to be a massive military and naval build-up by the British. Despite the recall of Ologun, Moor reported to the Foreign Office that Nana had failed to carry out the instructions contained in his letter (of 25 June). Because of this, reported Moor, 'I stopped the trading of Nana and his people in the Ethiope river, establishing a blockade against them at its mouth and siezing any of their canoes that attempted to pass.'[32] Nana was informed of Moor's decision in a letter dated 10 July 1894.[33] In order to prevent Nana from fighting back, Moor at once banned the use of war canoes on the waterways of the district, a war canoe being described for the purpose of the ban as 'any armed canoe or canoe carrying armed men'. Any such canoes found on the waterways would be liable to seizure and the chief to whom it belonged held guilty of 'hostility towards Her Majesty's Government of the Protectorate.'[34] The first physical sanctions against Nana and his town of Ebrohimi had thus been applied.

It does not appear as if Moor had at this time decided on full scale military action. He believed that the blockade would in time force Nana to come to terms since Nana and his people depended on outside supplies for food. He did not know, however, how well supplied Ebrohimi already was, nor could he guarantee how effective the blockade would be. Nana now wrote to Moor saying he had been informed by one Herbert Clarke, a messenger from the consular offices, that the government's intention was to deport him. He deprecated the plot against him and emphasised that he was now even less willing to entrust himself to the Consul by attending a meeting. He saw the ban on war canoes as tantamount to disarming the Itsekiri people and saw this as further proof of the hostile intentions of the British administration towards him. Still he made it clear that he had no intention of going to war against the 'whiteman'.[35]

Moor's next act was to isolate Nana. On the strength of a report to the effect that Nana intended to attack two friendly chiefs, Dogho and Dudu, Moor sent more soldiers to the Benin river, in late July, bringing the available force up to three officers and eighty-seven men. In addition he requested that the gun boat HMS *Alecto* be in attendance at the Benin river. From this position of strength Moor summoned a meeting of all leading Itsekiri traders for 2 August. The purpose of the meeting was to discuss the existing situation and to get the Itsekiri to sign another treaty similar to that of 1884. All the leading traders except Nana turned up and signed the treaty. This time, for obvious reasons, the Itsekiri traders accepted the entire treaty without reservation.[36] Nana's plea that one of the other traders, Ogbe, be allowed to represent him as well as his offer that he would consider himself bound by any agreement signed by all the Itsekiri elders[37] were turned down by Moor. He was told that he could sign the treaty but only at the vice-consulate.[38] Nothing could have been more calculated to confirm Nana's fears. At the same time his refusal to attend the meeting of the 2 August definitely singled him out as being in opposition to the British administration. Moor could now go on to convince the Foreign Office of the necessity of 'active measures' against Nana.

The day after the meeting of 2 August saw the first exchange of fire. British marines effecting the blockade had discovered that a strong barrier had been built across the only creek that led to Ebrohimi. There is no conclusive evidence as to when this barrier was built but it fitted perfectly into the obviously defensive posture which Nana and his men were to take throughout the impending encounter. This barrier was built of hard wooden logs placed very close together and driven deep into the bed of the creek. Nana claimed that his father had built the barrier as a defensive measure against enemies. It is equally likely that Nana himself had ordered the building of the barrier as he must have realised, with the arrival of the *Alecto*, that the British would try naval action. Be that as it may, Nana was ordered to remove the barrier as its presence was against the policy of keeping all the waterways of the protectorate free for use. Nana took no notice of the order. On 3 August, Lieutenant-Commander Heugh was ordered to remove the barrier with mines. During the removal operation there was an exchange of fire between the two parties. Nana's men had obviously taken position in the mangrove forest along both sides of the creek. Each side accused the other of firing first. There were no casualties reported. Heugh succeeded in removing the barrier but it required ten mines each with fifteen charges to blow it up.[39] The British were amazed at the strength of the barrier.

The first shots having been thus exchanged Moor prepared for a full scale offensive. A number of actions were taken against villages considered to be friendly towards Nana. Thus an Ijo village was razed to the ground by a party from the *Alecto*. Evhro (Effurun), hometown of Nana's mother, was burnt down by a combined military and naval force led by Moor himself on 8 August 1894.[40] There could be no more doubt about the ultimate military clash. Nana, without any trained fighting force and already forced to remain in Ebrohimi, sought the intervention of a third party. He sent emissaries to the Governor of Lagos to urge the latter to intervene and find a peaceful settlement. The Governor asked him to deal directly with Moor. So Nana put up a flag of truce and wrote to Moor stating his desire for a peaceful settlement.[41] Moor's reply contained nothing new. Nana would be left in his position only if he was 'prepared to carry out the directions and obey the orders of the Government'[42] and one of the 'orders' of the Government was that Nana should present himself at the vice-consulate. Nana would not obey this order.

Moor continued the military build-up. He left the Benin river for Calabar to secure more reinforcements: two officers and one hundred men. At the same time he cabled the naval authorities for another gun boat. The *Phoebe* arrived on 24 August in response to this cable.[43]

In the meantime Lieutenant-Commander Heugh continued to harass Nana. On 17 August he seized a number of hostile canoes some of them carrying food to Ebrohimi. On 19 August he led a force of 100 men against Oteghele, described by him as 'a large town of Nana's'.[44] The blockade continued though the people of Ebrohimi continued to defy it. Heugh was particularly struck by the open defiance demonstrated by an unknown man during this period. This man was suddenly seen one afternoon in a canoe closely hugging the mangrove bush. The man was ordered to stop and come alongside the British patrol boats. He paid no heed. The British party opened fire but, though hit, the man continued on his course, merely quickening his pace until he ran his canoe into a thicket, jumped into the bush and disappeared. When the canoe was picked up it was discovered that the man had lost a lot of blood. Heugh was amazed at the man's courage and his devotion and loyalty to Nana.[45] He came to the conclusion that Nana and his people were determined to resist to the utmost.

Heugh was soon to experience more of this determination. It had become clear that a full scale offensive would have to be mounted against Nana if he was to be broken. Heugh, therefore, against the express instructions of Moor, decided to reconnoitre the Ebrohimi creek with a view to discovering whether the town could be taken through a naval operation. He armour-plated his boat before setting out apparently not expecting anything more than desultory firing by wandering rifle men. He miscalculated badly. After going up the creek for some hundred yards, the British party ran into heavy fire from a masked battery somewhere in the mangrove swamp. Heugh's boat was pierced through in a number of places by shot which Heugh described in an exaggerated report as averaging 7–9 lbs. The British casualty list included two dead; one man lost a foot and another an arm; four others were injured. The boat was all but sinking by the time the survivors managed to get it back to the ship.[46]

Frederick Lugard, who was then in the service of the Royal Niger Company, was in the district when the above incident took place. His impressions recorded in his diary are an interesting commentary on the state of affairs at the time. There was, according to Lugard, considerable levity about the impending encounter with Nana. He thought little of the leadership of the British forces, noting that Captain Evanson, commanding the militia, was an officer 'with no experience at all'. Lugard had learnt enough about Nana and his town to reach the conclusion that Nana would be 'a hard nut to crack', but the British forces were 'looking forward to a great picnic', praying that Nana would not give in after all their preparations. Heugh's reconnaissance was a foretaste of the expected 'picnic'. The outcome, Lugard noted, was 'a great scare' and a considerable cooling of the martial ardour of the British forces.[47]

The above event demonstrated well the approach to the war of the beleaguered Nana and his people. They were fully aware of their inability to engage in a pitched battle with the British. Their only hope lay in preventing the British from actually reaching Ebrohimi while continued efforts were made to reach a settlement before a

major military defeat. Moor was greatly shaken by Heugh's misadventure and noted that the steadiness of the men was adversely
affected. Nevertheless there could be no going back. On 28 and 29
August, Moor ordered a 'reconnoitring in force'. Heugh's experience
had proved the folly of trying to reach Ebrohimi through the creek.
Moor now decided to cut a road through the dense mangrove swamp
to Ebrohimi.

On the 28th the work of cutting the road was led by 'a party of
friendly natives' supplied by Dogho and other Itsekiri traders who
stood to gain by the downfall of Nana, their over-mighty rival. The
cutting of the road proceeded until it was judged that the party was
nearing the masked battery which had done such damage to Heugh's
boat. Work was suspended until the next day when the entire force
available—military and naval—was landed. The aim was to take
Ebrohimi by land that day if possible. When the force had gone as
far as the point reached the previous day, scouts reported that there
was a powerful stockade some 200–300 yards off. This stockade was
eight feet high and 'had a face' of fifty yards extending for 300 yards
along the bank of the creek, very well masked by bush. It was made
of hard wood logs firmly driven into the ground in rows of two or
three. There were sleeping quarters for the stockade garrison.
Positioned at various points along the stockade were twenty-three
heavy cannon. The stockade was built during the months of July and
August. Moor described it as 'a most powerful construction'.
Little wonder the cannons had done so much damage to Heugh's
boat and party.

The British force now determined to take the stockade. Two seven-
pounder field guns had been supplied on request by the Lagos
Government. These were now brought into action against the stockade, the party advancing as the firing continued. Fifty yards from the
stockade the party encountered a deep creek. This had to be bridged
before the advance continued. Nana's men had apparently trained
their cannons on the creek. Knowledge of the land attack did not
reach the garrison until the 29th. It required considerable labour to
get some of the cannon turned away from the creek to the land, and
what was more Nana's men did not know the direction from which
the attack would come until the British opened fire (the mangrove
swamps could be just as much an advantage to the British as to
Ebrohimi). Ultimately the seven-pounder field guns were more than
a match for Nana's unwieldy cannon, not to talk of the marksmanship
acquired from disciplined training. It was not surprising therefore
that the garrison retreated in the face of this extremely heavy fire,

leaving the British to take the stockade, Ebrohimi's major defence position.[49]

Having taken the stockade the British advanced towards Ebrohimi. Once again they ran into a deep creek which took some four hours to bridge by the rough and ready method of felling mangrove trees into it. These creeks were part of Ebrohimi's natural defences and they had the result of increasing the task of the attacking party and so slowing them down. Meanwhile heavy firing was opened from Ebrohimi on the advancing party. As a result of this firing one African soldier was killed, a blue-jacket shot through the back, and one officer, Captain Scarfe of the N.C.P. force, shot in the head. The force pushed on de_pite these casualties and at 3 p.m. the outskirts of Ebrohimi became visible, but once again it was discovered that the way forward was 'a regular morass with a network of small creeks throughout'. The officers summoned a council of war on the spot. Heavy fire from Ebrohimi decided the British to fall back on the ships for that day. By 7 p.m. the entire force was back in the ships.[50]

Moor considered the 'reconnaissance' made on the 28th and 29th satisfactory. For one thing it had proved that it would be impossible to take Ebrohimi by advancing through the creek as this was the most easily defensible part of the ground to be traversed. Secondly, the experience of the 28th and 29th had clearly demonstrated that Ebrohimi had a reasonable supply of arms and ammunition and that its defences were well manned. It was the realisation of these facts that led Moor to request two more gun boats from the naval authorities.[51]

The lucky thing for the British was that the marksmanship of Nana's men was erratic. But for that the British forces would have suffered heavy losses on the 28th and 29th. Nana's Ebrohimi, built for defence and surrounded by mangrove forest, made it extremely difficult for the British to take aim at an enemy that was not visible. As for Nana, the events of the 28 and 29 August demonstrated to what lengths the British were prepared to go to break his power and position. The prevailing mood in both camps after the events of the 28th and 29th was one which favoured settlement. The letters exchanged on 30 August were the most sober written by both sides. Moor informed Nana that all he wanted was for peace to reign in the protectorate. The existing 'state of affairs was injurious to all' and he was 'therefore prepared on behalf of the government to make such settlement . . . as will allow of all persons carrying on their business without hesitation'.[52] Moor suspended all hostilities pending Nana's reply. Nana's reply reiterated the desire of himself and his people for peace. He asked to be told under what conditions the present hostilities could be terminated.[53]

It looked as if some settlement would now be reached, but this was not to be. Moor's conditions expressed in a letter of 4 September asked for unconditional surrender and the laying down of arms. The only guarantee he was prepared to give was that the lives of Nana and his men would be spared if he surrendered. Nothing was said as to what was to happen to Nana after his surrender. What was more, the first act of surrender was to be that Nana and his principal advisers should go on board HMS *Phoebe*.[54] Nana could not accept these terms.

Moor dared not attempt another attack until the extra force requested had arrived. In the meantime, negotiations having broken down, the shelling and blockading of Ebrohimi was intensified in the hope that Nana might yet be forced to surrender without the British having to undertake another march through dense mangrove swamps. But Nana did not surrender. Apparently he still had enough supplies of food in Ebrohimi; and anyway his men were much more familiar with the creeks and were obviously running the blockade successfully and bringing in further food supplies.

On 18 September HMS *Philomel* with the supreme commander of the African Squadron, Rear Admiral F. G. Bedford c.b., on board, arrived off the Benin river to take command of the expedition. Three days later HMS *Widgeon,* yet another gun boat, arrived.[55] Virtually the entire British naval strength in West Africa, together with all the military might of the Niger Coast Protectorate was thus concentrated on Ebrohimi—unquestionably the most impressive battle array assembled in the protectorate up to that time and in a sense a touching tribute to Nana's power and resilience. Moor was now in a definitely much stronger position than he had been on 28 and 29 August. He wrote to Nana giving him one final opportunity to surrender and go on board a British warship.[56] While Nana wrote saying he was ready for peace, he made it clear he would not go on board a British warship.[57] The die was finally cast. The time had come for the final showdown.

Rear Admiral Bedford himself took out another reconnoitring party on 21 September. He decided as a result it would be impossible to take Ebrohimi by approaching along the right flank of the town. On 22 September scouting parties (including guides sent by Dogho) were sent out in various directions. While the scouts did their work, Ebrohimi was kept under constant shell fire by the gun boats

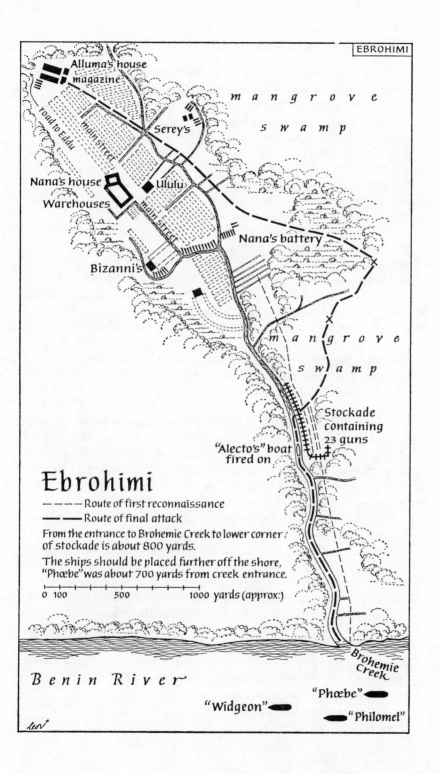

Alluma's house
magazine

m a n g r o v e

s w a m p

road to Eddu

main street

Serey's

Nana's house

Ululu

Warehouses

main street

Nana's battery

Bizanni's

X

X

m a n g r o v e

s w a m p

Stockade
containing
23 guns

"Alecto's" boat
fired on

Ebrohimi

– – – – Route of first reconnaissance

——— Route of final attack

From the entrance to Brohemie Creek to lower corner
of stockade is about 800 yards.

The ships should be placed further off the shore,
"Phœbe" was about 700 yards from creek entrance.

| 0 | 100 | 500 | 1000 | yards (approx:) |

B e n i n   R i v e r

Brohemie
Creek

"Phœbe"

"Widgeon"

"Philomel"

anchored off the creek. On 23 September it was again decided to cut a road to the town, care being taken this time to avoid the zone of fire from Nana's cannon. Even so Nana's men opened heavy fire on the working party. Ninety rounds were said to have been fired from cannons within one hour, in addition to rifle, machine-gun and blunderbuss fire.[58] But the firing was so erratic that no casualties were reported. Yet the situation was considered sufficiently threatening to warrant falling back on the ships. The next day the task was resumed and this time a track was cut right up to the outskirts of Ebrohimi.[59] The final onslaught was then fixed for 25 September.

The details of the final attack were carefully worked out by the Admiral himself. There was none of that levity of which Lugard complained in August. A general memorandum was circulated to all sectional commanders.[60] The stockade which the British had seized earlier on was to be the base of operations, 'housing' stores, ammunition and a field hospital. The attacking force itself totalled over 300 men with twenty-five officers not including the water party, which was to advance by boat after initial resistance had been overcome. The shelling of Ebrohimi was to continue while the land forces advanced. The exact strength of the defending forces was not known. The 2,000 people reported to have submitted after the fall of Ebrohimi included, women, children and other non-combatant personnel. What proportion of this total was actually involved in the fighting is difficult to say. It had become clear by this time, anyway, that the decisive factor in the impending encounter would not be sheer numerical strength but the nature of the weapons of war and the training, discipline and efficiency of the troops. In all of these regards the British had the advantage over Nana.

The final attack began as early as 5.30 a.m. on 25 September. The defenders were obviously on the alert for they opened fire on the attackers fifteen minutes after the advance began. Once again the firing, though heavy, was extremely erratic. No harm was reported to have been done. This meant that Nana's men were unable to stop the advance on their town as they had so far succeeded in doing. By 6.20 a.m. the track had been cut right into Ebrohimi itself and the advance into the town continued briskly. Rockets and Maxim guns were again brought into play to silence the Ebrohimi guns. A large number of thatched houses were set on fire by rocket fire. The main objective of the defenders had obviously been to keep the British from getting into Ebrohimi. Having failed to achieve this and in the face of Maxim and rocket fire, they gave up the defence of Ebrohimi. The town fell at 9 a.m.[61]

If the British forces thought that they would have the pleasure of capturing Nana, they were mistaken. Ebrohimi was largely deserted when it was taken, though people began to come in later. Nana himself had escaped from the town. While the British were planning the final stages of their campaign, Nana was busy working out his plan of escape in the event of failure to hold the British off. To escape through any of the well-known creeks was difficult because of the twenty-four hour patrol maintained by British boats. Nana therefore conceived the idea of cutting an artificial creek at the back of the town to link up with one of the major creeks at a point outside the patrol zone (see map p. 217). Work on this artificial canal or creek was all but finished by the time of the final attack on Ebrohimi. Nana and his immediate family and some friends succeeded in escaping from the town into the creeks of the mangrove swamp before the fall of Ebrohimi. Nana and his party endured many hardships in the swamp. Once Nana's canoe was chased by a patrol boat. He had to abandon the canoe with all property that he had managed to take with him. Ultimately having lost some of his relatives through disease or misadventure, he himself reached the Ijo village of Okotobo.[62]

Meanwhile Nana and his chief aides had been outlawed by the British, who had been cheated of their main adversary by his ingenious escape. A price of £500 was offered to anyone who captured and handed over Nana to the British.[63] 'Friendly chiefs' led by Dogho and Dudu sent their 'boys' round the country to gather information about Nana. Ultimately it was reported that Nana was in Okotobo. The British decided to leave the capture of Nana largely in the hands of the 'boys' of these 'friendly chiefs'. A force of 400 men mostly supplied by Dogho and Dudu and led by Dogho's head slave, Omota, was sent against Okotobo towards the end of October. Nana took his final stand against the British at Okotobo. The attacking force suffered some losses as did the Okotobo people in the one-day-long encounter. Okotobo eventually fell to the British force,[64] but once again while most of Nana's aides were taken, he himself escaped and found his way to Lagos where he put up with a friend of his, Seida Olowu.

In Lagos Nana was persuaded by Olowu and others to give himself up to the Governor of Lagos. It was apparently thought that such surrender would impress the British and so reduce the penalty that might be imposed whereas it was impossible to remain in hiding for ever. Nana gave in and surrendered himself to the Governor in Lagos.[65] He was ultimately handed over to the authorities of the Niger Coast Protectorate who tried him for making war on Her

Britannic Majesty, causing a breach of the peace and failing to keep his treaty obligations. He was found guilty on all counts and sentenced to deportation for life in addition to forfeiture of all property.[66] From December 1894 until August 1906 Nana was in exile; first in Calabar and then in Accra. In August 1906 he was allowed to return. By this time he was already in his fifties. For the ten more years of his life that were left to him, he demonstrated that he had not lost all the drive, energy and organisation that had won him a trading empire and the envy and hatred of lesser Itsekiri men and ambitious British empire builders. He died on 3 July 1916.[67]

The Ebrohimi expedition was, in some respects, similar to other expeditions mounted by the British against other rulers in West Africa. It demonstrated for example the weakness of West African military tactics in the face of the trained British who had better equipped forces. It demonstrated the inadequate experience of African non-professional soldiers in the handling of weapons acquired largely from the British themselves. Had Nana's men been good marksmen the British, by their own testimony, would have had an extremely uphill task.

On the other hand, the Ebrohimi expedition stands out by the sheer military build-up which was considered necessary if victory was to be won. The untrained gunners of Ebrohimi, taking advantage of such natural defences as they were blessed with, forced the British to withdraw on three different occasions. The final taking of Ebrohimi was, for the British, rather an anti-climax, the bird having flown before their arrival. Altogether Nana and his band of warriors were worthy adversaries who were beaten in war but most definitely not disgraced. The result of defeat was, however, the same here as elsewhere. An independent power was broken and a colonial administration was firmly foisted on the defeated and often unwilling party.

NOTES

1 For a general picture of the history of the Niger delta in the nineteenth century see K. O. Dike, *Trade and Politics in the Niger Delta,* London, 1956 and Obaro Ikime, *Merchant Prince of the Niger Delta* (The rise and fall of Nana Olomu, last Governor of the Benin River), 1968.

2 More details of Itsekiri Government can be found in Obaro Ikime, *Niger Delta Rivalry*, London, 1969, Chapter I.

3 *Ibid.,* Chapter II.

4 Jean Barbot, *A Description of the Coasts of North and South Guinea*, London, 1732, p. 377.

5 P. C. Lloyd 'Captain Landolphe and the Compagnie d'Owhere et de Benin', *Odu* No. 5, 1957, pp. 14–15.

6 Details of these wars are given in Ikime, *Merchant Prince* . . . Chapter 3. One of these wars was against Tsanomi. Olomu's crushing defeat of Tsanomi was one of the reasons for the family feud between Numa, Tsanomi's cousin, and Nana who succeeded his father. Dogho, Numa's son, carried on the feud to its bitter end by helping the British against Nana during the Ebrohimi expedition.

7 P. C. Lloyd 'The Itsekiri in the nineteenth century', *Journal of African History*, vol. 4, No. 2, 1963, p. 214.

8 Captain John Adams, *Remarks on the country extending from Cape Palmas to the Congo*, London, 1823, pp. 115–16.

9 Ikime, *Merchant Prince* . . . p. 13.

10 *Ibid.*, p. 8

11 Usually shortened to Tsanomi, the form used hereafter.

12 Ikime, *Niger Delta Rivalry*, Chapter I.

13 For details of the relations between the Itsekiri and the white traders see Ikime, *Merchant Prince* . . . pp. 15–25.

14 This is the shortened form of the full name Omadoghogbone.

15 See F.O. 84/1226, Mcleod to Vivian, 11th May 1870.

16 F.O. 93/6/10. For the full text of the treaty see Ikime, *Merchant Prince* . . . Appendix II, pp. 197–9.

17 F.O. 84/1940, Enclosure 8 in Macdonald to F.O., No. 11, 12 June 1889.

18 F.O. 2/64 Hewett to Nana, 24 February 1888, exhibit F at Nana's trial.

19 Ikime, *Merchant Prince* . . . Chapter III.

20 For more details of Itsekiri–Ijo relations see Obaro Ikime, 'The Western Ijo 1900–50, A Preliminary Survey', *Journal of the Historical Society of Nigeria*, December 1967.

21 George Neville, 'Nana Olomu of Benin', *Journal of the African Society*, vol. 14, 1914–15, pp. 162–7.

22 Ikime, *Merchant Prince* . . ., p. 36.

23 See map on p. 217.

24 F.O. 2/64, Gallwey to Nana, 1 December 1893.

25 F.O. 2/64, Macdonald to Nana, 5 April 1894.

26 F.O. 2/63, Moor to F.O., No. 22, 6 August 1894.

27 F.O. 2/64, Moor to Nana, 23 June 1894.

28 *Ibid.*, Nana to Moor, 24 June 1894.

29 *Ibid.*, Moor to Nana, 24 June 1894; Nana to Moor, 25 June 1894.

30 See J. C. Anene, *Southern Nigeria in Transition 1885–1900*, (London, 1966) pp. 82–92 for an account of the Jaja episode.

31 F.O. 2/64, Moor to Nana, 25 June 1894; Nana to Moor, 25 June 1894.

32 F.O. 2/63, Moor to F.O., No. 22, 6th August 1894.

33 F.O. 2/64, Moor to Nana, 10 July 1894.

34 F.O. 2/63, Moor to F.O., No. 22, 6 August 1894.

35 F.O. 2/64, Nana to Moor, 23 July 1894.
36 F.O. 2/63 see enclosure in Moor to F.O., No. 24, 15 August 1894.
37 F.O. 2/64, Nana to Moor, 1 August 1894 and 2 August 1894.
38 *Ibid.*, Moor to Nana, 2 August 1894.
39 F.O. 2/63, Moor to F.O., No. 22, 6 August 1894.
40 *Ibid.*, Moor to F.O., No. 23, 8 August 1894.
41 F.O. 2/64, Nana to Moor, 13 August 1894.
42 *Ibid.*, Moor to Nana, 15 August 1894.
43 F.O. 2/63, Moor to F.O., No. 25, 22 August 1894.
44 F.O. 2/64, Heugh to Moor, No. 6, 22 August 1894.
45 *Ibid.*
46 F.O. 2/64, Heugh to Moor, 25 August 1894.
47 M. Perham, *The Diaries of Lord Lugard,* volume 4 (London, 1960), pp. 75–8.
48 F.O. 2/63, Moor to F.O., No. 26, 31 August 1894.
49 *Ibid.*
50 *Ibid.*
51 *Ibid.*
52 F.O. 2/64, Moor to Nana, 8 August 1894.
53 *Ibid.*, Nana to officer commanding the expedition, 1 September 1894.
54 *Ibid.*, Moor to Nana, 4 September 1894.
55 *Ibid.*, Moor to Nana, 19 September, 1894.
56 *Ibid.*, same letter.
57 *Ibid.*, Nana to Moor, 22 September 1894.
58 F.O. 2/64 Moor to F.O., No. 28, 5 October 1894.
59 *Ibid.*
60 See Appendix.
61 F.O. 2/64, Moor to F.O., No. 28, 5 October 1894.
62 'Interview with Chief Nana of Benin (River)', *Lagos Weekly Record,* 3 November 1894.
63 F.O. 2/64, Enclosure in Moor to F.O., No. 28, 5 October 1894.
64 F.O. 2/64, Enclosure in Macdonald to F.O., No. 49, 13 December 1894.
65 F.O. 2/64, Macdonald to F.O., 12 December 1894.
66 F.O. 2/64, The Trial of Nana.
67 C.SO. 14/18, telegram from Resident Warri, the Secretary, Southern Provinces, 4 July 1916.

Appendix

General Memorandum on the Ebrohimi War.*

The Admiral will, acting with the Consul-General, exercise general supervision and direction of the movements.

2 Right Attack: Captain Powell will, on landing, immediately advance

* F.O. 2/64, Enclosure 1 in Moor to F.O. No. 28, 5 October 1894.

to the end of the road, and from there endeavour to get in the rear of the guns, and then make his way to the solid ground about Nana's house.

3 The Admiral and his staff will be with the column along the road.

4 Left and Centre Attack: Captain Campbell will establish his guns, and c., in the best position for harassing the enemy, but will not open fire unless they do, or in compliance with orders. He is to be prepared to advance up the main creek as opportunity offers. If possible, definite orders for him to advance will be sent, but in default of these he must act to the best of his judgement.

5 The stockade is the base, and the wounded are to be sent there. A reserve of water, and ammunition will be stored there.

6 As soon as the creek is open all communications between the two bodies to be by it.

7 The greatest caution is to be exercised when the town is gained to avoid casualties by explosion of small stores of powder which may be scattered about.

8 Any spirits found lying about to be immediately destroyed. Sentries to be placed on any store-houses.

9 The men are to be kept carefully in hand, and houses, and c., are not to be set on fire except by order.

The landing will be effected by 5.30 a.m. at the stockade.

The Niger Coast Protectorate troops and cutters to land outside the stockade below creek.

Right Attack: Force to advance along the road in the following order: Skirmishers:

50 Niger Coast Protectorate troops .. ⎫ Captain Evanson
17 ditto, with Maxim gun .... ⎭ and Mr. Roupell.
40 road cutters ...... Mr. Leckie and Mr. Campbell.
Rocket party........ Lieutenant Heugh and Sub. Lieutenant Harvey.
18 men, Maxim gun.. Mr. Staddon, gunner, Her Majesty's ship, 'Phoebe'.
37 marines.......... Sergeant of 'Phoebe' in charge.
'Philomel' .... 2 N.C.O.s and 14 privates.
'Phoebe' .... 2 N.C.O.s, 14 privates, and 1 bugler.
'Widgeon'.......... 1 N.C.O. and 5 privates.
50 seamen 'Phoebe'.. Lieutenant Hickley and Lieutenant Parks.
Ambulance .... Lieutenant-Surgeon Brown and Dr. Roth, Niger Coast Protectorate.
35 Seamen 'Widgeon' Lieutenant Grant-Dalton and Mr. Helihy, gunner, 'Widgeon' to remain at bend of the road until ordered to advance.

Left and Centre Attack: Landing party from 'Philomel', with

Maxim gun .... Lieutenant Gore Browne.
Lieutenant Clarke.
7-pr. gun .... Sub-Lieutenant Tomlin.

3-pr. gun .... Gunner Jennings.
Rockets .... Boatswain Tubb.
Explosive party .... Surgeon Maitland
Engineer Richardson will establish themselves in the stockade and advance when possible.

Lieutenant Marston, of 'Widgeon', assisted by Mr. Atkins, Assistant Engineer, 'Philomel', to be in charge of base at stockade under the orders of Captain Campbell, fifty carriers will be available to forward reserve stores to front.

The Surgeons of 'Widgeon' and 'Alecto' will remain to receive wounded at the stockade.

Staff Commander Maclean will be in charge of ships and will be responsible for the firing.

The men are to wear blue and hats; they are to take one day's provisions and 100 rounds of ammunition.

Portable bridges for crossing small creeks to be provided by 'Phoebe'.

Distinguishing signals: 'Philomel', three G's before and after bugle calls. 'Widgeon', two G's before and after bugle calls.

Details of arrangements to be made by officers in command of columns.

(Signed) FRED. G. D. BEDFORD
Rear-Admiral, Commander-in-Chief

'Philomel', at Benin, September 24, 1894
The respective captains and Officers
commanding Her Majesty's ships, &c., Benin River.

LA RAY DENZER

Sierra Leone–Bai Bureh*

By far one of the most difficult campaigns the British fought during the occupation of their West African possessions was against the Temne of northern Sierra Leone from January to November 1898.[1] Though the Temne army was small by West African standards, under the brilliant generalship of Bai Bureh, ruler of the tiny chiefdom of Kasseh, it held the initiative over the British for the first four months of the war and was not finally defeated until the capture of the leader ten months after the outbreak of hostilities. The secret of Bai Bureh's success was his appreciation that the only way to deal with invading troops with superior equipment was to use guerilla tactics. In exploitation of these his only peer in West Africa was Samori.

* Research on the general background of the Bai Bureh war was carried out by the author and Professor Michael Crowder at the suggestion of Dr. Robert I. Rotberg and Professor Ali Mazrui for inclusion in a symposium on the tradition of protest in Tropical Africa (see note 1). The author also reconstructed a 'diary' of the war based on the materials available in the Sierra Leone Archives for *Sierra Leone Studies*. She would like to thank the authorities of Fourah Bay College for generously providing her with a research assistantship to Mr. Crowder, when he was Director of the Institute of African Studies at Fourah Bay College, which enabled her to collect much of the background material on which this 'military' analysis is based. Since working on the above projects, the author has done more extensive research in the areas of Temne warfare and Temne response to the establishment of British rule. Both the articles referred to above are fully documented from archival sources, and only fresh archival material etc. is referred to here.

Bai Bureh's war, as the 1898 Hut Tax war in northern Sierra Leone was popularly known, was not strictly speaking a war against colonial occupation. Technically speaking Temneland had been under a British Protectorate for fifteen months when its people took up arms against the British. The ostensible reason for what the British regarded as a rebellion against their authority was their resistance to the imposition of a tax on every house in the protectorate. As we shall see, as far as it concerned the Temne, and indeed the Mende in the south who followed their example three months later, the 'rebellion' was a war to regain an independence which they had seen gradually slipping from their hands.

The war took the British completely by surprise. It interrupted what the British had been confident would be the peaceful transfer of sovereignty from the local African chiefs to themselves.

Until the declaration of the Protectorate in 1896, political relations between the chiefs in the northern interior and the British officials in Freetown, which had been occupied by the British from 1787, had been conducted along fairly amicable lines of near-equality and collaboration. Although they had yielded certain of their rights regarding foreign relations to the British Government before 1896, the chiefs still maintained their sovereignty within their own chiefdoms. In their dealings with the Freetown officials they had direct access to the Government Interpreter (later called the Secretary for Native Affairs) and through him to the Governor.

Discussions of matters involving either foreign relations or questions concerning British subjects resident in the chiefdoms took place in a manner not unlike that in which inter-chieftaincy disputes were settled prior to the arrival of the British. Chiefs and British officials met in one of the important chiefdom capitals (now including Freetown) to resolve their differences by arbitration.

The chiefs had agreed to limitations on their authority in a series of treaties in which they, as much as the British, hoped to gain greater advantages in trade through the construction and maintenance of roads throughout the interior. Like the Fanti in the Gold Coast, they welcomed alliance with the British as a means of containing their enemies in what is now Guinea—the Susu, Samory, and the French. In return for these advantages, the chiefs were quite willing to allow the Sierra Leone Colony Government the right to arbitrate, and if necessary, make final decision respecting the conflicts which might arise among their chiefdoms. In effect the Colony Government's demand that in return for its support it arbitrate inter-chiefdom disputes was an unexpected dividend, for this was in line with traditional diplomatic procedures but did not cost the chiefs as much. Among the peoples of the northern hinterland of Freetown, the leaders of one chiefdom or people would request the leaders of other chiefdoms or peoples to assist them both in waging war and making peace. It was customary to pay for such assistance in goods and in hospitality, an exchange which proved very expensive; the British Government, however, while adding much prestige to their deliberations, did not demand such payment. Only later did the chiefs discover that the real cost of British assistance was much higher than they were in fact willing to pay.

Throughout the period of growing British jurisdiction over the hinterland of Sierra Leone from the creation of the Government Interpreter's Department (later called the Native Affairs Department) in 1878 to the Proclamation of the Protectorate in 1896, British authority did not alarm the chiefs. Although in the area of their external relations with other chiefdoms and European powers, they had relinquished their rights to make war or treaties, they still possessed full powers in their own chiefdoms. In cases where chiefs did undertake preparations for war, the threat from Freetown that Britain would remove herself from treaty relationship with them was usually sufficient to return the chiefs to their agreement. They greatly feared that Britain would leave them to a worse fate at the hands of the French or Samory.

During the late 1880s and early 1890s the British Government was forced to exercise increasing authority over the areas of the northern interior (to which it laid claim on paper) lest the French try to occupy them on the grounds that the British did not effectively control them. Thus the Colony Government was compelled to devise institutions whereby it could ensure that the roads were kept clear and open to all travellers, and enforce the agreements already made with the chiefs. Of particular concern was the need to prevent chiefs within the British sphere of influence from making war across the much contested boundary between the French-claimed areas of south-eastern Guinea and those claimed by Britain in northern Sierra Leone. In 1890 the first steps were taken towards these ends. Two Travelling Commissioners, one for the northern interior and another for the southern, were appointed and the Frontier Police Force created.

The establishment of these two bodies began to abolish the right of free access to Freetown officials for the chiefs. Where the Secretary for Native Affairs or the Governor had heard cases involving disputes among chiefdoms and made judgements, now the Travelling

Commissioners undertook the responsibility. Where the chiefs had been held responsible for the ensurance of free passage along the roads, the prevention of any molestation of traders, and the prevention of war, these duties were now assumed by the police, who also provided the Government with reliable intelligence concerning chiefdom affairs.

Although the police were specifically admonished against interfering in the governments of the chiefs, they repeatedly overstepped the bounds of their authority, in many instances becoming little more than petty tyrants. Scattered throughout the interior, they were often left unsupervised by senior officers. Instead of maintaining peace, they not only insulted the chiefs and ill-treated the people, but also committed crimes ranging from unlawful arrest and flogging to thieving and plundering. They proved to be an extremely disruptive element, and the chiefs were constantly complaining about them to Freetown and to the Travelling Commissioners. More often than not the charges made against them proved to be correct, and only three years after the force was formed, the Creole Secretary for Native Affairs, J. C. E. Parkes, reluctantly urged that the number of men stationed in the interior be reduced and strict discipline enforced on those who remained.[2] Having recently proposed that a protectorate be established over the interior, he feared that the presence of these 'indiscreet and semi-civilised members of the native community' would considerably lessen the influence of the Government in the areas where they were stationed. Part of the problem derived from the fact that many of the police were slaves who had run away from the chiefdoms to Freetown where under British law they gained their freedom. It was in Freetown that they were recruited into the Frontier Police Force. Chiefs naturally resented such treatment from men who had once been slaves. Although police behaviour improved with the imposition of a stricter disciplinary code drawn up for the Force by Governor Cardew in 1894, there were still more than sixty recorded complaints against the police in the three years immediately preceding the war.[3]

The Protectorate was finally declared on 31 August 1896, a year after Great Britain and France had settled the boundaries between them in the area. The main objective of the Government was to establish public order on terms acceptable to British political ideals and practices. The Protectorate Ordinance provided for the division of the interior into five districts, and in each district vested supreme authority in a British district commissioner. It made major changes in two important areas of the traditional system of government, those of administration of land and justice, as well as those of prohibiting slave dealing and raiding. This prohibition did not come as a surprise to the chiefs: they had already agreed to it nine years earlier, and although there were many lapses on their part, they generally adhered to their agreement. The new regulations concerning land and their juridical rights, however, caused great alarm and consternation. These attacked the very foundations of the chiefs' sovereignty, and the chiefs immediately united to resist British encroachment on these aspects of their authority. They found that constitutional representations on their part won them no redress, and that the British Government fully intended to impose the new colonial authority on them. Only over the question of land was Governor Cardew prepared to admit that perhaps they had some foundation for complaint.[4] A full understanding of the bitterness felt by the chiefs over the new regulations concerning the administration of justice and of their lands is essential for an explanation of the ferocity and tenacity with which the Temne later fought the British.

Under the new regulations concerning court jurisdiction, three types of courts were created: (1) the District Commissioners' Court; (2) a court presided over by both the District Commissioner and the chiefs; and (3) the Chiefs' Court. The chiefs found that they were no longer allowed to try in their own courts cases which involved land titles, witchcraft, tribal disputes which might lead to armed conflict, slave dealing and raiding, murder, rape, and other major crimes. Although the chiefs could still try all civil cases which did not involve a land title, and certain lesser criminal cases, they feared that the new regulations would mean the loss of a good deal of their sources of revenue and loss of their powers of political sanction. Pa Suba of Magbele explained to the one-man Royal Commission for Enquiry under Sir David Chalmers, which was set up during the Hut Tax War to investigate its causes, that 'the king of the country however small if he cannot settle small matters is no longer king . . .'[5] The chiefs themselves interpreted these clauses to mean, 'That your petitioners are to have no more powers over their country. They are not to hear any cases relating to their lands, farms, and the boundaries of their country. This your petitioners take to mean nothing short of total dispossession of their country. . . .'[6]

With regard to the land regulations as well, the chiefs saw further loss of their authority in all its aspects: political, social, and religious. The, as yet unamended, Protectorate Ordinance stipulated that all grants of land made by countrymen or non-countrymen for collection of produce (rubber, palm kernels, etc.) must be approved by the Governor before the end of the year. The Government reserved the rights to exploitation of minerals for itself, and also assumed control of what it considered to be waste land. Finally, the Government levied a tax on houses. Originally this tax was fixed at the rate of five shillings a year for two-roomed houses and ten shillings a year for larger houses, but this was subsequently reduced to a flat five shillings for all houses having two rooms or more.

It was the tax which became the focus of attention during the war, occasioning as it did the first instance in which the newly established administration had to enforce its regulations over the entire territory. However, the entire body of land and court regulations had convinced the chiefs that the Government intended their ruin. After the Secretary of State replied to their June petition that they misunderstood the Ordinance, they said as much in a subsequent petition to the Legislative Council in which they declared that they interpreted the London decision to mean 'total ruin to themselves and their country generally . . .'[7]

Fully to appreciate the chiefs' attitude, it is necessary to understand what the concept of chieftaincy meant to the Temne.[8] When a Temne man was installed as chief, he became the focus of unity for his people. His person embodied their ideals of justice, wisdom, and humanity, and as such assumed a sacred character. One of the essential ceremonies at his installation was called *ankala na kawai rabai* (money paid for the chieftaincy) which symbolised his actual purchase of both the land and the people who inhabited it; thus establishing his right to the power of commanding their obedience. In pre-Protectorate days, before the role of chief was transformed from sovereign to government agent, the people had means of balancing his power, although in theory this power was absolute and he could dispose of either his land or his people as he desired. When the Government claimed and assumed ultimate authority over land through the Ordinance it was natural that the chiefs would regard it as being tantamount to their complete loss of authority.

According to traditional land law there was no concept such as that referred to by the British as 'waste land'. The chief owned all the land in his chiefdom whether it was cultivated or uncultivated. The uncultivated portion provided wild crops (fruit, palm kernels, etc.) which the people would collect. It also incorporated areas which were sacred to the people such as secret society bushes, the sacred burial grounds of the chiefs, and so forth. Beyond this, the uncultivated areas ensured the future of the chiefdom, for when the villages

became overcrowded or the cultivated land too poor for farm-
ing, the chief would allocate new fields and homesteads from
them.

Against this background, it can be appreciated that during the
course of the war the hut tax assumed an importance out of all
proportion to its meaning. At the beginning of the hostilities both
local administrators and the Colonial Office, as well as the traders and
press, believed that the primary cause of the war was the imposition
of the hut tax. The traders and press united in opposition to the
administration's policy, maintaining, not that the taxes were wrong,
but that the Governor had failed to explain himself adequately to the
chiefs, and that he acted in too great haste to collect the taxes. To the
chiefs this tax simply meant that the Government, having deprived
them of their legal functions and of their customary administration of
land, now meant to strip them of the last vestige of their authority
over their own houses.

The chiefs took the taxes to mean that now they must pay the
Government for a place to sleep, that they no longer owned their
own houses. No amount of explanation by the Governor and his
representatives could persuade them otherwise. W. T. G. Lawson,
the chiefs' lawyer and a member of a Temne regent family himself,
explained that they assumed themselves to be 'deprived of power in
their country' if they paid the tax on their houses.[9] They did not
reject the idea of taxation *per se* inasmuch as they possessed powers of
taxation themselves. When they hired Lawson to draft their petition
to the Secretary of State, he took great care to ascertain their exact
grievances.[10] He explained to them that the tax was necessary so that
the Government could pay for the maintenance of the police, but to
this they replied that 'if the Governor wanted them to help in the
maintenance of the police he would call and tell them so; that of
course, if they paid for a hut, they had no more right over it.'[11]
The chiefs themselves assured the administration that: 'Your
petitioners are not unmindful of the great expense the Government
must have undergone, and is undergoing, to bring about and maintain peace and order they are now enjoying in their country; . . . and
will not grudge any contributions in their power to lighten the
burden of the Government in any way.'[12] They rejected, however,
both the concept of a tax on their house, and the idea of paying it to
an alien administration. They begged the Governor to remember the
disaster of Quiah in 1861 when the British levied a tax on territory
ceded to them. The tax collector had proved to be an unscrupulous
person who plundered the people and created such a generally

unfortunate situation that the Freetown Government felt compelled to repeal the tax and return the ceded land to the chiefs.

Not only did the Ordinance infringe on traditional authority and its basis in every way, it now legalised what the Temne considered to be violations of the chief's *masem,* the set of prohibitions regulating the conduct of the people towards the chief, and the chief's conduct towards them.[13] Crucial were those which prohibited any person from beating, fighting or quarrelling with another in the chief's presence. To fight or quarrel with the chief himself would have been virtually unthinkable. Yet under the Ordinance the District Commissioners could, if a chief violated the Ordinance, flog, handcuff, or imprison him. The chiefs regarded this 'a terrible punishment for a right they had enjoyed from their forefathers,'[14] and feared that should such punishments be inflicted on them they would be so disgraced that they could no longer command obedience from their, subjects, domestic slaves, wives, and children. The Temne possessed no inanimate object such as the Ashanti Golden Stool which symbolised the soul of the people;* the chief's very person did just this. To protect him and their society from degradation the people would unite for war.

In the minds of the chiefs, therefore, the main issue was not the tax, but where authority lay. They constantly declared their loyalty, but it was that loyalty which they traditionally gave the Queen under their former treaty relationships. They maintained that the spirit of the present administration was 'so unlike the spirit of the English people, with whom they have had to deal now over one hundred and ten years.'[15] One chief explained it more simply when he told Sir David Chalmers that 'There is a difference between the white people that come now and those before: those who come now do not respect the Chiefs.'[16]

The principal desire of the chiefs, expressed in all their petitions was a return to their former relationship. They asked to be granted 'the enjoyment of the ancient privilege, accorded them from the first day the English landed on their shores, of appealing for protection direct to His Excellency the Governor and Administrator through the Colonial Secretary or the officer now known as the Secretary for Native Affairs'.[17] They assured the Government that they now knew the power possessed by the British and the benefits of peace, and no longer held any intention of making war. They guaranteed to maintain peace within their own countries, and towards this end were willing to allow one Government resident and a few police

* See p. 20.

officers to stay in their chiefdoms. Chiefs giving evidence before the Chalmers' Commission repeatedly made this point, and were quite confident that they could manage their own countries.[18] Cardew refused their request: 'The Government cannot leave your country to itself. If it were to do so—say withdraw the police and District Commissioners—slave raiding and inter-tribal wars would commence again, in a short time there would be such anarchy and confusion, and our neighbours would so suffer from the disturbances that they would step in and occupy and control your country themselves.'[18] He assured them that if England did not rule them, another European power would.

The Temne chiefs' initial protests were made through the presentation of a series of petitions. The chiefs of the Port Loko area, including Bai Bureh, presented the first petition to Captain W. S. Sharpe, the District Commissioner of Karene, only three months after the Ordinance had been proclaimed.[19] They drafted it immediately after Government representatives had come to Port Loko to explain the new Ordinance and its terms. Ten chiefs met for consultations and delegated Fodi Yunisa of Port Loko to write a petition.[20] It was not so well written as subsequent petitions, but the views contained in it were the same. The majority of these chiefs or their representatives united with other important Temne chiefs (while they were in Freetown for the Jubilee celebrations) to present another petition, this time to the Secretary of State through the Governor. So seriously did they regard its contents that they waited in Freetown for the Secretary of State's reply which did not come until October. When the reply arrived, they were not satisfied with it and drafted another letter of explanation, this time to the Legislative Council.

They decided to remain in Freetown until the Governor returned from England in November. Cardew met with them on 15 November, but his answer still did not satisfy them, and they wrote yet another letter explaining why they continued to protest.[21] Finally, they were convinced of the futility of supplication after they had received a curt reply to their last letter, in which the Secretary of Native Affairs told them that the Governor had discussed their grievances with them thoroughly, and that now the matter was closed.[22]

The chiefs manifested their opposition to the new administration in other ways than through petitions. Captain Sharpe complained that he had had little communication with the chiefs during that time, and that very few of them had taken advantage of the Ordinance to bring disputes to him for settlement.[23] A particularly instructive example of the hostility and resentment shown by the Temne to the new administration before the outbreak of war is given by the succession dispute in Sanda chiefdom. Shortly before the Ordinance took effect, the elderly Brima Sanda (ruler of Sanda) had died. When the new British District Commissioner took charge of the area, the chiefdom electors had still not chosen a successor. They remained deadlocked over the choice for more than a year, and finally, in exasperation, the District Commissioner gave them an ultimatum either to come to an agreement or be prepared for him to settle the matter for them. At the end of the time limit imposed by the District Commissioner they were no closer to a choice than before, and the District Commissioner made good his threat, recommending the election of Santigi Dura, the right hand man of the former Brima Sanda. The Governor approved his decision; however the people of the chiefdom itself were never satisfied with this usurpation of their prerogatives. Bokari Bamp, a chief of Port Loko, attempted to arouse them to take action against this administrative decision[24] since Santigi Dura had no right to the crown, but the District Commissioner checked his move. This same Bokari Bamp was to become a central figure in the opening days of the war, when he was arrested for refusing to collect taxes. The man who presumed himself to be the rightful successor was to apply to Bai Bureh to assist him in an attempt to take the chieftaincy. The people of the chiefdom were later to abandon their chief for Bai Bureh, leaving Santigi Dura, the Brima Sanda, in solitary loyalty to the Government.

Another early step taken by the new administration which caused resentment was to present the chiefs with gold-headed staffs of office in a ceremony devised to provide dignity to the chiefs' new relationship with the Government. Many chiefs refused to come to the ceremony, sending instead their messengers to receive these staffs. When they were forced to come in person, they protested that they did not understand this policy as they had always sent their messengers before. One of the most important of these chiefs who refused to come was Bai Foki[25] who was responsible for the installation of all the Port Loko chiefs, a relationship which would become a crucial point in the first attempts to collect taxes. Several times he had ignored the summons sent by Captain Cave Brown, the Acting District Commissioner, to come to Port Loko, but he was eventually forced to accompany a party of police constables who had gone to his town with orders not to return without him. Although this did not mean actual arrest, the police interpreted it as such. They handcuffed the chief, and imprisoned him in the barracks. His followers were greatly alarmed at the treatment given their chief, and a group of them, led by Bai Salamansa, forcibly removed him from the barracks.

Still another act of the administration which caused resentment involved the leader of the Temne opposing forces himself. Late in 1896, Captain Sharpe had summoned Bai Bureh to come to Karene to assist in the building of Barracks.[26] Several times Bai Bureh ignored the summons, coming only after Captain Sharpe sent a party of police to bring him back. After he arrived, Bai Bureh called on the District Commissioner who refused to see him, saying that he must first complete his work. Bai Bureh directed his men in their work but as soon as they completed their section of the barracks, he returned the insult by leaving the town without greeting Captain Sharpe.

Subsequent events demonstrated how little the District Commissioner and the Governor knew about the northern Temne people. Until well into the course of the war, Cardew remained blithely unaware of the gravity of the situation in the interior caused by his refusal to take seriously the grievances of the chiefs. He was completely unaware of the institutions possessed by the Temne for united, well-disciplined resistance. Given the changing trends in colonial practices, there was little possibility that another man would have acted much differently: the basic question involved was the transfer of ultimate authority. Conflict was inevitable if the chiefs still retained hope of keeping their sovereignty as they knew it. The Victorian views of progress and evolution, current among both missionaries and the new colonial officials, precluded any true assessment of tribal institutions or capabilities, Cardew's eloquent appraisal of the causes of the war, admittedly made four months after the outbreak of hostilities, gives a great deal of insight into this new colonial mandate:

> ... the true causes in my opinion ... are the desire for independence and for a reversion to the old order of things, such as fetish customs and slave dealing and raiding. It is practically a revolt of the Chiefs whose authority has been lessened and whose property has suffered through the abolition of slavery. They are sick of the supremacy of the white man as asserted by the District Commissioners and Frontier Police. . . . They see the old order of things passing away; the fear and reverence paid to their fetish customs and superstitions diminishing, their authority going from them, their slaves asserting their independence, their children

being taught by the missionaries a purer religion and the methods of civilisation and, on top of it all, comes the house tax which is the last straw that breaks the camel's back and hence the revolt.[27]

1

Although the Freetown officials came to understand the causes of the war, it took them a long time fully to realise the resilience of Temne military organisation. At first the Government officials and military officers were caught off-guard, but the military comprehended the seriousness of the situation long before the administrative officers would admit it. Governor Cardew assumed that a small demonstration of force conducted by the Frontier Police would reassert Government authority in less than a month. Not until he had experienced several months of fierce resistance did he personally appreciate the strength of Temne opposition. Temne competence in war won high praise from the British officers in the field. One of them, C. Braithwaite Wallis, a Frontier Police officer in Bandajuma, confessed his great respect for their abilities in his memoir of the war:

> ... if Bureh was an unusually smart man, so did the Timini prove to be in the events that followed. Savages they might be, but even in their very fighting they betrayed such admirable qualities as are not always to be found in the troops of the 'civilised' nations. They loved their chief, and remained loyal to him to the very last, whilst they 'understand bush-fighting as well as you and I do our very alphabet!'[28]

Steeped in the belief that the interior peoples would acquire the benefits of civilisation under British protection and guidance, the Freetown officials neither anticipated nor made preparations for a determined resistance. Even the officer most knowledgeable about the interior, the Secretary for Native Affairs, J. C. E. Parkes, had not expected resistance on the scale which developed. Yet in his department were kept many volumes of correspondence with the chiefs and memoranda analysing their political affairs. These covered a period of over twenty years, dating back to 1876. He was fully aware that as recently as 1892, the Temne, led by Bai Bureh himself, had conducted major war operations against the Susu in Limba country. More recently, the same Temne alliance, again led by Bai Bureh, had made preparations to attack the Susu in Moriah.

There is abundant evidence in these volumes concerning the organisational powers and military propensities of the Temne chiefdoms. Besides this contemporary information, there is a more recent historical analysis of Temne political structure made by V. R. Dorjahn which reveals some aspects of their past military institutions.[29] Although he limits his study to the Kolifa-Mayoso chiefdom in south-western Temne country, his description and conclusions do not differ greatly from what can be derived from the Native Affairs/Government Interpreters' documents or a few isolated interviews recently carried out in eastern Temne country.[30]

Temne military organisation centred on the war-chiefs *(kruba)*. These war-chiefs were usually heads of lineages or influential men who possessed enough power and wealth to supply food, men, weapons, and magical protection for a war party. They kept a retinue of a few personal warriors who protected their property and to whom was delegated the responsibility of organising the larger war parties.[31] Often they were sub-chiefs *(karp)* but it was not necessary that they should hold a position within the administrative hierarchy. A war-chief usually supported his paramount chief's authority, and would defend the chiefdom when it was attacked. However, if a war-chief possessed enough power, he could oppose the paramount chief if he felt that the latter was ruling unjustly and thus provided an important check on the latter's power.

Dorjahn claims that war-chiefs rarely accompanied their forces into battle, but instead would hire warriors of outstanding ability *(ankurgba)* to lead their army. These leaders could be from a different tribe or chiefdom. When making preparations for war, the war-chief would give their leading warriors a large amount of goods which was then taken to other chiefs in other areas, from whom the warriors would ask permission to recruit more warriors as well as pass through their countries with their recruits. Through these means warriors were collected from a variety of chiefdoms and peoples, and some would come from more distant places because the fame of the war-leader had attracted them. They were rewarded for their services with rights of plunder and a portion of the value of any slaves they might capture, although the percentage of goods distributed between warrior, war-leader and war-chief is vague.[32]

The occupation of warrior was clearly institutionalised. Boys were trained specifically for war duties through a system of apprenticeship. They were put under an established warrior's care for a number of years, during which they helped him in his farms and acquired the knowledge of the arts of warfare. An influential man might send his son to a successful war-leader or war-chief in a chiefdom other than his own, and in this way the young apprentice would acquire the basis of trans-chiefdom loyalties. The system of domestic slavery practised by the Temne would have encouraged the development of such a military aristocracy, for slaves could be entrusted with the maintenance of farms and farm villages while their owners were at war.

For purposes of war at the invitation of neighbouring chiefdoms, or at times when the entire group of northern Temne chiefdoms were threatened with attack, the various chiefdoms would form an alliance which usually consisted of the four chiefdoms of the Great Scarcies area (Mabwetie, Mambolo, Rowoola, and Digsaing), the two chiefdoms of the Small Scarcies (Robureh and Kasseh), and Port Loko.[33] This alliance was fairly stable, although when not allied for the purposes mentioned above they did engage in a certain amount of warfare amongst themselves, but this could usually be resolved in negotiations. It played an important part in the Susu civil wars throughout the entire period.

One of the prominent leaders in this alliance from 1865 onwards was one Kebalai, a warrior of part Temne descent. Later he would be installed as chief of Kasseh, and thereby assume the title of Bai Bureh. His career seems to have developed from war-leader to war-chief to paramount chief. Although Cardew would claim later that he really had no right to the chieftaincy by family, it is probable that he was related in some manner to a family eligible for office. However, the choice of a man renowned for his ability in war as paramount chief was quite common in Temne chieftaincy elections, particularly if there was no suitable candidate from the ruling families.

Kebalai's first major military successes occurred in 1865, when he led a contingent of warriors sent to aid Bokhari by Sattan Lahai, paramount chief of Rowoola, and other Scarcies' chiefs. Bokhari fought first to secure his title for himself in 1865. Later some of his sub-chiefs rebelled against his policy of imposing correct Koranic practices on his subjects, and Bokhari fought a *jihad* or holy war against them which did not end until his death in battle in 1885. Throughout the protracted war operations of twenty years, Kebalai was one of his most successful leaders, attracting followers from all over the Scarcies' interior and from more distant chiefdoms such as Yoni.

In 1886, he was installed as chief of Kasseh, a relatively small chiefdom on the left bank of the Small Scarcies river about twenty-five miles from Port Loko.[34] On acquiring office, he undertook the chiefdom's obligation of maintaining the terms of its treaty with the British which had been signed in 1871. It was incumbent on a new chief to carry out the agreements and court decisions made by his predecessor. As with other chiefs in the area, this treaty required him to keep the roads of the chiefdom open to traders and to refer any disputes with other chiefs to Freetown for arbitration. In return he received a small annual stipend of ten pounds from the Government.

It was not long before Kasseh, which had hitherto been a peaceful chiefdom, was involved in disputes with neighbouring chiefdoms. Three months after Kebalai's installation, Kasseh almost went to war with Binneh Sangkong, one of the Port Loko sub-chiefs; however the dispute was settled in Bai Bureh's favour by the Port Loko chiefs.[35] Not long afterwards Bai Bureh was involved in a serious land dispute with Bai Inga of Robureh.[36] Apparently, Bai Bureh utilised the political hierarchy of his chiefdom for military purposes, and soon built up an influential reputation throughout the Port Loko–Scarcies area. Several times he clashed with British authority, and twice British officials determined to arrest him, but failed in each attempt.

He led the Temne warriors in the Temne–Lokko–Limba coalition against Karimu, a Susu leader whom the French were encouraging so that their claims in the border area between Guinea and the northern Sierra Leone area would be furthered. When the British failed to negotiate peace between the two sides, partly due to Bai Bureh's refusal to participate in peace discussions, they determined to arrest him for his defiance of their authority, and to send an expedition against Karimu. They failed in this attempt. Later in 1892, when they organised their expedition, they were forced to seek Bai Bureh's assistance for political reasons. At that time, Bai Bureh's disciplined warriors and military organisation so impressed the British officer in charge of the warriors' section of the expedition that he praised Bai Bureh at great length in his report. During this expedition, Bai Bureh was able to observe the fighting techniques and organisation of the Frontier Police and the West India Regiment, knowledge of which was to be useful to him in his war against the British.

In collecting warriors and organising them to resist the British in 1898, Bai Bureh utilised the northern Temne alliance.[37] Important Temne chiefdoms in the southern area also gave their support, although they did not prepare their own chiefdoms for war.[38] All these chiefs had consulted together on a number of occasions, the most important of which were probably those when they met to draft petitions. Bai Bureh sent his head warriors through the chiefdoms to recruit warriors. Meanwhile other chiefs made arrangements to block river traffic and barricade the roads.

Warriors came from as far south as Funkdeh, Pamalap, and other towns near the customs station at Makela, on the south-western border with Guinea.[39] Susu warriors came from Moriah and Sumbuya in Guinea, giving assistance in return for Bai Bureh's earlier support in their unsuccessful wars against the French. Bai Farima of Safroko supplied both warriors and leaders, among them Pa Mana Saspo, who supervised stockade construction in some areas. Bai Simra of Kayimbo allowed his sub-chiefs to give refuge to many of Bai Bureh's wives. He was also instrumental in blocking river traffic. Bai Kura Hari of Tinkatupa and Alimami Baba of Rotata blocked the road to Falaba and refused to permit passage to Government messengers. Alimami Rassin of Binti prevented Government messengers from using the road. The chiefs of Port Loko and Rowoola joined in making their entire area a bulwark against British encroachment.

Most of the towns in the interior were built for maximum defence, situated in such a way as to derive full benefit from their natural surroundings.[40] In Temne country this meant that villages were built in extremely inaccessible places which were defended by means of intricate paths which converged on a single easily defended path as the village itself was approached. Towns were built on the rise of a hill or on the banks of a small river or creek wherever possible. Often the towns would be surrounded by swampy ground or thick bush. The huts were built very close together on either side of a single path which ran through the village. In times of war, the spaces between the huts would be barricaded, forming a temporary walled defence. The description of Romeni given by British officers is typical of this means of construction.[41] It was built on lower ground, and could easily be overlooked. Its central path was strongly barricaded between the huts, and through these barricades were inserted loop-holes which were used for firing.

The use of stockades was essential to Temne defence.[42] These were generally built at the entrance of the towns. There were seldom less than two, and quite often as many as four or five. They were constructed of short logs normally ranging from ten to fourteen inches in diameter which were embedded two to three feet in the ground, leaving six feet or more above the ground. Then they were solidly bound together. In front of the logs were placed large boulders or laterite stones which were piled three to four feet high. Funnels were made by cutting up bamboo poles into sections which were then pushed through the stones and logs to form a row of loop-holes near the earth. More loop-holes were placed at different heights above these. Just inside the stockade trenches were dug and from here men would take up firing positions. A pathway was cut in the rear of the stockades in case it was necessary to retreat. If possible they preferred to build their stockades where there was a slope running downwards from them, thus giving them additional firing advantages over an attacking enemy. With a large labour force, it was possible in two days to complete the number of stockades necessary to defend a town.

Bai Bureh adapted this mode of fighting to give him greater initiative over cumbersome British marching columns. Besides building stockades at village entrances, he also had them placed along the paths. Behind these Temne warriors would wait in ambush, and in this manner they inflicted considerable damage on British columns which were hampered by their ignorance of the terrain and their need to protect the carriers headloading supplies.[43] The shells of the British seven-pounder guns could not penetrate the thick walls of the stockades, and often broke into pieces upon impact. When attacked, the British troops were not able to pursue the Temnes because it took them too long to cut through the thick bush. Occasionally the British troops would send flanking parties to cut through the bush and attack from the rear, but there was not often time enough to put this plan into operation.

Over and above the construction of stockades, Temne preparations for war included removing canoes from rivers in order to stop the British using them, barricading the roads with brushwood, and laying in stores of gunpowder. All of this obviously took planning and organisation, and Captain Sharpe later estimated that Bai Bureh had been developing his defence system as long as six months in advance.

Bai Bureh also operated an extremely reliable spy system. Traditionally, spies were sent into a village to note its defence plans, the number of its inhabitants, and how best to attack it.[44] Sometimes they would obtain jobs with the enemy such as carrying water, and thus be able to move around with them and observe their movements. It was easy for Bai Bureh's men to infiltrate the British carriers, and thus observe preparations from close quarters: the British were often amazed at how well the Temne seemed to know their movements in advance. Other warriors took up positions along the paths and observed the movements of the British from their stations. Whenever a British column set out or halted three shots were fired to signal their movements. It seems possible, too, that some of the guides hired by the British were Bai Bureh's people, for since these men should be presumed to know the countryside well, it is remarkable how many times they led the British columns astray or missed village positions.

Temne warriors wore a distinctive dress consisting of *lankono* cloth which had been dyed red and a cap made from the same material.[45] They were armed with cutlasses, sling-shots, stone clubs, and guns of various types. Their guns were either of the variety made by Temne blacksmiths or trade guns, of which the ones provided by French traders were considered the best. Each man was responsible for his own weapons, but Bai Bureh's success was in large part due to his ability personally to provide his men with a large supply of guns and gunpowder. This ability to provide arms and ammunition meant a more dependable army, and one which was subjected to a higher degree of discipline than was to be found in many other parts of Africa at the time. Freetown traders, both Creole and European, provided a significant amount of gunpowder until March of 1898 when the Government forced them to stop their trade with the 'enemy'. These sources failing, Bai Bureh obtained what he needed from the French traders in Guinea, whom his son was often reported to have visited.

2

Neither Cardew nor the newly appointed District Commissioners expected more than a few isolated incidents at the beginning of the tax collection. These, they felt, could easily be put down by firm, quick action on the part of the police. They comprehended little concerning the depth of Temne feeling against the new administration, and even less about the organisational means which the Temne could and would activate when the time came. Only a few months before the collections began, Cardew demonstrated this when he wrote to the Secretary of State:

> I do not apprehend that the chiefs will combine to forcibly resist the collection of the tax, for they lack cohesion and powers of organisation, and there are too many jealousies between them for concerted action, but there may be isolated acts on the parts of some chiefs and their followers of forcible resistance to the tax which might spread to other tribes if not promptly suppressed by the Police. . . .[46]

From the commencement of collections in Karene District, Captain Sharpe experienced difficulties. He first asked his own contingent of police at Karene headquarters to pay. They protested, maintaining that it was unfair to be forced to pay taxes on houses which they had been forced to rent as the result of Government failure to provide them with proper housing facilities for themselves and their families. They paid reluctantly when it became apparent that Captain Sharpe would make no concessions. While the taxes were collected at headquarters, rumours came into the garrison that Bai Bureh planned to attack that night. No attack materialised, but a tense atmosphere pervaded the preparations for the next collection.

The next town in which Sharpe planned to collect taxes was Port Loko, the largest and most prosperous town in his district. Immediately after his arrival there on 5 February, he met resistance to payment which steadily progressed into war. It became clear that there was no hope of a peaceful collection. Port Loko was prepared for direct confrontation, but the chiefs stalled for as much time as possible. Bai Bureh was waiting in the neighbouring chiefdom to reinforce the Port Loko chiefs when the time came.

Sharpe met first with the traders, but they refused to pay and claimed that they feared reprisals from the townspeople who were intimidating them against making payment. During the course of the next five days, Sharpe held meetings with the traders and chiefs in the hope of settling the problem peacefully, but he was forced finally to resort to threats, detention and arrests. The traders continued to insist that the chiefs would not allow them to pay and that they had been threatened with evictions or worse. The chiefs, on the other hand, insisted that should the traders pay the tax, they would eventually claim ownership of the houses which they rented. Although at the time it appeared that the traders were genuinely afraid, Sharpe concluded later that the two factions were in collusion.[47] They would not specify who had threatened them, and after each meeting they could be seen in amicable conversation with the townspeople. Their later behaviour would confirm Sharpe in his opinion.

The acting chief, Bokari Bamp, employed traditional diplomatic gambits to stall direct confrontation. He could not, he maintained, give any direct answer to Sharpe's demands without the approval of the incumbent chief who was very ill. Furthermore, he would have to consult with Bai Foki in order to receive his approval as well. Finally Sharpe lost his patience and detained the chief, warning him that there would be serious consequences if he did not co-operate with the administration. Two days later he reluctantly released the chief who had half-heartedly promised not to hinder the tax collection. Meanwhile many reports had come in that the Port Loko people were gathering with the intention of rescuing their chief, and that one of his sub-chiefs had summoned Bai Bureh to assist them in their attempt.

The traders adamantly refused to pay, still claiming the fear of reprisals. They felt that the Government had not sufficiently ensured their safety. Sharpe ordered many of them to be arrested, charging them with refusal to obey the Government's orders. In defiance of this, the traders used various methods to annoy and hinder Sharpe, one of which was to refuse to speak in English or any other language for which he had an interpreter. Instead they spoke only in Aku (Yoruba)* or Mandingo. Their goods were detained, but when they were brought into court, Sharpe discovered that the traders had removed all their valuables, leaving behind only bundles of worthless rubbish. Amidst jeers from the women traders, Sharpe proceeded to try them, and fine them.

On 9 January he made a last unsuccessful attempt to bring the chiefs into line. Summoning them to a meeting, he explained in the presence of a thousand of their followers that he was through with waiting. He could permit no further delay, and demanded then and there the answer to two questions: 'Would Bokari Bamp let the traders pay?' and 'Would he immediately begin to collect the taxes in Port Loko?' Aware that there could be no further stalling, Bokari Bamp answered negatively to both questions. He was immediately arrested along with four of his sub-chiefs, and brought to trial that same day. They were convicted on three charges: incitement of disobedience, refusing to collect the tax, and attempting to overawe a public officer in the execution of his duty. Fearful that the towns-people would act as they had previously done in the case of Bai Foki, Sharpe had the prisoners sent forthwith to Freetown.

All through these proceedings, there had been constant rumours of impending attack from Bai Bureh. When Sharpe installed Sorie Bunki as acting chief in Bokari Bamp's stead, the frequency of these rumours increased. Sorie Bunki had been campaigning for many years for eligibility to the chieftaincy, and was quick to seize the opportunity now given him.[48] Sharpe justified his appointment by pointing out that he had enquired amongst the townspeople concerning a successor chief, and Bunki seemed to be the most respected man in the town. Bunki, in turn, demonstrated his loyalty to those responsible for his appointment and immediately began to collect taxes.

* Many of the Sierra Leonean traders were of Yoruba origin, having been sold after capture in the Civil Wars that plagued the Yoruba in the nineteenth century, and freed on their way to the Americas by the British anti-Slavery Squadron and resettled in Freetown.

However, it was a hollow victory as very few people remained in the town. Most of them had fled, leaving the town deserted for use as a battlefield.

The very first night of the new chief's administration was one of terror. Bunki reported to Sharpe that his messengers had come with news that Bai Bureh intended to attack Port Loko that night because of his collaboration with the administration. From the nearly deserted town, Sharpe wrote Governor Cardew that the situation was serious, and that he could not return to Karene until the danger of attack by Bai Bureh's forces was over. He next sent a letter to Bai Bureh order- ing him to collect Kasseh's taxes and have them ready for payment when Sharpe came. He had taken great care to choose a messenger well-known to Bai Bureh, and there was no mistaking what Bai Bureh meant when the messenger was returned to Port Loko by Temne warriors without being taken to their chief. Sharpe immedi- ately determined to arrest Bai Bureh, thinking that this was the only way to establishing peace in his district quickly. To facilitate this, he requested twenty additional police from Freetown, specifying that they be veterans since those police who accompanied him were new recruits who had not yet been trained in field manœuvres and some of them were not even trained in the use of their rifles.

While Sharpe finalised his preparations, Bai Bureh did likewise. Warriors poured into his chiefdom from every direction. Sharpe's reinforcements arrived in Port Loko under the command of Major Tarbet on 16 February, and they soon set out to arrest Bai Bureh.[49] All along the road they passed many groups of armed men travelling in the same direction. The warriors refused to make any communication with the British officers. Only one showed any response to Sharpe's attempt to talk with him. While they were talking, Temne warriors surrounded them, and it was not long before Sharpe decided that it would be best for him to return to his column. He forced the warrior to go with him thinking that he could interrogate him later, but when the other warriors crowded round them in support of their colleague, Sharpe decided to release the warrior from custody.

The Temne warriors followed the police as they continued their march, jeering at them from all sides. Some warriors, armed with slingshots, hurled stones at the police. When the stoning became intense, Tarbet ordered his rear guard to open fire. Panic soon ensued for when the advance guard heard the shots, they rushed to give assistance to the rear leaving the carriers unprotected. The Temne then fell upon the carriers and captured some of them with

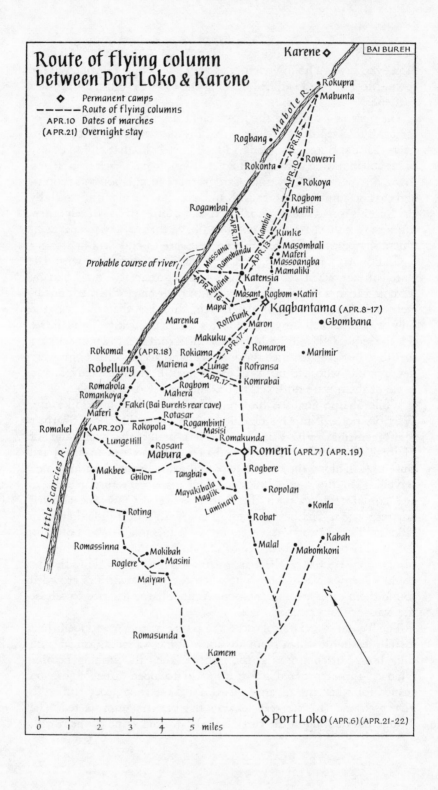

Route of flying column between Port Loko & Karene

BAI BUREH

◇ Permanent camps
------ Route of flying columns
APR.10 Dates of marches
(APR.21) Overnight stay

Karene ◇

Rokupra
Mabunta

Mabole R.

Rogbang
Rokonta
APR.10
Rowerri
APR.15
Rokoya
Rogbom
Matiti

Rogambai
APR.11
Kumbia
APR.13
Kunke
Masombali
Maferi
Massoangba
Mamaliki

Probable course of river
Massana
Ramobandu
Katensia
APR.16
Madina
Masant. Rogbom • Katiri
Mapa
Rotafunk
Kagbantama (APR.8-17)
Marenka
Maron
Gbombana
Makuku
Rokiama
APR.17
Romaron
Marimir
Rokomal • (APR.18)
Mariena
Lunge
Rofransa
Robellung
APR.17
Komrabai
Romabola
Rogbom
Romankoya
Mahera
Fakei (Bai Bureh's rear cave)
Maferi
Rotasar
Rogambinti
Masisi
Romakel
(APR.20)
Rokopola
Romakunda
LungeHill
Rosant
Romeni (APR.7) (APR.19)
Mabura
Rogbere
Makbee
Gbilon
Tangbai
Ropolan
Mayakibala
Maglik
Konla
Laminaya
Robat
Roting
Kabah
Romassinna
Mokibah
Malal
Mabomkoni
Roglere
Masini
Maiyan

N

Romasunda
Kamem

Little Scarcies R.

0 1 2 3 4 5 miles

Port Loko (APR.6) (APR.21-22)

their loads. It was reported later that several of the carriers had been sold as slaves in French territory in exchange for gunpowder. Some of the warriors returned the fire, and several volleys were exchanged before they retreated. Some informants attribute the beginning of the war to a warrior named Thambaili whose stone hit a British officer on the head.[50]

Temne warriors harassed Major Tarbet's party all the way to Kagbantama where they were met by a British party coming from Karene. Since the commanding officers of both parties reported the presence of many armed men on the road, they decided to delay the arrest of Bai Bureh until they could obtain more reinforcements. Temne warriors attacked the combined force as it forded the river at Kasumbala, but did not pursue it. The police arrived at Karene where they found the garrison expecting an attack from the Temne at any moment.

The result of the march from Port Loko to Karene was that the Frontier Police became much better aware of the strength and organisation of Bai Bureh's forces. It was evident that the entire countryside surrounding the garrison at Karene supported Bai Bureh in his open resistance to the administration. With a single exception, every town along the way was deserted. The large numbers of warriors on the road made it unsafe for anything but a large, well-guarded party to travel from Port Loko to Karene. Only Brima Sanda remained loyal to the British, but this was of little practical value since all his people had deserted him for Bai Bureh. He was rewarded handsomely for his loyalty for during the post-war pacification of the area he alone was given an almost free hand in his chiefdom's affairs.[51]

Meanwhile, panic prevailed throughout Port Loko. Rumours were rife that Bai Bureh's men had captured and killed Captain Sharpe. The small garrison of police left in Port Loko feared attack from the Temne. They were commanded only by a sub-officer who had little control over them, and they reacted wildly and with little forethought under the threat of attack. They disarmed everyone in the town, without ascertaining if they were friendly or hostile. As a result, there were several incidents, one of which resulted in the death of one of the townspeople who had refused to give up his sword. These incidents did little to reassure the remaining few townspeople of their security.

By 19 February, Bai Bureh's men had completely severed the British line of communication between Karene and Port Loko as well as seriously hampering communications with Freetown. They controlled the road and blocked the river, thus leaving the Government forces with only two means of communicating with Freetown: by carrier pigeon or by the circuitous route through Kambia.

Three days later Major Tarbet led a punitive expedition against those Temne who had blocked the river traffic by removing all but one of the canoes at Bokupru. The Temne now demonstrated the effectiveness of their hit and run strategy. Major Tarbet's party was able to do little more than harass their warriors. His party of forty-eight police had to cross the river in four relays in the single remaining canoe. As they crossed, the Temne deserted the village, retreating just outside the range of British fire. While the police rushed the deserted village, they held their fire, waiting until the police re-forded the river. Then they rushed back into the town and to the river bank where they fired at the police, taking advantage of the latter's need to protect the fording place. In this encounter the British discovered to their surprise that the Temne warriors were much better armed than they had anticipated. Instead of possessing only the trade guns which were sold by the British traders, it became apparent that they were armed with the superior make of trade guns sold by the French.

From this time until the end of March, Bai Bureh's army commanded the situation. The number of warriors joining him increased and so did the number of villages and towns which supported him. The simple tactics of Temne bush fighting, what would today be called guerilla warfare, proved to be very effective against the heavily encumbered West India Regiment whose officers knew little of the terrain over which they fought. The Temne concentrated on attacking the British columns engaged in maintaining communications between the two garrisons of Karene and Port Loko, and in keeping the former supplied with rations and ammunition. They paid particular attention to picking off the white officers and as a result many of these were either killed or severely wounded. In the early stages of the war there were not enough British troops to allow the British to undertake offensive operations, and they were thus limited to forcing their way back and forth between the two garrisons. They made an easy target for ambush by an attacking force which, as far as possible, avoided direct confrontation. Surprise attacks from ambushes and sudden raids were the order of the day for Bai Bureh's army.

A section of the Temne forces attacked Port Loko on 5 March. Another section attacked Karene the next day. They did not succeed in taking the two towns; however, the British troops guarding the garrison were powerless to do anything more than maintain their positions. In Port Loko the entire civilian population deserted the town, and did not return until they were sure that the British were in full command. Sorie Bunki fled when he heard that all the roads were blocked to Freetown and that an attack by Bai Bureh was pending. He sent several messengers to ascertain the situation, but they were all captured by Bai Bureh's men. Finally, he and one of his right-hand men determined to attempt the journey to Freetown. A party of warriors were sent by two dissident sub-chiefs to follow the fleeing chief. They overtook him on the river, and killed him, after which they tied a heavy stone around his body and threw him into the river, a particularly abominable burial for a Temne chief.[52]

In such circumstances the British could do little without more troops. At the beginning of March it was clear that the police did not possess enough force to restore administrative control, and on 2 March, Captain Sharpe had requested Major Norris to proclaim martial law in the district. Major Norris had just arrived with the first company of the West India Regiment, and by the end of the month, there would be six companies in Karene district; in effect this amounted to the full fighting force stationed in the colony. The officers in the field had become fully conscious of the seriousness of the situation quite early on. The first two companies, one commanded by Major Norris and another by Major Stansfeld, had completed several marches between the two garrisons, and each time they were forced to march through continual and persistent Temne ambushes and raids.

Only once during the month did the Government troops undertake offensive operations. Major Buck took out a flying column to march along the road from Port Loko and through the nearby villages. His policy was to raze to the ground every village and town which opposed his march, burning the huts and destroying the stockades. On the first day of his march, 13 March, he met no opposition. The Temne had concentrated their forces in the towns from Mahera onwards, and as the column approached these towns on their next day's march, they came up against full scale opposition. At Mahera, they fought a long, intensive battle against warriors who were commanded personally by Bai Bureh. Eventually the British troops took the town, but they were attacked later in the evening at Rutien. On the third day of the operations, Temne warriors withheld their resistance until the column approached Kagbantama. Here they were waiting in the stockades from which they launched an attack which the column was only barely able to resist. Afterwards, Major Buck concluded that he did not possess enough fighting strength to pursue the retreating warriors, and he decided to continue to Karene through the bush to the windward of the town. When the Temne discovered that the soldiers were not following them nor preparing for further battle, they attempted to burn the column out by setting fire to the grass and bush along the windward side of the road. As it was late in the dry season, it was not long before the entire countryside was in flame. The flying column countered the fire by setting fire to the bush on the leeward side of the path. This gave them enough space to wait out the fire, but they were unable to move until the next day.

The Temne warriors continued their intense resistance to the column's march on the next day, particularly at the stockade towns of Romaron and Katenti, two of the best defended Temne war-towns. The Government troops succeeded in fending them off by opening fire with the magazine gun, and for the remainder of the march the warriors restricted themselves to occasional sniping. Bai Bureh's army, however, had exacted a heavy toll on the fighting strength of the British.

When Cardew received report of this march, he became greatly alarmed at the systematic burning of the villages and towns by British forces. He was still concerned over the political aims of his Protectorate Government, and feared that such drastic activities on the part of the administration's troops would never win over the people. He urged Captain Sharpe and Major Norris to limit such action to Bai Bureh's chief towns. Both officers, however, had previously agreed to the column's procedure, and they assured Cardew that discretion had been used and only towns which offered resistance were destroyed by Major Buck. They felt that there was no other way of effectively putting down the resistance, since the whole area was up in arms. They did not have the opportunity to implement this policy again until April, however, for Temne resistance intensified and they were once again confined to maintaining communications along the Port Loko–Karene road.

Major Norris concluded that it would be impossible to defeat Bai Bureh's forces without making full use of the heavily equipped West India Regiment. Governor Cardew, on the other hand, disagreed with him, and had decided that the best policy would be to use the lightly-encumbered Frontier Police for field operations while the Regiment troops safeguarded the garrisons. He often interfered in the orders for the troop movements, and did not allow full use of Regiment troops until he could no longer ignore the fact that the Temne were fully in charge of the situation. Had he authorised the number of companies requested by the commanding officers in the field it is perhaps possible that they might have defeated Bai Bureh's forces earlier. When the first company of troops were sent to Port Loko on 22 February, Cardew, completely underestimating the strength of Bai Bureh's army, informed the Colonial Office that he was convinced that the armed resistance in Karene could not last the month.

The officers in the field were furious with Cardew's interference. On at least one occasion Major Norris was forced to apologise for his use of intemperate language in a report to Cardew.[53] The Governor did not fully comprehend the seriousness of the field situation until 19 March, when Temne warriors forced Major Stansfeld's column to retreat to Karene after their attack on the column at Magbolonta, a town six miles from Karene. Stansfeld had been in the process of conveying a large number of wounded soldiers and police as well as a large number of carriers back to Port Loko. The necessity to guard them greatly reduced his ability to counter the Temne attack, and he decided that it was best to return to Karene. Cardew did not entirely agree that this retreat was justified, but he could no longer deny the intensity of resistance. Consequently, on 19 March, he ordered Colonel Bosworth, the Commander of British Troops on the West Coast of Africa, to take a fourth company to Port Loko and assume personal command of field operations.

Colonel Bosworth decided to wait in Port Loko for Captain Carr Smith to return from his march to Karene, which he had begun on the 22nd. Three days later, Government messengers brought the report that an intense attack at Matiti had forced him to retreat to Karene. He, himself, together with one other officer had been wounded and there remained only one officer to command the column. Upon receipt of this report, Colonel Bosworth immediately set out for Karene to relieve the garrison. He also faced heavy resistance from Temne warriors at Malal, Romeni, and Kagbantama. At the end of the day's march the troops were completely exhausted from fighting and had still not arrived at Karene. They finally reached their destination in the night and, shortly after entering headquarters, Bosworth collapsed and died shortly thereafter of what was described as 'heat apoplexy'.

Cardew did not delay in appointing a successor to him, Lieutenant-Colonel J. W. A. Marshall, who had just come to Sierra Leone to take command of Karene's troops. He had previously ordered Major Bourke to take the fifth and sixth companies to Port Loko but was unwilling to believe Bourke's gloomy report of the situation. Marshall took the remaining forty soldiers with him to Port Loko arriving there on 1 April. He reported that he found the troops in Port Loko working under every possible disadvantage: many wounded lay in the hospital, morale was low, and all the officers were exhausted from constant fighting. Keeping the road open for supply transport and maintenance of communications had involved so much fighting and resulted in so many casualties that the main aim of tracking down the leaders of the resistance had almost been forgotten. Major Bourke had already advised that the Government abandon Karene garrison, thus relieving the troops of the burden of securing it and supplying it. Cardew refused to listen to the suggestion, and made it clear that he felt that Bourke exaggerated the gravity of the situation. He pointed out that political reasons dictated that Karene be maintained since it was the seat of the district government. In this the Colonial Office concurred, but the Secretary of State, Joseph Chamberlain, agreed with the officers in the field, and cabled Cardew to give his officers a free hand in their field operations.

In Port Loko, Marshall and the officers in charge there concluded that strategy must be revised.[54] It was impossible to continue to provision Karene as the columns had done all through March. The rains had begun, and continuing to send columns from Port Loko would not allow any free movement for offensive operations. In the preceding fourteen days, eight officers had been killed or wounded. Furthermore, at the beginning of April the Mende of southern Sierra Leone rose up against the hut tax, thus tying down government troops in the south. The Temne took full advantage of the delay in communications between the two posts, and rebuilt any stockades that had been destroyed or constructed new ones. Thus they maintained their ability to resist the British forces, and each column met with as much opposition as the one before. In order to break the power of the Temne, Marshall determined to establish two intermediate posts between Port Loko and Karene, dividing the distance between the garrisons into comparatively easy short marches. Thus security for the supply convoys was ensured, and a basis provided for a flying column to move out into the countryside. He put this plan into effect immediately and provided Karene with provisions for fifteen days. He then set out with a flying column to implement the second part of his strategy: a scorched earth policy, the same policy that had been earlier rejected by Cardew.

Lieutenant-Colonel Marshall experienced great difficulty even with a fighting force of close to seven hundred. For the first two weeks in April, he concentrated on the road. Every day he took out a flying column which worked its way through the villages near the road. Temne resistance increased in fierceness and strength; the opposition hitherto experienced was merely a shadow of what was now offered. Every village opposed the column, which had to fight three to four hard battles a day and destroy as many as twenty stockades. Particularly strong resistance was offered at Matiti on the 11th and Kagbantama on the 13th, but by the end of the two weeks Marshall commanded the road.

As the Government took control of the road, the Temne withdrew from that area and entrenched themselves in the villages beyond. In the last two weeks of April, they intensified their resistance still more, offering what amounted to last ditch stands in every village and town. The strongest defence was made at Mafouri on the 25th, but by then the whole of Kasseh had been overrun by the British; however, although Marshall now controlled the country, he had come no nearer the capture of Bai Bureh. He prepared to move into the neighbouring chiefdoms at the beginning of May. First he marched through Sanda country where he received a mixed response from the inhabitants who feared him and did not actively oppose his movements. In each village, Marshall assembled the inhabitants and explained what the West India Regent had done in Kasseh, and assured them that he would only destroy their towns if they attempted to prevent his march through them. He put great emphasis on assuring them that Bai Bureh would soon be captured.

From Sanda country he advanced into Rowoola chiefdom which was ruled by Sattan Lahai, an elderly war-chief for whom Bai Bureh had fought twenty years ago. As in Kasseh, the villages resisted the troops, but the Regiment troops quickly defeated them. By 10 May, the administration controlled the entire northern area of Temne country.

However, they were still unable to capture Bai Bureh. Throughout the war operations, Bai Bureh had remained a shadowy figure in the field reports. He was known to be on the scene directing operations against the British, but he always eluded them. Even an offer of a reward of fifty pounds, which was later raised to one hundred pounds, could not entice his followers to give information regarding his whereabouts to the Government. Though his country was ruined, he, his allied leaders, and a small band of warriors still remained at large. The Government's victory had been achieved at the cost of the complete destruction of Kasseh's countryside: the forces of 'civilisation' had demonstrated their worst aspect. However, Bai Bureh's ability in war and his army's capabilities were no longer questioned or glossed over.

Cardew hoped that the resistance was now finally broken, but he acknowledged that peace could never be fully established as long as Bai Bureh was at large. However, his capture had to be delayed until after the rains, which had become so intense that extensive military operations were no longer possible. There were a few isolated incidents during the rains, the most serious of which was an attempt by Temne to burn down the Karene barracks. Still the Governor was confident of ultimate victory, and made provisional plans to go on leave in October.

Bai Bureh had indicated that he was not opposed to mediation as early as mid-April, just when the British troops were moving beyond the road. He had requested the Rev. A. Elba, a C.M.S. missionary stationed at Bana Lokko, to come to him at Mahera. During an extended interview, Bai Bureh requested him to give a verbal message of peace to the Governor.[55] Elba had long respected the chief, and was convinced that he genuinely desired to come to terms with the Government. At about the same time, the chiefs of Port Loko, led by Alfa Yunisa, offered their services as intermediaries to the Government.[56] In May, Suluku of Bumban also offered his services.[57] To all of these offers, Cardew replied that the Government knew that some of these chiefs had assisted Bai Bureh and that he was prepared to accept nothing other than Bai Bureh's unconditional surrender.[58]

Cardew continued to reject offers for mediation even though Bai Bureh remained at large. Muslim leaders in Freetown passed on letters from Bai Bureh to both the Governor and Sir David Chalmers, who was at the time conducting his enquiry into the causes of the war. Chalmers also offered his services to the Governor as a mediator, but Cardew rejected any action that might lessen his authority. Chalmers had already by implication criticised the Governor on a number of occasions, and Cardew was not prepared to receive any assistance from him. He continued to insist upon unconditional surrender, and repeated his demand to the Freetown Muslim leaders.

3

Bai Bureh was finally tracked down in swampy, thickly vegetated countryside by a small patrolling party of the newly organised West African Regiment on 11 November. His Temne warriors resisted to the last, but they did not evade the troops for long. While warriors covered them, two men attempted to escape to the bush. A Sierra Leonean sergeant pursued them, concentrating his attention on the one moving slowest, and succeeded in capturing him. It turned out to be Bai Bureh himself. Tales which are still told about this event, however, give the war a more dramatic ending by relating that Bai Bureh ended the war himself by rushing out of the bush as the soldiers closed in, shouting 'de war don don'.[59]

The following day the captured chief was taken to Karene. He had lived in the bush for twenty-three weeks preceding his capture. Captain Goodwyn, the leader of the patrol party which captured him, had destroyed his bush camp earlier in November, and he had barely managed to escape. In London, the Colonial Office was relieved, since his capture greatly simplified matters for them. They had been planning to transfer a battalion of the West India Regiment from the Niger river, or alternatively a battalion from England for post-rains operations, but could now dispense with the plan.[60] They were confident that resistance in the Protectorate would now cease.

Only Bai Bureh's fate remained to be settled. The Government at first planned to bring him to trial in Karene, thinking that there would be too much excitement caused in Freetown if the trial were held there. Sharpe had planned to try him on a charge of treason, but the Colonial Office replied that there was some doubt as to whether Bai Bureh could be treated as a British subject, the necessary prerequisite for a charge of treason. Proceedings were delayed until the Colonial Office arrived at a final decision which declared that Bai Bureh had not committed treason since he owed no allegiance to the Queen, and he was never brought to trial.

Throughout these deliberations by the law officers, Bai Bureh was detained, at first in jail and then in a house next to that of the exiled Prempeh I* on the west side of Freetown. He had been removed from Karene after a Temne soldier in the West African Regiment had attempted to help him escape. Crowds flocked to his house, anxious to see the great hero whose legend was greatly developed during the war by the Freetown press. Finally, Sir Matthew Nathan, the Acting Governor, ordered his deportation to Gambia along with Bai Sherbro of Yoni and Nyagua of Panguma. He resisted any suggestion that Bai Bureh be allowed to return to Karene district. Such a move he considered would be a sign of weakness on the part of the Government. Bai Bureh's companion chiefs died while in exile, but

* See the chapter on Asante.

after two petitions to return, he himself was allowed back in 1905.[61] Elderly and seriously ill, he no longer posed much threat to the administration, yet they hedged his return with many conditions. He died only three years later.

4

Bai Bureh's war presented a well organised, disciplined resistance to the establishment of colonial rule in the Sierra Leone Protectorate. It occurred in an area which had been little affected by Western institutions such as education and Christianity, and was the culmination of many attempts on the part of the Temne chiefs to retain through peaceful means their traditional institutions of authority. They had been prepared to carry out British policies, but only on condition that they remained sovereign in their own local affairs; however, this was not consistent with the new design of colonial rule which would accept only their submission. As a proud people long experienced in the arts of warfare, they were prepared to respond with war if this were the only means left them to retain their independence.

NOTES

1 For a general background study of the Bai Bureh war see La Ray Denzer and Michael Crowder 'Bai Bureh and the Sierra Leone Hut Tax War of 1898' in Robert I. Rotberg and Ali Mazrui eds. *Black Protest*, O.U.P. London and New York, 1970. For a detailed military 'diary' of the war reconstructed from materials in the Sierra Leone Archives see La Ray Denzer 'A Diary of the Bai Bureh War' (in two parts) in *Sierra Leone Studies*, New Series, No. 23, July 1968 and No. 24, January 1969.

2 Parliamentary Papers (1899), vol. LX, Report . . . on the Insurrection in the Sierra Leone Protectorate, which is usually referred to as the C[halmers] R[eport]. See vol. II, Appendix IV, Memo from S[ecretary] for N[ative] A[ffairs] to C[olonial] S[ecretary], 28 July 1893.

3 CR, II, Appendix V, List of convictions of Frontier Police for offences against natives of Protectorate, February 1894–March 1898.

4 *Ibid.,* Appendix XXIII, Cardew's address to the Temne chiefs, 15 November 1897.

5 *Ibid.,* Evidence of Pa Suba, para. 4489.

6 *Ibid.,* Appendix XVII, Petition of Temne chiefs to Secretary of State through Governor, 28 June 1897.

7 *Ibid.,* Appendix XXII, Petition of chiefs to Legislative Council, 15 October 1897.

8 *Ibid.,* V. R. Dorjahn, 'The Changing Political System of the Temne', *Africa,* vol. 30, No. 2 (April 1960), pp. 110–39.

9 CR, II, Evidence of W. T. G. Lawson, para. 1753.

10 *Ibid.,* para. 1720–3.

11 *Ibid.,* para. 1756–7.

12 Petition, 28 June 1897.

13 Dorjahn, p. 119.

14 Petition, 28 June 1897.

15 Petition, 15 October 1897.

16 CR, II, Evidence of Alfa Saidoo, para. 2234.

17 Petition, 15 October 1897.

18 E.g., CR, II, Evidence of Port Loko chiefs, para. 4319–26.

19 *Ibid.,* Appendix XIV, Petition of Temne chiefs to Captain Sharpe, 17 December 1897.

20 *Ibid.,* Evidence of Port Loko chiefs, para. 2164–78.

21 *Ibid.,* Appendix XXVI, letter from SNA to Bai Suba *et al.*

22 *Ibid.*

23 CR, II, Evidence of Captain Sharpe, para. 3277.

23 *Ibid.,* para. 3773–6.

25 *Ibid.,* Evidence of Captain Sharpe, para. 3814–19.

26 *Ibid.,* Evidence of J. C. E. Parkes, para. 897–905; evidence of Captain Sharpe, para. 3481–95 and evidence of Port Loko chiefs, para. 5152.

27 S[ierra] L[eone] A[rchives]—G[overnor's] C[onfidential] D[espatches] to the S[ecretary] of S[tate], Cardew to Chamberlain, 28 May 1898.

28 C. Braithwaite Wallis, *The Advance of our West African Empire,* London, 1903, pp. 51–2.

29 Dorjahn, pp. 121–6.

30 These include eleven volumes of Government Interpreter's Memoranda and letters, 1876–89, and nine volumes of Native Affairs Letters Books, 1890–8, as well as the minute papers for both departments.

31 E.g., Howard Collection of Oral Tradition: Interview with Pa Santigi Taylor, Mange, 29 May 1968.

32 E.g., *Ibid.,* Interview with Pa Almamy Kamara, Mange, 29 May 1968.

33 For a history of these areas, see Great Britain, Parliamentary Papers (1886). Dispatch from the Administrator-in-chief enclosing information regarding the different districts and tribes of Sierra Leone and its vicinity, pp. 10–15 and 22–6. Also, see footnote 30.

34 SLA/A[rabic] L[etter] B[ook], Alikali Moroba of Port Loko to Governor Rowe, Trs. by Sanusi, 2 June 1886.

35 SLA/A[borigines] D[epartment] M[inute] P[apers], 14/86, statement of Santigi Bocary Bangura of Port Loko, 20 August 1886.

36 See Denzer & Crowder, Section II.

37 Evident through observing which chiefdoms gave him support.

38 Only Port Loko, Kasseh, Quiah, and Rowoola prepared defences in their towns, the rest co-operated with men, goods, blockades, etc.

39 SLA/C[onfidential] M[inute] P[apers], report of Customs Officer at Makela, 25 April 1898; SLA/CMP, 56/98, report of Customs Officer at Makela, 25 April 1898; CR, II, Appendix E, interview with Mr. T. Caldwell of the C.M.S., 12 May 1898; SLA/N[ative] A[ffairs] L[etter] B[ook], 165/98, SNA to Alimami Barbar *et al*, 14 June 1898; CR, II, evidence of Parkes, Cardew, Marshall, and Sharpe.

40 This description is based upon information included in the many field reports made by the Regiment officers during the course of the war. For full documentation of these reports see Denzer, 'Diary'. For an older description of Temne village situations, see Thomas Winterbottom, *An Account of the Native Africans in the Neighbourhood of Sierra Leone*, London, 1803, vol. I, pp. 78–88.

41 CR, II, evidence of Captain Sharpe, para 3789–91.

42 Description of stockade construction is based on CR, II, Appendix LVI, Report made on operations in Timini country by Lieutenant-Colonel Marshall to Officer Commanding Troops on the West Coast of Africa, 30 August 1898; and *Ibid.*, Evidence of Lieutenant-Colonel Marshall, para. 5804–30.

43 Howard Collection of Oral Tradition, interview with Pa Almamy Kamara, Mange, 29 May 1968.

44 *Ibid.*, interview with Pa Almamy Kamara, Mange, 29 May 1968.

45 *Ibid.*, interview with Pa Mamma Kamara and Pa Mayo Kamara, 19 February 1968.

46 SLA/GCDSS, 49/97, Governor to Secretary of State, 8 October 1897.

47 CR, II, evidence of Captain Sharpe, para. 3618–23.

48 In 1892, Bai Foki requested permission from the Governor to transfer the eligibility to the Alikaliship to the Sangkong and Bunki families. See SLA/ArLB, c. of NALB, 313/92, Parkes to Alikali of Port Loko, 21 October 1892.

49 Major Tarbet had previously had an encounter with Bai Bureh when he had commanded a party of police in an unsuccessful attempt to arrest the chief in 1894 for making war preparations against Moriah.

50 Howard Collection of Oral Tradition, interview with Pa Duramamy Cole of Port Loko, 1 April 1968.

51 His people, however, had the final revenge. When Brima Sanda died in 1914, they refused to bury him in the chiefs' burial grounds. I am grateful to Miss Emily Ann Langworthy for bringing this minute paper to my attention. SLA/MP, DC/K/90/1914, 11 September 1914.

52 CR, II, evidence of Siacho Furi, para. 6905–13.

53 SLA/L[ocal] C[onfidential] L[etter] B[ook], 38/98, Cardew to Officer Commanding Troops on West Coast of Africa, 17 March 1898.

54 CR, II, Appendix LVI, Report of Lieutenant-Colonel Marshall.

55 *Ibid.*, Evidence of Rev. Elba, para. 5643–6.

56 SLA/NAMP, 154/98, Alfa Yunisa to Governor through SNA, 18 April 1898.

57 SLA/GDSS, 110/98, Governor to Secretary of State, 2 June 1898.

58 *Ibid.*; also SLA/Local Letter Book, 405/98, Governor to C.S., 10 June 1898.

59 One of the most common tales concerning Bai Bureh in Sierra Leone, it forms a part of almost everyone's fund of stories.

60 SLA/CDSSG, CO/22674/98, enc., H. Bertram Fox to Under Secretary of State in the War Office, 19 October 1898, enclosed in GDSSG, 56/98, 19 October 1898.

61 Bai Bureh first petitioned for return in 1901, but the Governor of the Gold Coast, Governor Nathan, the man who had originally deported Bai Bureh from Sierra Leone when he was Acting Governor there, advised against the Governor of Sierra Leone allowing him to return. SLA/MP, 2429/1901. His second petition was presented four years later, which was accepted. SLA/MP, 2024/1905.

D. J. M. MUFFETT

Nigeria–Sokoto Caliphate

The last of the great states of West Africa to fall to the Europeans was the Sokoto Caliphate. Founded in the first decade of the nineteenth century, it covered most of what later became Northern Nigeria, as well as a considerable part of modern Niger and much of Cameroon.

With regard to population and size it was the largest of the African states which the Europeans conquered. Both the French and the Germans had cast covetous eyes on it, but at the Berlin Conference of 1884–5 it was held to fall within the British sphere of influence in West Africa, principally by virtue of the success of Sir George Goldie in eliminating his commercial rivals on the lower Niger. This hegemony was later reinforced by the treaties of 1885 which were signed between Sokoto and Gwandu on the one hand and Goldie's National African Company on the other.

In 1900 Great Britain abrogated the Charter which had been granted in 1886 to Goldie's company—now renamed the Royal Niger Company—and assumed direct administration over what became the Protectorate of Northern Nigeria. By March 1903, after a series of battles between the West African Frontier Force and armies of the constituent emirates of the Caliphate, the British High Commissioner, Sir Frederick Lugard, entered Sokoto. The final and decisive battle was fought at Burmi on 27 July 1903 when the fugitive Sultan Attahiru Ahmed was killed.

The Fulani-Hausa contingents proved no match for the smaller but much better equipped British forces. With few exceptions,

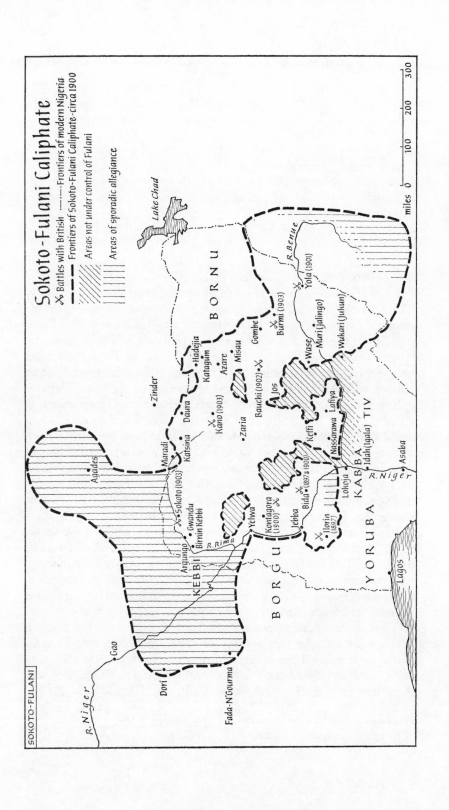

SOKOTO-FULANI

Sokoto-Fulani Caliphate

✕ Battles with British
------- Frontiers of modern Nigeria
▬ ▬ Frontiers of Sokoto-Fulani Caliphate·circa 1900
▨ Areas not under control of Fulani
▧ Areas of sporadic allegiance

R. Niger
Gao
Dori
Fada-N'Gourma
Agades
Maradi
Zinder
Lake Chad
BORNU
Argungu
Birnin Kebbi
Gwandu
Sokoto (1903) ✕
KEBBI
R. Rima
Katsina
Daura
Kano (1903) ✕
Zaria
Hadejia
Katagum
Azare
Misau ✕
Bauchi (1902) ✕
Gombe
Burmi (1903) ✕
Yelwa
Kontagora (1900) ✕
Jos
Wase
Muri (Jalingo)
Yola (1901) ✕
R. Benue
BORGU
Jebba
Bida (1897 & 1900) ✕
Keffi
Nassarawa
Lafiya
Wukari (Jukun)
Ilorin (1897) ✕
Lokoja
KABBA
Idah (Igala)
TIV
Asaba
R. Niger
YORUBA
Lagos

miles 0   100   200   300

victory came easily, though the Fulani fought with great bravery. This study will attempt to analyse the reasons why the Sokoto Caliphate failed to put up more effective resistance. To understand this failure it is important first to appreciate something of the way in which the Fulani-Hausa armies developed throughout the nineteenth century, and to achieve this, reference must necessarily be made not only to their origins but also to the more important aspects of their organisation and the logistic situation with which they had to deal.

1

The Sokoto Caliphate was established in the aftermath of a revolt by the Toronkawa Fulani of Hausaland against their Hausa overlords. These people had immigrated into Hausaland as early as the thirteenth century. Pastoral nomads, they came herding their distinctive Zebu cattle from the valley of the Senegal river, home of the Tokolor to whom they are closely related. The majority of the Fulani remained nomads, but over the centuries, a number of families settled in the famous walled cities of the Hausas and were converted to Islam.

Before the nineteenth century Hausaland consisted of a number of states claiming common ancestry whose relations with each other could best be described as those of a loose league. Sometimes they were at war with each other, at others they united against a common outside enemy. Each of these states was centred on a fortress nucleus— its walled capital. At the beginning of the nineteenth century the most prominent of these states were Kano, Katsina, Zaria, Zamfara and Gobir. It was in this last that the revolt began.

The rulers of these states were nominal Moslems, and the much more puritanical *Fulanin gida* (settled Fulani as opposed to *Bororoji*, the name by which the true nomads are known) who resided in them had become an important and influential élite. Many were rich merchants, scholars or political advisers to the Hausa Kings. The mass of the Hausa peasantry were, however, still devotees of the old religion of their forefathers, and their rulers were expected to cater to their subjects in this respect to the extent that many pagan practices permeated the religion of the Hausa ruling class.

To the Fulani Muslims, this was anathema and in Gobir they and their leader, the great scholar and divine, Usman d'an Fodio, suffered persecution at the hands of the Gobir Sarki, Yunfa, because of their opposition to his theological ecumenicalism.

In 1804, D'an Fodio, after fleeing from his home in Degel, issued an ultimatum to Yunfa and his fellow Hausa sarakuna (rulers) either to reform or suffer the consequences. Little, if any, notice was taken of this threat and the Fulani accordingly came out in open revolt. They elected Usman *Amir el Mumenin* or Commander of the Faithful and he, in his turn, leant heavily on the military prowess of his brother Abdullahi and his son Muhammed Bello, leaving the conduct of the war largely in their hands, whilst he himself formulated the principles which would underlie the governance of the territories they obtained as a result of their success in battle. He also adjudicated disputes between his emirs, to each of whom he gave a flag and his blessing.

From the point of view of the Hausa rulers, the rising constituted a rebellion against their authority on the part of a group of their subjects. The Fulani had been too long in the land to be regarded as foreigners. From the point of view of the *Fulanin gida*, who had rebelled, they were leading a holy war or *jihad* against Muslim rulers so lax in their observances that they could properly be considered no better than 'pagans'. From the point of view of the *Bororoji,* who joined their cousins from the towns, they were merely supporting their kinsmen in a fight against rulers who had on many occasions oppressed them.

The first major battle was that of Tabkin Kwatto,[1] in which the Fulani defeated Yunfa's Gobirawa. At this victory, which presaged their rise to dominion over Hausaland, the Fulani forces were composed exclusively of foot soldiers and bowmen.[2] The latter, particularly, wreaked havoc amongst the heavily caparisoned cavalry of the Gobirawa. As Johnston points out,[3] the formation into which the Fulani were constricted by the tide of the battle was that of a rough square, quite the best they could have adopted, given the discipline which their religious devotion inspired and their skill as archers inherent in their culture. The result was a foregone conclusion. But this foot- and archer-based army, however effective it may have been as the weapon of an insurgent élite concerned mainly with breaking the forces which opposed them, was not the most effective tool through which to govern and protect the territory which such victories bestowed.

Little by little therefore, the Shehu's lieutenants began to adapt the existing military organisation, until by the dry season of the following year,[4] the composition of their forces had changed considerably in character. By virtue of the accretion to them of horses, armour and chainmail as the spoils of victory, the formation of a Fulani cavalry arm, fully as well equipped as that of the Gobirawa, though naturally much less numerous, became feasible.[5]

Whether or not the leadership had learnt properly how to handle this new weapon in battle is, however, an entirely different matter and it may not be too fanciful to ascribe both the subsequent defeat suffered by them at Alwasa and the discordant argument on tactics which had preceded it, as being in major part attributable to this change in the basic composition of the military machine.

The Fulani counter-attack at Gwandu, when it came some four days after Alwasa,[6] was fought over ground which by its rocky and stony nature virtually precluded the use either of the re-formed Gobir cavalry, or of the camels of their Touareg allies, and they never fully recovered from the blow. One by one, the various Hausa states fell to the victorious Fulani, and by the autumn of 1808, the fortress city of Alkalawa, situated in the fork of the Gagare and Bunsuru rivers, where they come together to join the Rima, and a locality of enormous natural strength and strategic importance, fell to a direct assault.[7]

The defensive system of the Hausa states, which the Fulani had now toppled, had been evolving from the 10th century A.D. By the sixteenth century Hausa society had crystallised into a civilisation based on the famous 'walled cities', which were designed to provide defensive fortress nuclei for the protection of the surrounding countryside, whose intensive cultivation provided the basis of the wealth of these states.

Admirable as this system was against an invading army operating along extended lines of communication, which inevitably placed severe restraints on both the attacker's logistical and chronological arrangements, it was not fully effective against an internally based rebellion such as the Shehu had instigated. Insurrection had to be put down with dispatch. An invading army could hopefully, as a last resort, be starved out provided the fortress held, just as Soult's and Masséna's were when besieging the lines of Torres Vedras. Now that their initial victory was accomplished, the Fulani had to try to resolve this dichotomy of military interest between external and internal security arrangements. Here, to some extent, they were luckier than Yunfa and his Gobirawa in that the religious zeal which the Jihad had inspired among many Hausa tended to counteract the danger of spontaneous internal revolt within much of Hausaland.

For something like twenty years after the fall of Alkalawa the Fulani were pre-occupied with extending their conquests and consolidating the administration of the territory acquired thereby. It was not until as late as 1841 that the last emirate,[8] Adamawa, was finally secured, when its founder, Modibo Adama, built its fortress capital at Yola. In their expansion to the East, the Fulani came into head on collision with the people of Bornu, under their own Islamic reformer, Shehu el Amin el Kanemi. Bornu was to prove the major preoccupation of Sultan Bello, who succeeded his father as Commander of the Faithful in 1817, and who took the title of Sultan. It was he who administered directly the eastern emirates which shared a common frontier with Bornu, while his uncle, Abdullahi, administered the western emirates from Gwandu. Relations with Bornu had not been improved by 1837 when Bello died, and his successor, Sultan Abubakar Atiku, found that the strategic parameters which the situation demanded had already decided the pattern which his military organisation henceforth would be forced to follow.

The dilemma which confronted the Sultan and the Emirs lay in the duality of the roles to which they were militarily committed. In essence two problems arose, the solutions to which were to some extent mutually incompatible:

(I) To insure against invasion, and the risk to the base, a garrison army was required to defend the fortress. However, mere static defence of the fortress ran the risk of permitting the Hausa to break with their Fulani overlords and could thus largely be self-defeating. Moreover, neither the economy, nor the dictates of internal security, nor the agricultural cycle could readily condone too protracted a siege which might give scope for the re-emergence of Hausa antagonism. Garrison troops accordingly had always to be supported by an army capable of moving on to the offensive and of actually bringing the besiegers to bay and defeating them.

(II) In its role as an internal security force, however, a Fulani army had, of necessity, to be capable of operating as a *force de frappe*, able to strike punitively over long distances and with exemplary dispatch.

The first contingency thus demanded the establishment of armies of mass and necessitated the integration within them of the mass of the Hausa peasantry, and that of the other newly subjugated peoples, whilst the second required striking forces capable of considerable mobility and concentrated power.

The degree to which conflicting requirements had to be balanced, moreover, varied as between the Sultan and the Emirs and between Emir and Emir.

For the Sultan and his co-ruler, the Emir of Gwandu, with the intractible Kebbawa rooted in the marshy fastness of the Rima valley and poised on their western and northern flanks, and ever capable of driving a wedge between their two interdependent polities, defensive factors had constantly to be weighed against the much to be desired optimum of the eventual conquest and subjection of the enemy in his own heartland.

For the Emir of Ilorin in the south-west of the Caliphate, the principal concern was to hold the line against the Ibadan Yoruba. For him, as for the marcher emirs of the north and north-east— Katsina, Daura, Hadejia, Katagum, Misau, Jamaari, Bauchi, Azare and Gombe—considerations of defence and the maintenance of the frontiers were paramount.

In the east, Adamawa (Yola) and Muri were less concerned with protecting their frontiers than with raiding for slaves. Between Yola and Bornu lay a thick belt of 'pagan' country, difficult of access to either side and effectively acting as a buffer between them. To the east of Yola and Muri lay many 'pagan' groups, lacking any central- ised authority and, more important, any co-ordination of their resistance to incursion by the Fulani war parties. Such groups pro- vided fertile ground for the annual cropping of the human tribute which the slave economy demanded and which was due each year to Sokoto. [9]

Along the southern frontier of the Caliphate, that is along the Benue downstream from Ibi, and up the Niger valley north of the confluence, the great emirate of Nupe and the lesser fiefs of Keffi and Nassarawa had similar opportunities. The people to their south were in no position to offer much resistance and Nupe raided west into Kabba and Yagba with impunity.

The erstwhile might of the Jukun Empire had long since collapsed, the kingdom of Igala was now a broken reed, and the Tiv, a segmen- mentary people who began a migration in a northerly direction into the Benue valley as late as about 1830, had neither the political nor military capacity to deal with the Fulani, with whom in fact they achieved the status of *Abokin wasa*. [10]

Within the, geographically almost perfectly defined, quadrant of the flood plains of the Niger and the Benue, reinforced by the added geographical distinction afforded by the mountains of the Cameroon spine, there lay, moreover, the very considerable feature of the central massif of which Jos is now the principal focus, and which reaches into the borders of Zaria, Kano and Bauchi. This plateau served as a haven for another large group of pagan tribes, desirable quarry indeed as sources of slaves, and insufficiently organised to offer any real threat of counter-invasion. Around this island of refuge the emirates of

Zaria and Bauchi, and the tributary emirates of Jema'a, Wase and Lafiya (for all its Kanuri origin) lay like basking sharks, waiting for whatever pickings they could garner as opportunity arose.

Logistically and strategically, therefore, the reserve forces comprising the armies of mass were primarily domiciled either in Sokoto itself, or in the emirates of Gwandu and Kano, where the greatest population concentrations were to be found with a secondary reserve potential in Zaria and Katsina. The garrison troops were concentrated in Ilorin and on the eastern marches; and the raiding parties were gathered in Nupe, Yola, Muri and in the southern cluster of minor emirates, although Ilorin, Nupe and Yola could, if necessary put tens of thousands of men into the field at any given time from their own *levées en masse*. Nupe also provided a reserve capability for its overlord, Gwandu, which was actually called upon from time to time. Within this pattern, the Emir of Bauchi was also able to keep himself profitably occupied with raiding for slaves into the pagan enclaves around the Gongola valley, whilst Kano could and did wage almost interminable war with Ningi for the same reason, often with only varying good fortune.

It was such a strategical logistical situation that confronted the first Europeans who penetrated the area peripheral to the southern borders of the Caliphate when in 1841 an attempt was made under the auspices of the British humanitarians to set up a Model Farm at Lokoja, though those who bought the land from the local ruler, the Atta of Igala, for their unsuccessful demonstration that Africa could produce from its soil agricultural products for export in place of slaves, had of course no inkling of the fact. It is significant also that at this time Lokoja was under sway of the Atta of Igala, Ocheje. It is thus clear that the influence, whether military or political, which was subsequently exerted over the country around Lokoja by the Emirs of Nupe had not begun to make itself apparent at this time, but was in fact of later occurrence.

By 1859 when Dr. Baikie made his way up the River Niger in *Dayspring,* at the head of an official British expedition, it was from Masaba, Emir of Nupe,[11] that he sought and was granted permission to establish a trading station at Lokoja, almost precisely on the spot occupied some eighteen years earlier by the abortive Model Farm project. Some date during the period 1842–60 thus marks the establishment of the southern-most limits of the Fulani Empire along the Niger valley, and the year 1859 itself marks the precise date that Fulani military power first came into direct contact with the embryonic forces which would ultimately destroy it.

2

At the time, however, and for many years afterwards, Baikie and his successors, save for the vague support provided by the occasional visit of a gun boat, lived only on sufferance from the Emirs of Nupe. Masaba was well disposed towards them, and apart from milking them of a considerable annual commission, which he no doubt equated precisely to the slave tribute accruing from his other clients in the south, the traders had little to fear from the Fulani as long as he was alive. They were welcomed and regarded in particular as an especially valuable source of guns and powder, as will later become apparent.

Masaba's successors were more demanding, especially Maliki (4th Emir)—in fact he was disastrously so. But it was during the last years of the reign of Umaru Majigi (3rd Emir 1873–84) that an event occurred which marked a significant change in the relationship between the now consolidated United African Company of Sir George Goldie and the Fulani potentates. Before discussing this however, it is necessary to examine, in some detail, the military organisation with which Goldie and later Lugard came into conflict.[12]

As far as the Caliphate was concerned the backbone of the army was the *gayya* or *levée en masse,* consisting of the peasantry owing allegiance to the various *Sarakuna* (fiefholders). Each man was responsible for his own arms and equipment, as well as for a ten to twenty days' supply of 'iron rations'. The dress of these foot soldiers consisted of a *taguwa,* often dyed indigo blue, which in itself was a loose-fitting shirt-like garment with a circular neck hole and large arm holes, giving great freedom of movement. The skirts reached to about the knee, and were frequently gussetted, with the result that when it was secured around the waist by the usual rope girdle, *(d'amara)* the lower part of the garment flared over the hips and buttocks in an almost kilt-like effect. The *bante* (loin cloth) of cloth, or the *warki* (loin cloth) of leather, and a pair of *takalmi* (sandals) for the more affluent, completed the clothing, except that each man also carried a *bargo* (cotton or hair blanket) for wrapping round the body, similar to the Scottish plaid and usually slung over the left shoulder with the ends either tucked under the rope girdle or else loosely knotted in front. This item of equipment was so ubiquitous and essential, that the phrase 'I carried a blanket at ——'[13] has come to have almost the same connotation as 'I signed on for the duration with such and such a Regiment' has had in English.

Such foot soldiers *(dakarai)*[14], organised under a *sati* (non-commissioned officer) would be armed either with the bow *(baka)* or with spears, of which there were a considerable variety,[15] and sometimes with both. Those armed with spears alone carried two or even three. Strangely enough, the girdle was the more usual place for the knife, which one would have expected to have been strapped to the left forearm.

The bow was some five feet long and cut from a hardwood *(baushe)* of the genus *Combretaceae (Terminalia)*. It was then slightly flattened on the front edge whilst being reduced towards each end. The *tsirkiya* (bowstring) was of twisted raw-hide and the *kwari* (quiver), made from a tree of that name *(Anthocleista nobilis)*, normally contained some fifteen or twenty arrows, the shafts of which were cut either from two varieties of grasses called *kyamro* or *kyauro (Saccharun spontaneum)*, or *gazara*, a particularly tall grass, or else from the shrub *zamarke* or *ceceko (Sesbania punctata)*. *Kyamro* is also known as *abokin kibiya* (the friend of arrows) and is certainly in more common use to this day.

The arrow itself (generically) *kibiya* or (slang) *bakin maiki* (the griffon's beak) was unfletched and the head took several forms.[16] It was fastened to the shaft, into the centre pith of which its spike was pushed, by a binding made of the fibres of the *dorowa* pod *(Parkia filicordea)*—the African locust bean tree. The barbs *(kunne)* of the arrowhead were usually daubed with *dafi* (generic arrow poison) the principal and only essential ingredient of which was *kwankwani (Strophanthus hispidus)*.[17] Antidotes to this poison were *kirni (Briedelia Ferruginea)* and *makarin dafi* or *bi ta ka tsira*[18] *(Vangueria Dalzielii)*. These antidotes always had a high tannin content. The potency of the poison varied from district to district, the people of Bauchi being credited with an especially virulent form.

The archers themselves *('yam baka)* were proud of their prowess. Necessarily, the strength of the bow (with about a forty-five pound pull) and the use of an unfletched arrow limited the effective flight to a maximum of about a hundred paces. The author is acquainted, however, with a Fulani bowman named Umaru Kwa'a, from Argungu, who consistently grouped arrows around a twenty cigarette package at thirty paces, and by this standard the weapon was one of considerable accuracy. However, dead accuracy was not an essential criterion of effectiveness, especially against cavalry.

As for the horsemen, who now formed the élite shock troops of the Fulani-Hausa armies, the accoutrements and armour were both varied and picturesque, being divided into four categories.

    (a) Horse armour
    (b) Personal armour
    (c) Shields
    (d) Weapons

The *lifidi* (horse armour) consisted of protective quilting across the chest and around the shoulders of the horse, designed to give a measure of protection against arrow fire during a charge. This was made of homespun cotton stuffed with the fluff of the *gurjiya (Bombax Buonopozense)*—the red-flowered silk cotton tree, a variety of kapok. Only a small proportion of the cavalry forces were thus armoured, and they were usually the household slaves and retainers of chiefs, people whose role was closely analagous in many respects to that of the house-carl in Saxon England. Such *'yan lifida* (dragoons) were the élite of the mounted force, and their personal armour (*sulke*—any chain armour or *safa*—a quilted garment substituting for chain armour) took several forms.

The finest quality chain mail was known as *daudiya* or *badaudi*. Although most usually Mameluke in origin, a few examples still survive which are undoubtedly Crusader, whilst the word itself is derived from the name *Dauda* and connotes the mythical association of this class of fine chain mail with King David of Jerusalem.

A *safa*, on the other hand, was a sort of quilted jupon, again made of homespun, but with the quilts stuffed with tightly rolled wads of paper on which appropriate Koranic verses had been inscribed, and which were then encased in leather covers and sewn between the two layers of cloth. The result was both heavy and effective, with considerable stopping powers against a sword slash, but of less value against an arrow, which could readily find its way between the stuffing of the quilting. Another form of *safa* was the *kumakumi* which was a quilted corslet, rather tighter fitting, and worn as an alternative. Also a part of the quilted armour was the *banten lifidi*, a quilted loin cloth which encased the loins, abdomen and upper thigh of the warrior.

On the head, as far as the *'yan lifida* went, was worn a *kwalkwali* (a rag helmet), with the rags rolled in cylinders and then bound with brightly coloured cloth and adorned with the feathers of the ostrich and other birds. But the more usual head covering was a *malafa* (conical or round straw hat with brim) so large as to cover the turban completely and capable of being secured under the chin with a chinstrap. Some of these hats were reinforced with leather and were often

ornamented with great skill and charm. Combined with the volum-
inous folds of a turban, which they served to consolidate, a considerable protection for the head against sword slashes or the blows of a
mace was thus provided.

The shields which were carried by the cavalryman fell generically
under the name *garkuwa*. These were usually between four and five
feet high, roughly oblong in shape and some two feet wide, with a
neck indentation cut in the top. According to size and the material
used, the name often varied.[19]

Sometimes a cavalryman, instead of a *garkuwa* carried a *kunkeli*
(targe), a small round shield of very thick hide such as that of a bush-
cow, hippopotamus or elephant, or a *kutufani* or *kela*, a rather larger
round shield (buckler) of similar material. A few fortunate foot
soldiers might also carry a *kunkeli*.

The weapons of the cavalryman consisted principally of the
bugudun (broad-bladed spear) and of the *takobi* (sword), also called
kansakali, of which there was again a variety,[20] or the *gatta*, a form of
battle-axe. Swords were slung off the shoulder by a sling called the
hamili. The horseman armed with the *bugudun* frequently wore two or
three stone bangles of a pound or so each in weight on his spear arm,
which were designed to add deadweight to the downward thrust of
the spear when aimed at a man on the ground. In addition to the
sword and spear, a few of the cavalry and some infantry, carried a
short club or mace known as a *kulki*.[21]

The saddle *(sirdi)* was naturally an integral and important part of
the cavalryman's equipment. Again, there was some variety.[22]
The most usual pattern, however, was the *dan dumbulum*, with a deep
seat and a very high panelled peak at the back which provided a
great deal of support for the rider. It was secured in place by a
crupper strap *(ja kutur)*, usually of padded cloth which passed under
the horse's tail, and by girths *(bauji)* made of plaited leather with
wrought-iron ring fastenings. Associated with the saddle, but
utilised as a formidable weapon indeed, were the *wangami* or 'fighting
stirrups'. These were shovel-shaped stirrups, the front and rear edges
of which were honed to a razor sharpness. They were effective against
horsemen, to slash the belly of an unarmoured mount, but they were
equally fearsome to the man on foot. It was with a slash from his
wangami that D'an Ya Musa, the Magaji of Keffi, cut down the
notorious Audu Timtim, Captain Maloney's treacherous messenger,
in 1903.

The saddle was placed upon a quilted saddle cloth *(d'auki saka)*[23]
and often this was augmented by highly ornamented outer cloths,[24]

whose possession conferred prestige on their owner. Each horseman was accompanied by at least one squire *(zagi)*, whose duty it was both to care for the steed and to look after its rider and his weapons *(makamai)*.

The warhorse itself, was a particularly favoured animal, always 'entire' i.e. a full stallion, not having been gelded. In fact, the word for 'charger' *(ingarma)* and stallion are one and the same, the difference in connotation being usually merely a matter of the employment of the definite article coupled with the appropriate genitival participle.[25] These steeds were particularly well cared for, well fed and even coddled, and frequently were given pet names.[26]

Every man in the army was responsible for carrying with him up to three weeks' rations. They were usually in the form either of *yawara*, biltong (or jerky), *soye* chunks of offal fried in deep fat to especial hardness and capable of being kept for extended periods without wastage, or *dake dake* which was a sort of pemmican made by pounding cooked meat which had been dried. The most popular (and the best tasting) was undoubtedly *yawara*, the others being the staple of the less affluent.[27]

All this considerable accoutrement, this diversified vocabulary and extensive though primitive technology, added up to a significant military tradition of great organisational detail and to a marked pride both in skill and in achievement. A man who maintained his *makamai* in good condition was highly respected.[28]

An Emir who maintained his fortresses and keeps in similar repair was equally well regarded. The work necessary to accomplish this was phenomenal. Each year, the erosion of the rains was repaired, the ditch re-dug and the live thorn trees *(Sark'akk'iya=Dichrostachys platycarpa)*, deliberately planted in it, layered. The ramparts *(ganuwa)*, surmounted by battlements *(badala)*, overlooked the ditch. On the inside ran a ledge *(dakali)* on which the defenders could stand and shoot through the crenellations. In lesser fortifications, the earthworks *(tasam mahara)*[29] were combined with the ditch, the spoil from the one forming the other.

Considering the fact, for example, that Kano's walls encompassed almost ten square miles of territory—roughly half the size of Manhattan Island—and were forty feet thick at the base and from thirty to fifty feet high, with a double ditch in front,[30] the effort in maintenance that had to be expended was enormous. There were many fortifications which, if not equal to those of Kano, were not dissimilar.[31]

It would not be surprising therefore if this combination of the numbers and equipment of the soldiery, coupled with the appearance of impregnability which the walled cities and fortresses gave, induced something of a 'Maginot Line mentality' amongst the Sultan and his Emirs. Certainly, in the period up till almost immediately prior to the Berlin Conference of 1884, there was every reason for this to have been so.

The control exercised by the Caliphate was loose, but it was still very effective. Johnston suggests that the Kebbi wars represented the major threat to the strength and stability of the regime during the second half of the nineteenth century[32] before the Caliphate came into conflict with the British. This is probably true, but it is necessary to examine the circumstances a little more closely in order really to comprehend the effect which they had.

The threat which the Kebbawa posed was not one of major importance to Sokoto itself. There were already a whole group of fortresses on the northern and western marches similar to those on the east, and designed to keep the Kebbi in check. Such were Wamako, Tangaza, Binji, Silame, Kilgori and so on, and all of them were quite capable of slowing down an invasion—even if the Kebbawa could have mounted a serious one, which they could not—until the masses of the emirate-levies could be assembled. But the threat to Gwandu, the second partner, was much more real. To begin with, the Rima valley, with a flood plain as much as twenty-five miles across, full of marsh and reed and little-known channels, gave to the Kebbi fenmen a considerable mobility which the Fulani did not enjoy. Secondly, the Kebbawa in such circumstances were always operating from interior, and the Fulani, perforce, from exterior, lines of communication.

The necessity for the Sultan to prop up his Emirs was rendered all the more imperative by the administrative division of the Caliphate which the Shehu had decreed. Under it, Gwandu, in the person of the Shehu's brother Abdullahi, as we have seen, had suzerainty over the west, whilst Bello, his son, had the much larger and more populous east in his fee. Who was to bear the title of Amir al Mumenin was *not* decided. Abdullahi's subsequent recognition of Bello as Amir al Mumenin and also as Sultan after the battle of Kalembaina[33] and thus the *de facto* legitimisation of the cadet branch by the then senior branch, made Sokoto's support of Gwandu more than merely expedient. It was elevated to proportions of *wajibi* or 'inescapable obligation'.

Yet, on several occasions subsequently, it proved difficult for the Sultan to call up the support of his Emirs to assist in what was ultimately not a war of pitched battles, but very much, as Johnston describes it, 'a moss troopers war . . . (bearing) . . . striking resemblances to the border warfare of the English and the Scots'.[34]

Ilorin moreover, the first of Gwandu's major fiefs, was chronically engaged with Ibadan, and this left Nupe as the only substantial support for the Emir of Gwandu within the confines of his own suzerainty. Support from him to Sokoto was thus unlikely to be forthcoming in any strength. Support for him by Sokoto was not easy to muster either, however much the Sultan might desire to provide it.

The battle line therefore naturally tended to stabilise along the boundary marked by the complementary series of forts held by each side stretching from Aljenaari and Dakingari near the Niger in the south and northwards along the course of the Rima river to Silame and thence north-west through Tangaza till the aridity of terrain and lack of population forced a stalemate in an uncontested no-man's-land. It is little wonder then that Fulani attitudes solidified more and more on the rationale that their real security on this frontier lay in the maintenance of the strength of the fortresses and that border raiding was not capable of containment. Such an attitude reflected the same sort of thinking as that prevailing in France in 1939–40.

3

It is not proposed here to describe in detail the series of military defeats which the Caliphate suffered at the hands of the British, nor the diplomatic manœuvrings by which it attempted to avoid confrontation. Rather we shall try to answer the question: why did the vast, sophisticated military machine which we have described above, and which had been actively engaged in warfare for nearly a century before it was engaged by the British, succumb so easily to the comparatively very small forces of first Goldie, and then of Lugard?

As a prelude to this discussion we must consider the 1882 revolt of the Keddawa against Nupe, the only emirate to maintain direct and continuous trading relations with the Europeans, and the main centre for the acquisition of European goods and firearms for the Caliphate. The effect of this revolt was to upset the whole balance of power between Nupe and the European traders on the Niger and to presage the long series of military setbacks which the Caliphate was to suffer at the hands of the British.

In 1878/9 French traders, represented by the Counte de Semellé, attempted to break into the British monopoly of trade on the River

Niger. The Emir of Nupe, Umaru Magaji, saw this as an opportunity to play the French off against the British, represented by Goldie's United African Company, by granting the French not only permission to trade but land for a trading station.[35] However, his policy backfired. Quiet diplomacy by Goldie's representatives during 1879 succeeded in getting these concessions rescinded, but Semellé on his return to the coast persisted in his endeavours and on his death that year, his successor, Commandant Mattei was not slow to exploit dissident factions within the Palace itself, in order to pressure Umaru once again to change direction and to re-affirm his earlier concessions. The Palace revolt which led up to this was entirely minor, but not so the Kede Rebellion which immediately succeeded it.

Briefly, the *Keddawa* were the hereditary canoemen and ferrymen of Nupe, whose antecedents dated back to the legendary paddlers who had aided the first Etsu, Edegi, in his flight from Igala.[36] They formed a kinship group controlling a vital facet of the economic life of the Emirate, and their revolt, which began in the autumn of 1881 exerted an immediate stranglehold on all communications, commerical or military, between the Emir and a major portion of his dominions. By the spring of 1882 the rebels had complete control of the river banks on both sides of the Niger. Umaru, therefore, turned to the United Africa Company for help. Oral tradition has it thus:[40]

Some of the Nupe abandoned their allegiance to Umaru Majigi and rebelled against him. He sent his war chiefs, and later the Mayaki himself, to pursue them across the River Kaduna as far as Gwajibo. Then he heard that the *Keddawa* were also rising. Thus when, after the Mayaki had gone, it so happened that he (the Emir) heard that the *Keddawa* had joined in the rebellion—these were the people who controlled the boats and who ferried over our armies (to the west bank)—he accordingly summoned the European—whose nick-name was *Biri*[37]—from Eggan, saying that he should come. When he did—*Biri*—(the Emir) made a secret agreement with him. The gist of the matter was as follows: he said 'Now *Biri*, this is how it is! Our *Keddawa* are in revolt. What I want is that you cause your boats to be put at my disposal so that my men can get across and suppress the rebellion. Where, in all the Niger, is it easiest for you to embark the horses?[38]' *Biri* replied 'Giddi'—that is now Baro. . . . Then Umaru called Maliki,[39] and said 'Go such and such a day and meet the European.'

Maliki at this time was the Yerima. The war chiefs were gathered and went to Baro with him and there they found the company's boats and the European caused them all to be ferried across.

Flint's account[41] is somewhat different, in that he ascribes a much greater role to the ships—including a French one sent expressly by Mattei—and claims that it was the demonstration of European power, the cannon, the rifles and the Gatling guns which overawed the rebels, rather than the Fulani cavalry.

In the short run, the point is academic. In the long run, there is no conflict. The crucial element is that here for the first time the Emir needed the assistance of the Company, rather than the latter existing on his sufferance. From this day on, the exercise of power on the river changed hands, and things were never to be the same again. Thereafter, the Fulani-Hausa became involved in the European Scramble for Africa in three stages:

(1) The Royal Niger Company's Campaign of 1897 against Bida (Nupe) and Ilorin, the southermost emirates of the Caliphate.

(2) The establishment in 1898 of an *Imperial* force (the WAFF/ West African Frontier Force) with its headquarters at Jebba, in Nupe territory, independent of the Company, and their campaigns on both sides of the Niger Valley, and

(3) Lugard's campaigns, after the formal assumption of sovereignty over Northern Nigeria by the British, against:

    (i) Bida (Nupe) and Kontagora (1901)

    (ii) Yola (1901)

    (iii) Bauchi (1902)

    (iv) Kano (1903)

    (v) Sokoto (1903)

    (vi) Burmi (1903)

The Royal Niger Company's Campaign of 1897, against Bida and Ilorin, was undertaken ostensibly because of persistent raids into the Company's territories. The Company's force consisted of Major A. R. Arnold, commanding thirty-one officers and other Europeans, including Sir George Goldie himself, and 507 rank and file formed in seven companies, supported by 565 carriers and one 12-pounder B.L. gun and one 9-pounder B.L. gun (both Whitworth's), five R.M.L. (rifled muzzle loading) 7-pounder guns and six .45 Maxims.

The column which moved overland was supported by a flotilla under the command of Mr. W. Wallace, Agent-General of the Royal Niger Company, consisting of the following vessels: *Empire* and

Liberty (stern-wheelers, lightly armoured and fitted with two Nordenfeldt Q.F. guns on wheeled carriages); *Muri, Sudan, Florence, Borgu, Zaria, Bornu, Argus* and *Ribago* (launches); and *Frances* and *Busybody* (dispatch launches).

Against this array, Bida mustered a force of 25,000–30,000 men and Ilorin rather fewer.[42] Both were conquered, but Ilorin was left to administer itself after signing a treaty recognising the sovereignty of the Company. Nupe was forced to cede the southern half of its lands, and to accept, briefly, a puppet Emir, but remained otherwise independent.

The WAFF campaigns in the Niger valley in 1898/9 were much smaller operations, rarely more than one company strong. The objectives were mainly petty chiefdoms and comparatively minor towns such as Illo and Ngaske, and the motive was to secure free navigation on the Niger.

In Lugard's campaigns from 1900 to 1903 to take over effective control of the lands declared to be under British protection, the forces involved were as follows:

(a) Bida and Kontagora (1900): Colonel Kemball commanding 'a strong force'. All on foot. No fighting occurred at Bida. Kontagora was attacked and the number of the defenders is put at about 400 horse and 5,000 foot. The numbers actually in the town itself cannot be estimated.[43]

(b) Yola (1901): Colonel Morland commanding. Fifteen officers, four guns, four Maxims, 365 rank and file. River transport. Again the town was attacked. The Emir had sixty or so riflemen, armed with modern rifles, and two brass cannon which had been presented to him by the notorious French adventurer Lieutenant Mizon in 1892. No other estimates of the Fulani forces can be traced.[44]

(c) Bauchi (1902): Colonel Morland commanding. Thirteen officers, five British N.C.O.s, three doctors, 515 rank and file, two 75 mm. guns, four Maxims. River transport to Ibi thence on foot. No opposition at Bauchi. A detachment of the force, consisting of 100 men with a gun and one Maxim engaged the supporters of Mallam Jibrilla, a local Mahdi, near Burmi. The latter attacked with 100 cavalry and 600 foot and were beaten off with a loss of some ten per cent of the attackers as against only two wounded in the British detachment.[45]

(d) Kano (1903): Colonel Morland commanding. Twenty-two officers, two doctors, twelve British N.C.O.s, seventy-one artillerymen, 550 infantry, 101 mounted infantry, four 75 mm. guns and four Maxims supported by about 1,000 carriers. Kano forces were estimated by Morland as 800 cavalry and 5,000 foot.[46]

(e) Sokoto (1903): Colonel Kemball commanding. Twenty-five officers, two doctors, six British N.C.O.s, sixty-eight gunners, 439 infantry, eighty-nine mounted infantry, 195 gun and Maxim carriers, 400 general carriers, four Maxims and four 75 mm. guns, on foot.[47] According to local tradition, the Sokoto forces were put at some '30,000 extending in battle array for a good mile'.

(f) Burmi (1903): Major Marsh commanding. Two political officers, eighteen military, three British N.C.O.s, two doctors, 445 infantry, sixty mounted infantry, fifteen gunners, one 75 mm. gun and four Maxims. The defenders of the town numbered about 5,000 of whom about 900 were killed.[48]

While these campaigns were won by the British largely because of the superiority of their arms, the Caliphate, through Nupe, did have access to the purchase of a limited number of European weapons. Emirs of Nupe, from the days of Masaba onwards, had, as a result of their trade with Europeans, easy access to arms and ammunition. Flint points out that by 1871 there was a flourishing trade with several English firms, whose business consisted almost exclusively of dealing in arms and powder.[49] The Nupe army, he continues, was 'organised around a nucleus of 2,000 mounted men armed with European rifles, and Masaba's arsenal at the capital city of Bida boasted eight cannons, two of them six pounders'.[50]

Access to the free market in arms was, however, comparatively short lived. One of the main planks in Goldie's negotiations with the Government for the grant of a charter was that the Company should enjoy a monopoly in war materials. This demand never reached the legal draftsmen, but the fact remains that by 1888, a mere two years after the charter was granted, the trade in arms was extinguished— and Maliki was complaining bitterly of the fact. In 1886 he had received at least 400 guns and 400 barrels of powder, and the drastic reduction of the supply from this to nothing must have been a matter of considerable concern to him.[51]

If, however, we look at the question of the importation of these weapons not only from the limited viewpoint of the Emir of Nupe, but from the larger one of the Fulani-Hausa strategic and logistic imperatives already outlined, then we are entitled to ask whether or not the period between 1870 and 1900, and especially between 1890 and 1900, witnessed the inception and partial execution of yet another traumatic re-equipment problem for the Fulani military forces, this time one which was far more fundamental and far reaching than their previous switch from archer-infantry to cavalry.

There is a considerable body of evidence to support such an hypothesis. First, Simpson's description of Masaba's rearmament programme disclosed an extensive use of modern rifles complementing, if not superseding traditional weaponry.[52] Secondly, we know that this re-equipment was not confined to Nupe—certainly not after 1894 at any rate. Mai Maina of Jega[53] is specific on this point. He says, relative to his mission to Kano as a British spy in 1901–2 that:

'What brought my investigation about was that stories had been circulating in Lokoja to the effect that the Emir of Kano (Aliyu Babba) had in his service a number of trained soldiers from amongst his slaves, whom he had sent down to Lokoja to join the Army and be trained. These, on returning, were reported to be training his own soldiers in their camps in (modern) military tactics. It was also reported that he had purchased a large supply of guns and ammunition from Tripolitanians: Guns there certainly were in great numbers, but no sign of trained soldiers.'

In 1896, according to one informant,[54] a man named Malke who later became Kuta (chief) of the Kede as Kuta Yaya, was taken to the armoury on Stirling Hill at Lokoja by Wallace and Watts and shown the arsenal. This was done to impress upon him the Company's power. The informant continues:

'There was a certain brick building there—away from all the others at Lokoja—called "The Leopard House", and they took him there. He saw quick firing rifles, and guns innumerable and they said to him "How's that for weapons?" He replied "Huh. *You know there is one man in Bida who has equipment like this.*" (i.e. Emir Abubakar).'

A few months after this, when the city finally fell, Vandeleur[55] reported the capture of '350 rifles of all imaginable sizes and patterns, 550 barrels of gunpowder, 25,000 cartridges of all sorts and numerous loads of brass and heterogeneous articles'.

The same informant previously referred to further states:

'You are aware that Abubakar (of Bida) had guns? Ooh! From the South, mostly! There were proper repeating rifles from the Company, these he had got. There were short barrelled guns such as the people of Yakka make. There were guns from French country—we had a lot of these—right down to revolvers, he had them, but the majority of the guns, revolvers, or rifles, we got from the Europeans—from the Company, together with powder.'

When Kano fell, Lugard reported:[56]

'In the arsenal was found every conceivable kind of ammunition and a great quantity of powder. About 20,000 rounds of ammunition were destroyed and 350 firearms.'

Finally, Vandeleur, this time in respect to Ilorin comments:[57]

'Our casualties were very small, and it is difficult to understand why the Ilorins did not make use of the numbers of breech-loading rifles, amongst which there were even some curious magazine rifles, or of the quantity of ammunition which they possessed, and which was afterwards captured in the town.'

Although Vandeleur poses this question, he also, really, gives the answer. There is a world of difference between merely giving cavalryman a rifle, and actually making him even a moderately effective operator of or with it.

This dichotomy was emerging elsewhere throughout the era we are considering, and continued to exercise Western military thinkers right up to the middle of the First World War. The Boer War was to see the arguments on both sides fully exposed.

Basically, these were simply: 'If you give a cavalryman a rifle, what does he do with it without destroying his effectiveness as a cavalryman?'

The object of cavalry, in pitched battle as opposed to reconnaissance, is to effect the speediest possible transfer of a body of swordsmen or lancers from point A where the enemy is not, to point B where the enemy is, there to engage him in hand to hand combat. To achieve this end the cavalryman makes use of speed, coupled with the appearance of irresistible momentum which in its turn inspires a greater or lesser degree of terror according to the temperament and discipline of the troops being attacked. The rifle, on the one hand, or the bow and arrow on the other, represent the antithesis of the cavalry philosophy. Here the sole rationale is to prevent the development of hand to hand conflict.

As far as Western military theory went, the dichotomy was resolved prior to World War I by leaving the cavalry relatively untouched with their traditional weaponry and tactics intact, and then, if necessity arose, as in South Africa initially, creating 'Mounted Infantry Regiments' in which horses were used only to move the soldiery to the point at which they were needed, whereupon their riders then dismounted, and fought as infantry. That at least was the theory, though in practice in Nigeria, the mounted infantry were frequently used as cavalry proper.

The solution to this problem by the Fulani-Hausa generals did not achieve the more sophisticated analysis of the Western military schools, and it was never, in fact, resolved at all. Vandeleur makes quite apparent the paucity of technical skill in handling firearms, either at Bida or at Ilorin. The following quotations are amply sufficient to establish this point:

(1) 'The troops were surrounded on all sides and exposed to a constant, though ill-directed fire from the enemy's riflemen. These fortunately, aimed too high, or they would have inflicted far more damage than they did, the bullets usually whizzing harmlessly over the square.'[58]

(2) 'This camp would have been a nasty place in which to be attacked at night, but the ground was not suited to the tactics of the enemy, a fact of which we were unaware at that time . . . who preferred the open ground around Bida where they could attack with their cavalry which they believed to be invincible.'[59]

(3) '. . . we came under the fire of the enemy's riflemen who were posted in the village and clumps of trees to our left, and bullets were soon whistling over the square, which with its mass of people inside formed a large target.'[60]

Not all the shooting was wild, however, and Vandeleur also records: 'Some riflemen had posted themselves in the bushes, and fired into camp, wounding two or three of the carriers,[61] and later:

'more of our men had now fallen to the fire from the riflemen in the bushes, which was very harassing and could not be replied to on account (of the need to preserve dwindling supplies of ammunition). Captain Anderson in his white helmet, on our side of the square, seemed to be a target for the enemy, and though they invariably missed him, his vicinity was decidedly dangerous. The enemy now displayed a certain amount of indecision . . .'[62]

At Ilorin the pattern of inadequate technology was similar to that at Bida: 'The main attack (at the Oyon River) . . . came from the right front where one of the Baloguns was posted with his corps. . . . He advanced them . . . covered by a very ill directed fire from his riflemen.'[63]

Complementary to the technical inadequacy of the Fulani-Hausa's ability in employing firearms to the best advantage, the campaign of 1897 had seen a marked technological advance both in weaponry and in tactics on the part of the Company's forces. This development of new arms and the new tactics to accompany them set the pattern for all future confrontations with the Fulani in the open, and even, in the case of the West African Frontier Force's subsequent campaigns, for the approach marches relating to attacks on the fortresses.

Tactical deployment was based on the square, a formation dating back to the Peninsula War and brought to its previous maximum of effectiveness by Wellington at Waterloo. Curiously enough this was the formation which the Fulani, by *force majeure* had themselves adopted at Tabkin Kwatto. The logic of the square was founded on the extended reach which first the musket, and later the Martini-Henry carbine or the rifle and especially the Maxim provided. The troops literally formed a square with the fighting ranks, and in the space thus enclosed, the 'soft', vulnerable command, commissariat and headquarters personnel were able to operate in comparative safety and security.

Discipline and drill was so perfected that marching in square formation was perfectly feasible, and thus mobility, though perhaps slightly curtailed, was by no means precluded. But, as Waterloo had proved, the square provided not only virtually the only formation capable of withstanding a cavalry charge in the open, but also the only one capable of repelling one with such slaughter as to amount to defeat. This applied even to the highly trained and disciplined horsemen of Napoleon's army. Doubly so did it apply to less well-organised formations such as the feudal type levies of the Fulani-Hausa, no matter how brave they might be individually.

In considering the quality of the Fulani-Hausa military resistance, it must be made clear that many contemporary accounts were biased, including, and perhaps even particularly, those of Lugard. That those who opposed him were fired with great personal gallantry in the face of overwhelming odds as represented, after 1897, primarily by the Maxim gun[64] and the artillery, cannot now be disputed by any reasonable man. However, Lugard was not at any pains to accord them even this final compliment and in his reports makes reference to encountering any significant opposition on four occasions only: first at Yola, where he refers to deserters from Rabeh's and the French armies; secondly at Burmi when Mallam Jibrilla's following acquitted themselves with gallantry; thirdly at Kotorkwashi on the road to Sokoto where Wright won the V.C.;[65] and lastly, again at Burmi, in the final defeat of Sultan Attahiru, where according to him the town was the focus of 'a colony of aliens, who coming from the North and probably of Touareg origin, had settled there . . . these people were of a valiant race'.[66]

The reasons for Lugard's studied disregard for his opponents are not hard to seek. Plagued by the fear of prohibitive interference from a reluctant Colonial Office, and in the case of the Sokoto excursion, flying in the face, almost, of a direct instruction against offensive action, he was compelled at every stage to underplay the opposition with which his forces were confronted. Were he not to do so, then both his judgement and his discretion would have been called into question. Even Kotorkwashi—as he described it—bolstered his position since it was proof that a miniscule detachment of his troops was more than equal to the severest attacks which could be launched against them even when outnumbered by as many as 40 or 50 to 1.

From Lugard's point of view, there was a great deal of logic in this attitude. It is only to be regretted that the authority which he gave it and the unquestioned veracity which his eminence has commanded, should have led to the perpetuation of a myth of martial incompetence, and even of faint-heartedness, among the Fulani-Hausa. Hausa troops under British officers and N.C.O.s, it was argued, were paragons of military virtue. Under their own leaders, according to the myth, they were apparently almost entirely without any martial qualities.

Given the superiority in arms and in technique which the British demonstrated, the question must however be asked as to why the forces of the Caliphate did not resort to guerilla warfare, as Samori and Bai Bureh did, and as in fact, the Kebbawa had done for years in their wars with Sokoto. Clearly, a guerilla campaign would have made up for the one thing which the Fulani-Hausa lacked in their capacity to wage a successful encounter with this enemy, an opportunity to meet on equal terms.[67] Otherwise, the cavalry charge was the only tactic which could be employed against either the Company's Constabulary or the Frontier Force in encounters in the open, since it alone provided the sole and only hope of overcoming the disciplined invincibility of the stationary or moving square, or of breaking the advantage which the field guns and Maxims overwhelmingly bestowed.

Armies of far greater numbers and of much closer parity in weapons and support had been faced with the same choice of method and had arrived at the same conclusion. But a cavalry charge against a well-drilled square entailed either an iron-like discipline, comparable to that of the opposing infantrymen and an impeccably well-schooled horse, combined with good horsemanship, or else incredible courage and the highest standards of horsemanship alone. The first the Fulani-Hausa cavalryman did not possess. The second he did, and in abundance. Yet, all the time, as the Blackwell translations show[68] there was prevalent a sense of insecurity, a look over the shoulder, a questioning of the very basis of the legitimacy and propriety of resistance. This is the mentality that produced Sultan Attahiru's *Hijira,* or flight from the infidel, and it was classic in the simplicity of its Islamic traditionalism.[69]

From the point of view of the Sultan, pessimism as to the outcome of conflict with the Europeans is understandable. Though the French and Germans acknowledged, after 1885, British claims to the Caliphate, their close juxtaposition also constituted a threat to him, and in the event they occupied some of his outlying districts in what is now Niger and Cameroon. Sokoto was surrounded by Europeans. The Sultan knew of French successes in the Western Sudan, for followers of Ahmadu, ruler of the Tokolor Empire, whose royal house was related to his own, had taken refuge in the Caliphate, and Ali Bouri, Bourba Djollof, who had been defeated by the French in Senegal in 1890, had accompanied them. Sultan Abdurrahman is reported to have declared on hearing of Ahmadu's death: 'God has taken away a fine relation. He was the only support I had in the world.'[70]

There is, of course, also the question of the Kano Civil War of 1894, and of the singular ineptitude which Abdurrahman displayed on this occasion. Much weight has been given to this episode as indicative of the 'collapse' of the authority of the Caliphate. The incident has been grossly over-emphasised. The fact that immediately after the death of Danyen Kasko (Sultan Abdurrahman), the Emir, Aliyu of Kano found it necessary to go to Sokoto to make his peace with his successor, ought rather be the true measure of the incident's actual importance.[71]

Also present as a military consideration facing a Sultan at this period was the threat posed by Rabeh, the military adventurer from the Sudan who conquered Bornu in the name of the Mahdi. Initially, the threat was not an immediate one. In fact, Rabeh's invasion might well have been regarded as no threat at all, since it was the traditional enemy, Bornu, at whom his attack was directed and against whom all of his not inconsiderable military talent was brought to bear. If Bornu suffered too much, then an obvious ally would have been the Caliphate, both as a source of military and religious aid and comfort. But, at the same time, to counter an enemy such as Rabeh appeared to necessitate the continuance of the traditional formations of massive concentration of power. There was thus a reinforcement of the sense of security which the conservative military mind could draw from the existence of the armies of mass and the line of fortresses. To break them up to oppose the British by resort to guerilla warfare, even if successful, would only mean that they would not be available should a second threat to the integrity of the Caliphate emerge in the person of Rabeh.

What was not appreciated, of course, was that Rabeh's force was in fact a 'modern' one, with an artillery train of some fifty pieces and with at least three out of every five of his men armed with firearms. In the event Rabeh would thus have presented the Fulani-Hausa with much more serious problems than had been their usual experience in warfare with their neighbours. Moreover, as Johnston points out,[72] amongst Rabeh's captains was a descendant of Dan Fodio, Hayatu, who had joined Muhammad Ahmed's Mahdiyya sect and in respect of whom there is some evidence that the Mahdi, immediately before his death in 1886, was considering as a replacement Sultan for Sokoto. Even before he joined up with Rabeh in 1893, Hayatu had already repulsed attempts by the Emir of Yola to oust him from a foothold he had obtained in his emirate.

When in 1896, Rabeh, and his ally Hayatu, to whom Rabeh had given his daughter Hauwa in marriage, lunged at the Kanuri tributary state of Bedde, with an expedition commanded by Rabeh's son Fadr Allah, he was coming perilously close to the eastern line of fortifications which shielded the Caliphate. Thereafter, his intentions were unclear, but the trepidation which they engendered was very real.[73]

It cannot be concluded from this that Rabeh's threat was the only thing which prevented the Fulani-Hausa from moving to a more diffused and less formal type of warfare. Tradition also must have played a considerable part. The successors to Bello and Abdullahi were not likely lightly to dismantle the organisation which these great captains had created. To do so would have been to fly in the face of an established order which was of enormous strength and which had enjoyed remarkable success.

All in all, there is in fact no clear single reason which can be advanced as to why the Fulani-Hausa forces did not resort to a guerilla campaign. It is true to say, however, that it was not in character and was not a *modus operandi* with which the armies were well versed.

It could be, and has been, argued that the Fulani 'overlords' could not rely on the Hausa 'subject peasantry'—but this is very doubtful indeed. First, the claim of an essential antagonism on the part of the peasantry towards their rulers—which was a main plank in the Lugard platform—does not square up with the situation as Cargill, Popham Lobb and Temple saw it and reported it.[74] Second, there is ample evidence of the capacity of the refugees from the battles to disappear into the bush, and make good their escape, a factor which again does not support the existence of a hostile and unco-operative class of subject peasant-farmers anxious only to throw off an alien yoke.

The conclusion must therefore remain that the power to resist was eroded by circumstances which were purely military. These have been identified to some degree in the foregoing and to expand upon them now would be out of place.

In the last resort, however, no tactics, no personal gallantry and no resistance would have prevailed, since the 'Europeans'—and it is immaterial in this respect whether they had been British, French or German—or for that matter any other—had the Maxim gun and the artillery, and the Caliphate had not. Even Lugard pays tribute to the power of the machine-gun, and the awe in which it was held by his opponents. His description of its use on the occasion of the rising against his authority at Satiru in 1906,[75] though somewhat out of context in this discussion, includes an account by the Marafa Maiturare. Lugard obtained this from Major Burdon, the Resident at Sokoto, and it reads as follows:

'They came at us, and the horsemen gave way and went back. No one took any notice. I thought we were all going to be killed, as before. Someone gave an order. Everyone fired, then a whistle blew, everyone stopped and there was no one left alive in front.'[76]

It was by superior discipline and technology that the Fulani and the Hausa were brought to bay and that there fell the last of the great native polities of West Africa, in direct succession to those which had risen and fallen for nearly a millenium since the tenth century—Ghana, Mali, Songhai, Kebbi, and now Sokoto.

The Empire which toppled it lasted a scant fifty years. The conquest itself took barely six years. The first shots were fired in January of 1897 and the last, save for the episode of Satiru in 1906 and the punitive action against Hadejia in April of that year, by July 1903. Yet this brief span was sufficient to spell the difference for the Caliphate between survival as an entity and extinction.

The campaigns and those of other powers during the same period changed the map of Africa, and left only Ethiopia as representative of an indigenous political system. No one can judge what would have been the result if the Caliphate also had survived. Quite certainly, the salvaging of Ethiopia has not been without an almost unique value. Who can say that the preservation of the Sokoto Caliphate would have resulted differently?

NOTES

1 21 June 1804.
2 In confirmation of this statement, but in another context, see Mungo Park's *Travels in the Interior of Africa,* London, 1806. Amadi Fatouma's *Journal* pp. 368–9: 'We met a very strong army on one side of the river, composed of the Poul (Fulani) nation: they had no beasts of any kind.'
3 *The Fulani Empire of Sokoto:* H. A. S. Johnston, London 1967, p. 46.
4 Say September 1805.
5 Johnston *op. cit.* p. 5 *et seq.*
6 December 1805.
7 Readers of American History cannot fail to observe the almost precise analogy in the strategic setting of the main Gobir fortress at Alkalawa with that of Fort Duquesne in the time of the French–Indian Wars around 1756. Here the rivers Allegheny and Monogahela conjoin to form the Ohio, and gave the same natural strength to the French fortress-base as that which Alkalawa enjoyed.
8 Kontagora Emirate was officially recognised in 1859 by the fifth Sultan Ahmadu Atiku (Zaruku). It is sophistry however to claim that this was really the last Fulani Emirate to be established within the process which began in 1804. The circumstances surrounding its creation are entirely different from those for example of Yola, which was the capital of the conquered fiefdom of the Lamido, Modibo Adama.

   Kontagora on the other hand was made up of territory which prior to the appearance on the scene of Umaru Nagwamace (1806–76), son of the third Sultan Abubakar Atiku I (1837–42), was recognised either as the legitimate fief of Masaba, 2nd Emir of Bida or of Yakuba D'an Gajari, 33rd Emir of Yauri. Both were vassals of Gwandu.

True, a great deal of this territory was only loosely held and the Gwari and Bassa chiefs had considerable sway, but Kontagora Emirate was not a conquest *ab initio*. It was the result of an adjustment of boundaries within the Caliphate, and specifically at the expense of Gwandu since Kontagora's loyalty lay direct to Sokoto.

9 See D. J. M. Muffett, *Concerning Brave Captains*, London, 1964, p. 64 for a vivid account of the collection of annual tribute.

10 Literally, 'friends of play': known to anthropologists as 'the joking relationship'.

11 Muhammadu Saba, nicknamed Masaba. 2nd Emir of Nupe: 7th son of Mallam Dendo by a Nupe mother, Fatuma. Ruled 1859–73. It is probable that Baikie was originally given permission to settle at Lokoja by Usman Zaki (1st Emir 1832–59) who was officially recognised by the Emir of Gwandu in 1856, but it was with Masaba that all Baikie's dealings took place and with whom he achieved considerable rapport.

12 Most of the information set forth in this section is the result of notes and descriptions made by the author during the period 1947–63 when he served in the Administrative Service in Northern Nigeria. Much of the data was communicated to him by the late Sir Ahmadu Bello, who was a keen and perceptive student of military history and a considerable authority on that of his own people.

13 *Na d'auka bargo a . . . .*

14 Also *karma*.

15 E.g. generic 'spear'; *mashi, karfasa, katsungu, boyo, byallam* or *bellam, d'an tasawa*, with specialised types as follows: *asigiri* or *ausigir*=metal-shafted spear; *bugundun*=broad-bladed spear; *kambari*=a favourite of of the Kebbawa; *k'ok'obiro* or *k'okoburo*=a spear with a three-sided head, all sides being sharpened; *margi*=a throwing spear and *zululu*= a straight-headed one.

16 E.g. *Adullu*=blunt-pointed arrow; *Dunk'a* (Katsina) *k'unda* (Kano) arrow; *Gazara* or *gyage*=the narrow-headed small barbed arrow, with a shaft longer than others, always carried one to a quiver, from which it was thus the more readily drawn. It was *never* poisoned. The name of this arrow is derived from the grass from which its shaft was cut. *Tsaima*=a small long-pointed arrow; *Tsiko*=a barbless arrow and *surku*=a barbless arrow, but with serrations along its metal headshaft.

17 Other ingredients were *bijaje (Ficus populifolia)*; *gunguma* a plant of the *Amaryllideae* family; *gwaska (Erythrophloeum guineense)*; *ka fafogo (Uapaca guineensis), sainya (Securidaca longipedunculata)*; *tinya (Euphorbia unispina)*; the shrub *gazawa* and *zabo (Aloe Barteri)*.

18 'Find it and you escape.'

19 *Dangi* or *dingi*=an old shield of giraffe or white oryx hide, and often coupled with the epithet '*sha mai*'='drinker of oil', the name is derived from *dingi* meaning 'a male giraffe'. *Kulumbuwa*=a large shield made from tanned or untanned hide of no particular origin; *k'wangwara*=a white *garkuwa*; *tarman*=a new shield made from a

white oryx skin; *warwaji*=white oryx hide shield specifically, as opposed to *dangi*.

20 *Bisalami, hindi, hankaltilo, hankatilo, almulku*=a scimitar or sword like a sabre; *dunhu*=a sword devoid of all ornamentation or chasing; *fatefate*=a broad sword (also a foot soldier's weapon); *lafaranji*=a one-edged sword; *tama*=a cheap, shoddy sword: *tamogas* or *tamogashi*=a sword with channels cut into the blade; another variation was the *ʒabo*.

21 Also *gwama* or *gulma*.

22 *Bagariye*=a type of saddle originating in Bornu and having a curved pommel; *bacuncunam*=an inferior model of same; *k'warda*=another type of the same; *talha* or *talaha*=an ornate type imported from North Africa.

23 *Saka* or *salala*.

24 *Jalala* or *alkashafa, bisher, balliya, fantarna, ka k'i Bima*=ornamented or embroidered saddle cloths; *yifi*=an ornamented cover to be put over the saddle when the owner dismounted.

25 E.g. *Ingarman Sarkin Gobir*=a stallion of the chief of Gobir; *Ingarmanna Sarkin Gobir*=the chief of Gobir's warhorse. Occasionally other words such as *ʒutaki, ingaramniya* or *ingirma* denoted particularly fine large stallions and thence inevitably, by derivation, typical warhorses.

26 The Magaji of Keffi's charger was named *D'an Ashalu* (i.e. born with inherent fighting qualities). That of the Emir of Zaria was called *Mai Nasara* (the victor) and so on.

27 Varieties of *yawara* were: *kilishi* or *kilis*=thin strips of dried meat dipped in pounded groundnuts, condiments, and groundnuts oil and redried after each process, and then roasted; *margi*=the meat of game so prepared; *bagajigi*=long and broad strips. Meat prepared for drying or in the process of being dried was known as *raye, dango, jargi* or *kamsa*.

28 Muffett, *op. cit.*, p. 143. One of the facets of the character of Sultan Attahiru Ahmadu noted with approval by his contemporaries was that he kept himself and his accoutrements 'at all times fully prepared to take the field'.

29 'The scatterer of raiders.'

30 *Annual Reports,* 1902, p. 86.

31 E.g. Zaria or Katsina. Even Bin Yauri, a comparatively minor fortress, had walls encompassing three square miles; also, Lugard estimated that there were forty walled cities within a thirty-mile radius of Kano. For an excellent description of Kano City Walls see H. L. B. Moody, in *Nigeria Magazine,* March 1967, pp. 19–38. For a superb account of tactics against an equally armed and similarly accoutred force, or against a fortress, see Johnston *A Selection of Hausa Stories,* Oxford Library of African Literature, Clarendon, 1966, p. 142 *et. seq.*

32 H. A. S. Johnston, *The Fulani Empire of Sokoto:* London, 1967 Chap. 18.

33 See M. Hiskett, *Taʒyin Al Waraqat,* Ibadan 1963. Introduction to this edition of Abdullahi's work, pp. 18–20.

34 Johnston *op. cit.*, p. 193.

35 For details of this episode see J. E. Flint: *Sir George Goldie and the Making of Nigeria,* London, 1960, Chap. 3.

36 Oral data collected by the author in Bida in August/September 1966 and now being evaluated. It represents, of course, the 'perception' of an aged participant in the war. History is made of such perceptions. It is merely a matter of which particular set becomes accepted.

37 *Biri*=Monkey: He was Mr. Walter Watts, Senior Executive Officer of the Company at Eggan.

38 Note the emphasis on the cavalry, the 'terror' weapon—corresponding to a force of tanks or armoured cars today. c.f. the use of 'the dragoons' in civil disorder in England in the eighteenth and early nineteenth century.

39 Fourth Emir, 1884–95.

40 Oral data collected by author, 1966.

41 Flint *op. cit.*, page 39.

42 Source: C. S. Vandeleur, *Campaigning on the Upper Nile and Niger* London, 1898.

43 Source: *Annual Reports* and S. White *Dan Bana; The Memoirs of a Nigerian official,* London, 1966.

44 Source: *Annual Reports.*

45 Source: *Ibid.*

46 Source: Muffett, *Concerning Brave Captains.*

47 *Ibid.*

48 *Ibid.*

49 Flint *op. cit.*, p.25.

50 *Ibid.* Flint is quoting FO. 84/1351 Simpson to Granville 21 November 1871 pp. 3 and 21. See also Vandeleur, *Campaigning on the Upper Nile and Niger,* Methuen, London, 1898, p. 212: 'They (the defenders) had dragged out an old cannon from Bida, with which they attempted to retaliate with a great deal of noise but little result.'

51 Full details and sources regarding these transactions will be provided in the author's study of the Bida Wars, now in preparation. See also Flint *op. cit.* pp. 96 and 98.

52 See note 43.

53 See *Labarin Mai Maina na Jega, Sarkin Askira,* Zaria, 1958, pp. 13, 14.

54 Oral data collected by author, 1966.

55 C. S. Vandeleur: *op. cit.* p. 223.

56 *Annual Reports* 1900–11, p. 88.

57 Vandeleur *op. cit.* p. 276.

58 *Ibid.*, p. 207 (Bida).

59 *Ibid.*, p. 200 (Bida).

60 *Ibid.*, p. 215 (Bida).

61 *Ibid.*, p. 211 (Bida).

62 *Ibid.*, p. 216 (Ilorin).

63 *Ibid.*, p. 274. (Ilorin).

64 This fact is reflected in the contemporary statements such as that of Hilaire Belloc 'Whatever happens we have got the Maxim gun and they have not.'

65 See Muffett *op. cit.* Chapter 10 for details of this controversy and especially pp. 120 *et. seq.* See also I. F. Nicholson, *The Administration of Nigeria 1900–1960,* Oxford, 1969.

67 See Johnston, *Hausa Stories,* pp. 160–1. People like the Shemaki, or the Majidadi Babadarai (or his squire) would have made intrepid and valiant leaders of guerilla bands.

68 Blackwell H. F., *The Occupation of Hausaland 1900–04,* Lagos, 1927.

69 For a discussion of this point see Muffett *op. cit.* Chapter 10 and Hiskett M, review of same in Bulletin of S.O.A.S., (London) volume XXVII, pp. 670–2.

70 Cited by Michael Crowder *West Africa under Colonial Rule,* London 1968, p. 86 from Bendaoud Mademba, 'La dernière étape d'un conquérant (odyssée les dernières années de Sultan Ahmadou de Ségou racontée par san cousin et compagnon d'infortune. Mahammadou Hassimou Tall), trans. from the Bambara in *Bulletin du comité d'Etudes Historiques et Scientifiques de l'Afrique Occidentale Française,* 3, July–September 1921, p. 437.

71 Muffett, *op. cit.* p. 109.

72 Johnston *op. cit.* pp. 199 *et. seq.* This is an excellent and concise account of Rabeh's rise to power.

73 See Blackwell, *op. cit.* letters 93–9.

74 Muffett, *op. cit.*

75 14 February 1906.

76 *Annual Reports,* pp. 368–9.

Index